ORDERED TO DIE

**Recent Titles in
Contributions in Military Studies**

Jérôme Bonaparte: The War Years, 1800–1815
Glenn J. Lamar

Toward a Revolution in Military Affairs?: Defense and Security at the Dawn of the Twenty-First Century
Thierry Gongora and Harald von Riekhoff, editors

Rolling the Iron Dice: Historical Analogies and Decisions to Use Military Force in Regional Contingencies
Scot Macdonald

To Acknowledge a War: The Korean War in American Memory
Paul M. Edwards

Implosion: Downsizing the U.S. Military, 1987–2015
Bart Brasher

From Ice-Breaker to Missile Boat: The Evolution of Israel's Naval Strategy
Moshe Tzalel

Creating an American Lake: United States Imperialism and Strategic Security in the Pacific Basin, 1945–1947
Hal M. Friedman

Native vs. Settler: Ethnic Conflict in Israel/Palestine, Northern Ireland, and South Africa
Thomas G. Mitchell

Battling for Bombers: The U.S. Air Force Fights for Its Modern Strategic Aircraft Programs
Frank P. Donnini

The Formative Influences, Theories, and Campaigns of the Archduke Carl of Austria
Lee Eysturlid

Great Captains of Antiquity
Richard A. Gabriel

Doctrine Under Trial: American Artillery Employment in World War I
Mark E. Grotelueschen

ORDERED TO DIE

A History of the Ottoman Army in the First World War

Edward J. Erickson

Foreword by
General Hüseyin Kivrikoğlu

Contributions in Military Studies, Number 201

GREENWOOD PRESS
Westport, Connecticut • London

Library of Congress Cataloging-in-Publication Data

Erickson, Edward J., 1950–
 Ordered to die : a history of the Ottoman army in the first World War / Edward J. Erickson, foreword by General Hüseyin Kivrikoğlu
        p.   cm.—(Contributions in military studies, ISSN 0883–6884 ; no. 201)
 Includes bibliographical references and index.
 ISBN 0–313–31516–7 (alk. paper)
 1. World War, 1914–1918—Campaigns—Turkey—Gallipoli Peninsula. 2. Turkey. Ordu—History—20th century. I. Title. II. Series.
D568.3 E66 2001
940.4′15—dc21   00–021562

British Library Cataloguing in Publication Data is available.

Copyright © 2001 by Edward J. Erickson

All rights reserved. No portion of this book may be reproduced, by any process or technique, without the express written consent of the publisher.

Library of Congress Catalog Card Number: 00–021562
ISBN: 0–313–31516–7
ISSN: 0883–6884

First published in 2001

Greenwood Press, 88 Post Road West, Westport, CT 06881
An imprint of Greenwood Publishing Group, Inc.
www.greenwood.com

Printed in the United States of America

The paper used in this book complies with the Permanent Paper Standard issued by the National Information Standards Organization (Z39.48–1984).

10 9 8 7 6 5 4 3

Copyright Acknowledgment

All photographs used with the permission of the Military History and Strategy Research Center, Turkish General Staff, Ankara, Turkey.

To my wife, Melanie

Contents

Illustrations	ix
Foreword by General Hüseyin Kivrikoğlu	xiii
Preface	xv
Acknowledgments	xxi
1. Army on the Brink, 1908–1914	1
2. Plans	15
3. The Early Offensives, November 1914–March 1915	51
4. Under Attack, April 1915–January 1916	75
5. High Tide, January–December 1916	119
6. Strategic Pause, January–December 1917	159
7. End of Empire, January–November 1918	179
8. Conclusion	207
Appendix A. Commanders' Biographies	217
Appendix B. The Ottoman General Staff, Summer 1914	223
Appendix C. Ottoman Army Organization, 1914	225
Appendix D. The Ottoman Aviation Inspectorate and Aviation Squadrons	227
Appendix E. German Military Assistance	231
Appendix F. Ottoman Casualties	237
Appendix G. Turkey in the First World War-Chronology	245
Selected Bibliography	251
Index	257

Illustrations

A photo essay follows page 118.

MAPS

1.1 The Ottoman Empire in 1914	xx
2.1 Railroad and Road Networks in the Ottoman Empire, 1914-1918	18
3.1 The Sarikamiş Encirclement Operation According to the Third Army Attack Plan of December 19, 1914	56
4.1 General Situation at Gallipoli, First and Fifth Army Forces, End of August 1915	92
5.1 General Situation, Turkish Land Forces, 1916	132
6.1 General Military Situation, 1917	162
7.1 Third Army Operations, 1918	190

TABLES

1.1 German Military Mission	12
2.1 Ottoman Empire Population, 1914	15
2.2 1914 Coal Production	16
2.3 1914 Railways	16
2.4 Disposition of Turkish Forces, 1912	21

2.5 Disposition of Turkish Forces, July 1913   24

2.6 Disposition of Turkish Forces, August 1914   38

2.7 Days Required to Mobilize Turkish Corps versus Days Required by the Mobilization Plan   41

2.8 Disposition of Turkish Forces, November 1914—Concentration Plan   43

3.1 Available Offensive Strength—Third Army, December 22, 1914   57

3.2 Third Army Strength, March 24, 1915   64

4.1 III Corps Strength, August 2, 1914   77

4.2 Disposition of Turkish Forces, Late April 1915   86

4.3 Fifth Army Ammunition Expenditures Report, May 8-June 8, 1915   88

4.4 Third Army Effective Strength, June 4, 1915   106

4.5 Disposition of Turkish Forces, Late Summer 1915   109

5.1 Artillery Strength—Erzurum Fortified Zone, January 1916   124

5.2 Disposition of Turkish Forces, January 1916   126

5.3 Third Army Strength, April 28, 1916   129

5.4 Disposition of Turkish Forces, August 1916   134

5.5 Disposition of Turkish Forces, December 1916   154

6.1 Disposition of Turkish Forces, August 1917   170

7.1 Disposition of Turkish Forces, January 1918   181

7.2 The Fortress of Kars, April 30, 1918   185

7.3 Disposition of Turkish Forces, June 1918   188

7.4 Disposition of Turkish Forces, September 1918   197

7.5 Disposition of Turkish Forces, November 1918   202

8.1 The Cost of Defeat—Commonly Used Figures   208

8.2 Disposition of Turkish Forces, January 1919   209

8.3 Ottoman Casualties (Author's Estimates)   211

D.1 Aviation Squadrons, late 1915   228

F.1 Ottoman Casualties   237

F.2 Other Ottoman Casualty Figures   240

F.3 Consolidated Summary of Ottoman Losses   240
    in the First World War (Author's Estimates)

F.4 Consolidated Ottoman Losses by Year of the War 241
    (Author's Estimates)

F.5 Ottoman Army Strength 1918   242

F.6 Consolidated Ottoman Battle and Non-Battle Losses 243
    (Author's Estimates)

Foreword

TURKISH GENERAL STAFF
ANKARA

Lieutenant Colonel Ed Erickson's *Ordered to Die* is the first complete history of the Ottoman Army in the First World War to be attempted outside of Turkey. He has done an admirable job in assembling the complex pieces of this important story.

While we in Turkey may disagree with some of his fine points in this book, especially with the parts of the book which contain some assessments made by some academicians on the Armenian Rebellion, we still think that his account is fairly balanced and objective. I would maintain that *Ordered to Die* will stand as the definitive work in English on the subject of the Ottoman Army in the First World War for a long time.

The story of the Ottoman Army at war with the allies during the First World War is an incredible story. It is remarkable that the officers and soldiers of the empire managed to win both glorious victories and also to endure savage defeats under such difficult conditions. As the senior officer of the Turkish Armed Forces, I am extremely pleased that balanced and objective discourse on the subject of my nation's military performance during the First World War is emerging. Turkey's performance in the war has not been very well understood outside of Turkey. I hope this book will shed light on a subject long hidden from western eyes.

The Turkish Armed Forces and I are grateful to Lieutenant Colonel Ed Erickson for his hard work and dedication in bringing this story to the English-speaking world.

General Hüseyin Kivrikoğlu
Chief of the Turkish General Staff

Preface

I do not expect you to attack, I order you to die. In the time which passes until we die, other troops and commanders can come forward and take our places.

- Lieutenant Colonel Mustafa Kemal
Gallipoli, April 25, 1915
Gallipoli

There is no finer quote with which to summarize the battle history of the Ottoman Army during the First World War than that of Mustafa Kemal (later and better known as Atatürk) as he led the 57th Infantry Regiment forward into the hell of the Gallipoli beachhead. The Ottoman Army was a great fighting army that confounded its enemies during four years of war. It was an army that died with its boots on and endured great hardship and adversity. This was the army that after the dust settled on the prostrate armies of Russia, Austria-Hungary, Bulgaria, Serbia, and Romania was still on its feet and fighting a stubborn and determined fight.

A thousand years earlier, they had swept through the Middle East from the steppes of Central Asia and they had acquired Islam along the route. They were Turkmen warrior tribes from the Altai Hills whose fierce fighting qualities carried them to the gates of Vienna. They were the stuff of nightmare stories for the small children of Europe, and when they moved through an area only flames and destruction remained. Later, the tribes were molded into a nation by the Osmanli Dynasty, but they were generally not known to the common people by this appellation. For hundreds of years, feared by their neighbors, these fighting conquerors were known simply as "the Turks."

This book is about the Turkish Army, although it carries the title *A History of the Ottoman Army in the First World War*. Indeed, going back to that war the British, their most relentless adversary, always seemed to fight the *Turks*, not the Ottomans. British histories, as well as Australian, the New Zealander, and French, portray the enemy as the Turk or even as "Johnny Turk." This was partly due to the popular usage of the time, but in reality the term very accurately reflected the character of that army. Although it is true that the Ottoman Empire still existed as a legal entity and furthermore that many subject peoples, such as Arabs and Kurds, served in the army, the essence of the army was Turkish. Whenever the army got right down to the terrible matter of dying in the trenches it was usually the Turkish soldiers (Askers in Turkish) that accomplished the deed. Therefore, in this book, the term *Turkish Army* is used instead of the more proper term *Ottoman Army*, and associated terms such as the *Turkish General Staff* are used nominally.

There is a conspicuous void within the historiography of the First World War concerning the story of the Turkish war effort and particularly with the overall picture of the Ottoman Empire's strategic direction of the war. For the researcher who does not read Turkish, any serious attempt to explore these subjects in depth will usually fail in the face of an almost complete absence of materials that present the Turk's participation in the war in a continuous and unitary fashion. The researcher will also find that most of the available materials deal with the operational and tactical level of the campaigns with little analysis of overall Turkish strategy. The picture that emerges is episodic and incomplete since there is no overall framework on which to hang an understanding of the Turkish conduct of the war. This is a shortfall of no small consequence for both serious amateurs and for professional historians of the First World War. This book attempts to fill that void.

Given the overall backwardness of the empire, the nature of the its economy, its lack of modern lines of communication, and its sprawling geography, the Turkish war record in the First World War was an astounding achievement. During the war Turkey labored under many disadvantages. The geographic disadvantage alone is evident from an examination of Map 1.1. Nevertheless the Turks maintained their belligerent status almost until the bitter end of the First World War, outlasting Russia and Bulgaria and matching Austria-Hungary. Turkey absorbed punishing attacks from the Allies and sustained proportionately large casualties. Yet Turkey's armies never mutinied and the Turks inflicted huge numbers of casualties on their enemies. The Turkish soldier, *Mehmetçik*, often died where he fought. *Mehmetçik* literally translates as "the Mehmet" and was the Turkish equivalent of "Tommy" or "Doughboy." Turkey managed to field and sustain large fighting forces simultaneously on four fronts (and at times on a fifth) for most of the war, an accomplishment unmatched by any belligerent, save Great Britain. This was no small challenge and was an almost impossible strategic condition under which to engage in war. But Turkey, with its abysmal interior lines of communications, somehow consistently and successfully dealt with this unfavorable situation. Overall, the story of Turkey in the First World War is an incredible saga of fortitude and resilience. That these noble qualities are inextricably interwoven with the ineptitude and blunder of the Young Turks should not detract from the army's accomplishments. Turkey's story is not so much a story of failure, or of a crumbling antiquated empire, but rather a remarkable story of a long fight against impossible odds. It is story that begs to be told.

Although the campaigns on the Turkish fronts associated with the well-researched and well-written British and Australian official histories have been captured in great detail by historians, those campaigns fought on other fronts, against other enemies, are notably absent from available histories. The Gallipoli,

Mesopotamian, and Palestinian campaigns, for example, are thoroughly covered from the Commonwealth perspective and are also well covered by popular histories. However, historical appraisals of the Turkish view of these campaigns are nonexistent in western languages. Similarly, except for a single book published in 1953, a balanced and complete overview of the brutal campaigns in Caucasia is hard to locate. Farther afield, books about the Turkish contribution to the defeat of Romania and the operations in Galicia are impossible to find.

Of particular significance is the fact that a definitive history of Turkey's overall war effort, strategic direction, and command of forces has never been written. The solitary western work to attempt this subject was written in French in 1926 and is outdated today. The five-volume Turkish General Staff series, written by Turkish General Farhi Belen, titled *The Turkish War in the First World War* is superb but unfortunately has never been translated into English. Subsequent staff studies of the various campaigns and battles by the Historical Division of the Turkish General Staff have slowly trickled out from Ankara over the past thirty years. These too, if they can be found, are written in Turkish and present a partial picture of the unfolding events.

Because of the inadequacy of reliable western historical resources it was inevitable that an inaccurate picture of the Turkish Army at war has taken root over the past eighty-five years. This began when apologists sought to explain how and why the backward Turks had badly knocked about the more sophisticated allied armies during the war. Over the years, this picture has become peculiarly flawed by inaccurate histories portraying the Turks as prone to desertion, predisposed to massacre, and commanded mostly by Germans. Later, even popular cinema such as *Lawrence of Arabia*, *The Light Horsemen*, *Gallipoli,* and *All the King's Men* added more inaccuracies to this view. And in the last half of the century, a determined assault on the actual events of 1915 and 1918 has been waged by the descendents of the Armenians and Greeks subjected to Ottoman brutality.

All of this has given rise to myriad myths about the conduct of the First World War by the Turkish Army. One of the most prevalent myths is that the Turks held a numerical advantage over the allies during many of the important campaigns and another is that the Germans commanded many of the major operations. Another myth is that the Turks kept very poor records. Still another is the idea that Turkish units often "came apart" under pressure, disintegrating and crumbling because of mass desertion. Finally, there is the idea that the Turks wanted to regain their shattered and crumbling empire. None of these are true. In fact, in most cases, quite the opposite is true, showcasing the inaccurate picture that most westerners have of these people at war. Indeed, the Turkish Army in the First World War was a formidable fighting machine much feared by its enemies.

This book is the first full account in a western language in seventy-five years of the Turkish War and it attempts to frame the Ottoman war effort in a comprehensive and fully documented format. It examines Turkish war aims, strategic direction, and significant command decisions by theater of operation and evaluates the effects of these decisions on the Turkish war effort. It presents the Turkish land force structure and tracks its development and deployment from 1914 to 1918. Moreover, it considers the growth of Turkish military effectiveness as a function both increasing levels of Turkish experience and of German military assistance. This work evaluates the effectiveness of Turkish strategic direction during the war by focusing on the key decision points that changed strategic priorities and caused major force redeployments during the war. It assesses the overall success of the Turkish war effort, given the geographical and resource constraints of a primitive economy faced with a multifront, highly industrialized, technologically evolving, total war.

There are herein points of view, which at first glance, may seem to overly favor the Turks. The reader is reminded that findings are presented from the "Turkish side of the hill" and are based primarily and whenever possible on Turkish sources. In most cases, the enemy is deliberately referred to in the general sense as "the British" or "the Russians" in an attempt to show how western histories tend to present the Turks themselves. Readers interested in specific allied commanders, formations, and orders of battle will have to consult allied histories. This work purposefully focuses on the conduct of the war at the strategic and operational level of war. Except for the campaigns in eastern Europe, tactical details are generally omitted, since some of this information concerning individual battles may already be found in previous works in western languages.

Turkish source materials (archives and official histories) tend to focus on the physical elements of war rather than on the human dimension or on personalities. Contrary to expectations, the Turks did not overplay the role of Allied superiority in men and material in explaining responsibility for defeats. Neither do they exaggerate the role of Kemal Atatürk in explaining certain victories. Generally speaking, the Turkish material tends to align very well with Allied histories and chronologies. A notable exception, of course, is the Armenian deportation. Whenever possible, the Turkish version presented here has been corroborated with allied histories.

In a general sense, this book is intended to be a platform work for the future. It is a broad survey written in the hope of arousing in others an interest in exploring the complexities of the Turkish War. Furthermore, this book may be used as a starting point for understanding and identifying the depth and richness of the Turkish source material. The book is intended to present a unitary picture of the Turks at war and to complement other existing histories. Although most of the tactical details are absent, as noted earlier, the specifics of the planning and execution of the Sarakamiş campaign, the campaigns in Galicia and Romania, and the 1918 Caucasian campaigns are fully explained herein. Readers familiar with the contents of the official British and Australian histories and with the work of W. E. D. Allen, Paul Muratoff, and Commandant M. Larcher will find that *Ordered to Die* complements those works and completes the story of the Ottoman Army in the First World War.

To capture the flavor of the Ottoman world, modern Turkish script and spelling has been used for all individuals, in all place names and events, and titles. Exceptions to this rule are the use of commonly used western place names in use in 1914 for the major cities, these are: Constantinople (Istanbul), Adrianople (Edirne), Smyrna (Izmir), and Gallipoli (Gelibolu). The Turkish characters are pronounced as follows: Ş – an *sh* sound as in Pasha (Paşa) and Ç – a *ch* sound as in Chatalja (Çatalca), also, in Turkish, a C is pronounced as a *J* as in Chatalja (Çatalca).

Finally, this book creates a factual identity that characterizes the Turkish Army in the First World War. Probably the greatest injustice done to this magnificent fighting army was the gross distortion of its reputation, its ethos, and its character by erroneous historical perceptions. They were more than just the Turks; they were an *army* with all of the historical, psychological, and emotional weight that entails. This work translates anonymity into a tangible picture of decisions, fighting formations, and personalities that accurately portrays the Turkish Army at war.

Map 1.1
The Ottoman Empire in 1914

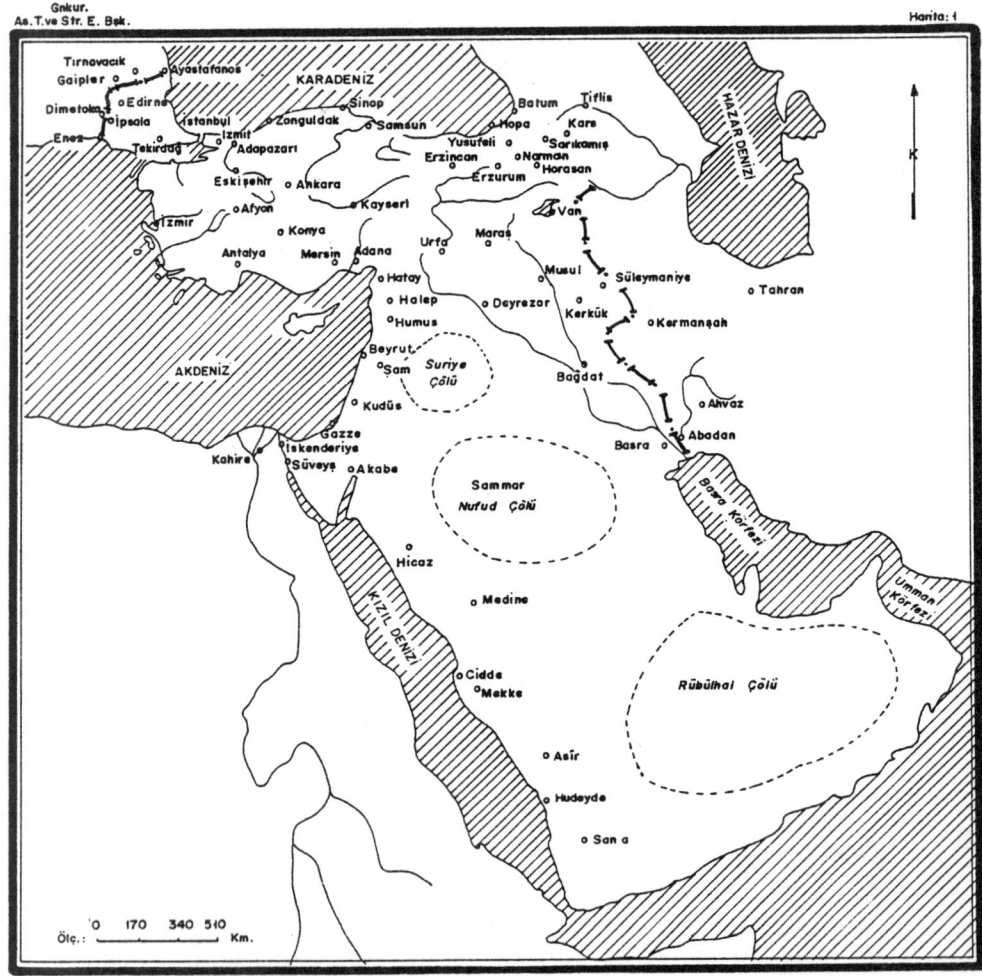

Source: Turkish General Staff, *Turk Silahli Kuvvetleri Tarihi Osmanli Devri Dünya Harbi Idari Faaliyetler ve Lojistik Xncu Cilt* (Ankara: Basimevi, 1985), Kroki (Map) 1.

Acknowledgments

The idea of this book was conceived in the early 1990s when I was assigned to NATO's Headquarters, Land Forces Southeast Europe in Izmir, Turkey. I had always been in interested in military history and I wondered why there did not seem to be a comprehensive book about the Turks in the First World War. I asked my Turkish officemates about this and was assured that indeed such books did exist--they just were not available in English! They then agreed to pick up for me some of the more recent Turkish official histories of the First World War the next time one of them went to Ankara. I first acknowledge these officers who in 1993 got me off to a good beginning by providing me with about ten volumes of the Turkish official histories of the Balkan Wars and of the First World War. They are Brigadier General Adem Huduti, Colonel Alaaddin Erk, and Colonel Orhan Yokuşoğlu of the Turkish Army, and I would not have ever gotten started without their support and encouragement.

To my longtime friend and teacher, Colgate University professor Tony Busch, I owe a large debt for encouraging me to continue on with this project and for also giving my first rough draft a critical look. Tony's unique understanding of Ottoman diplomacy and military history were extremely valuable in framing the events of 1914 and 1915. Friend and colleague Dan Callahan's careful reading of the manuscript was also very important in ironing out the fine details. I am indebted as well to Jim Minnoch in New Hampshire, Martin Kaeser in Germany, Bülent Yilmazer in Turkey, Geoffrey Miller in England, and to Dr. Yigal Sheffy in Israel for their comments and insights.

In Turkey, I am especially grateful to General Hüseyin Kivrikoğlu, the current chief of the Turkish General Staff. An old friend and my former commander, General Kivrikoğlu was instrumental in opening doors for me and for ensuring that I received VIP treatment while in Ankara. To the director of the Turkish General Staff's Archives Division, Major Tufan Yorgancioğlu, translator and researcher Ahmet Çalişkan, and Librarian Gülümser Mutlu, my thanks for making my research easier and far more fun that it probably warranted. At the archives, I had many fruitful conversations with geostrategist Colonel A. Rifla Ateşer, Turkish Air Force (retired), Bielefeld University Ph.D. candidate Mustafa Gencer, and Lieutenants Devrim Pinar and Tufan Günduz, all of whose insights were valuable and thought provoking.

There were many other friends who took care of me enroute and while I was working in Turkey: Chuck and Hulya Gillow in Adana, Turkey. Dave and Sally Pabst and Lisa Miller in Naples, Italy. Katherine and Tony Vass and Al and Liz Mitchem in Ramstein, Germany. I am also indebted to Colonel Raif Okutucu, Turkish Army, and Major Sami Gulunay, Turkish Army at the Turkish General Staff, for their assistance in scheduling office calls and to Colonel Selim Yüceoral, Turkish Army, and the entire staff of the Merkez Ordu Evi. I also acknowledge my good friends Mr. Steve Dawkins, U.S. Foreign Service (retired) and Colonel Rick Lorenz, USMC (retired) who encouraged me to start writing upon my retirement from active duty.

Any errors are my own as are any mistakes in the translation of Turkish documents. Finally, I owe an enormous debt to my wife, Melanie, without whose encouragement and support I could not have finished this book.

1
Army on the Brink, 1908–1914

THE YOUNG TURKS

Modern Turkish military history properly begins in 1908 with the accession of the Young Turks to power in the Ottoman Empire. As the antique Ottoman Empire entered the twentieth century, it was apparent to most educated Turks that radical political and economic reform was needed if the empire was continue its survival as a political entity. These modern thinkers formed political groups and gave rise to the movement called the Young Turks. The Young Turk movement attracted an unusual mix of Turks, including intelligentsia, liberal thinkers, as well as numerous military and naval officers. The most prominent of these groups was the Committee of Union and Progress (CUP). Naturally this movement was perceived as a threat to the sultanate of Abdulhamit II, who sought to suppress it both inside and outside of his empire. The army officers who secretly joined these groups maintained active cells in Damascus and Salonika.

In late 1907, the Second Young Turk Congress met in Paris. In attendance were CUP members, the Salonika Group, and Armenian Daşnaks. The delegates ended the congress by declaring that the sultan's regime should be deposed by violence if necessary and parliamentary rule established. Over the spring of 1908, conditions in the Ottoman Empire deteriorated, as well as Abdulhamit's grip on his people, and small revolts broke out. Salonika proved to be the hotbed of revolution and regular troops were sent to suppress it. Uprisings soon followed in the Balkans, and finally on July 23, 1908, the sultan agreed to Young Turk proposals and to work toward modernization. The revolution was almost bloodless.

The CUP was unprepared for such a quick about-face by the sultan and hurried to establish itself in Constantinople. Three members (part of a committee of seven) were sent to the capitol to influence the government, these were: Staff Major Cemal Bey, Talat Bey, and Cevit Bey. The impact of the Young Turks was immediate as comprehensive programs designed to modernize the empire were established. Preparations for reestablishing parliament were made, and for a time it looked as if the empire stood on the threshold of establishing full civil liberties for its minorities. Even democracy appeared to be within reach. Unfortunately, most of these plans were stillborn as the Young Turks fell out with the minorities and with the more conservative elements, which sought to slow the course of westernization and modernization.

In April 1909, a counterrevolution occurred when elements of the army supported the sultan and forced the Young Turks out. The Young Turks in the army now coalesced and marched on Constantinople to restore order. An improvised "Action Army" (Hareket Ordusu) commanded by Hüseyin Hüsnü, with Mustafa Kemal at his side took the capital and restored order. The commander of the Third Army, General Mahmut Şevket Paşa now took the reins of command and declared martial law. He reconvened parliament, which immediately deposed Abdulhamit on April 27, 1909. Soon thereafter the empire entered into a brief period of constitutional democracy.

Almost immediately problems erupted throughout the empire, particularly with dissident minorities in Albania, Macedonia, and in Eastern Anatolia. Further troubles occurred when Italy invaded the empire's sole remaining African possession of Tripoli (Libya) in September 1911. Several Young Turk military officers were then stationed there and distinguished themselves in the fighting, notably Enver Bey and Mustafa Kemal. This campaign did not last long and Italy claimed its prize on November 4. Concurrently, the CUP became embroiled in a coalition government and in doing so compromised some of its ideals, which internally fractured the party itself.

Unfortunately for the Ottoman Empire, other outside forces conspired to force crisis on an already overtaxed government. Serbia, a rising Balkan power backed by Russia, now sought to take advantage of the Turk's preoccupation with internal and external threats. The Serbs concluded a military alliance with Bulgaria on March 13, 1912 under which they would both receive Balkan lands at Ottoman expense. The Bulgarians in turn forged a second alliance with Greece on May 29, 1912, again splitting the remaining Ottoman possessions among themselves. Montenegro was persuaded to join the alliance in September and October. Anti-Ottoman Christian states had now forged a ring around the remaining Ottoman European possessions of the Sanjak of Novipazar, Kosovo, Macedonia, and the rump of Rumelia. These events found the Ottoman Army unprepared for war with about 250,000 men under arms.

THE BALKAN WARS

The First Balkan War began on October 8, 1912, with a Montenegrin attack on Novipazar; this was followed by a major Bulgarian offensive into Thrace. The Bulgarians defeated the Turkish First Army at Lüleburgaz in late October and then invested the Fortress City of Adrianople. The Bulgarians continued to march east until they were halted at the Çatalca Lines, about thirty kilometers west of Constantinople itself. The Serbs marched into Macedonia and Kosovo meeting the Montenegrins. By early November 1912, the Turkish Second Army was beaten and withdrawing into Albania. The Greeks pushed north taking the prize city of Salonika on November 8. In less than sixty days the two Ottoman armies had been defeated in detail and the empire's European possessions lost to the Christian Balkan states.

Negotiations began in London in mid-December in the hopes of bringing the war to a conclusion. The Ottomans had no bargaining position to speak of, their armies were shattered, hundreds of thousands of Muslim refugees were streaming into the empire, and Constantinople and Adrianople were on the verge of being lost. A sense of despair hung over the government and the Ottoman cabinet appeared hesitant and uncommitted to concluding a peace on any kind of terms favorable to the Turks. CUP members feared that the negotiations would give away too much and so they determined to act. On January 23, 1913, CUP member Enver Bey, led the famous "Raid on the Sublime Porte" and forced the grand vizier, Kamil Paşa, to resign at gunpoint. The CUP appointed Cemal Bey as Commander of the First Army defending Constantinople and also appointed Mahmut Sevket Paşa as the new grand vizier. The new CUP government was committed to retaining Adrianople, a condition that broke up the London Conference. Fierce fighting resumed in February 1913, and in March the Bulgars launched a determined attack on the Çatalca lines, which failed. Although the Turks planned and executed abortive counterattacks, the Fortress of Adrianople fell on March 28. Negotiations resumed and finally on June 10, 1913, the Treaty of London was signed. In this treaty, the Turks lost the Balkan lands they had held since the fifteenth century as well as Adrianople.

As a result of such unfavorable terms, considerable political opposition arose to confront the CUP. In an attempted counter coup, opposition gunman assassinated Mahmut Şevket Paşa. The CUP immediately suppressed the attempted coup and consolidated its grip on the Ottoman government. The CUP appointed Mehmet Sait Halim Paşa, an Egyptian prince, as the new grand vizier on June 12, 1913.

The Second Balkan War began when the erstwhile allies, Bulgaria, Serbia, Montenegro, and Greece fell out among themselves. The problem was the apportionment of Ottoman lands, especially the Aegean port city of Salonika, which the Bulgars coveted but were denied by their allies. On June 29-30, 1913, Bulgaria conducted a surprise attack on Serbian and Greek forces in Macedonia. Although the Bulgars seemed to enjoy a momentary advantage, Montenegro and the Romania joined the fight against the Bulgars. Bulgaria, now confronted with multiple enemies on both flanks, withdrew its army from Adrianople to oppose its former allies. The CUP took immediate advantage of this weakness and Enver ordered the army forward into Thrace. On July 21, the Ottoman Army seized Adrianople and the surrounding area. The Treaty of Bucharest ended the Second Balkan War on August 10, 1913. Thus, by the late summer of 1913, Serbia had doubled in size, Greece gained Salonika and much of Macedonia, Bulgaria gained only a small access to the Aegean Sea, and the Ottoman grip on the Balkans had ended.

The Balkan Wars served to solidify the CUP's hold on the government since it appeared to the public that the CUP was responsible for abrogating the London Treaty and for retaking Adrianople and Thrace. The leadership that would take the Ottoman Empire into the First World War was now established, with Sait Halim as prime minister (and grand vizier), Talat Paşa as the minister of the interior, Enver Paşa as the minister of war, and Cemal Paşa as the minister of the marine. Other CUP members were less successful in grabbing the reins of power. In particular, the ambitious Mustafa Kemal, who was at odds with Enver, was forced into semiexile as the military attaché in Sofia. Fethi Bey, another prominent CUP member, went to Sofia as well and other lesser CUP members went to obscure military postings at the fringes of the empire. As a group, the new CUP leaders of the Ottoman Empire were ambitious nationalists dedicated to westernizing and modernizing the empire. As individuals, they were young men in their late thirties and early forties, highly educated at either the Military Staff College or in universities, skilled in bureaucratic infighting. Unfortunately, they were also power hungry and beset by petty jealousies, which compromised their ability to work effectively together. As the events of 1914 unfolded, these traits, in combination, were to prove dangerous to the continued existence of the Ottoman Empire.

THE TURKISH GENERAL STAFF AND ARMY

At the apex of the Ottoman military structure was the Ministry of War (Harbiye) which had been established in 1826 after the suppression of the Janissaries. Within the ministry, there were offices for procurement, combat arms, peacetime military affairs, mobilization, and for promotions. Often staff coordination between these offices was poor or nonexistent.[1] From January 3, 1914, through October 4, 1918, Enver Paşa served as the minister of war (Harbiye Nazırı). Izzet Paşa filled this position from October 14, 1918 until November 11, 1918. The titular commander in chief of the Ottoman military forces was the sultan. However, the minister of war fulfilled this role as well by commanding all forces under the office of acting commander in chief (Başkomutanlik Vekaleti). The ministry did not, however, directly control the actual operations of the army, a general staff performed this function.

The Ottoman General Staff, hereafter referred to as the Turkish General Staff, was closely modeled on the Prussian General Staff. The General Staff fulfilled the classic staff duties then in use by all major European powers and was staffed by Kurmay Subay or General Staff officers. Carefully selected officers were highly trained in staff procedures at the War Academy in Constantinople. After completion of the War Academy, graduates were advanced in grade over their nongraduate contemporaries and immediately assigned to key billets. Almost all of the wartime Turkish corps and division commanders and chiefs of staff were trained General Staff officers. Reflecting the Prussian model, the most influential position within the Turkish General Staff was that of the chief of the General Staff. The staff itself was composed of various divisions, which specialized in a variety of military fields. The most powerful staff division was the First Division, or the Operations Division. There was also an Intelligence Division, and like the Germans the Turks had separate divisions for Railroads and Communications, and a variety of additional staff divisions to administer and supply the army. To help the chief of the General Staff, or to run the staff in the absence of the chief, there were two assistant chiefs of staff.

After January 1913, Enver Paşa served concurrently as minister of war and as the acting commanding general of the Turkish Army. He also served as the chief of the Turkish General Staff (Erkanı Harbiyei Umumiye Reisleri) from January 3, 1914, through October 4, 1918. Ahmet Izzet Paşa briefly held this post from October 4 through November 3, 1918, as did Cevat Paşa from November 3 through December 24, 1918. In August 1914, Enver Paşa was heavily engaged in the Ottoman diplomatic maneuvering which brought Turkey into the First World War. Based on what historians know of Enver Paşa's actions in the summer of 1914, probably the office receiving the least attention under Enver's competing portfolios was that of the chief of the Turkish General Staff. Fortunately for the Turks, in the spring of 1914, Liman von Sanders reassigned a highly trained German General Staff officer named Colonel Friedrich Bronsart von Schellendorf from a German Military Mission tactical assignment to the position of first assistant chief of staff of the Turkish General Staff. In the virtual absence of Enver Paşa, Bronsart von Schellendorf began immediate preparation of mobilization and war plans. The second assistant chief of staff was Turkish Colonel Hafiz Hakki Bey. Although they were both trained General Staff officers, as will be seen, there were intellectual divergences between these two men.

The active regular army force of thirty-six infantry divisions was divided up among the corps of four numbered armies. Turkish army corps had three infantry divisions, an artillery regiment, and a cavalry regiment. Turkish infantry divisions had three infantry regiments and an artillery regiment. All of these forces were mobile and were capable of sustained combat operations. Reserve forces were distributed throughout the empire and constituted a reserve manpower and small unit pool, which would be used to augment and to bring the regular forces up to their wartime strength. There were four fortress area commands: the western border city of Adrianople, the Dardanelles, the Bosphorus, and the eastern border city of Erzurum. A fifth fortress area was established at Çatalca during the First Balkan War to protect Constantinople, and although it was maintained in readiness it was inactive for most of the war. The fortresses were built of permanent concrete forts and entrenchments, except for Çatalca which was mostly built of earthworks and trenches.

Among the remainder of Ottoman military strength were the Light Reserve Cavalry Regiments. These units were the successors to the irregular Hamidiye cavalry formations, which were disestablished on August 17, 1910.[2] These new regiments were formed into seven cavalry brigades and three independent regiments and comprised mainly of Kurds, some rural Turks, and an occasional Armenian. Conventional-style military discipline had always been a problem with these irregular units and the Turkish General Staff was determined to end this with the establishment of the new reserve formations. After 1912, these brigades and regiments were consolidated into four reserve cavalry divisions placed in wartime under the control of the Third Army.

An important addition to the wartime strength of the army was the paramilitary Jandarma. Formed after the disastrous Russo-Turkish War of 1878 under a French training mission, the Jandarma was a powerful force. Its mission was primarily internal security and preservation of the borders. It was deployed throughout the empire. Every *vilayet* had a mobile Jandarma battalion, many large cities had mobile Jandarma regiments, and there were substantial numbers of static local battalions as well. The mobile regiments contained 2,371 officers, 39,268 men, and 75,395 animals, but total Jandarma strength including staffs, border guards, and support personnel greatly exceeded several hundred thousand men. Under mobilization, control of this substantial force transferred from the Ministry of the Interior to the Ministry of War.

The army was closely modeled on the German Army and included a large number of officer and noncommissioned leadership academies, branch training schools (including artillery, cavalry, infantry, signal, and engineer), technical centers, and regimental recruit depots. Basic training for soldiers was particularly severe and employed draconian discipline. Turkish soldiers spent the first half of their service undergoing training as individual soldiers and then spent the last half in unit training. Resources were scarce, soldiers typically were issued a single uniform and expended an annual total of only twenty to thirty rounds of rifle ammunition. Company and battalion-level training exercises were conducted throughout the year and the army conducted annual large-scale field maneuvers every October. Reserve infantry divisions were usually called to the colors to participate in these maneuvers and military attaches from the embassies in Constantinople were normally invited to observe these exercises. Frequently, however, western observers criticized the Turks because the maneuvers tended to be scripted and over controlled rather than using a free play methodology, which seriously tested commanders and units. The last full-scale maneuver of this type occurred in 1910 in Thrace near Lüleburgaz. The exercise pitted the First Army against the Second Army and lasted twelve days. The scenario had been planned in May and pitted the "Eastern Army" against the "Western Army" in October 1910.

In terms of military doctrine, the Turks tended to copy the techniques of their German teachers. Doctrinal march tables, frontages for attack and defense, tactics, and staff procedures were patterned on contemporary German methods. After the turn of the century, the great Ottoman fortress cities of Adrianople and Erzurum reflected German thinking on fortifications as well, as redoubts were moved father out and the forts became mutually supporting.

The strengths of the Turkish Army were primarily at the extreme ends of its rank structure. At its highest echelons, its highly trained General Staff officers were aggressive and well trained. At the bottom end, its rank and file were tough and capable of great feats of endurance, and were famous throughout Europe for their tenacity. However, it was in the middle ranks that the Turkish Army was the weakest. Unlike the British or the Germans, the Turks had no long-service corps of professional noncommissioned officers (sergeants), and there was no tradition of such service in the Ottoman forces. In peacetime, this made the effective and rapid training of recruits difficult. In combat, as junior officers were killed, this lack of professional depth meant that there were no leaders to step up and assume leadership responsibilities. This particularly hurt the Turkish Army when engaged in the highly attritional battles that characterized the First World War.

MOBILIZATION

In terms of human resources, the Turkish General Staff believed that the empire had a mobilization potential of about two million men.[3] However, this ambitious figure was in fact never achieved during the course of the war. In the summer of 1914, the classes of 1893 and 1894 (each age cohort was about ninety thousand men) had been called to the colors and the Turkish Army enjoyed a peacetime operating strength of about two hundred thousand men and eight thousand officers. Unlike some European powers, Turkey did not employ first-line formations in peacetime at war establishment, preferring instead to field a higher number of reduced establishment formations. This policy was systematically carried out by reducing the structure of all units below division level. Every Turkish infantry regiment was short one battalion (out of three) and every infantry battalion short one company (out of four). The average strength of Turkish infantry divisions, in the summer of 1914, was four thousand men out of a war establishment of ten thousand personnel. To bring the field army to war establishment the Turkish Army required a total of 477,868 men and 12,469 officers to completely fill out its divisions. This use of a reduced establishment or cadre structure (a lean and understrength organizational framework designed to be heavily augmented) was intentional and reflected a deliberate decision taken by the army after the Balkan Wars. There were no reserve artillery or reserve technical formations. In any case, the Turkish General Staff believed that approximately 1,000,000 men and 210,000 animals were easily available for recall and that, immediately upon full mobilization, the mobile field army would have an effective strength of 460,000 men, 14,500 officers, and 160,000 animals.[4] To this must be added the heavily armed and trained mobile field (seyyar) Jandarma of forty-two thousand men (twenty-five thousand gendarmes, twelve thousand frontier guards, and six thousand mule-mobile troops).[5] Altogether, Turkey planned to field about five hundred thousand men in mobile operational units, the remainder serving in fortress garrisons, coastal defenses, and in servicing the lines of communications and transportation.

In material terms, the army was ill equipped to fight a modern war. Most divisions had twenty-one or fewer of the 75 mm field guns that they were authorized out of an establishment of twenty-four. This artillery force was a mixed bag of French Schneider, German Krupp, and Austro-Hungarian Skoda pieces[6] and numbered about nine hundred field pieces. At corps level, most of the twelve 105 mm howitzers required for the three batteries of corps artillery were available. Overall, the army needed two hundred eighty field artillery pieces to bring itself up to war establishment. Additionally, in the fortresses of Adrianople, Erzurum, the Bosphorus, the Dardanelles, and Çatalca, there were an additional 900 fixed or semifixed coastal and fortress artillery pieces, which were ill placed for immediate use.

The machine gun situation was worse. Each Turkish Infantry Regiment was authorized four machine guns. Some regiments were short and the army needed two hundred to equip the regimental force to standard. At battalion and company level, there simply were no machine guns and the army estimated that it needed several thousand more to fill all requirements. At 1,500,000 in hand, rifles were a less critical shortage but the army still needed 200,000.[7]

Ammunition stockade was low and the Turks were unable to meet anticipated wartime demands. There were 150 cartridges available per rifleman, a further 190 available in corps depots, and for the entire army there were 200,000,000 cartridges in reserve. For the Turkish artillery, there were about 588 shells available per gun.

In service support, the Turkish Army suffered terribly. Each division was authorized a field medical unit, and each corps was authorized four field hospitals; however, these were never filled at established strengths. This deficiency was compounded by chronic shortages of doctors, medicine and medical supplies. The total Turkish hospital capacity was thirty-seven thousand beds, of which fourteen thousand were located in the city of Constantinople. Transportation was a critical weakness; especially short were supply wagons and draft animals. Motorization and aviation were almost nonexistent in the Turkish Army.

Upon the advice of the German advisor General von der Goltz, mobilization planning was based on peacetime conscription which provided a flow of trained individuals from the active army into the reserve forces. Active service in the peacetime Turkish Army was for a period of three years for the infantry and four years for the artillery and technical services.[8] Likewise, animals served for a period of four years and, in turn, were returned to civilian use carrying a lifelong obligation for national service. Non-Muslims were excluded from military service and were forced to pay a special military tax instead. By 1914, the period of active obligatory service was reduced to two years for infantry and cavalry and three years for the artillery. This decision was the result of reduced budgets and under this scheme the active army was maintained a lower strength. The military staff thought that a 50 percent bi-annual turnover was inferior to a 33 percent turnover every three years. In any case, the huge losses in trained leaders suffered during the Balkan Wars were reflected in the inability of the forces to adequately train replacements.

All men were liable for military service and were drafted as a group according to their chronological age as a class or cohort. This usually occurred annually in the late summer. Liability for service began on March 1 in the year when a man turned twenty and ended twenty-five years later. The Turkish military was divided into an active force (Nizamiye), a reserve force (Ihtiyat), and a territorial force (Müstahfız). The two youngest classes provided the manpower for the active army, the next sixteen classes provided the trained manpower for the reserve, and the oldest seven classes comprised the territorial forces.[9] The previous reserve system of the Redif (organized reserve units), begun in 1886, was discontinued in 1913. Some reservists and territorials were organized into units of battalion size or smaller and had local depots designated as mobilization stations, however after 1913 most were assigned as individual replacements. Turkey was not wedded to the idea of military units reflecting local character (as were the British or German armies), but in 1914 Turkish Army units were mainly composed of locally recruited men. This changed as the war progressed and men were sent as individuals or in levies to whatever units needed them the most. Unlike all other major European powers, Turkey did not have a large-unit reserve system which could field intact reserve corps composed of reserve divisions.[10] The use of permanently established reserve infantry divisions stationed in major cities having been discontinued in 1913 with the end of the Balkan Wars. Consequently, there was no major increase in the raw number of formations available to the Turkish Army immediately upon mobilization. There were several exceptions, those being the XII Corps (Independent), the 38th Infantry Division (Independent), and 1st, 2nd, 3rd, and 4th Reserve Cavalry Divisions. Later in the war, as the Turks needed more combat infantry formations, they simply mobilized more regular divisions. The identification of Turkish divisions mobilized after August 1914 as "reserve divisions" is erroneous. Likewise, the identification of some wartime Turkish divisions as "bis," or paired divisions, by British intelligence was in error. The probable culprit in both cases was likely to have been a misunderstanding of how the Redif changed in 1913.

There was also a residual volunteer system, called the Gönüllü Sistemi, which encouraged men to volunteer to fight together. While the last major use of this system was during the First and Second Balkan Wars, it remained in existence and there was some small use of it in the Caucasus and in Thrace. However, the Gönüllü Sistemi was used mainly in attempts to recruit from the many groups of Muslim refugees harbored in the empire. These Muslim volunteer groups would see action in the Sinai, in Persia, and in the Caucasus.

Between July 1913 and August 1914, the Turkish Army was undergoing an enormous reorganization and reconstruction effort as a result of the devastating losses suffered in the Balkan Wars. Compounding this huge task was Enver Pasa's determination to rid the army of older and less active officers, which he felt were an obstruction to modernization. Over thirteen hundred officers were involuntarily retired during this period.[11] The scale of this effort to rebuild the army must be explained in some detail because this reorganization of the Turkish forces provides the basis for understanding both the offensive failures of 1914 and the defensive successes of 1915.

Prior to the beginning of the Balkan War of 1912, the Turkish Army enjoyed a fair degree of stability based on a garrison system extending throughout the empire. A German military assistance group under General Colmar von der Goltz had restructured the Turkish Army and standardized the organization of

Turkish corps at a strength of three infantry divisions. In a prescient decision in 1910, von der Goltz also standardized the organization of the Turkish infantry division at a strength of three infantry regiments. Prior to this, the Turks had employed the European standard of two brigades of two regiments each within each infantry division. All European armies during the First World War would later adopt this triangular structure. In the Balkans, the twelve-infantry division strong Turkish Second Army provided security for Turkey's remaining possessions in the Vardar Valley and Albania. The equally powerful Turkish First Army (twelve infantry divisions) provided security for Adrianople and Constantinople. The smaller Third and Fourth Armies provided protection for Caucasia and Mesopotamia, and independent corps garrisoned Syria, Palestine, and Arabia. This powerful regular establishment was backed up by a reserve system that fielded infantry divisions in all major cities of the empire.

However, in less than a year, both the First and Second Armies had been destroyed. The Turkish Army had lost fourteen infantry divisions out of a beginning total of forty-three infantry divisions and the corps-sized fortress garrison of Adrianople was also lost. Additionally, eight regular infantry divisions and fifteen newly mobilized infantry divisions of reservists and territorials had been deployed to European Turkish Thrace to serve in the newly formed Çatalca and Gallipoli Armies. Several infantry divisions and a corps headquarters had been dissolved to provide replacements. Only six of the infantry divisions of the pre-Balkan War regular Turkish Army were spared the trauma of combat. In another context, 90 percent of Turkish infantry divisions mobilized participated in the Balkan Wars. Casualties from the wars exceeded 250,000 men. This was a military disaster of unprecedented magnitude for the empire, which all but destroyed the regular Turkish Army as an effective fighting force.

At the conclusion of the Balkan Wars, the condition of the Turkish Army demanded attention. Complete armies had been shattered, corps had been deliberately dissolved, and there were huge disparities in the fighting strengths of infantry divisions. There was a large number of ad hoc reserve divisional formations (named after their city of origin) composed of older reservists and territorials which had been mobilized to replace the lost regular formations. Training was at a standstill, as was weapons procurement. Finally, and not the least worrisome, almost the entire Turkish field army was deployed in European Turkish Thrace. These strategic and operational imperatives forced Turkey to immediately engage itself in a massive military reorganization effort in the aftermath of the Balkan Wars.

The reorganization of Turkish forces in 1914 was comprehensive and was designed to return the army back into its pre-Balkan War garrison locations and also to rebuild the divisional and corps base of the army. This was a gigantic undertaking and was incomplete on the eve of the First World War. In the reconstituted First Army, only the III Corps survived the war intact and retained its original organic pre-Balkan War divisions. The I Corps and II Corps lost a division each and each were rebuilding a new division. It is significant, and no surprise, that the combat hardened and intact III Corps was selected to defend the strategic Gallipoli Peninsula in 1915. Facing the Russians in Caucasia, of the Third Army's nine infantry divisions, three were being rebuilt from scratch and four were deployed there from Thrace that year. This hastily assembled and cobbled-together army was hurled against the Russians in December 1914 with predictably disastrous results. The Second Army was reconstituted in Syria and Palestine and was rebuilding two divisions while absorbing two more that were redeployed from Thrace. Altogether, fourteen of thirty-six Turkish infantry divisions organized in August 1914 were in the process of being entirely rebuilt, and eight divisions of the thirty-six had conducted a major redeployment within the year. The overall effectiveness of these twenty-two new or redeployed infantry divisions was low and would inevitably take time to remedy. However, events overcame preparation time and twelve of these divisions were involved in the early Turkish offensive disasters of 1914. Reciprocally, the single organizationally intact corps – the III Corps with its organic 7th, 8th, and 9th Infantry Divisions successfully defended the Gallipoli Peninsula in the spring of 1915. It could be argued that defeat in the Balkan Wars, and subsequent Turkish reconstitution and restationing efforts, set the stage for Turkish success or failure in the initial phases of the First World War.

THE GERMAN MILITARY MISSION

Essential to the rebirth of the Turkish Army as an effective fighting force was the continuing presence of the German Reform Mission[12] (hereafter referred to as the German Military Mission). By the summer of 1914, this mission, under the command of Major General Otto Liman von Sanders, consisted of about thirty officers and forty men. The mission had both teaching and operational responsibilities, and it was hoped that the assignment of high-ranking German officers to key command and staff positions would accelerate the reorganization of the Turkish Army. Although the outbreak of war initially and temporarily dried up the source of available German officers, the mission continued its work throughout the First World War. As originally structured, the German Military Mission (fully staffed) is depicted in Table 1-1.[13]

This manning plan was changed completely in 1914 and was adapted by Liman von Sanders to accommodate the circumstances of the regenerating Turkish Army. German commanders were assigned to three Turkish infantry divisions: these were the 3rd Infantry Division (Colonel Bronsart von Schellendorf), the 5th Infantry Division (Colonel Zadernstorn), and the 10th Infantry Division (Colonel Tronnier). In addition, Lieutenant Colonel Nikolai and Captain Stange were given command of the 3rd Artillery Regiment and the 8th Infantry Regiment, respectively.[14] The I, VI, and X Army Corps received highly trained German General Staff officers as their corps chief of staff. This arrangement front-loaded the bulk of the German talent into operational assignments in the First, Second, and Third Armies, with the I Corps in Constantinople receiving the most assistance.

In a remarkably prescient and highly effective move, Liman von Sanders reassigned Colonel Bronsart von Schellendorf from command of a Turkish division to the Turkish General Staff in the position of first assistant chief of the General Staff. From this position, Bronsart von Schellendorf exercised enormous power over the armies of the Ottoman Empire. Liman von Sanders, however, assumed command of the First Army in Constantinople in the early fall of 1914. In this position he was unable to affect the course of events as Turkey slid into war.

Table 1.1
German Military Mission

Command Group
1 commander [a]
1 General Staff officer (field grade)
2 aides-de-camp
3 other officers

Operational Assignments	Training Assignments
1 corps commander	3 General Staff officers (field grade)
1 division commander	1 director, Staff College
1 advisor – Rifle Regiment	2 instructors, Staff College
1 advisor - Cavalry Regiment	1 director, Infantry School
1 advisor – Field Artillery Regiment	1 director, Field Artillery School
1 advisor – Communications	1 director, Heavy Artillery School
	1 director, Cavalry School
	1 officer – Junior Officer School
	6 officers – for two corps headquarters
	2 commanders, Demonstration Regiment
	10 officers for technical advice [b]
	1 military doctor
	1 director, Gymnastics School
	3 commanders for NCO Schools

Notes: This plan only lists principal officers. Supporting noncommissioned officers and soldiers assigned to the mission greatly increased its personnel strength. Fully staffed, the mission would consist of about eleven hundred officers and men.
  a. The commander of the mission would serve in a dual role as the corps commander. In fact, Liman von Sanders was initially "double-hatted" as commander, I Corps.
  b. These specialties were railroads, motorization, telephones, telegraphs, engineers, logistics, and ordnance.

Source: Cemal Akbay, *Birinci Dünya Harbinde Turk Harbi (1nci Cilt) Osmanli Imparatorluğu'nun Siyasi ve Askeri Hazirliklari ve Harbe Girişi* (Ankara: Genelkurmay Basim Evi, 1991), 274.

NOTES

1. Turkish General Staff, *Turk Silahli Kuvvetleri Tarihi IIIncu Cilt 6nci Kisim (1908-1920)* (Ankara: GK Basimevi, 1971), 242.
2. Ibid., 130.
3. Cemal Akbay, *Birinci Dünya Harbinde Turk Harbi (1nci Cilt) Osmanli Imparatorluğu'nun Siyasi ve Askeri Hazirliklari ve Harbe Girişi* (Ankara: Genelkurmay Basim Evi, 1991), 127.
4. Ibid., 127.
5. Commandant M. Larcher, *La Guerre Turque Dans La Guerre Mondiale* (Paris: Chiron & Berger-Levrault, 1926), 66.
6. Ibid., 70.
7. Akbay, *Birinci Dünya Harbinde*, 135-136.
8. David Woodward, *Armies of the World 1854-1914* (New York: G. P. Putnam's Sons, 1978), 89.
9. Larcher, *La Guerre Turque*, 65.
10. Turkey, therefore, did not have units such as the "First Reserve Corps" or the "16th Bavarian Reserve Infantry Division."
11. Akbay, *Birinci Dünya Harbinde,* 121.
12. In Turkish, Alman Islah Heyeti, or German Reform Mission or German Improvement Mission.
13. Akbay, *Birinci Dünya Harbinde*, 274.
14. Ibid., 126.

2
Plans

RESOURCES

By 1914, the Ottoman Empire had fallen far behind the European Great Powers in every category of resources necessary for the conduct of modern war. The very term *empire* belied the ability of the beleaguered Turkish State to mobilize itself for a protracted war. Nevertheless, the physical landmass of the Ottoman Empire and its strategic geographic position forced upon it the roles and responsibilities of a Great Power. The empire was educationally backward, resource poor, industrially underdeveloped, and financially bankrupt. A brief comparison of population, coal production, and railways graphically shows the disparity between the Ottoman Empire and several of the Great Powers (Tables 2.1, 2.2, and 2.3). Of particular significance are the population figures for the Ottoman Empire contrasted with the actual numbers of ethnic Turks living within the empire.

Table 2.1
Ottoman Empire Population, 1914

Country	Population-World Almanac	Population-British Intelligence
Germany	65,000,000	
Britain	45,000,000	
France	39,000,000	
Ottoman Empire	22,000,000	20,000,000
Ethnic Turks	**12,000,000**	**10,000,000**

Sources: Press Publishing, *The World Almanac and Encyclopedia, 1914* (New York: Press Publishing, 1913), 224, and Intelligence Section Cairo, *Handbook of the Turkish Army*, *Eighth Provisional Edition, February 1916* (Nashville: Battery Press, 1996), 9.

16   *Ordered to Die*

The population of the Ottoman Empire in 1914 is generally estimated at about nineteen to twenty-three million people. This estimate is based on adjusting the 1908 Ottoman census figures upwards, taking into consideration probable birth and mortality rates and the loss of about a fifth of the empire's population as a result of the Balkan Wars. However, the actual number of ethnic Turks is perhaps the most useful statistic in comparing war making population potentials for Turkey during the First World War. As the Turks were to find out as the war progressed the empire was very often let down by the fighting performance of its subject minority peoples. In particular, the Arabs, the Kurds, and the Greeks were sometimes military liabilities when compared to their fellow ethnic Turk citizens.

Table 2.2
1914 Coal Production (tons)

Country	Tons of Coal
Germany	277,000,000
Britain	292,000,000
France	40,000,000
Italy	900,000
Ottoman Empire	**826,000**

Source: Press Publishing, *The World Almanac and Encyclopedia, 1914* (New York: Press Publishing, 1913), 244.

Table 2.3
1914 Railways

Country	Kilometers of Railways	Square Kilometers of Area
Germany	64,000	540,000
France	51,000	536,000
India	55,000	3,160,000
USA	388,330	7,739,524
Ottoman Empire	**5,759**	**2,410,000**

Source: Ahmed Emin Yalman, *Turkey in the World War* (New Haven, Conn.: Yale University Press, 1930), 85.

Production of pig iron and steel in the Ottoman Empire in 1914 was inconsequential;[1] therefore these critical indicators of economic potential are not presented. Additionally, there was literally no chemical production and very few petroleum refining facilities. For the production of military items there were only a single cannon and small arms foundry, a single shell and bullet factory, and a single gunpowder factory. All of these facilities were located in the Constantinople suburbs directly on the shore of the Sea of Marmara making them extremely vulnerable. The only items that the empire produced in adequate amounts were agricultural products, such as wool, cotton, and hides. Financially, the Ottoman Empire was almost paralyzed by the deficit spending patterns that constituted fiscal policy during the period 1911 through 1913. The actual Turkish deficit during these years was in excess of thirty-four million Turkish Pounds.[2] To compound matters, over 30 percent of the annual budget went to payments on the public debt. Although Britain, France, and particularly Germany with its Baghdad Railway, maneuvered for favorable positions in Ottoman railroad consortiums, there was little profit realized from these endeavors. Turkey, overall, was in an extremely unfavorable industrial and financial condition in 1914.

Consequently, the asymmetric Ottoman economy was incapable of sustained and independent industrial operations. Unlike all other major powers in the First World War, Turkey and its empire underwent almost no industrial expansion and remained dependent on imported weapons and war material until the end of the war. Until the restoration of continental landlines of communication after the defeat of Serbia in late 1915, the empire suffered terrible and crippling shortages of war supplies and raw materials. By any measurement of resources, save courage, the Ottoman Empire was unprepared to engage in a major war against Great Power opponents.

Lines of communications in the Ottoman Empire were extremely poor. As previously stated, the Turks were especially weak in their railroad system. This was compounded by the fact that various national consortiums had constructed the empire's railroad net over a prolonged period to various degrees of efficiency. It is significant to note here that all of the European Great Powers had railroad systems specifically designed to accommodate military mobilization. The Turkish system, designed by foreigners for profit motives, did not service the frontiers and it was not designed to deliver large numbers of men from their mobilization sites to concentration areas. There were different gages of railroad track in use, and there were also numerous types of German, French, and English steam engines, railway cars and equipment. In 1914, there were 280 engines, 720 passenger cars, and 4,500 freight cars in use in the Ottoman Empire.[3] The operationally ready rate for this small fleet was about 75 percent most of the time. Additionally, geography was not kind to the Turks, and the empire was spread over harsh and inhospitable terrain. Many of the railroads that had been started were incomplete and some had been abandoned. Several were cut by high mountain chains transversing the route through which tunnels had not yet been completed. The uncompleted gaps in railroad interconnectability (as illustrated by Map 2.1) at Pozanti through the Taurus Mountains and at Osmaniye through the Amanus Mountains particularly affected transportation going to Mesopotamia and Syria, since all cargo had to be transloaded through the mountains. These "choke points" afflicted the entire

Map 2.1
Railroad and Road Networks in the Ottoman Empire, 1914-1918

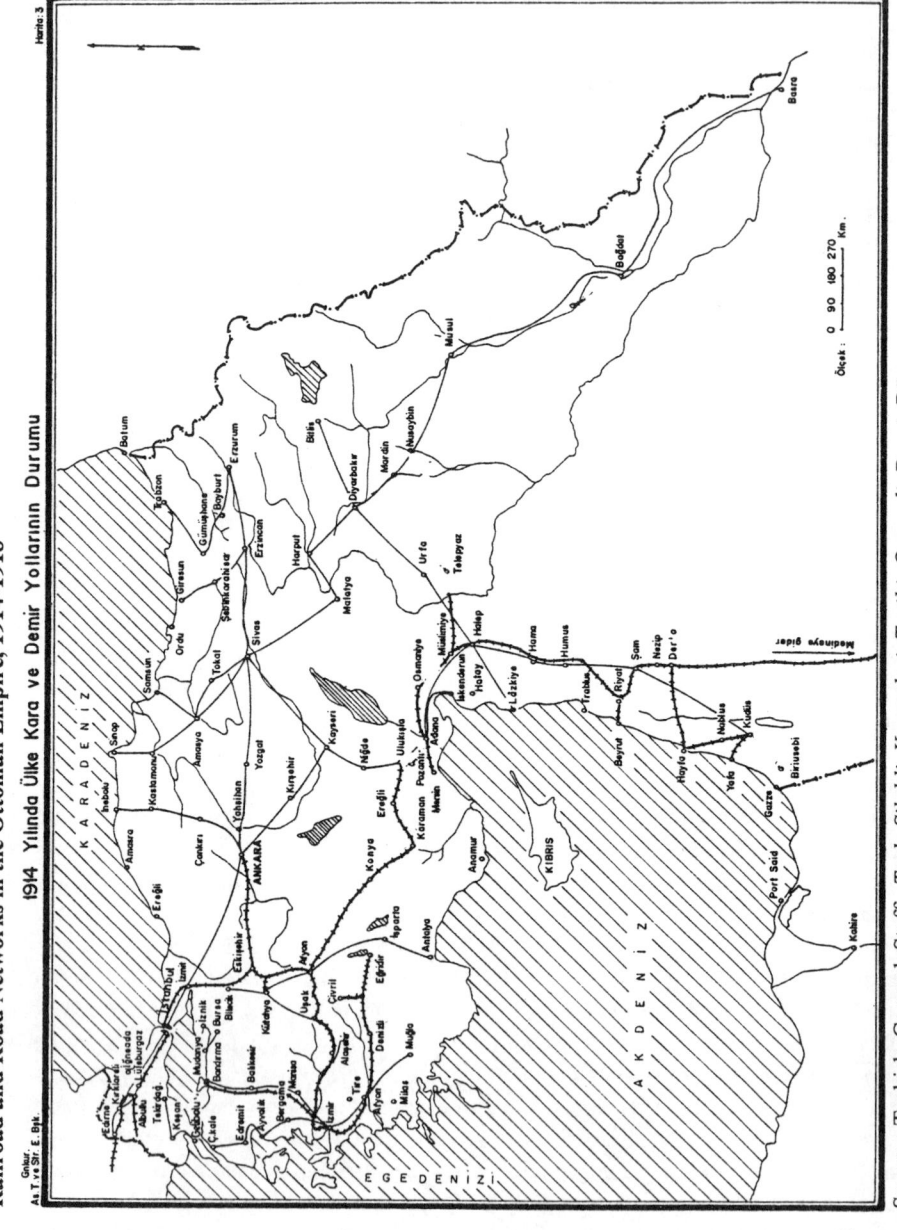

Source: Turkish General Staff, *Turk Silahli Kuvvetleri Tarihi Osmanli Devri Dünya Harbi Idari Faaliyetler ve Lojistik Xncu Cilt* (Ankara: Basimevi, 1985), Kroki (Map) 3.

Turkish war effort until the very last days of the war and greatly impeded military operations in the Caucasus, Palestine and Mesopotamia.

The road network was likewise haphazardly constructed and generally followed ancient caravan routes or terrain features. There were few paved roads. Unfortunately for the Turks, there were also huge gaps in the East–West lateral transportation lines linking eastern Turkey with Constantinople and the western reaches of the empire. On the Tigris and Euphrates Rivers, there were fairly well developed river steamer and boat lines, but these suffered from periods of seasonal flooding and low water. Prior to the outbreak of the First World War, much of the Ottoman Empire's economic commerce was seaborne between its port cities by a healthy coastal trade. However, in the Mediterranean and Aegean Seas this came to an abrupt termination as the Allies quickly blockaded the coastline. In the Black Sea the critical coastal trade carrying coal to Constantinople continued throughout the war, despite frequent Russian attempts at interdiction.

Of particular importance, Turkey, alone among the major powers, entered the First World War already exhausted from her involvement in the First and Second Balkan Wars. The significance of this fact cannot be overstated; it explains why Turkey, once again unique among the major powers, did not have mobilization plans designed to bring a mass of maneuver to a decisive point for early offensive operations (Britain's deployment of the British Expeditionary Force into France notwithstanding). By the end of the Balkan Wars, the Ottoman Empire had lost 32.7 percent of its territory and 20 percent of its population.[4] Furthermore, the empire was literally bankrupt and its army had been savaged by defeat in detail. By comparison, it would be hard to imagine France after suffering less damage proportionately, even with allies, renewing the war against Germany in 1872.

WAR AIMS

The entry of the Ottoman Empire in the First World War was an event of huge importance for several reasons. First, the entry of the Turks upset the careful calculations of strategic thinking that had characterized prewar military planning by all alliance partners. Russia and Britain, in particular, were unprepared for the nearly instantaneous creation of secondary fronts threatening vital strategic interests. Second, because of Turkey's geographic position, the relatively weak Turkish army became a magnet for Allied attacks which sought decisive and cheap victory over the apparently ill prepared and weak Turks. This drained deployable allied strength, particularly much of Britain's available strategic reserves in 1915 and a substantial part of the Russian strategic reserve in 1916. Third, Turkey's entrance into the war almost certainly propelled Bulgaria toward an active partnership with the Central Powers (this was not a foregone conclusion in 1914) by securing her rear in a war against Serbia. The entry of Bulgaria into the war was the death knell of Serbia and Romania. All of these events would have profound and unforeseen consequences on the conduct of the war. However, in 1914 Turkey had no elaborate mobilization plans designed to deliver large forces to a decisive point, nor did it have territorial or irredentist ambitions. In fact, beyond the simple act of the preservation of the state and the preservation of territorial integrity, the Turks seemed to have had no clearly defined war aims. The question of why and how Turkey entered the war begs an answer.

The most prolific author writing on the diplomacy of Turkey in this period is Ulrich Trumpener, whose main interests concern the role of Germany in Turkish affairs and the diplomacy of the Turco-German alliance. In *Germany and the Ottoman Empire 1914-1918*, Trumpener develops the theme that the secret alliance of August 2, 1914, provided the engine that separated Turkey from meaningful dialogue with the entente, while at the same time obligated Turkey to support Germany in an almost unavoidable slide toward war. He further develops the theme that the personal actions of Enver Paşa leading to the reckless naval attacks on Russian Black Sea ports on October 29, 1914, were primarily responsible for Turkey's involvement in the war. In *Eagles on the Crescent*, Frank G. Weber follows the same argument but further elaborates on the role of Austria-Hungary as agent provocateur in Turkey's entry into the war. However, neither Trumpener nor Weber precisely detail Turkey's war aims nor do they explain what the Turks hoped to accomplish or gain. Both of these authors leave out significant parts of the story, particularly Sait Halim's policy directives and the secret alliance between Bulgaria and Turkey. A. J. P. Taylor in *The Struggle for Mastery in Europe, 1848-1918* states that the Turks thought that a victorious entente would dismember the Ottoman Empire and reciprocally that Germany would guarantee its preservation. Taylor further states that war was an "all or nothing" bid by Turkey to resolve the issue of Black Sea power and control. Almost contradicting his own argument, Taylor also discusses the wildly vacillating Turkish diplomacy that characterized the months of September and October 1914. All of these themes intersect but none satisfactorily offer to explain what the Turks actually hoped to achieve by entering the war.

To understand the entry of the Ottoman Empire into the First World War it is necessary to consider the effect of the Balkan Wars of 1912 and 1913 on the Turks. Absent a hostile Great Power, the Turks entered the First Balkan War of 1912 under the worst possible strategic conditions, that is, against an alliance of every small Christian state in the Balkans. This hitherto impossible coalition of Bulgaria, Serbia, Greece, and Montenegro was temporary and lasted only long enough for the Ottomans to be ejected from the Balkan territory that they had held since the early part of the seventeenth century. The disposition of Ottoman forces shown by Table 2.4 illustrates the substantial investment that the Turks had committed to maintain a military presence in the Balkans by 1912. The First and Second Balkan Wars close forever this chapter of Ottoman history.

Table 2.4
Disposition of Turkish Forces, 1912

EUROPEAN THRACE
First Army
I Corps: 1, 2, 3 Inf. Div.
II Corps: 4, 5, 6 Inf. Div.
III Corps: 7, 8, 9 Inf. Div.
IV Corps: 10, 11, 12 Inf. Div.

CAUCASIA
Third Army
IX Corps: 28, 29 Inf. Div.
X Corps: 30, 31, 32 Inf. Div.
XI Corps: 33, 34 Inf. Div.

MESOPOTAMIA
Fourth Army
XII Corps: 35, 36 Inf. Div.
XIII Corps: 37, 38 Inf. Div.
Army Reserve: 42 Inf. Div.

SYRIA
VIII Corps: 25, 26, 27 Inf. Div.

ARABIA-YEMEN
XIV Corps: 39, 40, 41, 43 Inf. Div.

BALKANS
Second Army
V Corps: 13, 14, 15 Inf. Div.
VI Corps: 16, 17, 18 Inf. Div.
VII Corps: 19, 20, 21 Inf. Div.
Army Reserve: 22, 23, 24 Inf.Div.

[Callout: **Second Army**, stationed in the Balkans theater]

[Callout: **VII Army Corps**, assigned to the Second Army, comprising the 19th, 20th, and 21st Infantry Divisions]

[Callout: **Army Reserve**, assigned to the Second Army]

In *Caucasian Battlefields*, Allen and Muratoff state, "The result of the Balkan Wars was that the center of gravity of the Turkish State had been removed from Europe to Asia."[5] The significance of this event for the leadership of the Ottoman Empire in 1914 cannot be ignored.

Out of twelve prewar mobilization plans in 1912, seven Turkish Army mobilization plans centered on the Balkans.[6] Mobilization Plan Number 5 matched the actual threat and posited the First and Second Turkish Armies facing the combined armies of Bulgaria, Serbia, Montenegro, and Greece. In this particular plan, the Ottomans fielded 373 infantry battalions in Thrace (First Army) and 222 infantry battalions in Macedonia (Second Army) against an estimated 556 hostile infantry battalions. This plan was defensive and, although the Turks had a slight numerical advantage, invited defeat in detail. With a single exception, all twelve plans were strategically defensive and indicated Turkey's fundamental unwillingness to renew any irredentist claims from previous wars.

In Plan 5, the Second Army in Macedonia organized its three army corps into an area defense and at the tactical level simply attempted to hold key fortresses and cities.[7] Given a period of peace prior to the outbreak of war, reinforcements would come into Macedonia by rail and by sea from as far away as Yemen and Syria. Over half of the infantry strength of the 344,923-man Second Army would come from the reserves. Many never arrived.

The larger First Army defended Thrace from the fortress city of Adrianople. For this mission, the army had 466,453 men of which 54 percent of the infantry were reservists.[8] The Ottoman General Staff developed mobilization timetables, which mobilized most reserve infantry battalions within six to thirteen days and which used a combination of foot marches and rail transportation to deploy the units to their war stations. However, some units were not mobilized until the twenty-third day of mobilization. The disparity in personnel strengths of the two armies represented both the degree of difficulty involved in moving reinforcements from Anatolia to the Balkans, and also represented the strategic importance of Thrace as the main approach to Constantinople. Both armies were to fight on the defensive with the mission of holding ground while wearing the enemy down to exhaustion. The desired strategic outcome of Plan 5 was the collapse of the enemy coalition.

Unfortunately for the Ottoman Empire, Mobilization Plan Number 5 resulted in the defeat in detail of the First Army, the loss of Adrianople, and the near loss of Constantinople itself. Significantly, It also resulted in the nearly total destruction of the Second Army and the complete loss of the remaining Turkish possessions in the Sanjack, Macedonia, and lower Serbia. The effect that these twin losses had on Turkish military and diplomatic thinking were significant and would become important in the events of the late summer and early fall of 1914.

The Turkish Second Army headquartered in Macedonia was composed of the V, VI, and VII Army Corps, each of three infantry divisions and one cavalry brigade. The army had three additional infantry divisions in army reserve. It was an important and prestigious command and it was well supplied with proficient Turkish General Staff officers. Nevertheless, by the end of April 1913, the Second Army had been hammered down to a strength of less than twelve regiments and a few miscellaneous bits of units scattered about its former operational area.[9]

The larger Turkish First Army was composed of the I, II, and III Army Corps, each of three infantry divisions, and the Fourth and Fifteenth Fortified Zone Commands (corps equivalents), which together deployed two infantry divisions and four fortress divisions. The fortress of Adrianople itself had a corps-sized garrison of one infantry division, one fortress division, and three reserve infantry divisions. But by the end of July 1913, Adrianople and its garrison were lost and the First Army lay shattered and locked in a death struggle at Çatalca.[10] The defeated army headquarters element itself was renamed the Çatalca Army and fully half of its strength was composed of ad hoc reserve infantry divisions mobilized from the Anatolian heartland in a last ditch effort to defend the capitol. Table 2.5 illustrates the extreme differences between the balanced army dispositions of 1912 and the battered condition it found itself in 1913 after suffering both defeat and the loss of the Balkans.

The Treaty of London brought the First Balkan War to a close. The Second Balkan War began in June 1913 with the dissolution of the temporary alliance against Turkey. During that summer, Bulgaria attacked Serbia and Greece, and was in turn heavily attacked by those countries. Turkey took advantage of this momentary window of opportunity to exploit Bulgarian weakness in Thrace by retaking Adrianople. This action stabilized the Turkish frontier along its current boundary. The Treaty of Bucharest ended the Second Balkan War with Turkey holding Adrianople, Greece holding Salonika and Epirius, and Serbia holding Macedonia.

What was the overall effect on Turkey of these wars? First, the ponderous and operationally unsuccessful mobilization of 1912 brought home the lesson that timetable planning (as was used by the major powers of Europe) was unsuitable given the poorly developed lines of communications extant in the Ottoman Empire. Readiness of mobilized forces, therefore, became an event-oriented situation rather than a timetable-driven situation. Second, the immense losses suffered by the army had consequences of enormous impact. The losses in equipment, trained leaders, and experienced formations preordained the enlargement of the existing German Military Mission. This enlargement in early 1914, led by Cavalry Major General Otto Liman von Sanders, would have a dire effect on Entente perceptions of the events of the fall of 1914. Third, the loss of the *entire* Second Army of twelve regular infantry divisions and much of the First Army meant that the Turkish Army would have to focus in the near term on unit reconstitution rather than on training and preparation for war. This obviated any future mobilization that supported war plans aimed at early offensive operations. And although there was certainly some tactical benefit to a

Table 2.5
Disposition of Turkish Forces, July 1913

BALKANS
(All units lost in the spring of 1913)

EUROPEAN THRACE
Çatalca Army
I Corps: 2, 28, **Fatih Inf. Div.**
II Corps: 3, 5, 12 Inf. Div.
III Corps: 7, 8, 9 Inf. Div.
IV Corps: 29, Aydın, Ereğli, **Kayseri Inf. Div.**
Army Reserve: 51, Yozgat, Ankara,
    Selimiye, Amasya, **Asiret Inf. Div.**

Gallipoli Army
X Corps: 4, 31, **Aziz Inf. Div.**
I Fort Corps: 30, 32, **Mürettep Inf. Div.**
II Fort Corps: 27, Samsun, **Afyon Inf. Div.**
III Fort Corps: Çanakkale, **Edrimet Inf. Div.**

CAUCASIA
Third Army
IX Corps: 33 Inf. Div.
XI Corps: 34 Inf. Div.

RECONSTITUTION IN CENTRAL ANATOLIA
Vardar Army headquarters (Second Army)
V Corps headquarters
VI Corps: 16 Inf. Div.
VII Corps: 21 Inf. Div.

SYRIA
VIII Corps: 25, 26 Inf. Div.

MESOPOTAMIA
35, 36 Inf. Div.

Note: Units in boldface type indicate new formations.

seasoning of the army in the brutal school of combat, much of the surviving force was composed of older reservists, and as such, the army was tired out and worn down. Unlike her northern neighbors, Turkey did not enter the First World War to cheering crowds and garlanded regiments marching to the line of departure.

In the days following the assassination of Archduke Ferdinand in Sarajevo on June 28, 1914, Europe spiraled towards war. Diplomacy failed as ultimatums were followed by partial and then by full military mobilizations of the Triple Alliance (Germany and Austria-Hungary, but absent Italy) and by the entente cordiale (France, Great Britain, and Russia). War finally broke out on August 1 with Germany's declaration of war on Russia. Turkey, exhausted and recovering from the Balkan Wars, remained aloof from the running course of these events. The major European powers alternately attempted to either threaten or to encourage Turkey to enter the war or to remain neutral. There were mixed opinions in all camps about the military value of a friendly, a neutral, or a hostile Turkey. However, Germany had the greatest success in influencing events in the summer of 1914 and by late July had concluded a working understanding with Enver Paşa, the Ottoman minister of war. This understanding matured into a full biown but "secret" military treaty between Germany and the Ottoman Empire.

Much has been made of the Secret Treaty of Alliance between Germany and the Ottoman Empire, signed in Constantinople on August 2, 1914. This treaty was concluded in response to overtures made by the Ottomans to Kaiser Wilhelm in mid-July 1914. Detailed conversations, including the idea of keeping the treaty secret, were held on July 27. German Ambassador Hans von Wangenheim, the chief of the German Military Mission General Liman von Sanders, and the Ottoman Minister of War Enver Pasa met on August 1, 1914, to discuss the implementation of such a treaty. They reached an agreement that Turkey would stand on the defensive on the Caucasian Frontier and assemble an army in Thrace for operations against Russia, but with Bulgarian and Rumanian neutrality uncertain, alternatively against Greece.[11] The treaty itself was rather poorly worded and was vague in its meaning, or perhaps it was carefully crafted to serve other purposes. A careful reading of the Secret Alliance reveals it to be limited scope treaty similar to the Dual Alliance between Germany and Austria-Hungary in 1879. In reality, the Secret Treaty of Alliance was a very weak document with no operative power of enforcement and it was written only for the situational context of the ongoing Balkan crisis of July 1914. Under a strict interpretation of the terms of the Secret Alliance, Turkey was obligated to enter the war only under specific conditions. The treaty was, quite simply, overcome by events (having been drafted July 24) because it became activated only in the case of Russian intervention with active military measures against Austria-Hungary. In fact, Russia had only mobilized and had *not* intervened, when Germany declared war on her first. Wangenheim knew this before he signed the treaty for the Kaiser. Therefore, when Germany declared war on Russia on

August 1, 1914, the Secret Treaty of Alliance (which was signed the very next day) was in effect *invalid* on signature. By early morning on August 2, the Turks knew of Germany's declaration of war on Russia but went ahead and signed the treaty between 4 and 5 P.M. that day.[12] Although the treaty did not bring Turkey immediately into the war as an active participant, the real value of the document to Germany at this time was in the fact that the treaty was *secret*. The Secret Treaty of Alliance was reminiscent of Bismarckian diplomacy in which the very existence of treaties themselves became tools for leverage or were used to force other secondary actions. The Allies soon learned of the treaty's existence and consequently speculation began in London, Paris, and above all in St. Petersburg, concerning what *exactly* was in the treaty and which countries it was operative against. Many observers thought that the treaty was inherently offensive. The most prevalent allied thinking was that Turkey had been promised the recovery of parts of Bulgaria and Greece in return for entering the war against the entente.[13] By its very existence the treaty threatened the entente and created leverage for Germany over the Turks.

The treaty had only eight clauses. The parties (Germany and the Ottoman Empire) pledged to remain neutral in the conflict between Serbia and Austria-Hungary. Germany promised to leave its Military Mission in place in the event of war and in return the Turks agreed to let the Military Mission exercise general control over their army. Germany promised to defend Ottoman territory. There were ratification and expiration clauses and the final clause pledged both parties to maintain the secrecy of the treaty itself. The second clause was the operative clause which obligated Turkey to act in certain circumstances. A German version of this clause by Carl Muhlmann in *Deutschland und die Turkei, 1913-1914* appears as: "In the event that Russia should intervene with active military measures and thus should create a *casus foederis* with respect to Austria-Hungary, this *casus foederis* would also come into force for Turkey."[14]

There were different interpretations of what the second clause really meant. The treaty was written in French (the Ottoman diplomatic language of choice) for Germans and Turks to sign. That there would be varied interpretations was probably inevitable. A Turkish variant from Dr. Ahmed Emin Yalman contains a slightly different wording of this key clause: "If Russia intervenes and takes active military measures, and the necessity arises for Germany to carry out her pledges of alliance to Austria, Turkey is under obligation in such a case, to carry out her pledges made to Germany."[15] The original French text of this key clause was slightly different yet: "Dans le cas ou'nla Russie interviendrait par des mesures militaires actives et creerait par la' pour l'Allemagne le *casus foederis* vis-à-vis de l'Autriche-Hongrie, ce *casus foederis* entrerait egalement en vigueur pour la Turquie."[16]

In any event, Sait Halim, the grand vizier, was somewhat distressed to find the extent of the negotiations that Enver had carried on in the name of his government. Sait Halim was an Ottoman prince but more important was prime minister and foreign minister as well as grand vizier. He was not known to support Turkish involvement in the alliance process but was thought to lean toward the entente. It is almost certain that he did not want war. After it became clear that Germany had, indeed, declared war on the Russians first, Sait Halim had second thoughts about the alliance with Germany and belatedly exercised his prerogatives as prime minister and foreign minister. Furthermore, moving rapidly, Enver too was already attempting to negotiate a new less threatening agreement with the Russians by telling them that the ongoing Turkish mobilization was not directed against them.[17] Sait Halim resisted Wangenheim's insistent demands that Turkey immediately honor her treaty obligations. On August 6, 1914, Sait Halim pressed Wangenheim in a letter with six proposals for further German concessions in return for Turkey's activation of the Secret Alliance.[18] In the absence of a clear foreign policy or coherent military war plans, these six proposals probably come as close to defining Turkey's war aims prior to hostilities than any other document. Wangenheim, reluctant to endanger the proposed safe haven for the inbound squadron of Rear Admiral Souchon immediately agreed to Sait Halim's conditions. The six proposals were (1) Germany promises its help in the abolition of the capitulations; (2) Germany agrees to lend its support to understandings with Rumania and Bulgaria, and it will see to it that Turkey secures a fair agreement with Bulgaria with reference to possible spoils of war; (3) Germany will not conclude peace unless (all) Turkish territories, which may be occupied by its enemies in the course of the war, are evacuated; (4) Should Greece enter the war and be defeated by Turkey, Germany will see to it that the (Aegean) islands are returned (to the Turks); (5) Germany will secure for Turkey a small correction of her eastern border, which shall place Turkey into direct contact with the Muslims of Russia; (6) Germany will see to it that Turkey receives an appropriate war indemnity.[19]

It is immediately clear that the Turkish government was primarily interested in economic succor, notably the abolition of the capitulations, a fair share of the spoils of war, and also a war indemnity. The capitulations were favorable trading measures which relieved certain nations from the burden of Ottoman import tariffs, guaranteed trading rights, and granted legal extraterritoriality to that nation's citizens. The capitulations had been a crippling economic millstone and an emotional sore spot for the Turks for many years. They were widely regarded by Turkish nationalists as a significant obstacle to modernization. It is important to note that there was no mention of the recovery of any part of the Balkans lost in 1912 and 1913, or of the Armenian *vilayets* lost in 1877. It is also important to note that Turkey was not hostile to either Bulgaria or to Rumania.

Over the course of the next several days, the Germans pressed the Turks for guarantees of safe haven for the battlecruiser SMS Goeben and her consort, the light cruiser, SMS Breslau. The Germans also renewed pressing for an immediate Ottoman declaration of war against Russia. Sait Halim continued to harbor hesitancy toward what he increasingly believed was an ill-advised and mismanaged treaty with Germany. There was also strong opposition to active involvement supporting the Germans from influential military and naval officers; among them were Mustafa Kemal and Rauf Bey. In a meeting on August 9, 1914, with Enver Paşa, Cavid Bey, Cemal Paşa, and Talat Paşa, Sait Halim made it clear that he did not believe that the treaty imposed an obligation to enter the war to support Germany.[20] Later that same day, Sait Halim's thoughts coalesced and he directed the government to undertake a contradictory course correction in Ottoman foreign policy.   In this directive, Sait Halim sought to overcome the forces that were pushing the empire toward war. He wanted the text of the treaty with Germany examined from a legal point of view. He sought to conclude alliances with Bulgaria and Rumania and to convince the entente that Turkey meant to remain neutral. He directed that a special commission be formed to monitor food supplies. To mediate the uneasiness in the army, Sait Halim sought to gain time until the outcome of the war became clear. Importantly, he directed that the German ambassador not interfere with military affairs, or the German commander, General Liman von Sanders, with politics. He desired that under no circumstances would Turkey enter the war on any side, before concluding negotiations with Rumania, Bulgaria, and Greece. Finally, he directed that negotiations be reopened with the French and Russian ambassadors.[21]

This directive was important since it vividly demonstrated Sait Halim's unhappiness with the very existence of the secret treaty with Germany. There was absolutely no point for a legal review of the Secret Treaty of Alliance unless Turkey intended to abrogate all or part of the document and needed a legal reason to do so. Clearly, Sait Halim intended that Turkey would remain neutral for the near future and would not allow the Germans to tamper with Turkish political-military affairs. Sait Halim intended to buy time for Turkey and up to a point he was successful. This policy directive effectively marginalized Liman von Sanders, and to some extent Wangenheim as well. However, on August 11, 1914, a new player arrived on the field, Vice Admiral Wilhelm Souchon, whose presence and ships destabilized, in a very short order, Sait Halim's control over events.

One thing that Constantinople did not lack in the summer and fall of 1914 was an abundance of powerful personalities. Ulrich Trumpener and Frank Weber offer vivid portraits of the key players in the Ottoman diplomatic arena during those times. In particular, Weber's portrayal of Hans Freiherr von Wangenheim as a proactive and relentless advocate of German dominance in Ottoman affairs is compelling. With single-minded determination, Wangenheim maneuvered the reluctant and shifting Turks into an alliance, and when they balked he worked tirelessly to set up conditions which would bring them into the war. In retrospect, the Turkish entry into the First World War seems almost inconceivable with this pivotal individual.

A. J. P. Taylor paints a picture in which Liman von Sanders played a crucial role ("Sanders and his staff had a firm grip on the Turkish Army").[22] In actuality, the temperamental von Sanders was sidelined in early August 1914 after Enver Paşa reassigned him as the commanding general of the Turkish First Army, an important command, but one that took Liman von Sanders out of the critical high-level decision cycle. Von Sanders's memoirs reflect his frustration at the abysmal condition of his command and his inability to affect the course of events. He was completely surprised when his attaché relayed the news of the fleet actions of October 29, 1914, clearly showing how far from the nexus of power he really was.[23] Von Sanders himself had just arrived in Constantinople in December 1913 and the total strength of his Military Mission was only about seventy men altogether. With the exception of Colonel Friedrich (Fritz) Bronsart von Schellendorff (chief of staff of the German Military Mission), who also functioned in his capacity as the first assistant chief of the Turkish General Staff as a cross between the secretary of the Turkish General Staff and the chief of plans, no German officer actually exercised direct or indirect control over the strategic deployment of the land forces of the Ottoman Empire. Liman von Sanders was so unhappy with his role that in the middle of August 1914, he formally requested permission to dissolve his mission and to be allowed to return to Germany with his men.

Rear Admiral Wilhelm Souchon, Commander of the Imperial German Navy's Mediterranean Squadron, was a latecomer to the intrigues of Constantinople. He and his squadron arrived at the Dardanelles on August 11, 1914, and in his escape from the Royal Navy, Souchon had proven himself to be a resourceful commander. In a diplomatic charade, his ships were reflagged into the Turkish Navy (famously the Germans crews were given the Turkish fez to wear) and on September 24, 1914, Souchon was commissioned as a vice admiral in the Ottoman Navy. Souchon fell under the aegis of Ambassador Wangenheim, and unlike von Sanders, Souchon retained direct command of an instrument of war which Germany could wield independently.

The Turkish government was composed of a mixed bag of conservative, liberal, and ambitious men loosely known as The Young Turks. The most powerful among them, Mahmut Şevket Paşa, had been assassinated a few short months before the Sarajevo crisis. This inevitably led to a leadership crisis and internal power struggle as Enver, Cemal, and Sait Halim maneuvered for control. The death of Şevket Paşa left a vacuum in the power structure of the CUP, which seemed to set the committee at cross-purposes.

The most visible figure in Ottoman politics to the outside world at this time was Sait Halim. In most works, he is referred to as the grand vizier. This Imperial Ottoman title was a holdover from the Sublime Porte and was not reflective of his real position of power as prime minister and head of the CUP. Sait Halim also retained the portfolio of the Foreign Ministry. As the Ottoman foreign minister, ostensibly, all major diplomatic, military, and policy decisions were either made by him or with his concurrence. It is debatable whether he was intellectually up to the challenges imposed by these parallel cabinet responsibilities as Turkey spiraled towards war. He was considered to be anti-interventionist (pro-neutral) and slightly in favor of the entente, although Enver portrayed him as pro-German to Wangenheim. The events of August through November 1914 proved him to be hesitant and unable to control his own cabinet.

The most power hungry, volatile, and youngest member of the cabinet was Enver Paşa, who served as the minister of war. Enver had been served in Germany, spoke German well, and had close personal relations with Wangenheim. He was considered to be pro-German, although Trumpener considers his reputation as "the Kaiser's man" to be not altogether correct. Enver also functioned as the acting commander of the Ottoman Empire's armed forces. In this capacity, he exercised control over his own Ministry of War and the Cemal Paşa's Ministry of the Marine which further complicated matters. In 1914, Enver was riding a wave of public popularity and prestige from his reconquest of Adrianople.

The minister of the marine (navy minister) was Ahmet Cemal Paşa. After the war he was one of two Ottoman leader to write memoirs. Cemal Paşa was initially anti-interventionist and had personal connections to the chief of the British Naval Mission to the empire, Rear Admiral Sir Arthur H. Limpus. Limpus's mission was fundamentally dissimilar to that of von Sanders, and provided only administrative assistance as opposed to technical and tactical advice. However, the British Naval Mission would have matured into a full-blown assistance group when two battleships then being built for the Turks in British yards were completed and delivered. Instead, the seizure of the nearly completed Turkish battleships in August 1914 by the Royal Navy served to enrage the Turkish public, which had paid for them by popular subscription.

Talat Paşa was the very powerful minister of the interior and controlled the Jandarma (Gendarmerie). He was also responsible for all internal security functions and the police forces, as well. Considered somewhat pro-German, the cabinet chose Talat to pursue closer relations with Russia in the early summer of 1914. The minister of finance was Cavit Bey, who was anti-interventionist and definitely leaned in favor the entente. There were several other important Young Turks, including Mustafa Kemal, Kazim, and Fehti, however, these men had been marginalized in the power struggle and had been sent to remote postings.

True to Ottoman political styles of diplomacy, much of the work of conducting international dialogue was compartmentalized within the CUP. In his capacity as foreign minister, Sait Halim maintained direct contact with all of the major ambassadors in Constantinople. However, the Young Turks did not orchestrate foreign policy through a professionally staffed foreign ministry or foreign office, preferring instead diplomacy personally conducted by inner circle cabinet members. The period July through September 1914 was characterized by a series of Ottoman diplomatic initiatives which appear contradictory and confused. The central figure in this process was, of course, Sait Halim, who maintained ties to every important figure in Constantinople, except for von Sanders and Souchon (however, the pivotal player remained Enver Paşa who forged important links with the Germans). It is arguable that because of the Young Turks' propensity to conduct diplomacy (and their affairs in general) in isolation, that at any given time between August and November 1914, no single individual within the Turkish government (including either Sait Halim or Enver Paşa) had a global awareness of the entire diplomatic situation affecting the empire. This compartmentalization of awareness destroyed any chance of rational checks and balances which might have prevented war.

On the diplomatic front, under a mantle of tight security in Sofia on August 6, 1914, Talat Paşa and Ambassador Radoslavov concluded another secret treaty between the Ottoman Empire and Bulgaria. It should be noted that Talat Paşa was the minister of the interior and was not affiliated with the Foreign Ministry. This treaty was kept secret from the Germans until December 17, 1914. This treaty was a mutual defense pact that came into effect if either party was attacked by another Balkan power. It was also something of a nonaggression pact, as both parties pledged not to attack other Balkan countries without consultation with each other. In the absence of such consultation, the parties pledged benevolent neutrality in such a conflict. Furthermore, the treaty guaranteed Bulgaria that a bilateral or joint Turkish-Bulgarian agreement for Romanian neutrality would be negotiated. Bulgaria additionally agreed to notify Turkey of any impending military mobilization. The treaty would remain in effect for the duration of the war. Finally, both parties agreed that "the existence and tenor of the present treaty shall be guarded in the deepest secrecy."[24]

This treaty of alliance between Bulgaria and the Ottoman Empire was indeed a deep secret as evidenced by Sait Halim's instructions to his own government on August 9, 1914. It is interesting to compare the specificity of this treaty, negotiated by Talat Paşa, with that of the German treaty negotiated by Enver Paşa. Very clearly, Talat's treaty with the Bulgarians is much more finely drawn and functionally specific, and the weak wording in the German treaty was not to be found. Of interest is Article IV, which allowed Ottoman forces to cross Bulgaria to attack another power (perhaps Serbia or Greece) and Article V, which spoke to the mutual desire to avoid confrontation with Romania.

In early August the Austro-Hungarian Ambassador, Pallavicini, also began to press Sait Halim for a declaration of war against Russia. He had nothing to offer the Ottomans and pressed his case on the premise that history had presented the Turks with a favorable opportunity to rectify past injustices. Sait Halim and Pallavicini maintained a continuous dialogue until Turkey's actual entry into the war. At the same time, Enver Paşa opened renewed dialogue with Russian Ambassador Giers and on August 9, 1914, proposed an Ottoman-Russian alliance.[25] Trumpener, Weber, and Albertini all believe that Enver's proposal was a deliberate Ottoman ploy to draw attention away from the Secret Treaty of Alliance with Germany. However, Enver's actions were consistent with Sait Halim's policy decision of August 9, 1914. It is apparent through these initiatives that the Ottoman leadership, as a whole, was not absolutely committed to war and that the Turks were attempting to retain as many options available as possible.

Thus, immediately after the signing of the Secret Treaty of Alliance with Germany, the Ottoman leadership took several important diplomatic decisions, the most important of which were the decisions of August 6 and August 9, which established the direction of Ottoman foreign policy. Meanwhile, in the military arena, Enver Paşa, having appointed himself as the chief of the Turkish General Staff, ordered mobilization on August 2, 1914. The important point about this fact was that instead of ordering a limited mobilization, which supported the diplomatic framework envisioned by Sait Halim, Enver Paşa ordered general mobilization. This measure was widely misinterpreted by the entente as overtly hostile to allied interests.

Unlike the twelve complicated mobilization plans of 1912, the war weary and over taxed Turkish General Staff had but *one* mobilization plan in the summer of 1914. Bronsart von Schellendorff approved the staffing of this single plan on June 7, 1914.[26] The plan recognized the supreme strategic importance of the Turkish Straits and Constantinople and brought the bulk of the regular army into European Turkish Thrace. Out of twelve regular army corps in the Ottoman Army, six deployed to either Thrace or the Marmara region. A further corps went to Symrna. Three corps deployed against the Russians, and the remainder went to Syria and Arabia. None of the corps received offensive missions and like the 1912 plans, all were ordered only to defend Ottoman territory. Even though the weight of the army appeared to threaten Bulgaria, the Turkish General Staff had no plans for cross-border operations or offensive operations oriented toward the west. This mystified the entente attachés in Constantinople who had observed the mobilization of 1912 and thus confused reports emanated from the allied embassies throughout the Balkans. The British thought that the Turks were preparing to attack Russia on the Asiatic frontier, while trying to ally themselves with Bulgaria for an attack on Serbia.[27] However, as stated by Allen and Muratoff, the Turks were no longer focused on the restoration of a larger Turkey-in-Europe.

Because of their disastrous experiences with the mobilization plan of 1912, the Turkish General Staff realized that the underdeveloped railroads and lines of communications could not support timetable-based deployment schemes. As a result, completion of mobilization schedules became very problematic. It made no sense, for example, to plan on the VI Corps (which deployed from Aleppo to San Stefano) being ready to assume an operational role at the thirtieth day of mobilization if substantial elements on the corps were still on the road. Therefore the Turks now viewed mobilization an event driven affair. Units were not assumed to arrive at the scheduled times and were only counted in the line when physically reported as being ready. Bronsart von Schellendorff simply had no real idea of exactly when Turkish units would deploy from their peacetime mobilization stations to their wartime operational positions. As a result, the military began to push the diplomats for breathing time during which the slowly evolving mobilization plan could sort itself out.

Compounding these problems was the fact that the Turkish Army was engaged in a large unit reconstitution program, which was rebuilding the twelve divisions and the three corps headquarters lost during the First and Second Balkan Wars. This was further reason to delay the entry into the war for as long as possible. Because of all of these difficulties, mobilization proceeded slowly and was not complete until well into early November 1914. Even when completed, the mobilization plan of the Turkish Army resulted in the least concentrated deployment scheme of any of the major combatants.

Within the entente capitols, there were mixed feelings about the direction in which Turkey was headed. The British felt that the alliance with Germany and the presence of Admiral Souchon's squadron made dialogue with Turkey impossible. The Russians also believed that Turkey was not serious about a renewal of constructive dialogue. France almost ignored the Ottoman question and concentrated her efforts on bringing Greece into the war on the side of the allies. Winston Churchill felt that of all the intelligence pouring into Whitehall, the British were the most uninformed about the situation in Turkey.[28]

As the months progressed, Bronsart von Schellendorff received minor instructions to fine-tune the developing mobilization plan. On September 4, 1914, he was ordered to adjust the mobilization and deployment plan to accommodate a potentially hostile Greece.[29] Additionally, mobilization for many Turkish Army corps was delayed up to twenty-five to forty days beyond projections making detailed planning difficult. By the middle of October 1914, Bronsart von Schellendorf received further instructions to begin planning for a strategic attack aimed at seizing the Suez Canal. Unfortunately, the single-use mobilization plan of June 1914 had delivered the most proficient fighting divisions of the army to European Turkish Thrace.

In retrospect, the military deployment and concentration of forces available to the Ottoman Empire did not align well with the overall diplomatic situation, nor was the defensive nature of the empire's mobilization clearly understood by the allies. Thus, as either a useful tool for the diplomats or as an unsheathed sword for the generals, the Turkish Army's mobilization failed to meet the needs of the empire.

Probably the single most important ingredient in the mix of factors and forces involved in the Ottoman Empire's entry into the First World War was the presence of the Imperial German Navy's Mediterranean Squadron at Constantinople. U.S. Ambassador Henry Morgenthau thought that the passage of the SMS Goeben and the SMS Breslau through the Dardanelles created inevitable conditions that moved Turkey toward war.[30] Although the ships themselves were certainly an instrument of German diplomatic and military leverage over the Ottoman Empire, the powerful personality of Rear Admiral Wilhelm Souchon must be given equal weight in the diplomatic and strategic equation. Souchon was formally named as commander of the Ottoman Fleet on the day he handed over his ships to the Turks (August 16, 1914). However, this was a titular designation and Souchon was not at this time in actuality the commander of the Ottoman fleet, much in the same manner that the ships themselves were not Turkish (until 1918). Whatever Souchon's real title, it is clear that he reported directly to Wangenheim, had little to do with Liman von Sanders, and less to do with Ottoman Minister of the Marine Cemal Paşa. This point is not explained in any of the extant literature describing this period. It is unclear why, on September 14, 1914, Enver Paşa, rather than Cemal Paşa, authorized Souchon to take his ships into the Black Sea and attack Russian shipping.[31] Evidently there was a very strong informal link between Souchon and Enver Paşa (presumably exercising his authority as the acting commander in chief of the Ottoman forces), which seemingly bypassed Cemal Paşa, the minister of the marine. However, the intercession of Sait Halim aborted the proposed naval strike before Souchon could raise steam. With Wangenheim's approval, Souchon complained directly to the Ottoman government, requesting freedom of action to conduct training cruises. Sait Halim was very uncomfortable with this arrangement, despite the reassurances of Wangenheim.[32] Subsequently, discussions with Souchon were held on September 18, 1914, and the Germans were forbidden to exercise in the Black Sea. To achieve this understanding, the Ottomans proposed that Souchon receive a one-year appointment in the Ottoman service with the rank of vice admiral and furthermore that he take over the role of the Naval Mission, now vacant with the departure of Rear Admiral Limpus. In principle, this alleviated Sait Halim's fears because it brought Souchon and his ships directly under Ottoman control. The Germans approved this arrangement and on September 24, 1914, Souchon ostensibly reported for duty to Cemal Paşa.

The means for Turkey's entry into the war now lay with the weak and ineffective command relationship between Souchon and the Turks. Cemal Paşa's memoirs, published after the war, are very unclear about exactly which authorities he retained over the Ottoman Fleet and which authorities he delegated down to Souchon. In fact, Cemal's memoirs conveniently pause on October 12, 1914, and restart on October 30, 1914 (the day after Souchon's naval raid).

Throughout early October 1914, Sait Halim continued to press for Ottoman neutrality, and for a time Talat seemed to be with him. Enver, operating almost unsupported, secured several million Turkish pounds in gold from Berlin and continued to plan the opening move designed to force Turkey into the war.[33] This money probably went to buy the support of government officials wavering between war and peace. At a cabinet meeting on October 12, 1914, Cemal Paşa related that the inner cabinet felt that Turkey was faced with but two options, the first was immediate intervention and the second was to send Halil Bey and several others to Berlin to convince the Germans of the necessity of maintaining Turkish neutrality for another six months.[34] By late October 1914, however, Talat had swung back to Enver's interventionist clique.[35] In spite of the agreed on prohibitions, Souchon took his heavily flagged and bedecked ships out into the Black Sea again. Unfortunately for the empire, Sait Halim failed to act decisively to put an end to such excursions. Seizing this chance to overturn the prohibition, Enver issued instructions on October 25 to Vice Admiral Souchon authorizing him to conduct maneuvers in the Black Sea and to attack the Russian fleet "if a suitable opportunity presented itself."[36] The authority with which Enver did this, bypassing of the normal chain of command through Cemal's Ministry, is unclear today. At the same time, Cemal Paşa transmitted a secret instruction to senior Ottoman naval officers that Vice Admiral Souchon was entitled to issue orders to the fleet. Cemal's memoirs fail to address this key point. Importantly, Enver's orders called for an incident at sea and were based on the assumption that the Russians would rise to the bait of German ships steaming in the Black Sea. It is likely that Enver probably imagined a meeting engagement in the Black Sea between Germans and Russians that would result in shots being fired.[37] In any case, this abrogation of authority to Vice Admiral Souchon was the proximate cause of the Black Sea raids, which brought Turkey directly into the war.

At this time, there were still many men within the War Ministry and within the General Staff who were unconvinced that rapid entry into the war was in the empire's best interests. Many felt that time was on the side of the Turks and that the best course of action was to wait out developments. To counter this opposition, the number two and the number three officers from the Turkish General Staff, Bronsart von Schellendorf and Hafiz Hakki Bey were ordered to Belin for consultations on October 24.

On October 26, 1914, the Ottoman Navy received orders directing preparations for a reconnaissance exercise and was also provided with sealed orders from Souchon.[38] The fleet weighed anchor and departed Hyderpaşa the next day for its concentration areas. On October 28, 1914, the Ottoman fleet reorganized for combat by splitting itself into four task forces steaming for separate targets along the Russian coast. Vice Admiral Souchon with the Goeben and several Turkish destroyers opened fire on shore batteries at Sevastapol at 6:30 A.M. on October 29, 1914. The cruiser Hamidiye arrived at Feodosia at 6:30 A.M., and chose to inform the local authorities that hostilities would begin in two hours. The Hamidiye began shelling at 9 A.M. for an hour before proceeding to Yalta where she sank several small Russian vessels. Two Turkish destroyers attacked Odessa at 6:30 A.M., sinking two Russian gunboats and destroying several granaries. The cruiser Breslau and an accompanying destroyer arrived at Novorossiysk, and as at Feodosia, warned the locals. At 10:50 A.M., these ships opened fire on shore batteries and laid sixty mines. Seven ships in port were damaged and one was sunk.[39] As a result of these attacks, the Allies severed relations with Turkey and delivered ultimatums. Enver was quick to praise the returning fleet and wrote a congratulatory letter at 5:50 P.M. on October 29. In this letter he congratulated the fleet on its fine work and compared the action to the heady days of Ottoman naval supremacy under the Sultans. By his immediate action, Enver clearly knew of the scope and the objectives of the attack.⁴⁰ Several days later, on November 2, 1914, Russia declared war on the Ottoman Empire.

At the after action naval conference in Constantinople on November 1, German naval officers expressed disappointment at the limited success of the raids and were critical of Ottoman naval performance. However, it should be noted that while Souchon and the Goeben sank no ships, and the Breslau one ship, the Ottoman cruisers and destroyers bagged two gunboats and five merchant vessels. Any objective assessment of the raids might question the basic mission itself as one which had no viable strategic objective. The dispersal of the Turco-German fleet could lead to only one result and that was simply that at least some portion of the fleet would engage and deliver shellfire on the Russians. That the Turkish Fleet was never concentrated for a single decisive blow such as Togo's attack on Port Arthur or Nelson's attack on Copenhagen speaks to the nonstrategic nature of the mission. Unquestionably the weak and dispersed naval raids of October 29, 1914, could only have been seen as a political provocation, rather than as a serious naval operation. The Germans hoped that it would be enough to incite the Entente to act against the Turks. In that sense, the mission was a success.

The attacks provoked an immediate crisis with the Ottoman leadership, with Sait Halim and Cavit registering protests to Enver. This was followed by a firestorm of activity over the next two days, during which Sait Halim and several others offered resignations. Talat told Wangenheim that the entire cabinet, less Enver, opposed the naval action.⁴¹

This split finally resolved itself when Enver swayed Talat and Halil over to a pro-interventionist stance. Outfoxed by Enver and facing an aroused entente, Sait Halim was overcome by events as Russia, Britain, and France, in turn, declared war against the Ottoman Empire.

Thus, in the course of a three-month period, the Ottoman Empire drifted from a position of neutrality to that of full-fledged belligerence. With the exception of its partially mobilized armies, the empire was no more prepared to wage modern war than it was when the archduke was gunned down in Sarajevo. In a case unique among the major powers, the Turks had no definite or finely tuned war aims which reflected national policy objectives. The Ottomans did not covet the return of lost provinces (with the minor exception of some small Greek islands), nor did they expect to receive new lands. While they hoped for some financial remuneration and relief, this was not, of itself, a rational justification for going to war. The Turks simply tried to walk a neutral path for as long as they could. A. J. P. Taylor was wrong when he portrayed the Turks as willing to risk all or nothing to resolve regional issues. With the exception of Enver Paşa, Turkey went unwillingly to war and, absent the relentless determination of Ambassador Wangenheim and the accidental presence of Vice Admiral Souchon, might have successfully avoided involvement. Overall, maneuvering Turkey into the war was possibly the best strategic move that Germany made in the first two years of war, costing them almost nothing, while at the same time creating a strategic problem for the entente of enormous consequence.

WAR PLANS

On April 7, 1914, Bronsart von Schellendorf completed the staff work on the Primary Campaign Plan for the Turkish Army.[42] This plan was prepared prior to the events of the summer of 1914, and reflected the then-current strategic situation. The Turkish General Staff estimated that Turkey would simultaneously oppose both a renewed Balkan coalition of Bulgaria and Greece, and Russia. The mobilization plans subsequently developed supported this intelligence estimate. The Primary Campaign Plan specified that three basic tasks were to be initially accomplished by the military: (1) the army had to secure key terrain along the frontiers, (2) the army had to bring a majority of forces to decisive points, and (3) the army had to ensure that enough time was available to complete mobilization and concentration. The plan specifically forbade units being committed piecemeal.

According to Bronsart von Schellendorf's plan, the Turks would field an army of observation on the Greek and Bulgarian frontiers. Although this army was prepared to fight, it would not act provocatively, nor would it engage in offensive operations. In the east against Russia, the Turks would attempt to gain the tactical initiative by conducting limited attacks should favorable operational conditions exist in Caucasia. The plan recognized the supreme strategic importance of Constantinople and the Turkish Straits by prioritizing the establishment of the Çatalca Fortified Zone, covered by the Fortress City of Adrianople and the army of observation. Additional forces from Syria and Mesopotamia were earmarked for transfer to the Turkish Thrace to support this deployment. The principal weaknesses of the plan were perennial shortfalls in artillery and technical units. To increase combat potential against the Russians, the Turks increased their Jandarma strength in the east, and additionally planned to mobilize their entire reserve cavalry force of four divisions there as well.[43] Enver Paşa wrote to Bronsart von Schellendorf, "I see we are together in thought!"[44] and immediately forwarded the plan to the naval staff for concurrent action.

After the calamitous events of July 1914, Turkey found itself bound to Germany in a Secret Treaty signed on August 2, 1914. She then found herself tied to neighboring Bulgaria in a second secret treaty. These two treaties essentially negated the strategic principles which Bronsart von Schellendorf had formulated in the spring by eliminating Bulgaria and potentially adding the entente powers as opponents. In the meantime the army, as shown in Table 2.6, was well along in its reconstitution efforts, and had reestablished itself in garrison cantonments throughout the empire.

Table 2.6
Disposition of Turkish Forces, August 1914

EUROPEAN THRACE
First Army
I Corps: **1**, 2, 3 Inf. Div.
II Corps: 4, 5, **6** Inf. Div.
III Corps: 7, 8, 9 Inf. Div.
1 Cav. Bde.

SYMRNA
IV Corps: **10**, **11**, <u>12</u> Inf. Div.

ANATOLIA
V Corps: **13**, **14**, **15** Inf. Div.

SYRIA
Second Army
VI Corps: <u>16</u>, 26 Inf. Div.
VIII Corps: 25, <u>27</u> Inf. Div.

CAUCASIA
Third Army
IX Corps: **17**, 28, <u>29</u> Inf.Div.,
    9 Cav. Bde.
<u>X Corps</u>: 30, **31**, <u>32</u> Inf. Div.
<u>XI Corps</u>: **18**, 33, 34 Inf. Div.
    11 Cav. Bde., Van Cav.Bde.

MESOPOTAMIA
Sixth Army
XII Corps: 35, 36 Inf. Div.
XIII Corps: **37** Inf. Div.

ARABIA-YEMEN
VII Corps: <u>21</u>, **22**, **39**, **40** Inf. Div.

Note: Units in boldface type indicate new formations, units underlined indicate units redeployed since 1913.

Responding to these rapidly changing conditions, Bronsart von Schellendorf began to adapt the Primary Campaign Plan on August 20, 1914. The possibility of a direct attack on Turkish Thrace had receded with the signing of a Secret Treaty of Alliance with Bulgaria. Turkish forces would continue to concentrate in Thrace, but with an eye towards conducting possible operations with the Bulgarians against either the Romanians or the Serbs. Although Russia maintained strong forces on the Caucasian Front, the Turks thought that they would not be inclined to attack, since Russia was already heavily engaged against Germany and Austria-Hungary. As a result, the idea of a large scale Turkish offensive using the Turkish Third Army in Caucasia began to be seen as a viable option, in spite of the deplorable logistical and communications difficulties involved. Since eventual hostilities against Great Britain were likely, the Turks also began to consider the possibility of an offensive against Egypt and the Suez Canal. With the continuing security of a friendly Bulgaria and with the increasing likelihood of a neutral Greece, staff work and estimates continued supporting these twin offensives.

On September 6, 1914, the Primary Campaign Plan was formally and significantly changed. In Syria, the Fourth Army was ordered to plan an attack on Egypt with forces from the VIII and the XII Corps. In the absence of a Russian attack, the Third Army was ordered to plan for offensive operations toward Ardahan and Batum. Furthermore, it was decided that a wing of the Third Army would maneuver from a base formed by the Fortress City of Erzurum and crush Russian forces in the area of Sarikamiş.

As previously stated, there was an opposing point of view concerning overall Turkish strategy from the second assistant chief of staff, Turkish Colonel Hafiz Hakki Bey. On September 4, 1914, Hakki Bey revealed his own version of the Turkish Campaign Plan. This was an overly ambitious plan predicated on the Russian defeat at Tannenberg and the stalemate on the Marne. Hakki Bey thought that these events would paralyze both the Russians and the Anglo-French, thereby making large scale Turkish offensives possible. His plan involved deploying the I Corps and the V Corps from Istanbul, and the III Corps from Tekirdağ, by sea to Samsun and Giresun. From these locations, this army-sized force would attack toward Batum and Tiflis. In a supporting attack, the Third Army would attack to seize Ardahan, and reinforced by the XIII Corps from Mesopotamia, the Third Army would use the Van Jandarma Division and the four reserve cavalry divisions to attack into Azerbaijan.

Turkish forces remaining in Mesopotamia would guard Basra and would "menace" Afghanistan and India. In addition to the planned attack on Egypt, the VII Corps in Yemen would observe and threaten Aden.

This plan immediately ran into difficulty and it was shelved after the staff assessed that it would take until the late spring of 1915 to deploy the forces necessary for Hakki Bey's plan to be implemented. This did not deter the Colonel, and on October 4, 1914, Hakki Bey produced his Second Campaign Plan. In this plan, he retained strong forces in Thrace to watch Greece and he now planned to assist Romania and Bulgaria against Serbia in the spring. Hakki Bey also envisioned an attack on the Suez Canal and in addition advocated an offensive operation against Persia. As creative as these plans were, the Turkish General Staff (as a whole) felt that the inherent weakness of the Turkish Army was an insurmountable obstacle to the success of Hakki Bey's plans and his ideas were consigned to the dustbin.

Although Turkey was not immediately a belligerent in the First World War, the events of late July and early August 1914 were sufficient to cause Turkey to mobilize. By August 1, 1914, all major European powers and several minor powers were mobilizing their forces. Turkey followed suit by issuing partial mobilization instructions to the I Corps, in Thrace, and to the VII Corps, in Arabia. On Friday afternoon, August 2, 1914, the Turkish General Staff ordered general mobilization effective from 9:00 A.M. that day. For planning purposes, the following day, August 3, would be the first "numbered" day in the mobilization schedule. In theory, the army could be mobilized in about twenty-two days; however, the Turkish General Staff expected that delays and mismanagement would extend the mobilization window to about forty to forty-five days.[45] In addition to the missing regiments, battalions, and companies in Turkish divisions, the peacetime army had significant shortfalls in cavalry, communications, field bakery, and combat engineer detachments. Turkish divisions had no munitions reserves or depots. At corps level, severe shortages existed in animal depots, bakery detachments, telegraph detachments, and field hospitals. Only one corps had its allotted howitzer battalion, only one corps had a full strength telegraph battalion, and only one corps had its assigned cavalry regiment.[46] Crippling shortages of all kinds characterized the logistical capability of the Turkish Army to carry out mobilization. Thus, instead of delivering capable forces with timetable precision to battle positions on the frontier, the Turks simply lurched forward trying only to assemble major forces in army areas. The offensives sought by Bronsart von Schellendorf and Hafiz Hakki Bey were delayed indefinitely until the major commanders in the field reported their readiness.

By the middle of September, or over forty-five days into mobilization, the army was still not prepared for war. The I Corps reported that it was not ready and had severe shortages of artillery horses and transport. In addition, the reserve manpower the corps had received would not be ready "for a long time." The II Corps was short two thousand cavalry and had never received its infantry depot battalion. The III Corps was short uniforms, did not have enough soldiers and officers, and also had never received its infantry depot battalion. The IV Corps had similar shortages.[47] These four army corps were stationed in the western and most highly developed parts of the empire.

The Third Army's three army corps, located in eastern Turkey and unserviced by railroads, were in even worse shape. The IX Corps was missing officers and mountain equipment. It was also missing 1,823 horses, 1,324 oxen, uniforms and equipment. The X Corps was missing 229 horses and 130 wagons, 1,552 oxen and 779 oxcarts, and 448 camels. The Fortified Zone of Erzurum was short 150 infantry, 157 artillery, and 31 combat engineer officers. The fortress was short 9,000 rifles and for its 80 mm Krupp artillery, it was short 2,896 fuses and 14,728 shrapnel shells. The situation for its critical 120 mm artillery was in a similar state and fuse and shrapnel shortages were 444 and 8,700 respectively. The fortress was short 28,000 uniforms.[48] This was the army that would go over to the winter offensive in December 1914.

Critical shortages were even worse in units that were farther away from the Anatolian heartland, and the units in Mesopotamia, Syria, and Arabia suffered accordingly. Although the Turkish General Staff received reports outlining these shortages, there was little it could do to alleviate the problem. There were simply no war reserves, beyond limited munitions stocks, available to fall back on. In fighting the Balkan Wars of 1912 and 1913 Turkey had used up what little reserves it possessed, and in the intervening year, the nearly bankrupt empire was unable even to partially restock its war reserve of military equipment.

In due time, the army reported itself mobilized. The actual time required to mobilize the corps exceeded even the most pessimistic predictions. The actual number of days needed to mobilize the Turkish corps compared to the number of days required by the mobilization plan are shown in Table 2.7.

Table 2.7
Days Required to Mobilize Turkish Corps versus Days Required by the Mobilization Plan

Corps	Days Required	Actual Days to Mobilize
I	19	64
II	15	40
III	22	22
IV	27	27
V	20	36
VI	Not available	
VII	Not available	
VIII	26	36
IX	33	55
X	29	42
XI	30	42
XII	23	31
XIII	Not available	

Source: Cemal Akbay, Em.Tugg, *Birinci Dünya Harbinde Turk Harbi, Inci Cilt, Osmanli Imparatorlugu'nun Siyasi ve Askeri Hazirliklari ve Harbi Girisi* (Ankara: Genelkurmay Basimevi, 1991), 175,176.

CONCENTRATION OF FORCES

To support the Primary Campaign Plan, the Turkish General Staff had a Concentration Plan. It is important to distinguish this plan from the Mobilization Plan, which dealt with force generation and force readiness. The purpose of the Concentration Plan was to task organize the command and control of the Turkish Army and to position it to execute the Primary Campaign Plan.[49] In the planning endeavors of the more sophisticated armies of the major powers, these plans tended to merge into one nearly simultaneous effort. However, in the poorly developed Ottoman Empire, these plans were three distinct procedures separated in time, scope, and intent.

The Concentration Plan shifted major forces to European Turkish Thrace for the protection of the Turkish Straits, to Caucasia for the Third Army's winter offensive, and to Palestine for the attack on the Suez Canal. The Second Army headquarters deployed with the VI Corps to Constantinople and assumed responsibility for the defense of the Çatalca Fortified Zone and the Bosporus Straits. The V Corps was also deployed north from Symrna and was reassigned to the Second Army as well. The XIII Corps was slated to reinforce the Third Army and deployed northward from Mesopotamia. All of the reserve cavalry divisions and the Van Jandarma Division were also assigned to the Third Army. For the offensive into Egypt, a new Fourth Army Headquarters was formed in Damascus on September 6, 1914 and the XII Corps transferred to it from Baghdad for the attack. As economy of force measures to support these deployments, both Mesopotamia and the Symrna region were literally stripped of regular corps and divisions and were converted into area commands. The Concentration Plan put a severe strain on the already overtaxed railway system and like the Mobilization Plan, huge delays unavoidably afflicted the execution of the Concentration Plan. In particular, the XIII Corps, travelling by barge up the Tigris and Euphrates Rivers and then foot marching into the Anatolian hinterland, failed to arrive in the Third Army area in time to participate in the winter offensive. The Concentration Plan, illustrated by Table 2.8, reflected obsolete strategic priorities, and in his haste to enter the war Enver accelerated its execution. Thus, army units were moving to concentration areas before actual war plans were finalized. Although the Turkish General Staff successfully attempted to achieve some minor corrections, the plan failed to deliver the right combination of trained formations to the decisive points identified by the final versions of the Campaign Plan.

Presaging the events to come, the Turkish Mobilization and Concentration Plans provided several key indicators of future battlefield effectiveness, which are clearly evident in hindsight. In the winter offensive against Russia, the transportation and equipment shortages in the IX, X, and XI Corps proved to be

Table 2.8
Disposition of Turkish Forces, November 1914-Concentration Plan

THRACE
First Army
I Corps: 1, 2, 3 Inf. Div.
II Corps: 4, 5, 6 Inf. Div.
III Corps: 7, 8, 9 Inf. Div.
IV Corps: 10, 11, 12 Inf. Div.
19, 20 Inf. Div.
1 Cav. Bde.
Second Army
V Corps: 13, 14, 15 Inf. Div.
VI Corps: 16, **24**, 26 Inf. Div.

SYMRNA
Fortified Area Command

MOVING TO THIRD ARMY
XIII Corps: 37 Inf. Div.

SYRIA
Fourth Army
VIII Corps: 23, 25, 27 Inf. Div.
XII Corps: 35, 36 Inf. Div.

CAUCASIA
Third Army
IX Corps: 17, 28, 29 Inf. Div.
X Corps: 30, 31, 32 Inf. Div.
XI Corps: 18, 33, 34 Inf. Div.
Reserve Cavalry Corps: **1, 2, 3, 4 Reserve** Cav. Div

Van Jandarma (Inf.) Div.
2 Cav. Div.
Van Cav. Bde.

MESOPOTAMIA
Irak Area Command
38 Inf. Div.

ARABIA-YEMEN
VII Corps: 21, 22, 39, 40 Inf. Div.

Note: Units in boldface type indicate new formations, units underlined indicate units redeployed since August 1914.

disastrous when the Third Army was unable to logistically sustain itself at the Battle of Sarikamiş in January 1915. Additionally, the excessive number of days required for the newly reconstituted infantry divisions of these corps to mobilize also provides insight into their military proficiency and effectiveness. In January 1915, the inexperienced troops of these divisions were badly handled by the Russians in the Caucasian Mountains. The mismanaged offensive into Egypt was coordinated and commanded by the brand-new Fourth Army headquarters. Instead of leaving the Second Army and the VI Corps in place to conduct this logistically difficult offensive, the Turks chose to attack with a new and untested headquarters and the XII Corps redeployed from Mesopotamia. It is no surprise that the British beat the offensive back at small cost.

Singularly, it is worthwhile to point out that the III Corps met its "days required to mobilize" target of twenty-two days. The fact that the corps not only mobilized on time, but beat its nearest competitor (the VI Corps) by 6 days, attests to the efficiency of the III Corps. As previously noted, the III Corps was the only Turkish corps to survive the Balkan Wars with its original organic divisions intact. Mobilization was the first test of the Turkish Army in the First World War and the III Corps passed with flying colors. The British would meet the divisions of the III Corps on the Gallipoli Peninsula in April 1915.

Could the Turkish General Staff have done better? The simple answer is probably not. It is clear that the wildly ambitious ideas of Colonel Hakki Bey were not considered in serious contention to the solid staff work of Colonel Bronsart von Schellendorf. It would be all too easy to state that the best, and perhaps the only way, that Turkey might have increased the effectiveness of its General Staff would have been to import more Germans. However, the Turks were sensitive to the growing influence of the German mission, and the issue of adding Germans, who would have inevitably replaced Turkish officers would surely have caused ill feelings. It is very likely that additional German assistance in the form of more staff officers would have destabilized a relatively harmonious working relationship.

How realistic and how effective were the Turkish plans and the subsequent execution of those plans? The Turkish General Staff only had a single year to adapt itself to the loss of Turkey-in-Europe and to a reconfigured, and possibly more threatening, strategic situation. The former plans of 1912, a dozen in all, were hopelessly outdated and were replaced by a single mobilization plan. Although this did not speed up mobilization, it certainly streamlined the planning parameters and made subsequent staff work all the easier. This would seem to have been a sound decision.

Any further assessment of the effectiveness of the Turkish Mobilization and Concentration Plans must return to the Campaign Plan, since that document was the engine of the deployment scheme. Bronsart von Schellendorf's Campaign Plan delivered the preponderance of Turkish fighting strength to Thrace. Given the uncertainties of the Balkan situation in April 1914, in August 1914, and even as late as November 1914, this was a prudent strategic decision. It must be remembered that the loss of Adrianople, and the near loss of the Çatalca Line and Constantinople in 1913 was branded into the minds of the Turkish officer corps. It is probable that there were reserve officers on duty in 1914 who still remembered the near loss of Thrace because of the Treaty of San Stefano in 1878. This legacy and burden drove all strategic decisions for the Turkish General Staff in 1914.[50] While Turkey could trade space for time in all other theaters, she had no strategic margin for retreat in Thrace. Any possible campaign plan had to address this imperative before considering anything else. Although the deployment of the finest six out of thirteen active corps to sit idle in Thrace seems conservative beyond belief, it reflects the absolute necessity to defend, at all costs, the *strategic center of gravity* of Turkey.[51] What *could* be criticized in Bronsart von Schellendorf's final variant of the Campaign Plan was the decision to conduct simultaneous offensives on widely separated fronts. For the opening offensives, only three Turkish corps attacked in Caucasia and only a single corps attacked in the Sinai. Neither Germany, France, nor Russia contemplated conducting such weak offensives. The only major power attempting such operations as its opening campaign strategy was Austria-Hungary, which suffered similar disasters at the hands of the Serbs and the Russians. It is questionable whether Turkey possessed the military resources to conduct a single offensive in late 1914, and it is beyond doubt that Turkey could *not* reasonably expect success from two offensives. Surely the highly trained German General Staff Officer Bronsart von Schellendorf must have known this. It must be remembered here that both Bronsart von Schellendorf and Hafiz Hakki Bey journeyed to Berlin for consultation in late October 1914. Therefore, it may be considered as a reasonable speculation that the Germans intentionally encouraged the Turks to become actively involved against both the Russians and the British regardless of the overall possibilities of success. That some influential officers within the Turkish General Staff, notably no less an authority than the second assistant chief of staff, were ready to conduct even more wildly ambitious offensives indicates that Bronsart von Schellendorf did not really need to do very much encouraging at all. However, the endorsement of the offensive by the professional and admired Germans surely helped Enver Paşa and Colonel Hafiz Hakki Bey crush whatever advocates of a defensive strategic stance remained on the Turkish General Staff in the fall of 1914.

A single strategic offensive, either in the Caucasus or in the Sinai might not have succeeded, but more importantly, might not have resulted in the defeats which actually occurred. Overall, given Turkey's overall readiness posture to wage a multi-front war in the wake of the Balkan Wars, the most realistic campaign strategy may have been simply to sit tight on its borders, perhaps conducting corps-sized local offensive to seize key terrain or defensible ground. Turkey in 1914, of all the major participants in the First World War, knew the inherent strength of the modern defense and the fundamental weakness of the unweighted offensive. That Enver Paşa chose to disregard the evidence of the sieges of Plevna, of Erzurum, of Adrianople, and of the defense of the Çatalca

Lines speaks volumes about his junior officer background and his inexperience in strategic matters.

The Concentration Plan itself seemed to be fairly simple in transferring the centrally positioned corps, which were located in the interior of Anatolia, in Syria, and in upper Mesopotamia, to concentration positions on the frontiers. However, again movements were delayed and the plan proved slower to execute than expected. The IV, V, and VI Corps traveled over separate routes to Thrace but were still arriving in December 1914. The routes taken by the XII Corps actually overlapped and conflicted with the routes taken by the XIII Corps. This undoubtedly affected the deployment of the XIII Corps and delayed its deployment to the Caucasus for the Third Army's winter offensive. These slow movements presaged future problems with Turkey's inadequate infrastructure and weak transportation system.

Becoming convinced that the Turks would enter the war sooner or later against them, the British and the Russians used the time generated by the slow Turkish concentration to prepare measures against them. Both allied countries prepared to take the offensive immediately upon commencement of hostilities and both countries proved more capable than the Turks in their ability to position and to direct forces for immediate use. On October 31, 1914, several days prior to the official start of hostilities, Russian army units began cross border operations near Dogubeyazit and on the same day, Russian Ambassador Giers departed Constantinople. British operations began the following day in the Persian Gulf with the landing of troops near Fao and in the Mediterranean with a Royal Navy bombardment of Gaza.

A major Russian attack on the Third Army's defensive lines at Koprukoy began on November 5, and on November 7 major British forces landed at Basra. By November 19, the Turks had lost Basra in Mesopotamia and the Russians began larger operations aimed against Saray and Van. Obviously the allies had considered a hostile Turkey to be a likely outcome of the complex maneuvering of the fall of 1914 and had prepared accordingly.

Thus, the time gained by delaying the entry of the Ottoman Empire into the war still had not been sufficient to insure that Turkey would gain the initiative. As late as December 5, Enver was sending his final attack order to the Third Army and on the next day, he offered command of that army to Liman von Sanders. Liman von Sanders, a trained General Staff officer himself, wisely refused, thereby rendering his informal opinion on the ultimate success of Enver's offensive plans in Caucasia. Instead of remaining in the capital to direct the overall coordination of Turkey's widely scattered war fronts (now three in all), Enver Paşa decided to travel to the Third Army's area of operations to personally supervise operations there. He took both Hafiz Hakki Bey and Bronsart von Schellendorf with him. Fortunately for the remainder of the Turkish General Staff, German Field Marshal Colmar von der Goltz arrived in Constantinople on December 12, 1914, to carry some of the staff load caused by the exodus of senior leadership.

In any case, by mid-December 1914, enough forces with which to begin offensive operations were in position in the Caucasus. Longer distances and the change in Turkish headquarters from the Second Army to the Fourth Army in Syria delayed the Sinai offensive for another two weeks. Turkey was now poised for attack.

NOTES

1. *The World Almanac and Encyclopedia,1914* (New York: Press Publishing, 1913), 250.
2. Ahmed Emin Yalman, *Turkey in the World War* (New Haven, Conn.: Yale University Press, 1930), 93.
3. Ibid., 86.
4. Feroz, Ahmed, "The Late Ottoman Empire" in *The Great Powers and the End of the Ottoman Empire,* ed. Marian Kent (London: Allen & Unwin, 1984), 25. The Balkan Wars, in this statement, inclusively means the period from 1877 through 1913.
5. W. E. D. Allen and Paul Muratoff, *Caucasian Battlefields: A History of the Wars on the Turco-Caucasian Border, 1828-1921* (Cambridge: Cambridge University Press, 1953), 229.
6. Turkish General Staff, *Balkan Harbi (1912-1913)* (Ankara: Genelkurmay Basimevi, 1993), 185-190.
7. Turkish General Staff, *Turk Silahli Kuvvetleri Tarihi, Balkan Harbi (1912-1913), III Cilt, Garp Ordusu Vardar Ordusu ve Ustruma Kolordusu* (Ankara: Genelkurmay Basimevi, 1993), 59-132.
8. Turkish General Staff, *Turk Silahli Kuvvetleri Tarihi, Balkan Harbi (1912-1913), II Cilt, Edirne Kalesi Etrafindaki Muharebeler* (Ankara: Genelkurmay Basimevi, 1993), 45-71.
9. Ibid., Chart 12.
10. Ibid., Map 40.
11. Ulrich Trumpener, *Germany and the Ottoman Empire, 1914-1918* (Princeton, N.J.: Princeton University Press, 1968), 23.
12. Turkish General Staff, *Birinci Dünya Harbinde Turk Harbi, Inci Cilt, Osmanli Imparatorlugu'nun Siyasi ve Askeri Hazirliklarl ve Harbe Girisi.* (Ankara: GK Basim Evi, 1970), 49.
13. G. P. Gooch and Harold Temperley, eds. *British Documents on the Origins of the War, 1898-1914*, vol. 11, (London: HMSO, 1926), 311; Beaumont to Sir Edward Grey, August 3, 1914.
14. J. C. Hurewitz, *Diplomacy in the Near and Middle East: A Documentary Record: 1914-1956,* vol. 2 (Princeton, N.J.: Van Nostrand, 1956), 1-2.
15. Yalman, *Turkey in the World War*, 67-68. Dr. Yalman also noted that the treaty negotiations were never discussed during meetings of the Ottoman cabinet. Furthermore he noted that only five men in the government knew of its existence.
16. Commandant M. Larcher, *La Guerre Turque Dans La Guerre Mondiale* (Paris: Chiron & Berger-Levrault, 1926), 608-609.

17. Trumpener, *Germany and the Ottoman Empire*, 24.
18. Ibid., 25-26.
19. TGS, *Hazirliklari ve Girisi*, 54-55; Yalman, *Turkey in the World War*, 72.
20. Yalman, *Turkey in the World War*, 72.
21. Ibid., 72
22. A. J. P. Taylor, *The Struggle for Mastery in Europe, 1848-1918* (Oxford: Oxford University Press, 1971), 534.
23. Otto Liman von Sanders, *Five Years in Turkey* (London: Bailliere, Tindall & Cox, 1928), 31.
24. Luigi Albertini, *The Origins of the War 1914.*, vol. 3 (Oxford: Oxford University Press, 1952), 616-617.
25. Ibid., 619-620.
26. Cemal Akbay, *Birinci Dünya Harbinde Turk Harbe, Inci Cilt, Osmanli Imparatorlugu'nun Siyasi ve Askeri Hazirliklari ve Harbi Girisi* (Ankara: Genelkurmay Basimevi, 1991), 157-162.
27. Gooch and Temperley, *British Documents on the Origins of the War*, 306; Sir G. Barclay to Sir Edward Grey, August 4, 1914.
28. Winston S. Churchill, *The World Crisis* (New York: Charles Scribners, Sons, 1931), 280.
29. Akbay, *Hazirliklari ve Harbi Girisi*, 162-176.
30. Albertini, *Origins of the War*, 621.
31. Trumpener, *Germany and the Ottoman Empire*, 39.
32. Ibid., 40.
33. Geoffrey Miller, *Straits: British Policy towards the Ottoman Empire and the origins of the Dardanelles Campaign* (Hull, UK: University of Hull Press, 1997), 314-317.
34. Djemal Pasha, *Memories of a Turkish Statesman, 1913-1919* (London: Hutchinson, n.d.), 128-130.
35. Trumpener, *Germany and the Ottoman Empire*, 54.
36. Ibid., 54.
37. For the best presentation of Enver's machinations and the complete text of these secret orders, readers should look to Geoffrey Miller's excellent *Straits Policy* (Chapter 21, The Private War).
38. Bernd Langensiepen and Ahmet Guleryuz, *The Ottoman Steam Navy* (Annapolis, MD.: Naval Institute Press, 1995), 44.
39. Ibid., 44-45.
40. Miller, *Straits Policy*, 323. Miller notes that news of the attack was already common knowledge on the streets of Constantinople by the afternoon of October 29, 1914.
41. Trumpener, *Germany and the Ottoman Empire*, 58-61.
42. Akbay, *Birinci Dünya Harbinde*, 157.
43. These ill-trained and poorly equipped forces would be used in an economy of force mission on the southern flank of the Third Army's disastrous winter offensive in 1914.
44. Akbay, *Birinci Dünya Harbinde*, 158.
45. Ibid., 167.
46. Ibid., 171.
47. Ibid., 173.

48. Ibid., 174.
49. Ibid., 176–178.
50. The lack of strategic space in Thrace still affects the modern day Turkish General Staff, which in 2000 still stations four out of nine active corps in the area of the Turkish Straits and Istanbul.
51. In fact, the 1912 and 1913 defense of Thrace had involved ultimately five active army corps and four reserve corps of the Ottoman Army.

3
The Early Offensives, November 1914–March 1915

1914 AND EARLY 1915

In 1914 the Turks attempted to seize the strategic initiative with offensives in the Caucasus and in the Sinai with the limited forces in place under an outdated campaign plan. In their initial attacks, the Turks used nine infantry divisions in the Caucasus and parts of three infantry divisions in the Sinai, thereby committing only twelve of their thirty-six infantry divisions to combat. Additionally, many of these were newly raised infantry divisions with very limited experience. This was serious mistake but one which was not easily overcome given the realities of the Concentration Plan.

Like every other belligerent power's initial offensives, the Turkish offensives had also ended in failure. Although the Third Army suffered crippling losses in the Caucasian winter offensive at Sarikamiş, the front was stabilized and reinforcements were enroute to the Third Army. In Mesopotamia, Basra and Qurna were lost, but the British did not seem to be in any hurry to advance up river on Baghdad, and Turkish reinforcements were en route to Mesopotamia. The Fourth Army's ill-conceived Sinai attack on the Suez Canal failed, but losses were extremely light. The overall Turkish strategic situation in the late winter of 1915 was serious but not critical. On the positive side of the ledger, a Turkish expeditionary force had taken Tabriz in Persia. Taken as a percentage of available strength, the Turkish losses in the first four months of war were quite moderate when compared to the horrific losses suffered by the French, the Germans, the Austro-Hungarians, and the Russians.

Probably the most preventable and serious mistake that the Turks made in the early days of the war was the failure to provide an adequate defensive force in Mesopotamia. The decision to leave the Shatt-al-Arab poorly guarded opened the door for a British presence in Mesopotamia, which lasted the entire war. Although the British ultimately sent almost double the number of men that the Turks had in that theater, this was a dangerous situation that created competing strategic priorities for the empire for the rest of the war.

Although there remained a huge force of Turkish divisions in Thrace, there was a growing body of reports from Egypt that the British were bent on seizing the Dardanelles. Therefore, the First and Second Armies were maintained at nearly full strength and were retained in the vicinity of Constantinople. This decision would prove to be fortuitous in the coming spring of 1915.

Minister of War Enver Paşa and Minister of the Marine Cemal Paşa displayed a propensity to take leave of their administrative duties in Constantinople for more active roles as combat commanders. They also tended to bring their capable German advisors with them. In doing so they gutted the leadership of the Turkish High Command at a critical period. Of particular note, no exceptional leaders had emerged from the early offensives. Reciprocally, no leaders were identified as particularly deficient in military operations, and thus no major Turkish commanders were relieved of their duties.

Within the Turkish Army itself, regular Turkish infantry divisions, which had been afforded the time and opportunity to train for war, proved steady and capable of sustained combat effectiveness. Although logistical shortages continued to plague the army, the basic corps and divisional command structure of the Turkish Army appeared sound.

In assessing the operational effectiveness of the early Turkish offensives, the dispersion of Turkish strength appeared as the most critical determinant of failure. In attempting to conduct simultaneous offensives on widely separated fronts, the Turkish General Staff failed to achieve a decisive concentration of strength in any single theater. The poor condition of the Turkish lines of communications further complicated this dispersion and the Turks were unable to take full advantage of their favorable geographic interior position. As a result, the Turkish General Staff was left with inconclusive results on three active fronts.

SARIKAMIŞ

From a military standpoint, the geography in the Turkish Third Army's Area of Operations was rugged in the extreme. Physically, the mountains rose to heights of well over 3,000 meters and the land itself was barren and dry. There was little cover and concealment for troops. The narrow river valleys tended to channel operations along narrow axes of advance and the supporting road network was primitive. In the winter, the temperatures could plummet and remain at - 50°C and snow as deep as three to four meters could accumulate. The local population of about five million people consisted of mostly hardy Anatolian Turks and a sizable minority of Armenians--about seven hundred thousand. There were even several hundred thousand Greeks still living in the region.[1] These people lived mainly in the cities and villages that clung to life along the valleys. The inhabitants were poor, even by the standards of the Ottoman Empire.

Any military appreciation of the terrain in the Third Army's area would classify it as ideal for the conduct of defensive operations. The restrictive valleys became choke points hindering any advance and the barren ground was ideal for establishing defensive fields of fire. Operations in the surrounding mountains required elite mountain troops specially trained and equipped to deal with the unique physical and tactical problems. In an era of seasonal campaigning, the onset of winter imposed a set of additional problems as well. Units participating in winter operations in such an area required special clothing, extra food rations and fuel, and, above all, dynamic leadership at the tactical level.

Overall, the Third Army's area was totally unsuited for offensive operations, whether at the strategic, operational, or tactical level, yet it was here that Turkey struck its opening blow against the Russians. Because of the unfavorable geography, the question of intent or objective must be addressed. A case can be made that the provinces lost in 1878 made such an offensive in the east an emotional necessity and certainly an offensive in this area supported the greater political objectives of Pan-Turanism.[2] Whether either of these larger purposes was the true driving force behind the Turkish offensive in the winter of 1914 are unclear from Turkish records today. Speculatively, the operation's political objective was probably the restoration of the 1878 frontier, since the operation itself was portrayed as neither a crusade nor as a rallying symbol for Pan-Turanism. The attacking Third Army's geographic objectives were initially the key cities that lay about fifty kilometers across the border, and then as secondary objectives the former Turkish cities lying a further one hundred and ten kilometers beyond. Indeed, the primary purpose of the operation was simply to kill off a large part of the opposing Russian Army. It must also be considered that simply engaging the Russians with major forces in an outer theater was, for the Germans at least, a viable objective in and of itself.

The Turkish Third Army was commanded by Hasan İzzet Paşa and had a German officer, Lieutenant Colonel Guse, as its chief of staff. Brigadier General Ahmet Fevzi commanded the IX Corps, Mirliva (an old Ottoman term for brigadier general) Ziya Paşa commanded the X Corps. This corps also had a German chief of staff, Major Lange, and Mirliva Galip Paşa commanded the XI Corps. Colonels commanded the regular divisions in these corps. The unique Van Jandarma Division consisting of the Van Jandarma Regiment, seven regional Jandarma battalions, the Bitlis Jandarma Regiment (Independent) and the Diyarbakir Jandarma Regiment (Independent) was commanded by Major Ferit. The corps-sized Erzurum Fortress garrison of seven fortress infantry regiments, two heavy artillery regiments, and supporting arms detachments was commanded by Colonel Alaaddin. The effects of Enver Paşa's purge of older officers are immediately apparent—corps are normally commanded by lieutenant generals and divisions by major generals.[3] Although the retention of younger, and possibly more politically reliable, officers in high positions may have lent some greater degree of vigor to Turkish Army operations, the hemorrhage of experienced senior officers certainly must have had an offsetting deleterious and demoralizing effect.

Hostilities officially began on November 2, 1914, with the Russian declaration of war on the Ottoman Empire; however, the Russian offensive actually began the preceding day. The thin Turkish cavalry screen along the frontier came under heavy attack and fought delaying actions. The main Russian attack came along the Erzurum-Sarikamiş road, with a strong supporting attack from Oltu. Supplementary attacks were aimed at Karaköse and Beyazıt. Within a week, the Russians had advanced halfway from the frontier to Erzurum, where they were halted by determined defensive counterattacks from the XI Corps' 18th, 33rd, and 34th Infantry Divisions and the reserve cavalry divisions. By November 12, the IX Corps reinforced the XI Corps on its left flank and together with the cavalry the Turks began slowly to push the Russians back. By the end of November, the front had stabilized with the Russians clinging to a salient twenty-five kilometers deep in Turkish territory along the Erzurum-Sarikamiş axis. Losses were moderate.[4] The Russians had greater success along the southern shoulders of the Third Army and had taken and held both Karaköse and Doğubayazıt. Armenian formations fighting with the Russian Army were particularly visible in the seizure of Doğubayazıt.

On December 8, 1914, the Turkish cruiser *Mecidiye* brought Colonel Hafiz Hakki Bey to Trabzon. The second assistant chief of staff had been sent to energize the offensive spirit of the Third Army. The colonel personally gave Third Army Chief of Staff Guse (who was a German Lieutenant Colonel) instructions immediately to begin planning an offensive. The instructions reaffirmed the intent of the Turkish General Staff to deliver a crushing blow against the Russians. Guse was directed to prepare a plan that used one corps operating from the Erzurum Fortress to fix the strong Russian forces on the front lines. He was further directed to throw a wing of two corps around the left flank and behind the enemy.[5] Once this was accomplished, the Russians would collapse in a battle of annihilation.[6] The Third Army Commander, when briefed about this directive, felt that the operation would be very difficult to carry out.[7] The commander of the IX Corps also expressed misgivings about the feasibility of the plan. The weather notwithstanding, the Third Army had suffered serious personnel losses, which had not been replaced, especially in the reserve cavalry divisions.

On the basis of a German report that Hindenburg had sent to Berlin about the weakness of Russian headquarters, Enver Paşa and Colonel Hakki Bey were convinced that the Russians would collapse when encircled. The report, based on the Battle of Tannenberg (fought in late August 1914), noted that Russian headquarters were useless when surrounded and that, inevitably, command and control broke down. Both Enver Paşa and Colonel Hakki Bey wanted to duplicate Tannenberg and deliver another resounding defeat to the Russians at Sarikamiş. Furthermore, after winning this victory, they wanted to drive on Ardahan and the Fortress of Kars and destroy the Russian forces there as well. Planning began in earnest. To reinforce the offensive, the Turkish General Staff formed a special detachment from the 3rd Infantry Division, stationed in Thrace, consisting of two battalions of the 8th Infantry Regiment and two artillery batteries, which would deploy to the vicinity of Çoruh. The purpose of this detachment was to pin down the Russians on the coast near Batum. These troops came by sea, since at this early point in the war, it was still relatively easy for the Turks to move small transports along the Black Sea coast. This would allow the X Corps to relinquish its defensive coastal responsibilities and concentrate for offensive operations. The command of this detachment was placed in the hands of a German major named Stange (later lieutenant colonel), then assigned to the artillery command of the Erzurum Fortress. The detachment became known as the Ştanke Bey Müfrezesı. On December 12, 1914, Enver Paşa himself arrived in Erzurum and began to participate in the planning effort. He immediately began tinkering with the plan. After having decided to conduct large-scale offensive operations, Enver Paşa was now concerned about the large, and increasing, number of casualties sustained by the Third Army, which could not easily be replaced. He was also concerned about the wide frontage held by the Third Army, reaching from the Black Sea to Lake Van, which made concentration difficult. To compensate for these problems, Enver wanted aggressive commanders whom he could trust to overcome such difficulties. Later that month, Bronsart von Schellendorf and his chief of operations, Lieutenant Colonel Feldman would also come to Erzurum. There was no dearth of advice, or supervisory talent, for the unfortunate Third Army commander and his staff.

Unhappy with the leadership in the Third Army, Enver Paşa continued to change his horses in midstream by summarily and involuntarily retiring IX Corps commander Ahmet Fevzi Paşa. To replace him, Enver brought up the 34th Infantry Division commander, Colonel Ihsan Paşa. The commander of the X Corps, Ziya Paşa, was young, active, and intelligent. However, Ziya too, was out of favor with Enver, possibly for his slowness in mobilizing and concentrating his corps, or perhaps for his politics. In any case, the X Corps was chosen to lead the critically decisive left wing of the projected encirclement and required a commander who totally supported the plan. Consequently, Enver Paşa decided to place Colonel Hafiz Hakki Bey, who was conveniently lingering in Erzurum, in command of the X Corps replacing Ziya Paşa who was assigned to other duties. At this time, the young Hakki Bey was thought to be decisive, hardworking, intelligent, and hard driving.[8] As a result of these changes, the two Turkish Corps involved in the decisive left-wing encirclement against Sarikamiş had commanders who had little or no experience at the operational level of war.[9]

The Turkish Operations Plan was a single envelopment (Map 3-1) using two groups of forces; a weak group consisting of the XI Corps and the 2nd Regular Cavalry Division and a strong group consisting of the IX and X Corps (both of which now had new and inexperienced commanders). The weaker group would fix the Russian force in place while the stronger group would swing wide and encircle the Russians from behind. Neither the strong group, located on the left flank, nor the weak group located on the right flank received an overall wing or flank commander to coordinate operations. The plan involved much risk. The newly formed Ştanke Bey Müfrezesi would conduct highly visible operations

Map 3.1
The Sarikamiş Encirclement Operation According to the Third Army Attack Plan of December 19, 1914

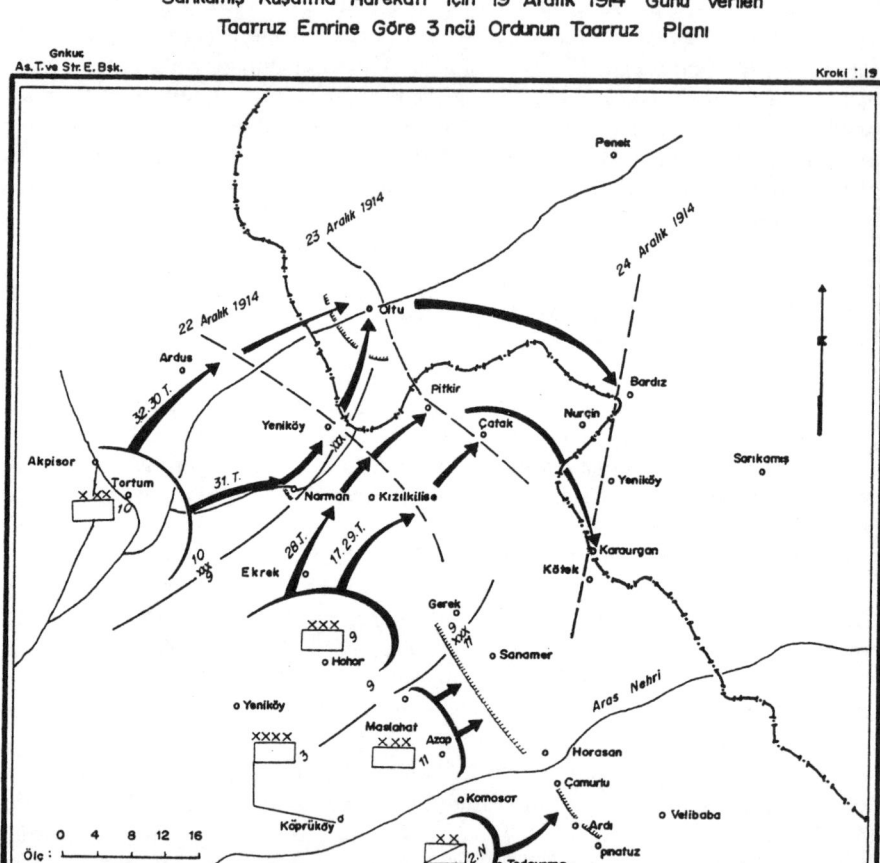

Source: Turkish General Staff, *Birinci Dünya Harbinde Türk Kafkas Cephesi 3 ncü Ordu Harekatı Cilt II Birinci Kitap* (Ankara: Genelkurmay Basım Evi, 1993), Kroki (Map) 19.

along the frontier to distract and pin Russian units. It was hoped that this activity would make the X Corps' drive on Oltu easier. To assist the weaker group of forces, the 2nd Cavalry Division was reinforced with four infantry battalions, a mountain artillery battery, and a 120 mm heavy artillery detachment. The XI Corps received additional artillery, as well. The forces were to be in position by December 19 and were to be ready for action not later than the following day. The operation was scheduled to begin on December 22, 1914.

The tempo of operations dramatically increased as all subordinate commanders and staffs began hurried preparations for a major offensive operation. Overall, the Third Army had about 150,000 men assigned to it in December 1914. However, many of these soldiers were assigned to the Erzurum Fortress and after a month of intensive combat, most maneuver battalions were weakening and short on ammunition. To make up shortfalls, the XI Corps had three border battalions and four Jandarma battalions assigned, and the X Corps had the Ştanke Bey Müfrezesi assigned to it. Six thousand replacements were sent to the XI Corps as well. According to returns, the Third Army had 75,660 men, 73 machine guns, and 218 artillery pieces available for mobile offensive operations (Table 3.1).[10]

Table 3.1
Available Offensive Strength—Third Army, December 22nd, 1914

Unit	Battalions	Riflemen	Machine Guns	Artillery
LEFT WING				
X Corps	33	28,000	20	56
IX Corps	27	21,000	23	58
RIGHT WING				
XI Corps	34	22,274	16	94
2d Cavalry Division		4,386	14	10
TOTAL	94	75,660	73	218
Other Combatants		37,000		
Replacements available		6,000		
THIRD ARMY TOTAL		118,660		

Source: Turkish General Staff, *Birinci Dünya Harbinde Türk Kafkas Cephesi 3 ncü Ordu Harekatı Cilt II Birinci Kitap* (Ankara: Genelkurmay Basım Evi, 1993), 383-384.

It would appear that the average rifle strength of Turkish infantry divisions involved in the Sarikamiş offensive was about seven thousand riflemen per division (out of an authorized strength of about ten thousand). Machine-gun availability was notably weak in all corps, as was artillery in the critical IX and X Corps (fifty-eight and fifty-six out of seventy-two guns authorized to be on hand, respectively).

The Turks estimated that the opposing Russian force, which they hoped to entrap and destroy, was in a similar condition. Their intelligence estimated that the Russian Sarikamiş Group had a rifle strength of about sixty-five thousand men, organized into eighty-four infantry battalions. The Turks estimated that the Russians also had 36 cavalry squadrons and 172 artillery pieces available. If these estimates were correct, the Turks had a small superiority in infantry and artillery, which *if* properly employed could tip the tactical balance in their favor.

However, it was also estimated that the Russians could call in one hundred thousand fresh reinforcements, if necessary.

The morning of December 22 began with auspiciously mild weather and little fog or snow. The X Corps began its movement toward Oltu at 4 A.M. The XI Corps attacked at 9 A.M., while the divisions of the IX Corps attacked between 6 and 8 A.M. Enver Paşa went forward to view the action at 8 A.M. and arrived at the front near Hahor at 3 P.M. It was a successful day and the evening reports to the Third Army were extremely encouraging. The next day too went well and by December 24, the Turkish left wing was beyond Oltu and still advancing. The XI Corps and 2nd Cavalry Division were advancing as well. By Christmas, the IX Corps reached the outskirts of Sarikamiş and the X Corps had reached the point where it would pivot toward the southeast to outflank and envelop Sarikamiş. Thus far, the offensive was an astounding success, with the X Corps marching a hard seventy-five kilometers in just over three days. In a night attack on December 25 and 26, the 29th Infantry Division entered the town of Old Sarikamiş. By December 28 the X Corps had seized blocking positions at Selım, on the road from Sarikamiş to Kars. The weather conditions were now turning for the worse, the X Corps reported one and a half meters of snow and temperatures of - 26°C.

Unfortunately, the XI Corps attacks were not pressed hard enough and the corps failed in its basic mission to pin the Russians in their forward positions. The Russians were quick to take advantage of this and thinned the lines in front of Erzurum to send a force of several regiments of infantry and cavalry back to Sarikamiş before the Turks arrived. These forces arrived in the nick of time and were able to hold the city in the face of repeated Turkish attacks. Unlike their ill-fated First and Second Army counterparts in the forests of East Prussia, the Russian army and corps headquarters maintained a solid grip on the situation, bleak as it was, and retained effective command and control over their forces. Russian reinforcements were also arriving quickly at Benli Ahmet to block any further advance of the X Corps.

December 29 saw the high-water mark of the Third Army. Enver Paşa had accompanied the army forward and had assumed direct command of the operation. From his field headquarters to the north of Çerkez köyü, Enver ordered a renewed all-out effort to complete the envelopment. However, the Turkish attacks seemed to be getting nowhere and, worse yet, the Russians did not seem to be in danger of collapse, as had happened at Tannenberg during the previous summer. By the next day, it was apparent that the Russians were bringing up fresh relief forces from Kars and from the southeast. Additionally, attrition and casualties were weakening the Turkish divisions, the troops were exhausted, and the weather was worsening.

As the forces weathered the new year and 1915 began, the operational and tactical initiative changed. Large Russian forces had been brought to bear along the flanks of the X Corps and in front of the IX Corps. On January 2, 1915, the Russians launched an offensive of their own. This was trap within a trap, and the enveloping IX and X Corps now became the object of a crushing Russian encirclement. The situation for the Turks declined overnight and became desperate. Enver Paşa reacted by forming the IX and X Corps into a single operational detachment called the "Left Wing" and he placed Hakki Bey in command. Enver also promoted Hakki Bey to Brigadier General, so that he would outrank Ali Ihsan Paşa, the commander of the IX Corps. Evidently, Enver now believed that centralized command in the rapidly forming Turkish cauldron would help salvage the situation. To the south, the XI Corps continued to attack, but it too was subjected to repeated Russian counterattacks. Enver still maintained a sense of optimism and allowed the Dutch Attaché Westenek and Norwegian Army Major Hoff to visit the Third Army area on December 31 in premature expectations of success.

By January 4, the Turkish situation verged on total catastrophe, as the Russian attacks steadily pressed the IX and X Corps into a smaller and smaller area. It was apparent that the Turks must retreat or be annihilated and Enver Paşa approved a withdrawal. The IX and X Corps began immediate withdrawals under severe Russian pressure. Fighting a desperate rear guard action, the IX Corps was now literally destroyed as a fighting unit. Surrounded by the Russians, the remnants of the 17th, 28th, and 29th Infantry Divisions, as well as the IX Corps headquarters itself, were cut off and forced to surrender. Ali Insan Paşa, his chief of staff Lieutenant Colonel Şerfi, and his aides were captured. Hafiz Hakki noted that there was *"one road out of the Turnagel Woods* (the scene of the IX Corps disaster) *that night and only the X Corps returned–the IX Corps did not return."*[11] It was a major disaster for the Third Army as fully one-third of its combat power was eliminated almost overnight. January 7 saw the Turks in full retreat. Losses due to combat and weather were horrendous. On that day, the strength of the X Corps was worn down to a pitiful twenty-five hundred riflemen and sixteen artillery pieces, of which one thousand to twelve hundred rifles were to be found in the 32nd Infantry Division.

Enver Paşa departed the Third Army on January 8, 1915. His farewell message to the army began encouragingly with "Friends!" and noted that the army had fought the weather and the terrain, as well as the enemy. Enver congratulated the army on its performance, which he claimed, rivaled the glorious days of the early Ottoman Empire. He told them that he was returning to Constantinople. He wished the army Allah's blessings and much success in beating the Russians. Enver ended his message by reminding the troops not to forget that Allah's help was with them at all times. Before leaving, Enver placed Hafiz Hakki Bey in command of the Third Army and placed cavalry colonel Yusuf Izzet in command of the X Corps. When Enver departed for Constantinople at 7 A.M. on January 9, 1915, he brought Bronsart von Schellendorf back with him. Returns indicated that on that day, the Third Army could field about ten thousand riflemen.

The operation had been incredibly costly and harsh. In the high mountains, especially in the IX and X Corps zones, the temperature had dropped to - 40°C and there were 50 to 60 centimeters of snow. The most commonly used western figures for Turkish casualties seem to come from Commandant Larcher's 1926 history and historians often use the same figures today–90,000 dead and 40,000 to 50,000 captured, leaving a total remaining of 12,400 men. However, the operational returns compiled by the Third Army's chief of staff, Lieutenant Colonel Guse, are quite different—thirty thousand dead and seven thousand captured.[12] This left twelve thousand men in the Fortress of Erzurum and forty-two thousand in the vicinity. It is quite possible that Commandant Larcher's numbers include killed, wounded, and missing (many of whom later showed up as stragglers). Since the number of wounded soldiers generally outnumber the dead, it is reasonable to assume that there were significant numbers of Turkish wounded among the Third Army's survivors. The military hospitals in the Erzurum area had nine hundred patients before the campaign, After the battle, the hospitals were full to overflowing with fifteen thousand sick and wounded men. The Turkish official history lists twenty-three thousand dead, ten thousand died in hospital, seven thousand prisoners, and ten thousand wounded for a total of some fifty thousand casualties.[13] In any event, the casualties were huge in proportion to the force engaged.

On February 14, 1915, the Third Army counted forty-two thousand effectives. The army artillery force was in much better shape than the maneuver battalions and counted about 170 assorted types of artillery. One hundred forty-one artillery pieces had returned from the Sarikamiş campaign (losses were twelve field artillery pieces and fifty mountain artillery pieces).

In many respects the Turkish campaign to annihilate a major portion of the Russian Army in the Sarikamiş pocket was a remarkable accomplishment. In the preliminary planning phases, the Turks concentrated three army corps for the attack in a very short time, including reinforcements from as far away as Constantinople. In concept, the Turkish plan was no less ambitious than the French Plan XVII or the Austro-Hungarian offensive into Galicia or the Russian offensive into East Prussia. The weather, terrain, and logistics involved come under the general heading of "factors affecting the operation" and, while relevant, did not appear to have fundamentally caused the plan to fail. A case may certainly be made that the Turkish means were exceeded by these factors affecting operations; however, the root miscarriage of the Turkish plan was caused by flawed assumptions and planning parameters concerning Russian command and control. Embedded in the assumptions of the Turkish plan was the idea that Russian command and control would waver and fatally disable the Russian ability to react to the changing situation. The Turkish plan went off as scheduled and remained very much on track until December 28, 1914, when the Russians managed to pull several infantry and cavalry regiments off the Erzurum line in time to rush these units northwards to garrison the city of Sarikamiş. This timely Russian reaction was probably the most important reason that the Turkish plan failed—absent strong Russian forces in and around Sarikamiş on December 28, the city would have undoubtedly fallen to the Turkish IX Corps. Faced with a Turkish corps astride its lines of communications and with hard weather coming on, it is very likely that the Russian will to fight would have, indeed, collapsed. The fact that the Turkish envelopment came within a hair's breadth of snapping shut as planned validates their basic operational concept.

The Turkish plan certainly involved much risk. The decision to conduct economy of force missions along the Black Sea coast with the Ştanke Bey Müfrezesı, and along the southern shoulder of the offensive with the 2nd Cavalry Division was in itself inherently fraught with risk. The choice of a deep objective, rather than a closer objective, was a risk—the more time it took to reach Sarikamiş and beyond, the more time the Russians had to react. The force ratio was less a risk, because with the element of surprise in the Turk's favor, the small disparity in overall force levels became less significant, since the Turks could pick their ground for larger local tactical superiority. However, that must be tempered with the nature of the Turkish force itself, which was, in the main, a hastily assembled melange of newly formed divisions. Finally, the Turks depended on the Russians to react in a predetermined way based on German reports from Tannenberg. This was an exceedingly dangerous gamble and there was ample evidence available from the recent Russian successes against the Austro-Hungarians, that the Russian Army remained capable of decisive action. Did the risks outweigh the real chances for success? Again, the relevant indicator is that the Turkish operation almost succeeded and this serves to validate the Turkish staff estimate.

Could the Turks have done better? The short answer is probably not—it would be hard to exceed the overall Turkish performance. The approach marches of the IX and the X Corps, under arduous conditions, were superb examples of what the Turkish soldier was capable of achieving. Turkish command authority, in the persons of Enver Paşa and Hafiz Hakki Bey, was "on the spot" and exercised immediate and decisive tactical influence over the operation. However, the absence of strong coordination at the operational level between the three Turkish corps meant that these formations fought widely separated battles rather than mutually supporting engagements. Nevertheless, the Turkish commanders rapidly brought the majority of their forces to the right places and that is hard to improve on. To criticize the Turkish Army itself for its inherent logistical and material weaknesses is fruitless because those problems were largely unsolvable and could only be remedied by compensatory factors such as leadership and surprise. Beyond their faulty estimate of how the encircled Russians would react, if the Turks could be criticized, it would be for not maintaining an operational reserve. A reserve force might have favorably tilted the tactical balance on Christmas Day 1914 in favor of the Third Army. Perhaps the Turks could also be criticized for not taking most of their field artillery forward beyond Oltu (almost all of the artillery pieces lost in the retreat were mountain howitzers,[14] indicating the absence of field artillery with the forward elements). Whether bringing the field artillery over the mountains southeast of Oltu was physically possible is questionable, but having only short range, smaller caliber artillery forward at Sarikamiş and on the road to Kars, certainly hurt the Turkish offensive capacity at that critical point.

The Turkish campaign to envelop the Russians between Erzurum and Sarikamiş was a remarkable achievement in every sense. As a campaign, it bears a close similarity to Chancellorsville, which was fought during the American Civil War in May of 1863. Joseph Hooker, the Union commanding general envisioned a wide flanking movement with his army which would envelop Robert E. Lee's Army of Northern Virginia and crush it against the anvil of Sedgewick's Corps on the Rappahannock. Although Hooker got off to a fine start and initially gained the element of surprise, Lee's quick reactions saved his army. Hooker was caught in a trap within a trap and was barely able to extract his army. What is notably different, and what further highlights the Turkish accomplishment, is the fact that Hooker enjoyed both huge material resources and numerical superiority over Lee—and it was the warm month of May in Virginia. Yet Hooker also failed.

In the wake of the Third Army's disaster, the Turkish staff fully expected the Russians to exploit their success and launch an all out attack on Erzurum. Hafiz Hakki Bey began immediate and energetic measures to reconstitute the shattered Third Army. This proved very difficult because there were no local reserves available. Additionally, the Fortress of Erzurum had been stripped of all available resources to support the offensive. Fortunately for the Third Army, the Russians were exhausted too, and operations ground to a halt. To compound Hakki Bey's difficulties, the Armenian population grew restless and acts of violence in the Third Army's area began to increase, possibly as a result of Russian subversion and possibly encouraged by the Sarikamiş disaster. Turkish intelligence tracked the rise of large numbers of smuggled weapons into the area and the Turks feared an armed uprising behind their wafer-thin lines.

The most immediate problem confronting the Turkish General Staff in late February 1915 was the outbreak of a spotted typhus epidemic in the Third Army area. The aggressive, charismatic, and newly promoted Third Army commander, Brigadier Hafiz Hakki Bey, died in this epidemic on February 12, 1915.[15] Liman von Sanders again was offered his post as commanding general of the Turkish Third Army but again declined. The problems with the Armenians continued and on February 24, 1915, the Turks were forced to send the Harput, Diyarbakir, and Bitlis Jandarma Battalions to the city of Van, where a revolt appeared imminent.[16] There were also terrorist bombings in the rear at Kayseri.

Further reinforcements for the Third Army were enroute from Thrace. The First Army commander had been ordered on December 3, 1914, to prepare a reinforcement force to be dispatched to the east—destined for upper Mesopotamia, where it would advance toward Tabriz.[17] This force was put together from assets belonging to the IV and V Corps, and was enhanced by freshly trained and well-disciplined reservists. It comprised of the 37th, 40th, and 43rd Infantry Regiments, three cavalry battalions, two machine-gun detachments, a mountain howitzer battalion, three artillery batteries, a field hospital, a telegraph detachment, two hundred camels, and the twenty-eight-man musical band from the Turkish War Academy. The force was designated as the Halil Bey Division and was under the command of Constantinople Area Commander Lieutenant Colonel Halil Bey (later Halil Paşa). The division departed from the Haydarpaşa train station on December 11, 1914 bound for the east. From his forward headquarters in Köprüköyö on December 15 Enver Paşa sent the force an order exhorting it to drive on Tabriz and then drive on Azerbaijan! Enroute, on December 26, 1914, the division was redesignated the 5th Expeditionary

Force and ordered to the vicinity of Diyarbakir and Bitlis. In early January 1915, the force had reached the city of Akçakale and on January 11, it was assigned by Enver Paşa to reinforce the battered Third Army. Since the units were already routed east on Turkey's abysmal railroad system, it took time to reroute them northward, and even further movement problems were encountered marching on the winter storm afflicted roads. Finally, on February 2, 1915, the tired and cold units of the 5th Expeditionary Force began to arrive in Erzurum, many of the soldiers showing the first signs of typhus. Halil Bey and his staff arrived on February 8. The following day the force began moving to its assembly area south of Erzurum, where it concentrated on February 20 and began field training on February 23. On paper, the 5th Expeditionary Force had a strength of 248 officers, 10,920 soldiers, 6 machine-guns, and 12 mountain howitzers (of which 8 were quick firing guns). The Third Army also sent a column of 700 camels to increase the mobility of the force. However, on the difficult journey from Constantinople, the 5th Expeditionary Force had lost 102 men dead from sickness and injuries, was missing 1,041 deserters, and had left 1,040 men behind in hospitals along the route. Additionally, there were 2,708 men who were sick but remained with their units. The 5th Expeditionary Force was present in theater, but was clearly not combat ready.

Enver Paşa had ordered the formation of a second provisional force on December 11, 1914.[18] This second force was formed from the II Corps in Adrianople as the Kazim Bey Division, under II Corps Chief of Intelligence Lieutenant Colonel Kazim Bey (later Lieutenant General Kazim Karabekir). This force was composed of the 7th and 9th Infantry Regiments (from the 3rd Infantry Division), a cavalry detachment, a field hospital, a transportation unit, and an intelligence section. From II Corps assets, it also took with it a mountain howitzer battalion of two batteries, a telegraph section, a field bakery, and a uniform and equipment repair battalion. From the I Corps, the force received a replacement depot and transportation assets. Although it had less infantry than the 5th Expeditionary Force, the Kazim Bey Division was structurally more self sufficient and capable of independent operations. The division received a variable mission to be prepared to go to either upper Mesopotamia for operations against Tehran, lower Mesopotamia for operations at Basra, or to the east for operations against Tabriz. The force departed Constantinople on December 19 by train and was bound for Aleppo. On December 25, 1914, the division was redesignated the 1st Expeditionary Force.

Due to the gaps in the Turkish railway system, the 1st Expeditionary Force had to march by foot through the Taurus Mountains and through the Osmaniye Gap (see Chapter 1). While marching near the sea at Iskendurun, the force was bombarded by the British Royal Navy, with the 9th Infantry Regiment suffering its first war casualties. While in Aleppo, on January 10, the force was alerted for an assignment to the Third Army in Erzurum; however, since the 5th Expeditionary Force was tying up all available rail transport, the Turkish General Staff informed the 1st Expeditionary Force that it probably would not move until mid-April 1915. However, on January 19, Enver Paşa, who had returned to Constantinople, sent the 1st Expeditionary Force an order titled "The

Primary Mission Continues" and on January 22, the force found itself enroute to Erzurum by way of Mosul (in Mesopotamia). It was expected that the force would make its way, by a roundabout route to Akçakale, where it would rendezvous with the 5th Expeditionary Force. Enroute, it was hoped that additional strength could be garnered as the force passed through the Mosul Vilayet. It was March 13, 1915, by the time the 1st Expeditionary Force was able to reach and depart from Mosul, and with its final destination once again redesignated, it finally arrived in the vicinity of the city of Van on March 23, 1915. While enroute, it had indeed garnered strength and added the 44th Infantry Regiment, three thousand animals, and eight hundred camels to its rolls. It continued to march towards its assembly area.

The returns of the Third Army on March 24, 1915, showed in increase in fighting strength.[19] Major combat unit strength is shown in Table 3.2.

Table 3.2
Third Army Strength, March 24, 1915

Unit	Officers	Soldiers
IX Corps	261	7,806
X Corps	235	3,513
XI Corps	251	4,206
5th Expeditionary Force	113	8,944
TOTAL	860	24,469

Source: TC Genelkurmay Başkanlığı, *Birinci Dünya Harbinde Türk Kafkas Cephesi 3 ncü Ordu Harekatı Cilt II Birinci Kitap* (Ankara: Genelkurmay Basım Evi, 1993), 567.

There were a further thirty-five to forty thousand personnel in the Erzurum area assigned to the fortress garrison and to the lines of communications. The battered cavalry forces were consolidated into two divisions—the 1st Reserve Cavalry Division and the 2nd Reserve Cavalry Division. The total strength of these divisions had been worn down to a total strength of only seventy officers and two thousand men. Although the 1st Expeditionary Force was in theater, it was still marching toward its assembly area and was therefore not yet counted as an asset.

The story of the Third Army's winter offensive in 1914 and spring recovery in early 1915 would not be complete without returning to the Ştanke Bey Müfrezesi and its operations during this time period. The detachment departed from Haydarpaşa on the battle cruiser *Yavuz* (ex-SMS *Goeben*), the cruisers *Mecidiye* and *Hamidiye*, and other assorted ships on December 5, 1914, bound for Trabzond. By the December 17 it was in contact with the enemy along the Black Sea coastal front. In support of the Sarikamiş offensive, the Ştanke Bey Müfrezesi conducted an active attack towards the east to take the pressure off from the X Corps, then advancing towards Oltu in the south. With the 8th

Infantry Regiment in the lead, the hard-driving German commander exceeded all expectations and actually seized the key city of Ardahan on December 27. Unfortunately for the Turks, the detachment was simply too small to hold the city, nor were there any reserves available to reinforce this brilliant success.[20]

Within days, three Russian infantry regiments and a cavalry regiment counterattacked Ardahan, driving the detachment back. However, the detachment continued to fight a strong delaying action, falling back on successive lines. It delayed increasingly stronger Russian forces for almost two months, finally arriving back at its start line on March 1, 1915. From March 7 to March 16, the detachment was under heavy attack by the newly formed Russian Nineteenth Turkistan Army, but it only yielded about ten kilometers of ground. The Ştanke Bey Müfrezesi had accomplished its mission and more.

The final chapter in the winter saga of the Turkish Third Army was the First Invasion of Persia. While planning the Sarikamiş Battle, Enver Paşa was also scheming to launch his "Pan-Turanian" Invasion of Persia. Enver hoped to beat the Russians into the key cities of Persia. From there, he would shift his forces northward and, perhaps, invade Azerbaijan, all the while raising rebellion among the oppressed Turkic peoples held in thrall by the Russians and Persians. It was a wildly ambitious idea. Nevertheless, seeing a window of opportunity open in December 1914, Enver ordered his forces forward into Persia. Unfortunately, the only force then available, and even remotely near the Persian frontier, was the Van Jandarma Division. This paramilitary formation was lightly equipped with artillery and machineguns, and was only suited for internal security functions, rather than for an invasion of a neighboring country. However, by December 15, 1914, the Van Jandarma Division had crossed the frontier and was holding the Persian town of Kotur. The division's lines of communications fed back through the Turkish town of Saray and then back into the city of Van. To the south, an ad hoc regiment-sized force under Cevat Bey had occupied an additional corner of Persian territory. The Russians responded very quickly by sending several divisions to occupy Tabriz and Tehran.

Enver planned to send the newly constituted 1st and 5th Expeditionary Forces to reinforce the invasion force in Persia. Meanwhile, the Van Jandarma Division pushed father east to Zori and began to dig in. Unfortunately, after the Sarikamiş disaster, Enver rerouted the 5th Expeditionary Force, which had reached Diyarbakir on January 10, 1915, north to the Third Army. The 1st Expeditionary Force soon followed. These forces had been projected to attack Tabriz, via the Van Jandarma Division's bridgehead at Kotur. However, without their presence, the proposed invasion plan collapsed. The Jandarma troops remained at Kotur for several months, until they were attacked by greatly superior Russian forces on March 7. They were gradually pushed back beyond the Turco–Persian frontier, as was the Cevad Bey detachment. By April 18, 1915, all Ottoman forces had been pushed back out of Persia. Enver's First Invasion of Persia had failed. He would try again.

MESOPOTAMIA

The operational area of the Mesopotamian campaigns in the First World War was composed of the ancient and fertile lands watered by the Tigris and the Euphrates Rivers. Beset by seasonal flooding, malaria and pestilential swamp fevers, and terrible summer heat and humidity, it was a difficult area in which to conduct military operations. Agricultural irrigation networks and swamps made travel near the rivers difficult and where the irrigation ended, the desert began. The inhabitants, although Muslim, were predominately Marsh Arabs rather than Turks, and there was a sizable sprinkling of Kurds, Armenians, Syrians, Jews, and Arabs as well. The Ottomans had conquered the region in the early 1500s and had divided the area into three *vilayets*, centered on Mosul, Baghdad, and Basra. The area was famous for the quality of its agricultural produce and also for the inefficiency with which the Turks administered the region.[21] In the wake of the Balkan Wars, the Turkish General Staff garrisoned Mesopotamia with the XII Corps at Mosul and the XIII Corps at Baghdad. The divisions of these corps were distributed along the river cities for ease of administration and also for internal security missions. Along with the remote Turkish garrisons in Arabia, the Mesopotamian theater was a sleepy backwater for the troops of the Turkish Army.

In the intelligence estimates of the Turkish General Staff, the possibility of war with Great Britain was assessed as unlikely. The Mesopotamian theater, therefore, was judged to be a secure rear area from which the Turkish Army could draw reserves for more active roles. In fact, the Turkish Campaign Plan and the Mobilization Plan did just that, and stripped Mesopotamia of most its prewar Turkish garrisons. By November 1914, The entire XII Corps was redeployed to Syria and the XIII Corps and its 37th Infantry Division were both enroute to the Third Army. The Sixth Army headquarters, under the command of Cevit Paşa, itself was scaled down and became the Irak Area Command with the new 38th Infantry Division forming under its command.

The newly formed 38th Infantry Division relied heavily on locally raised Arab levies to fill its ranks and by the beginning of hostilities had only six of its normal complement of nine infantry battalions. The Irak (Iraq) Area Command also had one independent battalion of the 26th Infantry Regiment, eight battalions of frontier guards, and nine battalions of Jandarmes. Although the total Turkish strength in the area was over twenty-three thousand men, actual mobile strength in the region was only about sixty-five hundred riflemen, three old machine guns, and thirty-three artillery pieces.[22] Equally important in the equation of the Irak Area Command's low fighting potential was the poor discipline and questionable loyalty of the force that was made worse by inadequate levels of equipment.

By early fall in 1914, it was very apparent to the Turkish General Staff that the empire would soon be at war with Great Britain, as well as with Russia and France. Therefore planning proceeded for an early Turkish attack on the Suez Canal and for an aggressive offensive in the Caucasus Mountains of eastern Turkey. The bulk of the remaining army concentrated in Thrace to await uncertain developments in the Balkans. Since the Turkish General Staff thought that Great Britain lacked the resources to concentrate its scarce land forces in France and Egypt, while simultaneously conducting offensive operations against Turkey, Mesopotamia continued to rank low in the order of military priorities facing the empire. Belatedly, in November 1914, the Turkish General Staff became aware of the plans of the Indian Army to land troops in the Shatt al Arab to protect British Persian Gulf oil interests. In fact, preliminary British plans envisioned only the early seizure of Abadan Island, where the Anglo-Persian Oil Works were located, and Basra by a reinforced infantry brigade.[23] However, it soon became clear that the Indian Army could deploy, at the least, an entire reinforced infantry division for operations in Mesopotamia (the 6th "Poona" Division). The British estimated Turkish strength in the area at 10,000 rifles, 114 guns, and 6 machine guns (almost double the actual Turkish strength) and it was thought that the Turks would concentrate most of this strength at Basra.[24] By late October, the British received intelligence confirming the departure of the Turkish XII Corps and the XIII Corps. The British expedition convoyed to the head of the Persian Gulf to await the outbreak of war.

In the meantime, the Turks, under the command of Süleyman Askeri Bey, redeployed portions of the 38th Infantry Division to positions at the mouth of the Shatt al Arab to await the expected British assault. The main Turkish defense force, consisting of the 38th Infantry Division and a reinforced infantry regiment, was stationed in the vicinity of Basra and fielded forty-seven hundred riflemen, eighteen field guns, and three machine guns. The key to the Shatt al Arab was the old Turkish fort at Fao and, inexplicably, here the Turks stationed only 350 men and four 87 mm cannon. A second detachment of 160 men was stationed on nearby Abadan Island. A Turkish Major named Muhammad Amin, later wrote that the flawed Turkish dispositions were the result of a decision to maintain strength against the Russians and the Persians, thereby dispersing Turkish strength.[25] The remainder of the Turkish force was deployed to oppose a potential overland thrust from Kuwait.

The British commander, General Delamain, received orders to commence hostilities against Turkey on October 31, 1914, and began combat operations shortly thereafter. The British naval force bombarded the old fort at Fao and landed troops on November 6, which took the fort later that day. The Turkish battalion withdrew safely up river. After destroying the guns and the installation, the small landing force withdrew on November 7. Larger forces followed and by the middle of November, about half of the 6th "Poona" Division was ashore and the remainder were en route to the Shatt al Arab as well. The Turks established a regiment-sized blocking position between Basra and the sea but the British brushed it aside on November 14, 1914. Encouraged by their early success, the British decided to seize Basra, which fell on November 20, with a Turkish loss of twelve hundred prisoners and three guns. As a result of this unexpected and easy success, the India Office began to propose further advances up river to Qurna. The military secretary at the India Office felt that this would afford the oil works additional protection, have a moral affect on the Arabs, and offer strategically valuable ground to the British.[26] Approval followed quickly, and plans were put in train to deploy more Indian Army units to Mesopotamia and by early December the British were advancing on Qurna. Several regimental scale battles were fought, with the Turks partially successful in each but gradually being pushed back inside the town. Qurna fell on December 9, 1914, with the surrender of a further forty-five officers and one thousand men, and the loss of six cannons.[27] The Turkish 38th Infantry Division had been defeated in detail and was soon reduced to shattered debris. The surviving Turkish forces retired toward Amara.

Disturbed by the increasing problems in this theater, Enver Paşa notified Lieutenant Colonel Süleyman Askeri Bey to go by steamboat to the front. On January 2, 1915, he took command of the Irak Area Command. Greatly alarmed by these developments, the Turkish General Staff also reversed the deployment orders of the 35th Infantry Division and ordered its return to Mesopotamia. This division began to arrive in Mesopotamia in early January 1915 and its presence enabled Süleyman Askeri Paşa to reform his army into two wings for the defense of the region. Additionally, the battered 38th Infantry Division was reinforced and partially restored to effectiveness. These two divisions then became the framework on which the Turks built two separate defensive columns. The right wing guarded the Euphrates River and was composed of the reconstituted 38th Infantry Division. This force defended the approaches to Nasiriya and was directly under the command of Süleyman Askeri Paşa. The left wing guarded the more important Tigris River, which led to Baghdad. This vital route was entrusted to the fresh 35th Infantry Division under the command of Mehmed Fazil Paşa, who also had irregular cavalry and Arab infantry battalions under his command as well.[28] With these forces in place, the Mesopotamian front stabilized.

SINAI

After the tumultuous staff disputes between Bronsart von Schellendorf and Hafiz Hakki Bay concerning overall Turkish strategic direction, Enver Paşa approved the plan for offensive operations against the Suez Canal. Unfortunately, the Turkish Second Army and the entire VI Corps were now entrained and moving toward their war stations near Constantinople. This was because the Turkish plans had never foreseen a multifront war, in which Great Britain was an adversary. Syria, with its Sinai front, was seen as a reservoir in the Turkish force pool, which could be safely drained to support other requirements. However, with the Sinai front projected as the launching point for a major offensive, there now existed a requirement for a controlling army-level headquarters and additional troops with which to conduct the attack. While the Turkish Second Army and the two division VI Corps were deploying northward toward Thrace, a new army headquarters was formed in Syria and the two division XII Corps was deployed to Syria from Mesopotamia. Additional reinforcements, in the form of the first-class 8th Infantry Division from Rodosto (Tekirdag) and the well-trained 10th Infantry Division from Symrna, were ordered to Palestine. The 22nd Infantry Division, from Hedjaz, was also put on orders for Palestine. In the midst of this, a brand new infantry division, the 25th Infantry, was formed in Palestine to add weight to the VIII Corps. Thus forces from Syria went north and forces from the northwest went south to Syria sometimes crisscrossing each other enroute. The carefully designed Concentration Plan was coming apart at the seams.

The new Turkish Fourth Army was formed on September 6, 1914, and was assigned the mission to begin planning and preparations for an attack on Egypt. On November 18, 1914, Minister of the Marine Cemal Paşa arrived from Constantinople to take command of the army for the offensive. With him came Colonel von Frankenberg to act as his chief of staff for the new Fourth Army and Lieutenant Colonel Freiherr von Kress to act as the chief of staff of the VIII Corps. Planning went ahead for the offensive and the campaign plan envisioned a single corps thrust across the Sinai Desert to cut the Suez Canal almost at its midpoint of Ismailia. The remaining corps in the Fourth Army would garrison Syria, Palestine, and guard the long and vulnerable Mediterranean coastline.[29]

The geography of the Sinai Peninsula was not conducive to either sustained operations or to the movement of large forces across its breadth. There were only two semi-improved roads leading from Palestine, one along the northern coast, and the second along the ancient Route of the Patriarchs, in the arid and desolate middle of the peninsula. The second route led to Ismailia on the canal. The terrain was waterless and afforded no fodder for the draft animals, which meant that everything that the army needed for survival had to be brought forward. Water, in particular, consumed in large quantities by both men and animals, posed a particular problem.

The mature Turkish plan for the attack on the Suez Canal envisioned a daring coup-de-main seizure of Ismailia by a single infantry division, which would force a passage over the canal itself. This division would immediately be reinforced by a second infantry division, which in turn would be supported on either flank by two additional divisions remaining on the east bank of the canal. A further division would be available to reinforce the bridgehead on the West Bank of the canal, if needed. The Turks hoped that by cutting the mid-point of the canal that they could mediate the effects of the gunfire of Royal Navy warships, which would inevitably assist any British counterattack. Furthermore, they hoped that such an audacious maneuver would incite the Muslim populations of Egypt to rise in revolt against the British.[30] The plan was not without risk. The British were rapidly bringing the Australian and New Zealand Army Corps (Anzac) into Egypt, along with several brigades of the regular Indian Army. This sizable British and Imperial force, combined with the logistical difficulties involved with crossing the desolate Sinai Desert, meant that the Turks might have to fight at a severe numerical disadvantage. Nevertheless, planning for the attack went forward.

To cut down on unnecessary movement, as the VIII Corps deployed into southern Palestine for the attack, the XII Corps, arriving from Mesopotamia, took its place in Aleppo, Damascus, Homs, and along the coastline of Palestine. At the disposal of the VIII Corps were the 8th, 10th, 23rd, 25th, and 27th Infantry

Divisions. Contingents of fellow Muslims were recruited to accompany the expedition forward into Egypt, hopefully to raise revolt there in support of the Turks. Among these contingents were Sinai Bedouins, Druses, Kurds, Mohadjirs, Chercassians from Syria, and Arabs. Also accompanying the expedition were military Imams (Muslim religious chaplains) and two thousand refugees from Lybian Tripoli. The force numbered about fifty thousand men and reportedly the morale was high.[31] Because of the chronically poor Turkish railroads and communications, the assembly of this force took considerably longer than had been projected and preparations were not completed until mid-January 1915. The VIII Corps concentrated at Beersheba for its movement forward across the frontier.

As finally constituted, the VIII Corps assembled an first echelon of about thirteen thousand men with which to force passage across the Suez Canal. The heart of the force was the reinforced 25th Infantry Division, augmented by volunteers from the 23rd and 27th Infantry Divisions, fifteen hundred Arabs, and eight batteries of field artillery. Accompanying this force across the Sinai were about one thousand horses, twelve thousand camels, and about three hundred oxen. The second echelon comprised the 10th Infantry Division with twelve thousand men. Flank guards were provided by the 23rd Infantry Division. Thus, before it even began the projected five-division attack was scaled back to a mere three, although somewhat stronger than normal, Turkish infantry divisions.

Movement forward began on January 14 and for the first week movement was conducted in daylight. The Turks advanced with three columns abreast with the main effort in the center. Huge water tanks and storage depots were moved forward in an unprecedented and sophisticated logistical operation. Although the British had received intelligence reports of Turkish movements and reinforcements in Palestine, they remained unaware that a major attack was imminent.[32] Because of the danger of discovery by British reconnaissance hydroplanes (seaplanes), the Turks decided to conduct the final approach march under the cover of darkness. In a series of rapid night marches conducted over the next seven days, the 25th Infantry Division (the main center column) reached its planned assembly area, ten kilometers east of Ismailia, on January 31 1915. There the force rested while the supporting engineers and trains brought forward pontoons, boats, and bateaux, which had been requisitioned in Gaza and laboriously transported across the desert from Beersheba. The Right and the Left Wing columns, in regimental strength, also reached their flanking assembly areas.

On the night of February 2, 1915, the 25th Infantry Division moved forward to its assault positions on the east bank of the Suez Canal. There an assault force of two infantry battalions brought forward boats and prepared to cross the canal between the towns of Toussoum and Serapeum. The Turkish attack plan envisioned a classic water crossing operation. In fact, the attack graphics (military map symbols used for planning) were strangely reminiscent of more recent amphibious operations such as Normandy or Iwo Jima and depicted a very orderly and precise military operation.[33] The eight batteries of field artillery were also brought forward to support the attack. To the north, the flanking 23rd

Infantry Division would conduct diversionary operations, which would appear to threaten the town of Ismailia. The second echelon 10th Infantry Division lay in reserve.

The Turks had achieved complete surprise at all levels, but upon entering the water, the Turks disturbed a small British observation post, which immediately opened fire. The soldiers of the 25th Infantry Division, almost completely untrained in water crossing operations, panicked. Some of the men jumped out of the boats and fled inland and some dropped their boats even before entering the water. The carefully prepared attack plan disintegrated. In spite of these difficulties, about two companies of Turkish soldiers actually reached the West Bank of the Suez Canal. This drew an immediate and strong British reaction. Despite these strong and repeated British counterattacks on the ground, and under incessant naval gunfire from Royal Navy units in the Great Bitter Lake and Lake Timsan, the Turks attempted to press the attack. The 10th Infantry Division was brought forward in readiness to attempt to reinforce the tenuously small bridgehead. Throughout the day of February 3, the Turks held their small bridgehead against counterattacks from Indian and Sudanese troops. However, by 4 P.M. that day, it became apparent that the British were rapidly gaining the upper hand and that the Turkish bridgehead would eventually be wiped out by superior forces. Cemal ordered the VIII Corps chief of staff, Colonel von Kress, to begin withdrawal of the corps to its assembly area ten kilometers to the rear. While the disengagement was conducted successfully, the bulk of the boats and pontoons were abandoned, ending any hopes that the Turks might have had of renewing the offensive. About three hundred Turkish soldiers were captured. Turkish casualties were relatively light, with 192 dead, 381 wounded, and 727 missing or captured, for a total loss of about 1,300 men.[34] After the action, the British thought that they had simply countered a reconnaissance-in-force rather than a major Turkish offensive aimed at severing the vital Suez Canal on which Imperial communications depended. Cemal Paşa decided to retreat back to an advanced line to be established near El Arish–Magdaba and which would be held by three infantry battalions and two batteries of field artillery. From there, he hoped to be able to harass and interdict British shipping on the Suez Canal with mobile columns. This was a prudent decision, taken in light of the fact that due to the prolonged preparation time taken by the Turkish Fourth Army, the British had greatly reinforced their Egyptian garrison. In fact, by January 1915, the British had over 150,000 troops on hand from India, Australia, New Zealand, and the United Kingdom assembling in Egypt. While many of these troops were almost completely untrained, they were lavishly equipped and close to permanent bases of supply. This gathering British host numbered far in excess of the original Imperial garrison of about twenty thousand men that the Turkish Fourth Army expected to confront in Egypt.

By the middle of February 1915, the VIII Corps was pulled back to Gaza and the 10th Infantry Division was stationed at the end of a Turkish defensive line at the ancient wells of Beersheba. The aggressive and ill-conceived Turkish attack on the Suez Canal had ended in failure. Later in 1915, the Fourth Army itself would be stripped of its trained combat divisions as the 8th, 10th, and 25th

Infantry Divisions were transferred to the critical Gallipoli front. In their place, the Fourth Army would raise the new 41st, 43rd, and 44th Infantry Divisions.

NOTES

1. TC Genelkurmay Başkanlığı (Turkish General Staff), *Birinci Dünya Harbinde Türk Kafkas Cephesi 3 ncu Ordu Harekatı Cilt II Birinci Kitap.* (Ankara: Genelkurmay Basım Evi, 1993), 31-32. This is the Turkish General Staff Study of the Third Army's operations in the Caucaus Mountains..

2. Pan-Turanism expresses the idea of a larger Turkish ethnic identity including the Turkic peoples residing in the Caucasian republics and the Trans-Caspian republics.

3. Turkish General Staff, *3 ncu Ordu Harekatı,* 39-53. Enver Paşa had involuntarily forced 2 marshals, 3 lieutenant generals, 30 major generals, 95 brigadier generals, 184 colonels, 236 lieutenant colonels and majors, and some 800 captains and lieutenants into retirement in the year prior to the outbreak of war.

4. Turkish General Staff, *3 ncu Ordu Harekatı,* losses for the Koprukoy battle were: 1,983 killed, 6,170 wounded, 3,070 prisoners, and 2,792 deserters (two of which were Armenian officers). Of note, an estimated 10,000 men from the reserve cavalry divisions deserted and returned to their villages, 322. Because of this, the Turks dissolved the Reserve Cavalry Corps on November 21, 1914, 302.

5. The "Schulenburg legend" mentioned by W. E. D. Allen and Paul Muratoff, *Caucasian Battlefields: A History of the Wars on the Turco-Caucasian Border, 1828-1921* (Cambridge: Cambridge University Press, 1953), 249-253, suggesting that the German Count von der Schulenburg was partly responsible for the operational concept and terrain analysis of the Sarakamiş operation is not corroborated in the Turkish official histories.

6. In Turkish, the phrase is *büyük kuşatma harekatı,* which translates to "large envelopment operation." The root word *kuş* means "bird" and invokes a mental image of two large wings enveloping the prey along the lines of a classic Cannae type of battle of annihilation.

7. Turkish General Staff, *3 ncu Ordu Harekatı,* 348-349.

8. Ibid., 352.

9. At this time, most corps commanders in the German, French, and British armies were experienced senior lieutenant's general, who were, on average, about fifty-five years old.

10. Turkish General Staff, *3 ncu Ordu Harekatı,* 383-384.

11. Ibid., 512.

12. Ibid., 535-536.

13. General Fahri Belen, *Birinci Cihan Harbinde Turk Harbi 1914 Yili Hareketleri Incu Cilt* (Ankara: GK Basimevi, 1967), 192.

14. I base this conclusion on the nature of the terrain between Oltu and Sarikamiş, which precluded bringing anything larger than mountain howitzers over the mountain tracks. These guns were probably then left behind in the Turkish retreat, which would explain why the loss ratio of field artillery compared to mountain artillery was so lopsided.

15. Liman Von Sanders, *Five Years in Turkey* (London: Bailliere, Tindall & Cox, 1928), 49.

16. Turkish General Staff, *3 ncu Ordu Harekatı*, 565-566.
17. Ibid., 569-579.
18. Ibid., 575-582.
19. Ibid., 567.
20. Ibid., 601-605. On December 29, the strength of the detachment was 58 officers, 2,896 men, 398 animals, 3 howitzers, and 2 captured Russian machine guns--it was a shoestring operation. To accomplish this, the cost to the detachment was 149 dead, 411 wounded, and 15 missing.
21. Brig. Gen. F. J. Moberly, *The Campaign in Mesopotamia, 1914–1918*, vol. 1. (London: HMSO, 1923), 1-15. Brigadier Moberly quotes a Turkish General Staff report stating that the Turks had seventeen thousand rifles and forty-four field guns in Mesopotamia, but this obviously included Jandarma and frontier guards.
22. Commandant M. Larcher, *La Guerre Turque Dans La Guerre Mondiale*. (Paris: Chiron & Berger-Levrault, 1926), 323–325.
23. Moberly, *Campaign in Mesopotamia*, 85-88.
24. Ibid., 100.
25. Ibid., 352– 55. Brigadier Moberly's Appendix 6, Summary of a pamphlet "The Turco-British Campaign in Mesopotamia and our mistakes," by Staff Binbashi Muhammad Amin, published by the Turkish General Staff, contains a comprehensive analysis of the strategic, operational, and tactical options available to the Turkish command in Mesopotamia in 1914 and 1915.
26. Ibid., 136.
27. Turkish General Staff, *Birinci Dünya Harbinde Turk Harbi Irak-Iran* (Ankara, GK Basimevi, 1970), 107.
28. Larcher, *La Guerre Turque*, 326–327.
29. Ibid. 248–250.
30. Ibid., 251.
31. Ibid., 251.
32. Otto Liman Von Sanders, *Five Years in Turkey*, 44.
33. Fahri Belen, *Birinci Dünya Harbinde Turk Harbi 1915 Yili Hareketleri 2ncu Cilt* (Ankara: GK Basimevi, 1967), Diagram 1.
34. Larcher, *La Guerre Turque*, 254.

4
Under Attack, April 1915–January 1916

1915

1915 was characterized by the loss of the strategic initiative to the allies as the Turks were forced to respond to their incursions and attacks. Overall, 1915 was a brutal year for the Turkish Army, in which it weathered major offensives by the British and French at Gallipoli, by the Russians at Erzurum and Malazgirt, and by the British and Indians in Mesopotamia. Almost 100 percent of the Turkish Army was committed to combat in 1915 and the total losses of killed, seriously wounded, and missing sustained from all theaters probably exceeded 500,000 men. The Turks had little to show for these losses and lost significant amounts of terrain in the Caucasus and in Mesopotamia. However, Gallipoli was reclaimed as empire territory, but at a terrible cost and effort.

At the operational level, the Turkish Army was savaged by a year of brutal and costly combat. Although the number of active Turkish infantry divisions had reached a total of fifty,[1] many of these formations were worn down to the size of regiments. However, the Turkish Army, although badly knocked about, was still a force to reckoned with and still retained its combat effectiveness. At the strategic level, the Germans and the Austro-Hungarians defeated Serbia and persuaded Bulgaria to join the Central Powers. These two events allowed the establishment of a continuous landline of communications from Central Europe to Turkey. Much was expected by the Turkish General Staff from this development.

Importantly, the Turks were learning that they could stand in the line toe to toe with the allies and win. They were also learning the fine art of high command at corps and army level. Assisted by able German staff officers, the Turks were becoming adept at organizing ad hoc groupings of forces to address crisis situations. This capability would continue to mature as the war continued. Turkish commanders of ability were emerging through the hard school of combat. Gallipoli veterans, in particular, would prove extremely able and would move up to important command responsibilities later in the war.

GALLIPOLI

For the Turks, the Çanakkale Savaş or the Gallipoli campaign, evokes the same kinds of memories as Gettysburg, the Somme, Verdun, or Leningrad do for the Americans, British, French, and Russians, respectively. It was a victory of huge physical and psychological importance and it is vividly remembered in Turkey today. When discussing the subject of the First World War with almost any Turk, invariably, the first subject to arise is Çanakkale. The campaign is also similarly embedded in the psyche of the people of Australia and New Zealand who continue to celebrate Anzac Day. For all three nations the battle represented a coming of age of a people about to test themselves against the currents of the twentieth century.

The straits of the Dardanelles are approximately forty miles in length and are dominated on the west side by the commanding heights of the Gallipoli Peninsula. To the east, the low rolling hills of Asia provide enough cover and concealment to hide an army. On the peninsula itself, the high hills in the center provide the dominant terrain. To the north and behind these hills, the peninsula narrows to a tiny waist only a little over a mile in width before merging into the plains of Thrace. The Dardanelles themselves are only fifteen hundred meters wide at the narrows of Çanakkale. Although the ground seems ideal for defense, the long coastline provides a naval adversary with many opportunities for flanking attacks and makes resupply and communications difficult. Finally, the possession of the high ground in the middle of the peninsula negates the military value of the low ground along the interior of the straits. It is not easy ground to defend.[2]

In peacetime, the defense of the Dardanelles was in the hands of the commander of the Çanakkale Fortified Area Command. This was a fortress command, which had control over a string of elderly forts and over a brigade of three heavy and medium artillery regiments. The forts and guns were generally clustered at the mouth of the Dardanelles and at the narrows and, in times of peace, were manned at very low levels. Just to the north of the peninsula, the Turkish III Corps lay in the garrison city of Tekirdag, on the Sea of Marmara. The III Corps had the 7th, 8th, and 9th Infantry Divisions assigned to its rolls, and also the 9th Field Artillery Regiment, the 3rd Cavalry Brigade, and a corps support command. This corps was the only corps in the Turkish Army to emerge intact from the Balkan Wars of 1912 to 1913.

Neither of these major units was ready for war in early August 1914. Following the July crisis in the summer of 1914, the Turkish General Staff decided to conduct military mobilization as a precautionary measure, even though Turkey was not yet at war. The Turkish General Staff sent mobilization orders to the Commander of the III Corps, in Tekirdag, at 1 A.M., on August 2, 1914. The commander was Esat Paşa who roused himself out of bed and read the orders at 0245 hours in the morning, which offers a glimpse of that officer's professionalism and concern for his mission. He began immediate preparations for war. The following day, which was the first numbered day of mobilization (August 3), the III Corps began to mobilize. However, its initial strength returns reflected the low condition of peacetime readiness that the Turkish Army operated under (Table 4.1).[3]

Table 4.1
III Corps Strength, August 2, 1914

Unit	Officers	Soldiers	Animals
7th Infantry Division	200	5,021	724
8th Infantry Division	173	5,622	508
9th Infantry Division	138	3,427	913

Source: Turkish General Staff, *Birinci Dunya Harbinde Türk Harbi, Vncu Cilt, Çanakkale Cephesi Hareketi, Inci Kitap (Haziran 1914 - 25 Nisan 1915),* (Ankara: Genelkurmay Başım Evi ,1993), 54.

Upon mobilization, the 9th Infantry Division was attached to the Çanakkale Fortified Area Command to act as mobile reserve. Technically, it still reported to the III Corps, but for all intents and purposes, fell under the command of the fortress commander. The divisions of the III Corps were the only units in the Turkish Army that met their mobilization timetables.[4] By August 21, 1914, the III Corps strength had swelled to 28,945 men and 7,402 animals. The 7th Infantry Division reported 12,937 personnel and 2,540 animals on hand, and the 8th Infantry Division reported 13,061 men and 2,354 animals, respectively.[5] The Çanakkale Fortified Area Command had a more difficult time with its mobilization, in particular having difficulty with filling the required number of specialized personnel and with animals. However, by August 17, the command reported that its all-important heavy artillery regiments were at war establishment strength. On August 27, the commander of the 9th Infantry Division began conversations with the commander of the Fortress concerning the deployment of his division to the Gallipoli Peninsula and by mid September 1914, the division was moving towards the peninsula. The 7th Infantry Division followed on October 29 and the III Corps headquarters moved from Tekirdag to the town of Gallipoli itself on November 4. The 8th Infantry Division was alerted for service on the Sinai front and began preparations for departure. In its place the III Corps was given the new 19th Infantry Division, then forming in Tekirdag.

In spite of these preparations, the defense of the Dardanelles remained weak due to the poor condition of the fortifications, the antiquity of many of the cannons, the scarcity of ammunition and supplies, and the lack of good coordination between the fortress command and the corps headquarters. To rectify these deficiencies, the Germans dispatched Vice Admiral von Usedom, who was an expert in seacoast defenses. Accompanying the admiral were about five hundred Germans who were specialists in coast artillery, communications, and mines. German Army engineer and defensive specialist Colonel Weber was also assigned to assist the commander of the Çanakkale Fortified Area

Command. The Germans likewise dispatched limited quanities of war material to Turkey through the neutral countries of Romania and Bulgaria. On November 3, the Royal Navy briefly bombarded the Turkish forts at the entrance of the Dardanelles. This attack achieved no objective of military value, and indeed, only served notice on the Turks concerning the vulnerability of the straits. In effect, the British attack thoroughly alarmed the Turkish General Staff, and provided them with good reason to accelerate the program of fortification and defensive improvements.

Defense planning and training, particularly anti-invasion drills, now began in earnest, and the troops began to improve the seaward defenses and also to construct roads and interior communications. By February 1915 the fortress command had (including the 9th Infantry Division) over 34,500 soldiers, armed with 25,000 rifles, 8 machine guns, and 263 cannons, on the peninsula. The mobile III Corps (now including only the 7th Infantry Division) had 15,000 soldiers in position, armed with 9,448 rifles, 8 machine guns, and 50 cannons. The 19th Infantry Division remained in the Tekirdag garrison where it was undergoing intensive training under its new commander, the young and aggressive Lieutenant Colonel Mustafa Kemal Bey.[6]

At the onset of mobilization the fortifications of the Dardanelles consisted of the outer defenses, the intermediate defenses, and the inner defenses. The outer defenses were two very old forts at Kum Kale on the Asiatic side and Seddelbahir on the peninsula. These forts had a total of thirteen heavy guns and seven medium guns, which were mostly obsolete. The intermediate defenses were positioned to protect the interior minefields, and fielded four medium guns, and sixteen lighter quick-firing guns. The purpose of these intermediate defenses was to prevent enemy minesweeping activities within the straits. Most of these guns were positioned on the north face of small hills, which screened them from enemy ships coming up from the south. The final inner defenses were very powerful and comprised seventy heavy and six medium guns; however, like the outer defenses, many were antiquated and ammunition was scarce. After the November 3 bombardment of the outer defenses, it was very apparent to the fortress commander, Major General Cevat Paşa, that his fortifications required augmentation.

Throughout the winter of 1914 and 1915, many much needed Turkish reinforcements poured into the area. By mid-February 1915, the British confronted a significantly more powerful defensive force. In particular, the 8th Artillery Regiment commanded by German Colonel Wehrle, which was equipped with 150 mm howitzers, was deployed to reinforce the defenses. The howitzers of this regiment were capable of firing from behind protective terrain and delivering plunging fires on the weakly armored decks of enemy ships. As such, they were almost invulnerable to naval gunfire and were themselves, deadly to ships caught within the narrow confines of the straits. The 1st Battalion of the regiment, with twelve guns, was positioned on the peninsula, and the remaining 2nd and 3rd battalions, with a further twenty guns, were positioned on the Asiatic shore, between the outer and the intermediate defenses. The Turks had also been busy over the winter and had laid additional minefields, one of which was laid inshore on the Asiatic side and parallel to the coastline near Erenkoy (as well as parallel to the direction of the enemy fleet's advance). Nine previously laid belts of mines were laid across the channel at its narrowest points. The unorthodox parallel line of mines at Erenkoy lay directly under the guns of the 8th Artillery Regiment. [7]

On February 19, 1915, the Royal Navy began its attack and on February 25 landed troops at the Kum Kale and Seddelbahir forts, which had been abandoned by the Turks under the heavy British fire. The guns in these old forts were destroyed, and the British withdrew. Again, this action provided the Turks with further worry and only provoked them to work harder in preparing their defenses. Additional guns were brought in from as far away as the fortresses of Erzurum and Adrianople. There were now three cornerstones to the Turkish naval defensive concept. First, groups of mobile howitzers would deliver plunging fire on the fleet entering the Dardanelles. Hopefully, this would damage or sink some of the ships, and would keep the enemy from deploying their unarmored and vulnerable minesweepers ahead of the oncoming fleet. Second, underwater mines and antisubmarine nets were laid in successive belts within the constricted narrows and were heavily covered by quick-firing guns. Finally, the inner defenses, comprising heavy coast defense guns would deal with any ships that managed to break through the mine belts. Altogether, the Turks had 82 guns operational in the fixed fortress defenses, and additional 230 guns operational with artillery units posted along the shores. Ammunition availability remained a problem for the Turks. The 150 mm howitzers of the 8th Artillery Regiment were organized into three operational Howitzer Groups, under Major Rifat on the north shore, and Captain Ali and Major Halit on the south shore. Major Rifat received an additional six 120 mm howitzers. A fourth group of eight 120 mm howitzers, under Major Haspi, was also positioned on the Asiatic side. These howitzer groups divided the area between the entrance of the straits and the narrows into sectors and registered pre-planned concentrations of fire into the area.

On March 18, 1915, the Allies made a concerted attempt to break through the Dardanelles into the Sea of Marmara. A combined Anglo-French fleet, under the command of Admiral de Robeck, attempted to force the straits using minesweepers to clear lanes through the mine belts through which the larger battleships might pass. After a running battle lasting most of the morning, the Anglo-French warships had silenced most of the Turkish forts; however, plunging fire from the 150 mm howitzers of the 8th Artillery Regiment remained heavy. As the battleships turned to starboard to allow the minesweepers access to the mine belts, disaster struck the Allied force. In quick succession, three Allied battleships struck the unexpected mines of the new perpendicular minefield and sank within minutes. Three other battleships suffered severe damage from both mines and artillery fire. Essentially, the Turks had ambushed the Allied ships by the unorthodox positioning of the new minefield. Encouraged, the Turks from the fixed fortifications returned to their guns and renewed fire. Reluctantly, the Allies called off the attack and concluded that the navy could not carry the Dardanelles alone. Turkish casualties had been relatively light in comparison to the Allied losses: fifty-eight killed and seventy-four wounded. Additionally, the Turks had lost nine artillery pieces and had one artillery redoubt destroyed against the severe naval losses suffered by the Allied fleet. The Turkish ammunition situation was of some concern since the Turks had expended about a sixth of their available shells during the daylong battle.[8] The distribution of the remaining shells especially was a problem with some of the guns, particularly those on the higher elevations, having only three shells remaining and others, at lower locations, having as many as eighteen to fifty shells remaining. The variety of types and calibers of the Turkish artillery inventory was also making itself felt, and the spare parts inventory was dropping because the intensity of firing had caused mechanical difficulties for some guns that required repair parts. Eight of the underwater mines had also been detonated. Not knowing if the Allies would press the attack, the Turks went to work to redistribute ammunition and to repair what damage they could. The Allies now began serious preparations for an amphibious landing intended to seize and hold the Gallipoli Peninsula, which, with its high ground, would dominate and make untenable the Turkish fortifications below.

During this period, the Turkish General Staff, in Constantinople, was awash in bad news from the active fronts. The Third Army's winter offensive had collapsed with crippling losses, as had the Fourth Army's attack on the Suez Canal (although with very few casualties), and the British had taken Basra and Qurna in Mesopotamia. The Armenian population in eastern Anatolia was also thought to be preparing to rise in rebellion. Amid this background of competing misfortunes, it became apparent both from Allied activities in the northern Aegean Sea, and from intelligence agents in Egypt, that the Allies were preparing a major amphibious invasion to seize the Dardanelles. To counter this, on February 20, 1915, Enver Paşa ordered a restructuring of the Turkish armies guarding Thrace and Constantinople. Enver ordered that the First Army defend the northern coast and the west side of the Turkish Straits and the Second Army to defend the south coast and the east side of the Turkish Straits. In the words of Liman von Sanders, "it was the feeblest imaginable defensive measure."[9] This plan split the Turkish Straits through the center on a north–south axis, and violated the principle of unity of command. Liman von Sanders protested vigorously to Enver, arguing for a single command which would be responsible for repelling an expected Russian assault near Constantinople, and another command, which would be responsible for repelling the Anglo-French at the Dardanelles. Enver failed to agree with Liman von Sanders's recommendations, and on March 1 made further adjustments to the Turkish dispositions. Enver withdrew the II Corps from Adrianople to Çatalca and the IV Corps from Bandirma to the Gulf of Izmit (positioning them closer to Constantinople to repel an expected Russian amphibious invasion from the Black Sea). Liman von Sanders again protested, because these troops were the closest reserves to the Dardanelles and felt that they would be needed to assist in fighting off the allies.[10] However, in the wake of the Allied attempt to force the Dardanelles on March 18, Enver changed his mind and decided to form a new army headquarters, which would be directly responsible for the defense of the southern straits. On March 24, 1915, the Turkish General Staff activated the Turkish Fifth Army. Enver asked General Liman von Sanders to relinquish command of the First Army and take command of the new Turkish Fifth Army, which he did on March 25. Liman von Sanders departed Constantinople, taking a small part of the First Army Staff with him, among whom were Lieutenant Colonel Kiazim Bey as his chief of staff and his two German aides—Captains Muhlmann and Prigge. Field Marshal Freiherr von der Goltz took over command of both the German Military Mission and the Turkish First Army in Constantinople. Liman von Sanders arrived by sea at the port of Gallipoli on March 26 and established himself in the headquarters of Esat Paşa's III Corps.

The new Fifth Army was a powerful force and had as its main components the III Corps, the XV Corps, the 5th Infantry Division, and an independent cavalry brigade. The III Corps retained its 7th, 9th, and 19th Infantry Divisions, and the XV Corps commanded the 3rd and 11th Infantry Divisions. Both the 5th Infantry Division and the cavalry brigade were kept as army reserves. The Çanakkale Fortified Area Command continued as a separate operational command. Under this command arrangement, the III Corps defended the Gallipoli Peninsula itself, with the 7th and 9th Infantry Divisions watching the beaches and the 19th Infantry Division held in corps reserve near Eceabat. The XV Corps held the Asiatic coast with the 3rd and 11th Infantry Division defending the vulnerable flat beaches. The XV Corps headquarters, with two infantry regiments as the corps reserve, was located at Calvert's Farm near Ciplak, the site of Heinreich Schliemann's archaeological excavations of Homer's Troy.[11] Farther north, the 5th Infantry Division guarded the critical and narrow isthmus of Bulair, and the independent Cavalry Brigade screened the long beaches of the Gulf of Saros. The headquarters of the new Fifth Army remained in the town of Gallipoli. Cevat Bey's Fortress Command continued to command the forts and most of the artillery. The March attack had alerted the Turks to the extreme dangers of an Allied attack and, over a four-week period, Liman von Sanders worked tirelessly to improve the tactical situation in his new army area. He concentrated on realistic preparations which were within Turkish capabilities, such as improving the road network, camouflaging troop concentrations and artillery batteries, and improving the fortifications along the likely landing beaches. He commandeered tools and barbed wire fences from the local farmers in order to fortify even more areas.[12] He worked to improve the existing hospital situation so that by mid-March 1915, there were a total of 1,050 beds available to treat casualties.[13] In between the grueling periods of building fortifications, at night, and in inclement weather, the troops were endlessly subjected to anti-invasion alarms and drills. Although ammunition for some of the larger calibers of artillery was in short supply, morale in the Fifth Army and in the fortress was high. Given the resources at hand, Liman von Sanders and his subordinate Turkish commanders used their time well in preparing the force to meet the Allies.

Liman von Sanders judged that there were three areas of particular danger to his command, these were the Isthmus of Bulair and the Gulf of Saros, the coast of Asia near Kum Kale, and southern tip of the Gallipoli Peninsula. He therefore broke his command into three operational groups, which would defend these three key areas. Apparently uncomfortable with some of the senior Turkish commanders, Liman von Sanders placed highly trained German officers in tactical command of several of these groups. Colonel von Sodenstern with the 5th Infantry Division and the independent cavalry brigade was assigned the Gulf of Saros sector. Colonel Weber was given the XV Corps, composed of the 3rd and the 11th Infantry Division to defend Kum Kale and the Asiatic shore. The Gallipoli Peninsula itself remained under the operational command of Major General Esat Paşa's III Corps. This corps deployed the 7th Infantry Division along the vulnerable isthmus of Bulair, the 9th Infantry Division along the southern tip of the peninsula and maintained the new but well-trained 19th Infantry Division as a reserve.

One of the prevalent myths of the campaign is the idea that Liman von Sanders was instrumental in rationalizing and solidifying the defensive arrangements of the Gallipoli Peninsula in his short first month of command. His own memoirs and most histories credit him with an exaggerated role in this sense, and it is generally unknown that the Turks had established defensive plans for the peninsula in 1912 and 1913 during the Balkan Wars. As the Bulgarians isolated the Gallipoli Peninsula during their advance on the Çatalca lines in November 1912, the Turks began defensive preparations to guard the straits against an amphibious assault by the Greeks. Elaborate plans evolved employing four reserve infantry divisions guarding the vulnerable beaches of the peninsula and the Asiatic shore as well.[14] Two reserve infantry divisions, employing a system of mutually supporting company and battalion strong points, guarded the two areas later famously known as Cape Helles and Anzac. Regimental reserves were positioned in covered ground for immediate counterattacks. A third reserve infantry division guarded the Asian shore at Kum Kale. Behind them on the peninsula at Ecabet, the fourth reserve infantry division lay in general reserve (a position later occupied by the 19th Infantry Division in 1915). In total, the three reserve infantry divisions of the 1912-1913 peninsula defense contained approximately the same combat strength as the later 9th and 19th Infantry Divisions that performed the same missions in 1915 (the Kum Kale position was greatly reinforced in 1915). Although these plans were never actively exercised they were retained and improved on as the empire went to war in 1914. A comparison of the dispositions between 1912-1913 and the final Fifth Army dispositions of April 1915 reveals very close similarities in unit deployment and combat strength.[15] It is noteworthy to mention that these plans were completely the products of Ottoman commanders and General Staff officers.

At the strategic level, the Fifth Army knew that the allies had embarked and were about to launch a large multidivisional Anglo-French expeditionary force somewhere either in European Thrace or in the Asian Troad. However, Liman von Sanders did not know exactly where the main effort would be and the dispositions of the Fifth Army reflected this weakness in intelligence at the operational level. Nevertheless by mid- to late April 1915, an almost continuous series of alarms and invasion scares had raised Turkish troop readiness to a very high level.

Tactically, the Fifth Army deployed a light infantry screen in outposts sited on the dominating terrain overlooking potential landing beaches. These forces were usually in platoon strength and were well dug in with wire and prepared trenches. The Turks did not intend to stop the allies on the beaches with these troops. Instead, regiment-sized forces were positioned three to five kilometers behind the beaches in protected ground. As the outposts slowed the enemy landing and channeled their advance, these larger forces would counterattack the enemy. It was hoped that these counterattacks, conducted immediately or as soon as possible, would throw the unwary invaders back into the sea. At all levels the Turkish commanders rehearsed these counterattacks in detail. The Fifth Army was ready to receive the enemy.

In the early hours of April 25, the allies conducted landings at six separate locations on the Gallipoli Peninsula and at Kum Kale on the Asiatic shore. Furthermore, a highly visible and creative deception was staged in the Gulf of Saros. The invading Allied troops were heavily supported by intense naval gunfire. Reports and alarms poured into the Fifth Army headquarters; however, Liman von Sanders could not yet pinpoint the main enemy attack. Reports from the III Corps indicated that the 9th Infantry Division was holding its ground but that the situation was dangerous. Liman von Sanders ordered Esat Paşa to go forward to Seddelbahir at the southern tip of the peninsula and to take direct command of the battles raging there. Arriving there, Esat found that Colonel Sami, the 9th Infantry Division commander, had put all of his reserves into the fight, and so Esat urgently requested reinforcements. At Ariburnu, the Anzac came ashore and made contact with the Turkish coastal defenders. This brought an immediate and strong reaction. In a famous incident, which propelled Lieutenant Colonel Mustafa Kemal into the limelight, the 19th Infantry Division was alerted and deployed to halt the Anzac attack that threatened the critical high ground dominating the narrows. In what would later prove to be the decisive maneuver for the Turks on the first day of the campaign, Mustafa Kemal intuitively sensed the strength of the Anzac attack and, seizing the initiative, committed his division to battle without waiting for orders. He led his division forward into the fight and personally commanded the 57th Infantry Regiment at the critical point in the battle. It was here that he issued his famous order, "I do not expect you to attack, I order you to die! In the time which passes until we die, other troops and commanders can take our place!" It was inspired and heroic leadership and the final result of the battle probably rested on this single dramatic action. The Anzac's failed to reach their objectives. Kemal would later note that the 57th Infantry Regiment was, "a famous regiment this, because it was completely wiped out."[16]

Meanwhile, at the very tip of the peninsula another tale of heroism was playing itself out. Notably absent from the official Turkish histories of the First World War are the mention of any participants below the rank of captain, and especially absent are the rank and file. One notable exception; however, is the story of Yahya Çavus or Sergeant Yahya, who was assigned to the 12th Company of the 2nd Battalion of the Turkish 26th Infantry Regiment defending the heights named Ay Tepe and Gözcübaba Tepe. These small and adjacent hills overlooked the infamous and deadly V Beach and had been heavily entrenched and defensively wired into a single strongpoint. Towards the early evening (5:40 P.M.) of April 25, Irish troops began a strong attack on these positions. Sergeant Yahya found himself with five squads of infantry, and his position on Gözcübaba under assault by a large column of enemy infantry. With his officer down, the mission to defend the position fell on the shoulders of Sergeant Yahya. The sergeant was described as "intelligent and heroic" and was also an instinctive fighter.[17] He beat back several determined attacks on his hilltop position until the enemy finally quit. Later the British broke into the adjacent Ay Tepe position and tried to outflank and surround Yahya's Gözcübaba position. Reacting immediately, Yahya personally led a bayonet attack, which restored the situation. He survived to tell the story and his name is inscribed on a contemporary memorial at the site. Eventually that evening the Turks lost the Ay Tepe/Gözcübaba Tepe position when the British were able to bring heavy enfilading machine gun fire on the hills. Nevertheless, the Turks remember the singularly heroic exploits of Sergeant Yahya in their histories of the battle.

Liman von Sanders personally rode to the threatened northern sector to gauge for himself the strength of the Allied effort. By late afternoon, the situation became clearer and he was now almost convinced that the Allied presence in the Gulf of Saros was merely a diversion. He ordered the 7th Infantry Division, then deploying to the heights overlooking Bulair, to halt and turn toward the south in response to Esat's plea for reinforcements. Additionally, he ordered the 5th Infantry Division to send a regiment south, as well. Incoming reports from Colonel Weber in Asia indicated that the situation there was well in hand and that he required no major assistance.

As darkness closed in on the Fifth Army on the night of April 25, the tactical situation appeared threatening but favorable. The British landings had been contained to five very small beachheads and the Turks held commanding positions over them. Turkish reserves were deploying to reinforce the thin defensive lines holding the invaders. In Asia, the French landing had been contained at Kum Kale. Although Liman von Sanders did not know it, not a single Allied objective had been reached.

The next morning, even more convinced that he had correctly anticipated the Allied assaults, the Fifth Army Commander dispatched regiments of the 5th and 7th Infantry Divisions to the Seddelbahir front. He also ordered an uncommitted regiment from the 11th Infantry Division in Asia to be brought to the Anzac beachhead. The reinforcements sent earlier were now on hand and were immediately pressed into the fight by Esat Paşa. Liman von Sanders himself went forward to Esat's camp at Maltepe (only four and one-half kilometers from the front lines) to better understand the battle. In Asia, the situation had stabilized, with German Lieutenant Colonel Nicolai's 3rd Infantry Division inflicting heavy loses on the French and completely driving them off by April 29. This success enabled the Turks to bring another regiment of the 11th Infantry Division and two regiments of the 3rd Infantry Division across the narrows in successive detachments to further reinforce the main battle.

According to Liman von Sanders memoirs, the confusion of the first several days of battle forced him to feed reinforcements into the fight without regard to formal command arrangements.[18] Regiments from the 5th and the 11th Infantry Divisions were fighting with the 19th Infantry Division and regiments from the 3rd, 5th, 7th, and 11th were fighting in the 9th Infantry Division sector. This meant that, potentially, the III Corps was in danger of losing control of the battle. The safest way to keep this from happening was to form new operational groups under trusted commanders, who would control the battle on the spot. On May 1, 1915, Liman von Sanders created corps-level group headquarters to weld together these disparate formations into ad hoc but coherent combat groups. He placed Colonel von Sodenstern in command on the Seddelbahir front (Cape Helles) and placed Esat in command on the Ari Burnu front (Anzac beachhead).

Thus, a combination of prompt reactions by subordinate Turkish commanders at lower levels and carefully weighed decisions by the senior Turkish and German commanders enabled the Fifth Army to accomplish much in the decisive initial phase of what would become known as the Çanakkale Savaş (Gallipoli campaign). Despite overwhelming odds and heavy naval gunfire support, the well-drilled Turkish *askers* had stopped the British cold at the landing sites. Correctly anticipating Allied attacks, Turkish and German divisional commanders boldly committed their reserves to halt Allied progress. Lieutenant Colonel Mustafa Kemal and Colonel Nicolai fall into this category of audacious combat leaders without whose presence a Turkish victory is questionable. At the highest levels, the almost immediate reaction of Liman von Sanders and Esat in diverting and committing reserve divisions proved decisive in stopping Allied attacks on the second day of the battle. By the end that second day, the Fifth Army had five of its six infantry divisions in contact with the enemy. On the third day of battle, every Turkish infantry division had regiments in action. By the end of the fourth day, only two infantry regiments remained in Asia and two infantry regiments remained at Bulair and on the isthmus narrows. Taken as a whole, it is hard to imagine a better performance by the Fifth Army.

The first major breakout attempt by the allies occurred at the Cape Helles beachhead (at the southern tip of the peninsula) and was aimed at the capture of the village of Krithia on April 28. This attack failed in the face of a dogged Turkish defense by the 9th Infantry Division and both sides suffered heavy losses. Several days later, with the arrival of regiments of the 3rd, 7th, and 11th Infantry Divisions, Colonel von Sodenstern launched a two-division night attack on the British lines. Because of the scarcity of artillery ammunition, a very brief preparatory barrage lasting only a few minutes preceded this attack, which merely succeeded in waking up the British in their trenches. The attack was repulsed with heavy loss to the Turkish divisions.

Faced with allied landings at the Dardanelles, Enver Paşa was forced to make hard choices with the with the fourteen divisions of the unengaged Turkish First and Second Armies (Table 4.2). These armies had been withheld in the Constantinople area to protect the capital from either a Russian amphibious assault from the Black Sea or from a possible invasion from the Christian Balkan states in Thrace. Another possible deployment for these forces was to

Table 4.2
Disposition of Turkish Forces, Late April 1915

THRACE
First Army
I Corps: 1, 2 Inf. Div.
II Corps: 4, 5, 6 Inf. Div.
IV Corps: 10, 12 Inf. Div.
20 Inf. Div., 1 Cav. Bde.
Second Army
V Corps: 13, 14, 15 Inf. Div.
VI Corps: 16, **24**, 26 Inf. Div.

GALLIPOLI
Fifth Army
III Corps: 7, 9, 19 Inf. Div.
XV Corps: 3, 11 Inf. Div.
5 Inf. Div.
Independent Cav. Bde.

MOVING TO THIRD ARMY
37 Inf. Div.

SYRIA
Fourth Army
VIII Corps: 8, 10, 23, **25**, 27 Inf. Div.
XII Corps: 38 Inf. Div.

ARABIA-YEMEN
VII Corps: 21, 22, 39, 40 Inf. Div.

CAUCASIA
Third Army
IX Corps: *17, 28, 29 Inf. Div.*
X Corps: *30, 31, 32 Inf. Div.*
XI Corps: *18, 33, 34 Inf. Div*
36 Inf. Div.
2 Cav. Div.
3 Reserve Cav. Div.
Van Reserve Cav. Bde.
Van Jandarma (Inf.) Div.
1st Expeditionary Force
5th Expeditionary Force

MESOPOTAMIA
Sixth Army
35 Inf. Div.
Provisional Inf. Div.

Note: Units in boldface type indicate new formations; units underlined indicate units redeployed since December 1914; units in bold italic indicate seriously understrength units.

counter an expected attack on Symrna. Since none of these possibilities seemed to match the danger posed by the Fifth Army's ongoing battle, Enver had little choice but to reinforce Liman von Sanders. At the end of April, the Turkish V Corps, with the 13th, 15th, and 16th Infantry Divisions was ordered to Gallipoli. The 4th Infantry Division was ordered to join the Fifth Army, as well. At the same time, the Turco-German fleet sent two sections of twenty-four machine guns to join in the defense of the peninsula. The Turkish General Staff also scrapped the bottom of the barrel to locate and deploy more howitzers to support Liman von Sanders. The divisional pool in Thrace, so carefully assembled by the Concentration Plan, was slowly being emptied.

The 11th and the 15th Divisions were thrown immediately into costly assaults upon their arrival at the front as the Turks attempted to drive the invaders back into the sea. Although these attacks also failed, the Turks continued to attack throughout the first week of May 1915.

The British decided to try once again to seize Krithia and on May 6 launched a second assault on the Turkish lines. This assault too failed and became known as the Second Battle of Krithia. The British official history notes this battle as the end of the first phase of the Gallipoli campaign.

On May 10 the 2nd Infantry Division was brought forward from its garrison in Constantinople. This division was regarded by the Turks as a very well trained division and was placed in tactical reserve behind the Anzac front. During the night of the May 18 to 19 the 2nd Infantry Division and the 3rd Infantry Division, now entirely having been brought over from Asia, launched a major attack on the Anzac beachhead. Esat Paşa commanded this attack, and he was extremely confident of success because he had numerical superiority at the point of attack using two fresh and highly regarded Turkish infantry divisions. However, the Australians and the New Zealanders had been warned by aerial reconnaissance and by observing preparations in the front-line Turkish trenches. The Turkish attack began at 3 A.M. in the morning and was concluded by dawn. Not only had the attack failed, but the Turks had taken over thirteen thousand casualties, of which over three thousand lay dead in front of the Anzac trenches. The 2nd Infantry Division alone had lost over nine thousand men killed, wounded, or missing.[19] For the first and only time in the Gallipoli Campaign, the local British commander asked for and received permission for a Red Cross-supervised truce in which to bury the dead. Liman von Sanders agreed and on May 23, both sides suspended hostilities to bury the mounds of dead.

On June 4, 1915, the British again took the offensive in the Third Battle of Krithia, sending several divisions to attack the 9th and 12th Infantry Divisions holding the Turkish lines. That morning the Turkish trenches came under a naval bombardment beginning at 8 A.M. By 11:45, the 12th Infantry Division reported that its entire front was under fire from three battleships and that an enemy attack was imminently expected.[20] The British attacks began at 12:10. Most of the attacks penetrated 200 to 450 meters into the Turkish defenses. The farthest went about a kilometer and the 12th Division reported that its soldier's morale was "shaken."[21] All attacks were finally repulsed and the front stabilized about 8 P.M. The Turks estimated that the British suffered forty-five hundred casualties and the French another two thousand on that day. Expecting the British attacks to continue, the 5th and the 11th Infantry Divisions moved into staging areas behind the lines to be ready for a massive counterattack in the event of an Allied breakthrough. Fortunately, the Allies quit, leaving the front relatively unchanged. The Turks lost three officers; forty-nine men were killed and sixty-two officers and 4,903 men were wounded.

On June 9, 1915, Liman von Sanders requested fresh forces from the Turkish General Staff. Enver replied by telegraph on June 12 saying that because of the political situation it was not possible to send fresh forces to the Fifth Army. There had been continuous bombardments by the Russian Navy of the Turkish Black Sea ports throughout the months of April, May, and June and many in the government were worried about the possibility of a Russian amphibious invasion on the Black Sea coastline. Enver promised to send instead individual reinforcements and reservists (private soldiers). Further, he suggested that the Fifth Army consider rotating the divisions in Asia and at Saros into the battle area, especially the 3rd Infantry Division which had sent to Asia to recover after the costly May battles. Enver also offered to exchange regiments of the Fifth Army's divisions with the uncommitted II Corps on a one-for-one basis.[22]

The fighting during the first weeks of the Gallipoli campaign was fierce. The Turkish defenses had depended largely on manpower and rifles rather than on machine guns and artillery. In particular artillery ammunition had to be carefully husbanded because of limited quantities on hand. On June 22, 1915, Liman von Sanders reported to Enver Paşa that he now had now had enough troops on hand but was experiencing difficulty with artillery ammunition availability, especially for his field howitzers.[23] A Fifth Army report to the Turkish General Staff on June 23 highlighted the problem (Table 4.3).

Table 4.3
Fifth Army Ammunition Expenditures Report, May 8–June 8, 1915

Type	Shells Expended	Shells On Hand
Field artillery guns	29,462	19,500
Mortar	1,868	788
Mountain howitzer	2,446	unknown
120 mm gun	1,548	72
150 mm quickfire	765	97
120 mm howitzer	486	173
150 mm howitzer	446	259
105 mm mortar	4,142	1,169
210 mm mortar	165	26

Note: Field artillery guns and mortars were not listed by type or caliber in this report.

Source: Turkish General Staff Archives (ATASE), Fifth Army Report to Turkish General Staff, June 23, 1915. Archive 4/8749, Class 3474, Folder H-11, File 7-8.

A careful examination of this report reveals several severe problems with ammunition availability. The apparent mountain of field artillery ammunition was for guns with low or flat trajectories, which were not particularly useful in fighting trench warfare. The most useful artillery types in trench warfare were howitzers and mortars, which had high-arcing trajectories. In most of these critical categories, the Turks had very small inventories of shells on hand and of these most useful types fewer than ten thousand shells had been fired in the thirty-day period shown. During this period the strength of the Fifth Army had swollen to ten infantry divisions. Given this density of Turkish forces fighting on the peninsula, the total number of Turkish shells expended (roughly eighteen thousand) from early May through early June is actually quite small. To alleviate the growing scarcity of shells the Çanakkale fortress sent 105 150 mm howitzer shells, 1,320 150 mm gun shells, and 750 210 mm shells to the Fifth Army.[24]

A major and costly French attack at Seddelbahair on June 21 and 22 also failed. Later in the month (28-29 June), the British attempted an offensive from the Anzac beachhead. Turkish losses were about one thousand and Liman von Sanders happily reported the repulse of the Anzac attack. He attributed this defensive success to two Turkish officers, Faik Paşa and Albay (Colonel) Refet, both in the 11th Infantry Division.[25] This attempt to break the deadlock failed. Heartened by their defensive success, the Turks counterattacked the Anzac beachhead but were bloodily repulsed. Between June 28 and July 5, the Fifth Army lost sixteen thousand men, about fourteen thousand of whom were lost in the Anzac sector. Concerned over these huge losses, the Turkish General Staff dispatched the 13th Infantry Division to assist the Fifth Army. Enver Pasa was beginning to register concern as well about the way in which the defense of the peninsula was being handled. On July 4, 1915, Enver sent a telegraph cipher to Liman von Sanders suggesting that due to the tired condition of the Fifth Army that it would be a prudent measure to turn over the peaceful Saros Bay sector to the uncommitted Second Army.[26] Liman von Sanders promptly registered his strong disagreement and reconfirmed his belief that the peninsula was best defended by a single commander. Another British offensive followed at Cape Helles on July 12, which failed with very heavy casualties. Turkish strength at the Cape Helles was then five full infantry divisions backed by seventy-two field artillery pieces and twenty-two mountain howitzers.

Neither side made any progress during these costly summer battles, as the European experience with World War I trench warfare asserted itself in the Mediterranean. In spite of their local superiority of 150,000 effectives, backed by powerful naval forces, against the Turkish total of about 120,000 effectives,[27] the allies were unable to break the deadlock at the tactical level. In Constantinople, Enver continued to repeat his call for continued Turkish offensives against the small allied beachheads. Many of the Fifth Army's infantry divisions were depleted by months of continuous combat to regimental strength. As a result, the Turkish Second Army sent a steady stream of replacements to the front and, in July, also sent its chief of staff, Vehip Paşa, to relieve Colonel Weber at the Cape Helles front. Vehip was the energetic younger brother of Esat Paşa and this relationship fostered better coordination between the two operational groups in contact with the British. Vehip immediately began to visit his divisions and to send inspirational messages to his soldiers. The continuing battles were absorbing a large quantity of available Turkish resources and Liman von Sanders now commanded a total of seventeen Turkish infantry divisions. In addition to the original six Fifth Army infantry divisions, the 2nd, 12th, 15th, and 16th Infantry Divisions had arrived in May, the 1st, 4th, and 6th Infantry Divisions had arrived in June, and in July the entire staff of the Second Army, the V Corps with its 13th and 14th Infantry Divisions, and the XIV Corps with its 8th and 10th Infantry Divisions had arrived. Upon its arrival, the Second Army staff merged with the Southern Group staff which greatly augmented and increased the group's capability. On July 28, 1915, the Fifth Army had a total of 250,818 men and 69,167 animals under its command. However, the beleaguered Fifth Army seemed to gain no respite and began to hear rumors about a second allied invasion force assembling on the island of Lemnos.

Concerned about their losses and their continuing inability to break through the Turkish lines, and under considerable political pressure at home, the British decided to attempt to force a solution at the operational level. The British had come to the belated conclusion that the small size of the Cape Helles and the Anzac beachheads negated the allied manpower and reinforcement superiority, and therefore decided to conduct a second major amphibious operation in an attempt to outflank the Fifth Army. Plans were set in motion to assemble a force which would conduct an invasion at Suvla Bay, immediately to the northwest of the Anzac positions. This force would flank Esat's defensive lines and thrust across the peninsula to the narrows. The British felt confident because the Suvla Bay area was known to be lightly held by the Turks. There, in fact, Bavarian Major Willmer was in command of an extremely light Turkish screening force guarding the Suvla beaches. Willmer commanded two understrength infantry battalions and a Jandarma Regiment, and four artillery batteries, which was a very small force for such a critical area. Apparently, Liman von Sanders regarded the Gulf of Saros as a far more likely landing spot and stationed the entire 7th and 12th Infantry Divisions in that location. Esat Paşa, too, regarded the Suvla site as an unlikely landing objective, although Mustafa Kemal had pointed out its vulnerabilities to him during the midsummer.

On the evening of August 6, the British landed at Suvla Bay, with a force that finally grew to five full divisions. Willmer's tiny force held the high ground but could not effectively guard the long sandy beaches which were put under observation by individual posts. The British came ashore in force very quickly, but, inexplicably from the Turkish point of view, failed to seize rapidly the thinly held dominant terrain of the Kuçuk and Buyuk Anafarta ridgelines.[28] Reacting with his typical sense of urgency, Liman von Sanders put the 7th and the 12th Infantry Divisions of the XVI Corps on the road south by the end of the day. The nearby 9th Infantry Division was ordered into action to assist Willmer's troops. The following day, to the surprise of Liman von Sanders, the XVI Corps Commander appeared early and reported that he had double marched his corps southwards and that he was ready to join the fight a day earlier than expected. He was immediately ordered to bring his 7th and 12th Infantry Divisions into line; however, due to the exhausted condition of his troops, he failed to execute this order in a timely manner. Liman von Sanders now determined that he needed to energize this critical sector and he gave command of the newly formed Anafarta Group to Colonel Mustafa Kemal, in whom the German commander had full confidence. The Anafarta Group controlled the XVI Corps, the 9th Infantry Division, and the Willmer Group. By the morning of August 9, the Turks had four infantry divisions in line against the British. Mustafa Kemal launched immediate counterattacks, personally leading one himself on August 10, which pushed the British back to within one kilometer of the landing beaches. Anzac and Seddulbahair seemed to be repeating themselves. Supporting British attacks coming out of the Anzac beachhead were also beaten back by East Paşa with great difficulty. However, the Suvla Bay forces succeeded in establishing contact with the Anzacs. Although the Turks were outnumbered in the new Anafarta sector, the British had committed every unit they had available to the fight. This allowed Liman von Sanders to bring critical reinforcements from the Asiatic side.

Strong British attacks followed on August 12 and again on August 15, The final largescale British attack occurred on August 27. All failed to achieve decisive results. In spite of these frequent largescale British attacks, Turkish casualties in the Anafarta Group during this period were relatively light with a total of 3,860 killed and wounded.

Both sides were now exhausted, both physically and psychologically. Although hard fighting continued and attacks were maintained at the tactical level, the fighting on the Gallipoli Peninsula slowly atrophied into a dogged stalemate with no end in sight. The Fifth Army held the key terrain in every sector, which compensated for its lack of artillery, artillery ammunition, and machine guns. The everchanging Turkish command arrangements had now solidified into four operational groups of various sizes, the Anafarta Group under Colonel Mustafa Kemal, the Ari Burnu Group (Anzac sector) under Esat Paşa, and the Seddelbahır (Cape Helles) Group under Vehip Paşa, and the Asia Group under Mehmet Ali Paşa. During August further Turkish reinforcements had reached the peninsula, the I Corps headquarters commanded by Mirliva Hilmi Pasa, the VI Corps with its 24th and 26th Infantry Divisions, the XVII Corps with its 15th and 25 Infantry Divisions, and Field Marshal von der Goltz with most of the headquarters personnel of the First Army. At the end of August 1915, the Turks had twenty infantry divisions committed to the campaign (Map 4.1).

In September Bulgaria joined the Central Powers, thus opening the way for German material assistance, especially for much needed artillery ammunition and spare parts. On September 9, a battery of Austrian 240 mm howitzers, a battery of German 150 mm howitzers, and a mortar battery arrived at the western rail terminus of Uzunköprü. Along with this artillery, about five hundred German and Austrian technical specialists arrived. The flow of highly trained German General Staff officers, abruptly cut in the summer of 1914, was

Map 4.1
General Situation at Gallipoli, First and Fifth Army Forces, End of August 1915

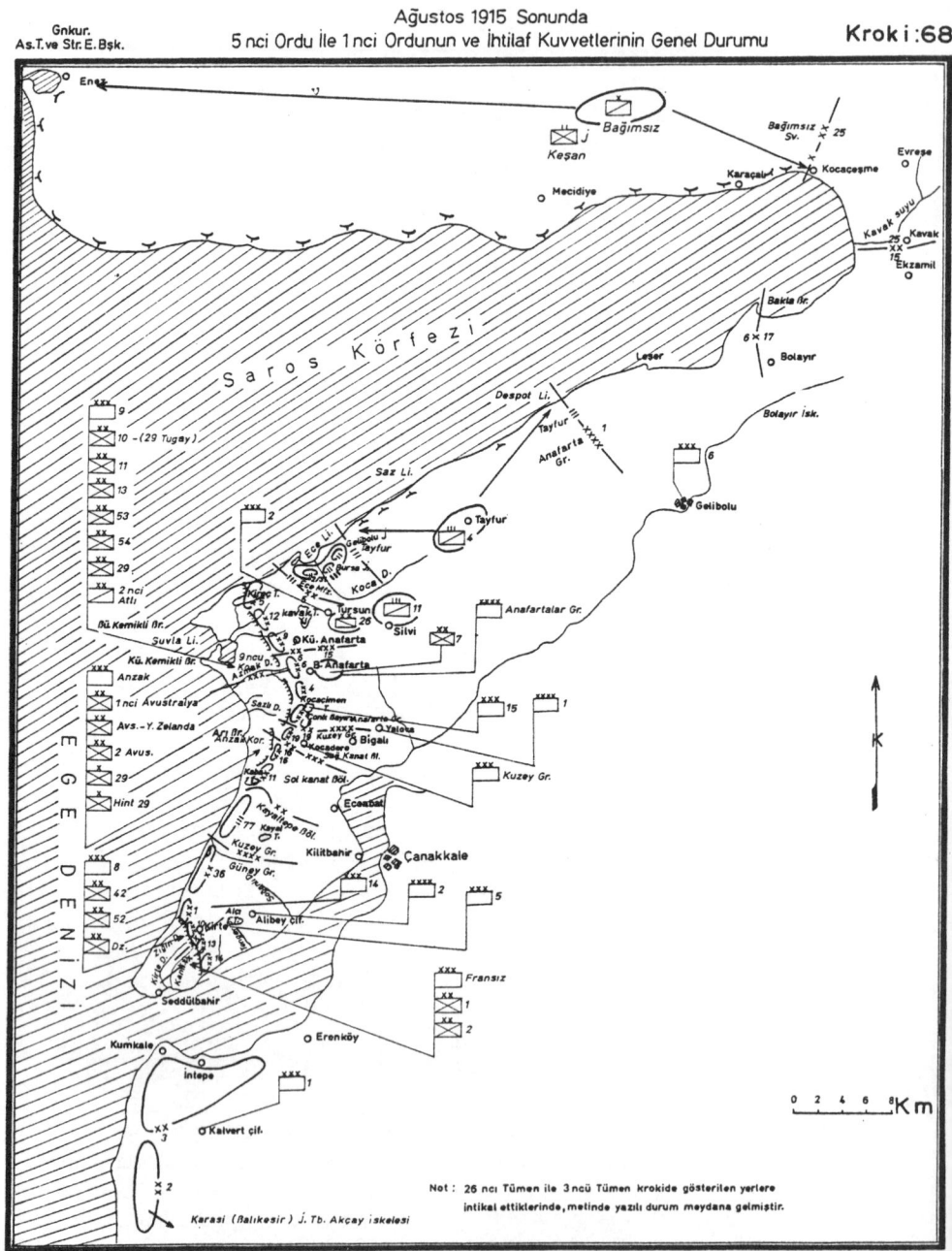

Source: Turkish General Staff, *Birinci Dunya Harbinde Turk Harbi Vnci Cilt Çanakkale Cephesi 2ncu Kitap* (Ankara: GK Basimevi, 1978), Kroki (Map) 68.

now restored with the arrival of three such officers (this was an extremely important development). In the second half of September, the troops of the Second Army began to be replaced by troops of the First Army. With these troops departed Vehip Paşa and the Second Army staff, who were replaced by Cavid Paşa and no staff. Although the tempo of the campaign appeared to be slowing down, interest at the Turkish General Staff continued unabated. On September 4, Enver informed the Fifth Army that substantial Italian forces were massing to reinforce the Allies at Çanakkale. He noted that thirty-seven thousand troops at Brindisi, twenty thousand at Naples, and a further twenty thousand at Rhodes were preparing to embark for this attack. The source of his information was not revealed to Liman von Sanders.[29] The Turkish 20th Infantry Division, stationed at Symrna, was sent to the peninsula and the Operations Division of the Turkish General Staff alerted a cavalry brigade and two infantry regiments to prepare for deployment to the battlefront. As late as September 29, 1915, Liman von Sanders thought that the greatest threat was a simultaneous landing in Asia and at Saros Bay against which he would be unable to concentrate his reserves.

The long awaited artillery ammunition began to arrive in November, along with several batteries of heavy Austrian howitzers. Encouraged by these reinforcements, Enver and the Turkish General Staff began to push for an all-out offensive to push the allies back into the sea. Fortunately for the *Mehmetçıks*, who would have to carry these assaults to the enemy, the Allies decided in the late fall of 1915 to withdraw their forces from the Gallipoli Peninsula.

In a brilliant series of withdrawals carried out under conditions of extreme secrecy, the allies evacuated the Suvla Bay and Anzac beachheads during the night of December 19-20. This evacuation was planned and executed right under the noses of the Turks, and depended on both a great deal of luck and on a series of detailed deception operations. At 4 A.M. on the morning of December 20, Yuzbasi (Captain) Ali Remzi was notified by field telephone from his forward outposts that the enemy trenches appeared empty. News was immediately relayed to the Fifth Army Headquarters and the Yuzbasi was ordered to investigate. He went forward and penetrated 150 meters into the British trench system, finding it indeed empty and filled with dummy soldiers. At this point the Fifth Army staff woke up Liman von Sanders and told him the news. The Turkish official history simply notes that he replied "God be praised." [30] The entire enemy force, and most of the artillery, was gotten away quite successfully, but large quantities of stores and supplies fell into Turkish hands.

As the new year approached, it seemed certain that the Allies would evacuate the Cape Helles beachhead also. Despite intense Turkish observation and interest, the Allies repeated their successful withdrawal from this position on the night of January 8-9, 1916. Again, large amounts of military supplies, horses, tentage, and rations fell into Turkish hands. Liman von Sanders noted that it took two years for the Turks to organize and carry away the material that they captured. Thus ended one of the most original strategic conceptions of the First World War with the Turks again in possession of the peninsula.

In a ciphered message from the Fifth Army to Enver Paşa, Liman von Sanders reported that at 8:45 A.M., January 9, 1916, the Gallipoli Peninsula had been cleared of the enemy.[31] It did not take the Turks long to begin moving their battered formations out of the combat area. Between January 9 and January 20, eleven Turkish infantry divisions were moved out of the battle zone and north into Thrace. Liman von Sanders himself left on January 15. As calm returned to the Gallipoli peninsula, the Turkish General Staff reduced the strength of the Fifth Army to a level below its preinvasion strength. By the end of January 1916, Mirliva Cevat Paşa commanded a smaller Fifth Army composed of the VI Corps with the 24th and the 26th Infantry Divisions and the XIV Corps with the 25th and the 42nd Infantry Divisions. The strength of the fortress command remained more or less the same. Later in the war, as these divisions recuperated and were brought back up to full fighting strength, they were sent to more active fronts and new divisions raised in their place.

The official British account of the campaign attributes two important factors in the British failure to carry the Dardanelles.[32] These factors were the dogged defensive fighting qualities of the Turkish soldiers and the brilliant leadership in the Turkish Fifth Army. This is certainly an accurate appraisal. The campaign slipped away into the histories as one of the great "what ifs?" of the First World War. In tallying the balance sheet, it appeared that the combatants lost nearly equal numbers of casualties. The British lost a total of 205,000 men, of whom 43,000 were killed or missing. Of the seventy-nine thousand French engaged, forty-seven thousand became casualties. British accounts of the battle note a total Turkish casualty figure of 251,000 men, while Liman von Sanders estimated 218,000 Turkish casualties, of whom 66,000 were killed. He also noted that about forty-two thousand of the Turkish wounded returned to duty. The official British campaign history of the battle speculates that because of careless Turkish record keeping, that perhaps as many as 350,000 Turks became casualties. However, Turkish record keeping was quite meticulous, and the final count for the period of April 4, 1915, through December 19, 1915, was 595 officers and 56,048 men killed, 1,018 officers and 95,989 men wounded, and 27 officers and 11,151 men missing.[33] Fahri Belen's figures match these and he adds that twenty-one thousand died in hospital and that a total of sixty-four thousand became sick during the campaign.[34] Therefore Liman von Sanders's figures would appear to very close to the actual final Turkish casualty figures for the Gallipoli campaign.

In terms of forces committed, the Allies sent 489,000 men to the Dardanelles.[35] Most British, Australian, and American authors credit the Turks with committing five hundred thousand men to the campaign over the nine-month course of the battle. Given the deployment of the Turkish Army in 1915, this figure is, perhaps, on the high side, and disguised the allied humiliation suffered at the hands of the Turks. From the Turkish records and from Liman von Sanders's account, it is doubtful that the Turks ever had equal numbers of combat troops engaged (except for a brief period in the early summer of 1915). Indeed, the opposite was probably the case: the Turks were outnumbered most of the time. The highest strength that the Turks had on the peninsula occurred in

October 1915 when a total of 5,500 officers and 310,000 men were listed on the rolls of the Fifth Army.[36]

There were several outcomes from this campaign. The first and most well known was that British never attempted another amphibious attack on Turkey during the remainder of the war. A second was that it focused the British high command on the idea of winning the war on the western front and those advocating peripheral campaigns fell from power. Finally, the British came away from the battle with a renewed respect for the Turkish Army. From the Turkish perspective, there were several other important outcomes which were generally ignored by the world at large. Probably the most significant result for the Turkish Army was the emergence of a group of combat-tested commanders with proven abilities. Many of these individuals would make important contributions to the Turkish war effort later in the conflict. The second important outcome for Turkey was that the Turkish leaders drew renewed confidence in the continuance of the war and the ultimate victory of the Central Powers. The deployments of the Turkish Army in 1916 would reflect this increased optimism and commitment to victory. Finally, there emerged from the Gallipoli battles a hard cadre of veteran Turkish infantry divisions that would see tough action on other fronts and that would prove difficult to defeat in subsequent campaigns.

ARMENIAN REBELLION

There is huge body of historical literature concerning the "Armenian genocide" that maintains that the Young Turks, in particular Enver, Talat, and Cemal, intentionally sought to exterminate the Armenian citizens of the Ottoman Empire. This case against the Young Turks rests on the premise that they intended to racially purify the empire by purging or exterminating its minorities, particularly the troublesome Christian Armenians. Moreover, the literature maintains that under the pretext of wartime emergencies and threats to national security, the Young Turks took advantage of circumstances to conduct genocide against the Armenians. Using a combination of methods ranging from massacre to starvation, the Young Turks then deliberately and intentionally caused the deaths of several million Armenians. Much of this literature is emotionally charged and a large percentage of it is directly generated by the descendents of the survivors of the events. The genocide itself has, over the past eighty years, become a highly political issue in most western countries, as Armenian descendants seek legislative condemnation of the modern Turkish Republic. Because of this transgenerational campaign to establish that an Ottoman genocide (defined as an intentional and systematic attempt to exterminate a people or a race) against its Armenian subjects occurred, balanced and objective discourse on this subject becomes difficult.

In many quarters of academia, debate has more or less settled on the acknowledgment that the genocide occurred as a matter of historical fact.[37] Without question, a large number of innocent Armenians, including women and children, died during the First World War at the hands of the Turks.

Documentation on this point is incontrovertible and was witnessed by too many neutral observers, many of whom wrote reliable and immediate narratives and reports. Because of this, the Young Turks have been intellectually equated with Adolf Hitler and the Holocaust, and secondarily, the Turkish Army with the German SS. The Turkish position on the matter is that the Armenians were actively engaged in terrorism and in outright insurrection beginning in April 1915.[38] Military necessity therefore justified the deportation of the Armenians. Both sides conducted unsanctioned massacres, but to this day the Turks deny that the Ottoman government sought, with premeditated intent, to exterminate the Armenian people.

It is beyond the scope of this book to assess or to comment on whether or not there was a deliberate or systematic genocide of the Armenian people during the First World War. This section focuses on the role and the responsibility of the military in identifying and reacting to the Armenian Rebellion of 1915 and 1916. Only a fraction of the massive Turkish archival holdings are available to researchers, and these are carefully controlled by the Turkish authorities. The records available to researchers in the Turkish General Staff's archives describe a rising pattern of civil unrest, followed by an armed rebellion. The available records also show an escalating response by the military culminating in the mass deportation of the Armenians.

As a prelude, there had been considerable recent conflict between the Armenians and the Ottoman government in the immediate aftermath of the revolutions of 1908 and 1909. During this turbulent period, Ottoman restrictions against minorities first relaxed and then tightened. The hopes of the minorities, especially the Armenians and the Greeks, who had thought that the ending of the sultanate and the establishment of a modern constitutional structure would lead to greater autonomy and political inclusion, were shattered when General Mahmut Şevket Paşa seized power. Disorder broke out throughout the empire among minorities disappointed with this development and with increased taxes and restrictions of civil rights. In particular, Armenians in Adana rose in revolt on April 14, 1909, and the army and the Jandarma in quelling the uprising subsequently killed many thousands.

The Armenian population of the Ottoman Empire in 1914 approached several million and the Armenian population of the northeastern Ottoman *vilayets* was probably about 1.3 million people.[39] There had been numerous Armenian uprisings beginning in the late 1700s and culminating in the 1890s in infamous and widely reported massacres. While many of the Armenians were loyal and law abiding citizens of the empire there had existed for many years subversive Armenian societies dedicated to the establishment of an autonomous Armenia. After 1909, internal dissent accelerated interest in these societies. In 1910, the Daşnaks (a revolutionary Armenian nationalist society) launched a campaign of terror in eastern Anatolia.[40] Both Armenians and Turks were killed in the thousands, and the army again was called upon to help restore order. Similar problems arose in Albania, Kosovo, and Macedonia as other minorities became disaffected as well. The Balkan Wars of 1912 and 1913 brought an end to Ottoman control of its European empire, thus eliminating a substantial part of its minority problem. However, the Armenians remained within the now truncated empire. By 1914, nationalist/revolutionary Armenian societies were operating openly in Europe and in Russia and were receiving support from many sources that sought the dismemberment of the Ottoman Empire.

Within the empire itself, the Armenian community was increasingly alarmed by a resurgent interest in Pan-Turanism, in particular, by the Turkish nationalist theories of Ziya Gökalp, who advocated the imposition of the Turkish language and culture on the empire. Certainly a case can be made that these ideas appealed to some members of the CUP, especially Enver Paşa. This cult of Turkish nationalism and modernization found many adherents within the army as well. Gökalp's supporters even made contact with non-Ottoman Turks outside the empires boundaries. The Christian, linguistically and culturally different, Armenians received the ideas of Gökalp with great foreboding. Perhaps equally worrisome to the hard working and industrious Armenians was Gökalp's advocacy of greater Turkish participation in the economy. In any case, it was perhaps more than idle speculation by 1914, that the Turks intended to consolidate their hold on the remaining empire in the Anatolian heartland, and that they intended to impose some kind of cultural, linguistic, and economic Pan-Turanic program on the empire's population. In the spring of 1914 the Turks intercepted letters from Armenian committees expressing concern over these developments. Other letters sent by the Taşnak Committee requested weapons from the Russians. In July 1914, the Ottoman Consulate in Kars intercepted a telegram outlining the smuggling of four hundred rifles into the Elişkirt valley.[41] Also during the summer of 1914, the Armenian Committees conducted the important Erzurum Congress under the leadership of the Taşnaks. Armenian representatives from every major Eastern Anatolian city were present. Ostensibly conducted to peacefully advance Armenian concerns through legitimate means, the Turks regarded the Congress as the seedbed for later insurrection. It was here, the Turks were convinced, that strong Armenian–Russian links solidified into detailed plans and agreements aimed at the detachment of Armenia from the Ottoman Empire.

By September the commander of the Erzurum Fortress received a report that the Armenian regiments in the Russian Army were mobilized and were conducting war-training exercises.[42] Indicators of potential violent intent accumulated as Turkish authorities found bombs and weapons hidden in Armenian homes. The 4th Reserve Cavalry Regiment patrolling from its lines in Köprukoy discovered Russian rifles cached in Armenian homes in Hasankale on October 20. The tempo of army operations against Armenian dissidents accelerated.

In early October 1914 (prior to the commencement of hostilities), the Turkish Third Army was receiving reports of Armenians who had been ex-Russian soldiers returning to Turkey with maps and money.[43] There were reports from infantry battalions concerning Armenian meetings at which large numbers of aggressively nationalist people were gathering.[44] In late October 1914, the Third Army staff informed the Turkish General Staff that large numbers of Armenians with weapons were moving into Muş, Bitlis, Van, and Erivan.[45] Additionally disturbing to the military staffs at all levels was an increasing recognition that thousands of Armenian citizens were deliberately leaving their homes in Ottoman territory and traveling into Russian held territory with most of their earthly possessions. Although Turkey was still officially at peace with Russia, many Turkish officers were by now convinced that Russia was actively conspiring to foment an Armenian revolt.

The situation went from bad to worse as Russia declared war on Turkey in November 1914. Throughout November, December, and into January 1915, many similar reports to the Turkish General Staff outlined the danger posed by armed Armenians in the Third and in the Fourth Army areas. Incidents of terrorism increased, particularly bombings[46] and assassinations of civilians and local Turkish officials.[47] On February 25, 1915, a ciphered cable went from the Operations Division of the Turkish General Staff to the First, Second, Third, and Fourth Armies; the Irak Command; I, II, III, IV, V Army Corps; and to the Jandarma Command. The cable contained the chief of the Operations Division's newly issued Directive 8682 titled Increased Security Precautions.[48] This directive noted increased dissident Armenian activity in Bitlis, Aleppo, Dortyol, and Kayseri, and furthermore identified Russian and French influence and activities in these areas. The Operations Division directed that the Third and the Fourth Armies increase surveillance and security measures. All recipients of the cable were instructed to increase coordination among themselves. Finally, the cable specifically directed that any ethnic Armenian soldiers should be removed from Turkish headquarters staffs and taken out of important Turkish command centers.

The final measure contained in Directive 8682 was probably taken in response to a report from the Ministry of the Interior's Intelligence Division to the Turkish General Staff's director of intelligence.[49] In this report it was noted that the Armenian Patriarchate in Constantinople was transmitting military secrets and dispositions to the Russians. From February through July 1915, a great many additional reports from provincial officials and lower level army units reinforced this pattern of allied intelligence gathering as well.

In the Third Army area, the disastrous Sarikamiş offensive had created a deplorable military situation. The army staff was trying to restore combat effectiveness to its shattered infantry divisions while at the same time trying to hold a very long front. Fortunately for the Turks, the battered Russians were in a similar condition; however, the Russians were winning the reinforcement battle because of their superior lines of communication. A massive Russian offensive was expected following the spring thaw in 1915. Overlaid on this dismal situation was the increasing belief by the Turks of an Armenian rebellion in the rear areas of the Turkish Third Army. For the staff of the Third Army this represented a catastrophe of unimaginable proportions. The main Armenian centers of population (and thus of potential armed resistance) lay directly astride the only two metaled roads leading into the Third Army's area of operations. Sivas, Erzincan, and Erzurum interdicted the northern route into the area and Diyarbakir, Bitlis, and Van interdicted the southern route. Each of these cities included substantial Armenian populations. Some contained Armenian majorities. Furthermore, Armenian activity in Konya, Adana, and Aleppo (in the Fourth Army's area) interdicted the only railroad bringing food, war material, and reinforcements from the west, through which the Third Army's supplies flowed as well. Since the Third Army had only limited quantities of food, medicine, and military stores on hand, interdiction of these key communications arteries spelled disaster. There was also the distinct possibility of organized and armed Armenian groups rising in the Third Army's rear to actively support and assist the anticipated Russian spring offensive. This was particularly worrisome given the large numbers of Armenian men who had joined the Russians, many of whom had left relatives and friends behind in Ottoman territory. The Armenian threat affected the military situation not only for the Third Army, but potentially for the Fourth Army in Syria and the Sixth Army in Mesopotamia. These concerns, therefore, had to be addressed by the planning staffs of the Turkish Armies as they prepared for operational contingencies.

It is difficult to pinpoint exactly when and where the rebellions broke out first. Many western writers and historians[50] have concluded that the Turks themselves deliberately instigated the revolts by enforcing intolerable conditions on the Armenians. These acts included murder, rape, and lesser humiliations, which served to provoke an Armenian reaction. The Turks dispute this and today claim that it was the Armenians, encouraged by the Russians and French in the aftermath of Sarikamiş, who first rose in revolt.

In fact, armed revolts by the Armenians soon broke out. The most famous incident occurred when the Druzhiny, an Armenian nationalist movement, seized the lakeside city of Van in fierce fighting on April 14, 1915.[51] The Turks responded by rushing the Van Jandarma Division to the city to contain and to crush the rebellion. There was bitter fighting as the Turks besieged the city. Simultaneously the Russian Army began its long awaited offensive into the region. This Russian army contained a large number of Armenians organized into a several army divisions of well-trained and highly motivated infantry regiments. Although these soldiers were recruited mainly from the Armenian *vilayets* lost to Turkey in 1878, their ranks included numerous expatriate Armenian citizens from the Ottoman Empire who had fled to fight against the Turks. The Turks believed that the Russians deliberately recruited these people because of their knowledge of the terrain and peoples within the Ottoman Empire. The tactical situation around Van and its approaches appeared so critical that the Turks rerouted the 1st Expeditionary Force to assist in crushing the rebellion. Two Jandarma battalions assigned to the 28th Infantry Division were also pulled off the line and sent to Van. Fighting around Van lasted into late May, when the Russians finally broke the siege and relieved the Armenian defenders of the city. Other Armenian centers of population soon followed suit and over the next several months revolts broke out in the cities of Bayburt, Erzurum, Beyazit, Tortum, and Diyarbakir. Most of these revolts were traced to the support and instigation of the Armenian nationalist committees.[52]

Horrible massacres of Armenian males were committed in the Van region which were widely reported by numerous neutral observers. Most of these were attributed to Kurds and Circassians, although some were ascribed to Turkish forces. Rafael De Nogales, a Venezuelan soldier of fortune fighting with the Turks, claimed in his memoirs to have been told that local Ottoman officials had received secret orders to exterminate all Armenian males of twelve years of age and older.[53] Other witnesses, including Americans and Germans with direct access to the ruling elite, claimed to have been told about similar orders. Documentation on this point is contested by the Turks. De Nogales remarked that the Armenians reciprocated in kind by slaughtering large numbers of Muslims and also noted that the Armenian rebels were well equipped with arms, ammunitions, and explosives. He claimed that the semi-automatic Mauser pistol seemed particularly abundant, and was an Armenian weapon of choice in the close hand-to-hand fighting within the city of Van itself.

Turkish reaction to these armed rebellions escalated in the late spring and the early summer of 1915. On April 20, Enver Paşa sent a ciphered message to the Third Army headquarters[54] confirming that Armenian and Greek soldiers were deserting to form dangerous rebel bands. Enver noted that it was undesirable to use either regular Turkish troops or the mobile Jandarma regiments against these rebels (these troops were then badly needed at the front). He therefore directed that the local and permanently based (static) Jandarma battalions be used to help capture the rebels. He also recommended that a reward system of one Turkish lira per every captured rebel be established to encourage local inhabitants to turn in the rebels.

A message from Muammer Bey, the Governor of Sivas, exposed a serious problem with this plan. The governor noted that in his *vilayet*, although about fifteen thousand Armenians of military age had departed to join the Russians, another fifteen thousand Armenian men remained in the *vilayet*. Unfortunately, conscription of all Turkish men up to the age of 50 years old had left the local villages practically unprotected and vulnerable to Armenian depredations.[55] This condition made hunting down the rebels problematic. The greater need by far, at least in Sivas, was simply to provide for the protection of the Muslim villagers themselves, and the local Jandarma were hard pressed to accomplish this.

On April 24, 1915, Enver Paşa in his capacity as the chief of the Turkish General Staff issued an important directive[56] that noted that the Armenians posed a great danger to the war effort, particularly in eastern Anatolia and outlined a plan to evacuate the Armenian population from the region. This directive also confirmed the Armenian's worst fears about the direction of Ottoman policy regarding their status as a discrete cultural entity within the empire. It specified that Armenian males between sixteen and fifty-five years of age would be deported. Furthermore, all Armenians would be directed to learn and speak Turkish and Armenian schools would be forced to accommodate this. All Armenian newspapers throughout the empire would be closed immediately, although this may have been a moot point since Enver had rounded most of the Armenian intelligentsia (over three hundred in Constantinople alone) previously on April 20. The April 24 directive specifically identified the six eastern Anatolian *vilayets*, Zeytun, and the area south of Diyarbakir as the operational area affected by the evacuation plan. It was intended to move the Armenians to the Euphrates Valley, Urfa, and Süleymaniye. The order specified that the goal was to create an eastern Anatolian demographic situation in which the ratio of Armenians would drop to 10 percent of the local total of Turks and local tribesmen. Almost mocking the inhumanity of the directive, it was specified that the Armenian families would draw lots to see who would have to leave. Finally, the directive concluded by reminding all concerned that the Armenians would be treated in a proper manner.

It would appear from this directive that the Turkish General Staff intended that this evacuation would be orderly. Further guidance from Enver soon followed on April 29. In a ciphered instruction to the Ministry of War, all army commanders, all fortress commanders, and to the Irak Command, Enver directed that all Armenian leaders and "malicious" Armenians be arrested immediately. The Daşnak, Hunçak, and similar Armenian Committees in Constantinople and in the *vilayets* would immediately be closed down and those who were regarded as harmful would be made to stay in a more "suitable location." [57]

Outside forces now conspired to exaggerate the growing problem of an actively hostile Armenian population in eastern Anatolia. In Mesopotamia, on April 14, the British began an offensive that would take them to the very gates of Baghdad itself. On April 25, 1915, the British and French came crashing ashore at Gallipoli creating a critically important fourth front that immediately threatened the power center of the empire. The long anticipated Russian offensive in Caucasia began on May 6 with a major attack down the Tortum Valley toward Erzurum. A second major Russian attack also started toward the city of Van. These twin Russian attacks seemed aimed at Turkish cities containing large Armenian populations. Indeed, the Armenians in Van had already risen in rebellion. Furthermore, the timing of the allied attacks, nearly simultaneously on three widely separated fronts, indicated allied coordination and mutual support hitherto unseen by the Turks. There was a sustained period of crisis for the Turkish General Staff in 1915–it began on April 25 and it lasted until the fronts were stabilized in the fall of 1915. During this period almost every Turkish Infantry Division would be committed to combat in a strategic situation akin to the Dutch boy plugging the dyke with his finger. Quite literally in the very middle of this sea of competing priorities and in a position to interdict the military lifelines of the empire, lay the Armenians, a subject people heavily armed, belligerent, and now actively engaged in open rebellion.

The strategic dilemma of early May 1915 caused a major shift in the philosophical and practical basis of the government's policy toward the Armenians, as Enver Paşa reevaluated the mounting problems and decided to take a radically different approach. This shift in policy would have severe and heartbreaking consequences for the entire eastern Anatolian demographic landscape, and it produced unintended effects that linger into the contemporary world. On May 2 Enver wrote to the Ministry of the Interior outlining his thoughts on the best way to tackle the Armenian situation.[58] He thought it necessary either to drive the Armenians, then living around Lake Van, into Russian territory or to disperse them throughout the Ottoman Empire. Enver's preference was to drive the rebels, their families and their headquarters away from the Russian border and then to resettle the area with Muslim refugees from abroad (Turkey had still not fully assimilated the millions of Turkish and Balkan Muslim refugees who had fled into the empire after the Balkan Wars). Finally, Enver asked the Ministry of the Interior to select an appropriate plan, practices, and methods to accomplish these ends.

Clearly what had begun as a temporary and partial evacuation of rebellious Armenians had now changed, philosophically and practically, into a mass deportation of a more permanent nature. Moreover, it was now apparent that the military was attempting to involve or to include the Ministry of the Interior in the promulgation of the deportation. As the full scope of the Van rebellion and associated Armenian rebellions in the Third Army area became apparent the military tried to enforce and adhere to the existing policies. However, the existing security measures were inadequate to deal with the problems at hand, in particular, the pressing enemy offensives drained almost all regular Turkish military power into the front lines. As Enver's new policy ideas began to take hold in the capital, the military grappled with ways to come to terms with the dilemma. Turkish reactions grew harsher. A new provisional law was passed on May 27, which established military responsibility for crushing Armenian resistance. The military was also fully empowered to round up the Armenians, either collectively or individually in response to military needs or in response to any sign of treachery or betrayal, and to transfer populations.[59] It is important to note here that this law still maintained the operative notion that direct action against Armenians would only be in response to military necessity or in reply to hostile behavior.

On May 30, 1915, the now infamous Regulation for the Settlement of Armenians Relocated to Other Places because of War Conditions & Emergency Political Requirements[60] was established under the oversight of the Department of Settlement of Tribes and Immigrants in the Ministry of the Interior. This regulation fixed responsibility for transportation with local officials and additionally charged them with the protection and lives of the Armenians enroute to their new homes. Importantly, the regulation established that the new areas and the new villages for the Armenians would be established at least twenty-five kilometers from the route of the Baghdad Railroad. It was clearly specified that the health, boarding, and welfare of the deportees would remain a high priority.

Thus cumulatively, the mechanism for the deaths of many deportees enroute was now established. There was no central headquarters in overall charge of the deportation. To the military fell the responsibility to round up the rebellious Armenian population. To local officials fell the incredibly difficult responsibility of arranging transportation, lodging, feeding, and health care for an unwilling Armenian population of mostly women, children, and the elderly. To the Ministry of the Interior fell the responsibility of finding suitable locations at the end of the journey for the deportees to reestablish their lives. Compounding this critically flawed organizational command structure was the military mandate to relocate the Armenians to a place somewhere other than near the route of the Baghdad Railroad. There is nothing in the record to indicate that the military, the Ministry of the Interior, and local officials coordinated their efforts to alleviate the horrible conditions suffered by many of the deportees.

A human disaster of huge proportions loomed on the horizon. Administratively such a scheme wildly exceeded Turkish capabilities. Even had the Turks been inclined to treat the Armenians kindly, they simply did not have the transportation and logistical means necessary with which to conduct population transfers on such a grand scale. Military transportation, which received top priority, illustrates this point, when first-class infantry units typically would lose a quarter of their strength to disease, inadequate rations, and poor hygiene while traveling through the empire. This routinely happened to regiments and divisions that were well equipped and composed of healthy young men, commanded by officers concerned with their wellbeing. Once again, in a pattern which would be repeated through 1918, Enver Paşa's plans hinged on nonexistent capabilities that guaranteed inevitable failure.

Compounding the implementation of these policies was the continuing Armenian Rebellion, which included bombings, assassinations, and the wholesale slaughter of Muslim Turkish villages. In some places the rebels even gained the upper hand. The rebels in the city of Van were ultimately relieved by advancing Russian forces. At Musa Dağ in Cilicia, highly organized Armenians fought the Turks for forty days.[61] These events were bound to inflame an already angry Turkish population and bureaucracy. In spite of this, the Ministry of the Interior continued to muddy the organizational waters by establishing further regulations[62] that safeguarded the homes of the deportees. According to the ministry, the homes of the deportees were to be sealed and possessions left behind were to be cared for. If the Armenians' homes were used as temporary lodging for Balkan immigrants the new occupants would be liable for any accrued taxes and for damages. Certainly there were many mixed messages with all of their associated and unsaid complexities to be found in the rapidly evolving legal mechanisms which governed the deportation and relocation of the eastern Anatolian Armenians. The ponderous and complex wheels of the relocation process now began to grind the Armenians into dust.

At the highest levels, Enver Paşa and the military staffs appear to have generated the basic idea of the forced evacuation of the Armenians in response to a military problem which threatened the security of the Turkish Third Army and therefore of the empire itself. It is beyond question that the actuality of the Armenian revolts in the key cities astride the major eastern roads and railroads posed a significant military problem in the real sense. In point of fact, there were heavily armed and organized bands of Armenians operating in concert with their Russian allies.[63] This problem in combination with the allied offensives in Caucasia, Mesopotamia, and at Gallipoli caused an acceleration of the Turkish will to deal with an issue of growing military concern. The main body of the army itself appears removed from the Armenian deportations because of the strategic crisis of 1915 which kept regular army units at the front and away from the implementation of the Armenian directives. Most of the mobile Jandarma regiments and battalions would likewise have fallen into this category. As to the question of which military units actually participated in the initial consolidations and delivery of Armenians into the pipeline, the answer is not clearly established in Turkish official histories. It is likely that the work was done by local Jandarma units and Ministry of the Interior forces which remained in the *vilayets* for village and area protection. Kurdish and Circassian volunteers who probably had axes to grind with their Armenian neighbors usually augmented these units. De Nogales says as much in his memoirs.[64] The highly visible deportations began in earnest in the early summer of 1915 and, as detailed by numerous German and American observers, violence against Armenian noncombatants began almost immediately. By the early fall, formal reports of abuses against Armenians were beginning to filter up the military chain of command to the Turkish General Staff and to the Ministry of War.[65]

By mid-1916, most of the Armenian population had been forcibly removed from the eastern Anatolian *vilayets* and from the key cities along the east-west railroad. At this point, the Armenians ceased to be a military concern for the Turkish military staffs. Numbers of Armenian males remained alive as the Turkish Army continued to use Armenian manpower in its labor battalions until the end of the war. This is particularly true of the western, and predominately Catholic, Armenian population of the empire. Additionally, large numbers of eastern Anatolian, primarily Orthodox, Armenians survived by fleeing to join the Russians.

In the end, hundreds of thousands of Armenians died during the Armenian Rebellion and deportation of 1915-1916. A similar number of Muslim Turks also died during the Armenian revolts and during the Russian occupation of Erzurum, Van, Erzincan, Trabzon, and Malazgirt. To be sure, many Armenians, particularly leaders and men of military age were immediately killed or massacred early on before entering the deportation flow. Many more, especially the elderly and the infirm, died en route from apathy and neglect, or were murdered outright, as the deportees were passed from local official to local official in an ambulatory pipeline that resembled a decaying daisy chain. Finally, the geographic constraints imposed on where the Armenians could ultimately be allowed to settle imposed long term starvation as they were sent to arid locations outside the fertile and well-watered route of the Baghdad Railroad. It was a recipe for disaster with profound historical, moral, and practical consequences which persist into the present day.

CAUCASIAN OFFENSIVES

The Third Army commander, Brigadier General Hafiz Hakki Bey, died in the spotted typhus epidemic on February 12, 1915. He was replaced by Mirliva Mahmut Kamil Paşa, who retained the indomitable German Major Guse as the Third Army chief of staff. After the disastrous winter offensive, the first order of business for the new commander was to put his shattered army back into a semblance of fighting order. For this purpose, individual replacements were arriving monthly from the First and Second Armies. The 36th Infantry Division finally arrived from Mesopotamia and took up positions along the southern flank of the Third Army near Lake Van. The 37th Infantry Division, at one time enroute to the Third Army, never arrived because it was diverted to take advantage of the occupation of Tabriz by a group of Turkish volunteers and Kurdish irregulars.[66] By mid-March, the Turks had somewhat restored the situation and had put the X, and XI Corps back in line, albeit with combat strengths hardly exceeding normal infantry divisions. A new IX Corps was also reconstituted from the surviving artillery and support units that had been left behind the mountains at Oltu, and it was also given a defensive sector. The four reserve cavalry divisions had performed badly and had never achieved the desired levels of discipline necessary to be considered as reliable formations. They were therefore dissolved and the best reserve light cavalry regiments consolidated into a single stronger division (the 3rd Reserve Cavalry Division). As the Third Army entered the month of April 1915, the strategic situation seemed stable with the Russians standing nearly on the 1914 frontier in the north but firmly in possession of the Turkish cities of Elişkirt, Ağri, and Doğubeyazit in the south.

This relatively stable situation enabled the Turks to maintain defensive lines with the reforming X and XI Corps, and to move the still shattered IX Corps to the rear near Erzurum for unit reconstitution and training. The 5th Expeditionary Force was held reserve, while only the thin screen of the 2nd Regular and 3rd Reserve Cavalry Divisions held the long vulnerable front between Lake Van and Erzurum. The Van Jandarma Division and the 1st Expeditionary Force held the front to the south of Lake Van. May 6 brought a major Russian offensive down the Tortum Valley toward Erzurum. This offensive was beaten back by the 29th and 30th Divisions, but the Turks lost about fifteen kilometers of ground. The Russian offensive ground to a halt on May 24, 1915. Determined to regain the lost ground, the Third Army began a flanking attack on the Russian salient using the X Corps on June 11. By June 13, the Russians had been pushed back to their starting positions.

The Turks had less success in the south. During the month of May, the 1st Expeditionary Force had been pushed back from its positions on the frontier, as had the Van Cavalry Brigade. The Russians took the city of Van itself on May 17 and continued to press the Turks. To the north of Lake Van, the 1st and 3rd Cavalry Brigades were pushed southwards, losing the city of Malazgirt on May 11. The growing Armenian Rebellion was also beginning to affect the army's strategic posture as units began to experience logistical shortages caused by the interdiction of lines of communication. By June 5 the Russians had reached the northern shores of Lake Van and were threatening the avenues to Muş. These double losses to the north and to the south of Lake Van created a huge Russian salient in the southern flank of the Third Army area of operations. The terrible numerical weakness of the Third Army was being ruthlessly exposed and exploited.

At this point in time, the campaigns in the Caucasus region were fought by armies which looked strong on paper but which were very weak in actual fact. W.E.D. Allen and Paul Muratoff credit the Russian commander, General

Yudenich, with having more men and cannon on hand in the summer of 1915, than he had on hand at the onset of hostilities. They note that the Russian armies had a total of 130,000 infantry and 35,000 cavalry, backed by 340 cannon.[67] But on June 4, 1915, the Turks estimated the effective Russian strength in infantry between 64,800 and 73,600 men and in cavalry between 8,400 and 9,240 men, for a total of somewhere in the area of 73,200 to 82,840 effectives. Likewise, the Turks estimated that the Russians only had around 130 cannon. Regardless of the exact size of the Russian host, the Turks only had 52,351 effectives (infantry and cavalry combined) and 131 cannon available, with which to hold a front in excess of 600 kilometers. When this obvious strength disparity was combined with the length of frontage over incredibly difficult terrain, the depth of the Turkish strategic dilemma was painfully apparent. The total strength of the Third Army mobile formations on June 4, 1915 is shown in Table 4.4.

Table 4.4
Third Army Effective Strength, June 4, 1915

Unit	Strength
Lazistan Detachment	6,836[a]
IX Corps	11,338
X Corps	4,887
XI Corps	5,624
2nd Regular Cavalry Division	1,710
3rd Reserve Cavalry Division	1,248
5th Expeditionary Force	4,745
1st Expeditionary Force	7,500
36th Infantry Division	5,403
Van Jandarma Division	2,500
Baghdad Regiment	560
TOTAL	52,351[b]

Notes: These figures do not include the Erzurum Fortress garrison and do not include line of communications troops (however, neither do the Russian figures previously quoted).
a. The detachment formerly commanded by Major Stange was subsumed into the Lazistan Detachment.
b. About 75 percent of these troops were concentrated in the northern portion of the Third Army sector, for the defense of Erzurum and the road to Erzincan.
c. The success of the efforts to rebuild the IX Corps are apparent as are the negative effects of keeping the X and XI Corps continuously in the line after Sarikamiş.

Source: Turkish General Staff, *Birinci Dünya Harbinde Türk Harbi, Kafkas Cephesi 3ncu Ordu Hareketi, Cilt 1 (*Ankara: Genelkurmay Başım Evi ,1993), Kroki (Map) 51.

Sensing the great weakness in the southern part of the Third Army area of operations, the Russians shifted their center of gravity to the southeast for a concerted push on the Turkish city of Muş. On July 10, 1915, the Russians opened a major offensive northwest of Lake Van driving from Malazgirt toward

Muş with the better part of a Russian army corps. However, the Russian attack was channeled in between Nazik Lake and Haçi Lake, which made the Turkish defensive preparations both simpler and more effective. Unknown to the Russians, the Third Army Staff, extremely concerned about the deteriorating situation in the southeast, had dispatched the rebuilt and rested IX Corps, with the 17th and 28th Infantry Divisions, to the area northeast of Muş. They had also repositioned both the Turkish 1st and the 5th Expeditionary Forces in battle positions on the southern flank of the Russian attack force. So, on the opening day of the Russian offensive, powerful Turkish forces were available for counterattacks. The Turks had also established a Right Wing Group, under the command of Mirliva Abdulkarim Paşa, to command the newly arriving forces. This operational level grouping of forces was then removed from the Third Army's control and became an independent force operating directly under Enver Paşa. The Right Wing headquarters was in position in Demirçi on July 11 and was set to assume command of the battle. The Mirliva's Right Wing Group also had command of the 2nd Regular and the 3rd Reserve Cavalry Divisions, the 36th Infantry Division, the Van Jandarma Division, and the Baghdad Infantry Regiment. Altogether, he had almost thirty-five thousand of the fifty-three thousand men available to the Turkish Third Army in mobile field units. It was a masterful assembly of forces, conducted in secret under difficult circumstances. Allen and Muratoff attribute the Turk's success in maintaining secrecy to the Russian commander, General Yudenich's failure to use the "numerous and pro-Russian Armenian elements in the area of action."[68] The Erzurum front was denuded of reserves in an economy of force mission designed to concentrate forces where the Russians did not expect to see Turkish strength. By July 16, the Russian offensive had stalled and the divisions of the Turkish IX Corps, coming from the northwest, combined with the fresh 5th Expeditionary Force hammered the Russians to a halt. Merliva Abdulkarim Paşa continued to attack and savagely forced the Russians back to their starting lines, with heavy losses. He kept on attacking until the Russians gave up the city of Malazgirt on July 26. However, the price of victory had been costly to the Turks also, with Third Army losses, since May, nearing fifty-eight thousand men.[69]

Excited by his stunning victory, Abdulkarim wired Constantinople for permission to continue his offensive. Enver, needing little encouragement, concurred and urged Abdulkarim onward. He ordered the Right Wing Group to attack toward Elişkirt and Karakose and to clear the frontier area as far north as the Aras River in Russian territory. Enver called this wildly ambitious plan "The Bull's Eye Directive."[70] In the first week of August 1915, the Right Wing Group attacked into the Elişkirt Valley. By August 5, the group had made progress, advancing about twenty kilometers northward, but the Russians counterattacked into the exposed left flank of the IX Corps. Repeating the mistakes of the Sarikamiş campaign, the Turks had committed almost everything to the attack and had not maintained sufficient tactical or operational reserves with which to counter the Russians. Fortunately, the third division of the IX Corps (the 29th Infantry Division) arrived on the battlefield from Erzurum at this time and relieved the pressure on the Turk's left flank. Now threatened with encirclement,

Abdulkarim called off the attack and ordered a retreat. The Turkish forces fell back, and once again Malazgirt passed into Russian hands. During this retreat, the Turkish forces lost many stores and part of their field artillery. Finally, by August 15, the front once again stabilized along the line of lakes to the northwest of Lake Van. The operations south of Lake Van had been somewhat more successful, with the Van Jandarma Division pushing the Russians back to the southeast tip of the lake. The total Turkish losses suffered in "Directive Bull's Eye" were approximately ten thousand men killed and wounded, and about six thousand taken prisoner.[71]

In the wake of the intensive battle around Malazgirt, the Turkish General Staff ordered a general restructuring of the Third Army, further breaking it up into operational groups and detachments (Table 4.5). The terrible losses suffered in the campaigns of 1915 could not be made up in the immediate future by either replacements or by reinforcements. The massive battles then ongoing in the Gallipoli Peninsula were pulling every available formation and replacement into that fight. The ill-starred IX Corps would never regain the strength that it had so carefully built back up in the spring of 1915. For the remainder of the year, the weak X and XI Corps made up the bulk of Abdulkarim's effective strength. The Russians too were hard hit by casualties, which at this point in the war could not easily be made good either. Therefore this condition of joint weakness imposed a lull in the operational tempo of the Caucasus front and both sides settled into a period of recuperation and planning which lasted until January 1916.

Over the course of 1915, in the Third Army's area of operations, the Turks had displayed great resiliency in recuperating from savage defeats and huge losses. Additionally, they had shown great skill in the formulation of operational level movements and attacks, involving corps-sized and group-sized formations. The corps counterattacks during the Russian summer offensives and the secret formation of the Right Wing Group are evidence of this capacity for large-scale planning. However, as in the Sarikamiş campaign, the ends exceeded the means. Enver Paşa, in particular, displayed an exaggerated sense of what the Turks could accomplish with the troops at hand. Enver's strategic concepts involving the seizure of Tabriz, and the operations to move into the Elişkirt and Aras River valleys, wildly exceeded any realistic appraisal of Turkish capabilities. In practical effect, these Turkish offensives caused the local front, corps, and group commanders to commit almost every available mobile unit to the attack. This resulted in the absence of adequate reserves, with which to weight the battle at the critical moment, or with which to respond to Russian counterattacks.

On balance, the year ended with the Russians in a much better geographic position than when they had started. The huge salient at Malazgirt was strategically dangerous to the Third Army and required a serious diversion of Turkish strength. However, given the disparity of resources, especially in the numbers of mobile formations, the Turkish performance was admirable and Turkish infantry divisions and corps had shown the capability for both defensive and offensive operations.

Table 4.5
Disposition of Turkish Forces, Late Summer 1915

THRACE
First Army
1 Inf. Div.
20 Inf. Div.
1 Cav. Bde.
Second Army
VI Corps: 16, 24, 26 Inf. Div.
Forming: XIV Corps, XVI Corps
Forming: **43, 44, 47, 48** Inf. Div.

GALLIPOLI
Fifth Army
I Corps: **2**, 3 Inf. Div (XV Corps merged)
II Corps: **4, 5, 6** *Inf. Div*
III Corps: 7, 8, 9, 19 *Inf. Div.*
IV Corps: 10, 11, 12 *Inf. Div.*
V Corps: **13, 14, 15** *Inf. Div.*
25 Inf. Div.

SYRIA-PALESTINE
Fourth Army
VIII Corps: 23, **24**, 27 Inf. Div.
XII Corps: **41, 42, 46** Inf. Div.

CAUCASIA
Third Army
IX Corps: 17, 28, 29 *Inf. Div.*
X Corps: **30, 31, 32** *Inf. Div.*
XI Corps: **18**, 33, 34 *Inf. Div*
2 *Regular Cav. Div.*
3 *Reserve Cav. Div.*
Van Cav. Bde.
Van Jandarma (Inf) Div.
1st Expeditionary Force
5th Expeditionary Force
36th Inf. Div.
37th Inf. Div.

MESOPOTAMIA
Sixth Army
XIII Corps: **35,** 38 *Inf. Div.*
XVIII Corps: **45** Inf. Div.

ARABIA-YEMEN
VII Corps: 21, 22, 39, 40 Inf. Div.

Note: Units in boldface type indicate new formations; units underlined indicate units redeployed since April 1915; units in bold italic indicate seriously understrength units.

THE FIRST BATTLE OF KUT

During the months of February and March 1915 in Mesopotamia, there were several small meeting engagements between the Turks and the British, but neither side could make these fights work to their advantage. Alarmed by the seemingly effortless seizure of the lower Tigris and Euphrates basin by the Indian Army, the Turks began to contemplate offensive operations designed to push the British back down river. The Turkish area commander, Süleyman Askeri Bey, then in direct command of the Turkish Right Wing, decided to conduct a flanking attack on the British positions at Basra. In doing so, he could avoid the main British positions at Qurna, and perhaps achieve local numerical superiority. At Basra, the British maintained a cavalry brigade, which held the town of Shaiba, on the southern approach to the city of Basra. Süleyman Askeri began movement south in early April 1915, but this movement was noticed by the British, who were able to make stronger defensive preparations. At 5 A.M., on the morning of April 12, the Turks attacked the British fortified camp at Shaiba. The Turks began their attack with a brief bombardment from the twelve field guns that they had brought forward. The Turkish infantry went into action shortly thereafter. This attack failed but relentless Turkish infantry attacks continued throughout the day. The Turkish attacks continued the following day with similar results. Finally, a British cavalry counterattack provided the Turks with enough reason to call off the attack. Of thirty-eight hundred Turkish soldiers engaged, approximately one thousand were killed or wounded, and the British captured four hundred men and two field artillery pieces. The Turkish force fled to the north in great disorder.[72]

Deciding to exploit their success, the British advanced on the Turkish defensive works on April 14, 1915. Although the first line of Turkish trenches were taken, mainly due to excessive Turkish casualties and the mass surrender of Arab soldiers drafted into the Turkish Army, the second line of trenches held. Over these three days of fighting, the Turks lost almost six thousand men killed or wounded, including two thousand Arab tribesmen, and lost over seven hundred officers and men as prisoners. The Turks withdrew to Khamisiya, about one hundred twenty kilometers up river. There according to the official British campaign history, Süleyman Askeri Paşa, in pain from being wounded earlier in the campaign and now semi-invalid on his camp bed, assembled his staff. Depressed at the failure of his plan and angrily denouncing the performance of the Arab levies, Süleyman Askeri Paşa then shot himself rather than endure defeat. The official Turkish campaign history mentions the suicide of Suleyman Askeri but it is not explained in great detail. However, it was noted that he was concerned about the discipline and fighting performance of his Arab levies and also about their overall numbers in his infantry divisions.[73] It was a bleak day for the Turkish Army and interim command of the forces fell on the shoulders of Mehmet Fazil Paşa.

However, all was not ended for the Turkish forces in Mesopotamia. A new Turkish Army, the Sixth, was formed from the staff of the XIII Corps in mid-April. At the same time, the Turkish General Staff began to send reinforcements to the region and the newly formed XVIII Corps began to arrive augmenting the new Turkish Sixth Army. Although incomplete at that moment, both corps would gain strength throughout the remainder of 1915.

Largely due to their unexpected success in Mesopotamia, the Indian Office and the Indian Army's General Staff decided in late April 1915 to continue the advance upriver to Amara on the Euphrates and to Nasiriya on the Tigris. General Townshend arrived in Qurna to command this endeavor. Once there and seeing the effects of the seasonal flooding, Townshend determined that a single advance up the Tigris was the best course of action. Driving onward, he captured the river port of Amara on May 3. The Turks contested the advance with a small fleet of armed river streamers. In June, after the worst of the seasonal flooding was past, the British took Nasiriya on the Euphrates, as well. Over the late spring, a second Indian Army infantry division arrived to reinforce the expedition. Because of the political repercussions from the already failing Gallipoli campaign, both the British War Office and the India Office began to view the Mesopotamian theater with renewed interest. Although aware of the shortage of troops in Mesopotamia, London began to push for further advances, possibly resulting in the seizure of Baghdad itself. Checked on the Euphrates by strong Turkish forces, the British began to make preparations for moving on the port of Kut al Amara, some one hundred twenty kilometers upriver on the Tigris. Facing them were the debris of the Turkish 38th Infantry Division, a total force of about five infantry battalions, at Kut al Amara.

Unknown to the British, however, Turkish prospects in Mesopotamia were rapidly changing for the better. A new Sixth Army Commander, Nurettin Paşa (or Nur ud Din Pasha in the British histories) arrived to take command of the Turkish forces. Throughout the summer he worked tirelessly to rally the battered Turkish infantry. Reinforcements, slow to arrive, were nevertheless finding their way to Mesopotamia. The 51st Infantry Division, formed in Constantinople in the late fall of 1914 from First Army assets as an expeditionary force, was dispatched to the region from the Third Army. The newly formed 52nd Infantry Division would shortly follow. In Baghdad, the Turks formed the new 45th Infantry Division around a core of five thousand Jandarma and several miscellaneous battalions of frontier guards. However, these forces would not be ready for combat operations for some months, and in the meantime, Nurettin had to rely on the remnants of the 35th Infantry Division, now numbering only three thousand men, and the 38th Infantry Division, with thirty-five hundred men. Along with a handful of cavalry and artillery, Nurettin had a total effective strength of about seven thousand men available to deal with the renewed British offensive.

The British began to move on September 1, 1915. The brutal heat of the Mesopotamian summer was behind them and the rivers were low—it was a good season to campaign in the area. By September 26, General Townshend had closed on the river town of Kut al Amara. The town was then defended by six battalions of the 35th Infantry Division on the right bank of the river and by six battalions of the 38th Infantry Division on the left bank of the river. There was a reserve of four battalions and some cavalry. Most of these soldiers were local

Arabs, who had been drafted into the Turkish Army, and their morale was not high. For an artillery, the Turks had a total of thirty-eight guns. Townshend moved his force closer in a night march, and attacked the Turkish redoubts early in the morning on September 28, 1915. By midday, the British had broken into the Turkish lines, and also had outflanked them in the north. The Turks committed their reserve, which was defeated, and by dark, the Turks were in full flight. Townshend pursued the retreating Turks and by October 5, had reached Aziziya, one hundred kilometers above Kut. The British operations had been extremely rewarding and at little cost to themselves had cost the Turks about four thousand men, of whom about twelve hundred men were captured, along with fourteen Turkish cannon. The First Battle of Kut had been a resounding British victory.

CTESIPHON

The relentless British advance continued, fighting the delaying actions of the survivors of the 35th and 38th Infantry Divisions. By early November 1915, Townshend's force, now numbering about eleven thousand men, reached Ctesiphon (or Selman Pak as it was known to the Turks), which was only about twenty miles south of Baghdad. It was here that Nurettin chose to make his stand. Over the fall, the 45th Infantry Division completed its training and was now combat ready. After a five-thousand-kilometer roundabout journey through the Third Army area taking almost ten months, the newly designated 51st Infantry Division arrived on November 17, with seven fresh infantry battalions and a group of Schneider howitzers. This division was formerly called the 1st Expeditionary Force, which had been diverted to the Third Army while en route to the Irak Area Command. Full of combat veterans, this formidable fighting force finally arrived in Mesopotamia. Additionally, one regiment of the 52nd Infantry Division had also arrived at Mosul and the remainder of the division was due shortly. The 52nd Infantry Division was the former 5th Expeditionary Force, which had also been redesignated as a normal infantry division. Like its brother formation (the 51st Infantry Division), this division was composed of combat veterans, whose morale and fighting capability was high. Nurettin now had a total effective strength of twenty thousand men, armed with nineteen machine guns, and fifty-two cannons. He also had a small cavalry force available of about four hundred men. More important, he now had in his hands several of the best fighting divisions in the Turkish Army.

Nurettin chose a defensive line at Ctesiphon, where he could solidly anchor his right flank on the Tigris River. He established two defensive lines in depth. The first line was about ten kilometers in length and had fifteen defensive redoubts studding its length. These earthwork redoubts were connected by deep trenches and were covered with barbed wire. The 38th and the 45th Infantry Divisions garrisoned this line and it was a formidable work. Three kilometers to its rear lay the second Turkish defensive line which was also strongly constructed. The 51st Infantry Division lay in reserve behind this line. On the south side of the river, the 35th Infantry Division held positions, and on the left flank of his entrenchments Nurettin positioned his cavalry. Although well dug in and possessing a healthy number of troops, Nurettin was far from confident of the result.[74] There were several reasons for his uncertainty; firstly he had an almost total lack of knowledge of the size and composition of the enemy force which lay before him and secondly he was concerned about the hitherto poor fighting record of his troops.

In the early hours of November 22, 1915, General Townshend's 6th "Poona" Division attacked the Turkish lines at Ctesiphon. Townshend organized his force into four columns. Townshend knew that he was outnumbered but was relying on the demonstrated propensity of the Turkish formations in this theater to break at the critical moment. He had no idea of the caliber of reinforcements that Nurettin had received in the form of the 51st Infantry Division.[75] It was a bitterly cold morning as the Indian and British columns began their advance under the cover of artillery and naval gunfire. The British thought they had achieved surprise and thought that they observed numbers of Turks fleeing the lines. Nothing could have been farther from the truth as Turkish artillery, machine guns, and rifles by the thousand opened fire on the attacking forces. Townshend continued to press the attack all morning long despite mounting losses, which now began to include a number of officers. At 11:30 A.M., he launched his cavalry brigade in an attempt to outflank the Turks, but was met by the Turkish cavalry and the 51st Infantry Division. About noon, the battle for the first Turkish line shifted in favor of the British, and by 1:30 P.M., they held most of the Turkish front line trenches and redoubts. Nurettin had lost most of the 38th and 45th Infantry Divisions in this fight. At this point in the battle, Nurettin committed his reserve, the 51st Infantry Division under Cevid Bey, to the counterattack. Cevid Bey led his forces forward in a furious counterattack. The fighting continued all afternoon and as darkness fell, the British and Indian advance was finished. Losses on both sides had been horrendous. Townshend's losses were 130 British officers out of 371 engaged and 111 out of 255 Indian officers engaged. In the ranks, he had lost forty-two hundred men out of eleven thousand. His field hospitals, equipped to handle four hundred wounded, had to accommodate ten times that number.[76] Nurettin estimated that he had lost forty-five hundred men killed and an equal amount wounded, and had twelve hundred men taken prisoner. These losses amounted to half of his available strength. That evening both the Turkish and the British commanders were profoundly depressed.

The next day fighting resumed, with Townshend attempting to continue his breakthrough and also attempting a second cavalry flanking attack. That morning, a fierce sandstorm blew up, which badly affected the visibility of both armies. The battle continued, as Nurettin threw the reformed remnants of the 35th and 45th Infantry Divisions back into the fight. Dusk brought a halt to the fighting as both sides sank into exhaustion and inactivity. By the morning of November 25, the fighting had ended. Although he still held the first line of Turkish trenches, Townshend determined that he could not break through. He thereupon made the fateful decision to withdraw his force back downstream to

Kut al Amara. The final Turkish casualty figures were put at 6,188 killed and wounded, the earlier estimates having been found to be exaggerated. The 51st Infantry Division lost 12 percent of its strength, and the 35th and 45th Infantry Divisions lost 25 percent and 65 percent respectively. It was a savage encounter, but it ended the British threat to Baghdad in 1915.

Townshend withdrew his battered force down river through Aziziya and on into the dubious refuge of Kut al Amara. Most of his force arrived there by December 3. The town itself lay in the bend of the Tigris River and contained a total of seven thousand Arab residents. Townshend began to fortify the town and began to off load his supplies from river steamers. On December 6, aware now that Nurettin was on his trail and that he might have to endure a siege, Townshend sent his cavalry downstream. This left Townshend with about 11,600 combatants and 3,350 noncombatants in the town of Kut al Amara. He had sixty days of full rations available, along with plenty of ammunition. He also had the powerful Royal Navy squadron of river gunboats and steamers on the Tigris, and he knew that several additional Indian infantry divisions were arriving at Basra. Therefore, on this day, he was not alarmed about the possibility of being besieged in Kut.

The Turks, in the meantime, had reorganized the Sixth Army into two corps for the investment of Kut and Enver Paşa named German Field Marshal von der Goltz to replace Nurettin, who was apparently regarded by Enver as being somewhat timid. The Turkish Sixth Army slowly pursued Townshend's army into Kut, closing on the northern approaches on December 7 and by the end of the day the 51st Infantry Division had penned up the British in Kut. The 38th and the 45th Infantry Divisions were coming up in support. The 35th Infantry Division crossed the river to the south, completely encircling the town by December 9, and then proceeded down stream. Additionally, the Turks pushed a cavalry screen fifteen kilometers father downstream from the 35th Infantry. Kut al Amara was now cut off from Basra, and the Sixth Army began to dig a series of entrenchments across the neck of the bend in the Tigris in which the town lay. There was a smaller British enclave across from the town of Kut on the southern bank which was held in check by the 35th Infantry Division. The Turks launched strong attacks on December 10 and 11, 1915 with regiments of the 38th, 45th, and 51st Infantry Divisions, which were repulsed. On December 12, von der Goltz arrived at Nurettin's headquarters. By December 23, about twenty-five thousand Turkish soldiers were ringing the town of Kut al Amara and they had about fifty cannons with them. Von der Goltz went off to inspect his forces in Persia, and in his absence, Nurettin, irritated by inactivity, launched another Turkish attack on the town on December 24, 1915. He was repulsed with over thousand casualties. At the end of December, another attack by the XIII Corps' 35th and 52nd Infantry Divisions met a similar fate.

Thus the campaign in Mesopotamia in 1915 ended on a favorable note for the Turks. General Townshend was bottled up in Kut al Amara, and although the British were assembling a relief force at Basra, the Turkish 52nd Infantry Division had arrived in force in Mesopotamia. Like the 51st, it was also highly regarded for its fighting reputation. With the arrival of these divisions the ethnic composition of the combat formations in the Sixth Army shifted from predominately Arabic to predominately Turkish. This would shift the balance of power in favor of the Turks in the defensive battles ahead. Field Marshal von der Goltz, a German whose experience with the Turks extended back into the 1880s, had also arrived. Although von der Goltz was seventy-two years old, he was vigorous, and the Turks expected much from him. Finally, with the Gallipoli campaign winding down, the Sixth Army had increased expectations of receiving further reinforcements in 1916.

NOTES

1. General Fahri Belen, *Birinci Cihan Harbinde Turk Harbi 1918 Yili Hareketleri Vnci Cilt* (Ankara: GK Basimevi, 1967), unnumbered chart following page 250. During the course of the war the Turks organized a total of sixty-two numbered infantry divisions. By the end of 1915, fifty-two infantry divisions had been activated and two infantry divisions had been deactivated.
2. Brig-Gen. C. F. Aspinall-Oglander, *Military Operations Gallipoli*, vol. 2. (London: HMSO, 1929), 21.
3. Turkish General Staff (TC Genelkurmay Başkanlığı), *Birincı Dünya Harbinde Türk Harbi, Vncu Cilt, Çanakkale Cephesi Hareketi, Inci Kitap (Haziran 1914-25 Nisan 1915)* (Ankara: Genelkurmay Basımevi,1993), 54.
4. See Chapter 2I for the III Corps mobilization timetables.
5. Turkish General Staff, *Çanakkale Cephesi Harekati*, 56.
6. Ibid., 38-40.
7. Otto Liman von Sanders, *Five Years in Turkey* (London: Bailliere, Tindall & Cox, 1928), 55. Liman von Sanders named a Turkish mine expert, Lieutenant Colonel Geehl, as the officer responsible for having laid this important minefield. Modern Turkish official histories do not mention this individual at all; an unfortunate omission since this officer's contribution to the defense of the straits in March 1915 was decisive.
8. General Fahri Belen, *Birinci Cihan Harbinde Turk Harbi 1915 Yili Hareketleri Iincu Cilt* (Ankara: GK Basimevi, 1967), 149.
9. Otto Liman von Sanders, *Five Years in Turkey* (London: Bailliere, Tindall & Cox, 1928), 53 – 54.
10. Ibid., 54.
11. Turkish General Staff, *Çanakkale Cephesi Harekati*, Kroki (Map) 15.
12. Liman von Sanders, *Five Years in Turkey*, 62.
13. Turkish General Staff, *Çanakkale Cephesi Harekati*, 272.
14. Turkish General Staff, (TC Genelkurmay Başkanlığı), *Türk Silahli Kuvvetleri Tarihi Osmanli Devri Balkan Harbi, Iinc Cilt 2nci Kisim 2ncu Kitap, Şark Ordsu, Ikincii Çatalca Muharebesi ve Şarköy Cikmarasi (Ikinci Baski)* (Ankara: Genelkurmay Basimevi, 1993), 66-67.
15. Ibid., Kroki (Map) 19.
16. Michael Hickey, *Gallipoli* (London: John Murray, 1995), 119.
17. Turkish General Staff, *Birinci Dunya Harbinde Turk Harbi Vnci Cilt Çanakkale Cephesi 2ncu Kitap* (Ankara: GK Basimevi, 1978), 261.
18. Liman von Sanders, *Five Years in Turkey*, 68.

19. Commandant M. Larcher, *La Guerre Turque Dans La Guerre Mondiale* (Paris: Chiron & Berger-Levrault, 1926), 221.
20. Turkish General Staff, *Çanakkale Cephesi Vncu Cilt*, 44.
21. Ibid., 46.
22. Belen, *Turk Harbi 1915 Yili Hareketleri*, 99.
23. Ibid., 142.
24. Ibid., 99.
25. Turkish General Staff, *Çanakkale Cephesi Vncu Cilt*, 176.
26. Ibid., 218.
27. Larcher, *La Guerre Turque*, 222.
28. Later the British IX Corps commander, Lieutenant General Stopford came under intense criticism for his failure to push his troops hard enough on the initially successful endeavors of August 6. This failure perhaps cost the British the campaign.
29. Turkish General Staff, *Çanakkale Cephesi Vncu Cilt*, 468.
30. Ibid., 492.
31. Ibid., 499.
32. Aspinall-Oglander. *Military Operations Gallipoli*, vol. 2. 484.
33. Turkish General Staff, *Çanakkale Cephesi Vncu Cilt*, 500.
34. Belen, *Turk Harbi 1915 Yili Hareketleri*, 252.
35. Alan Moorehead, *Gallipoli* (New York: Harper & Row, 1956), 361.
36. Turkish General Staff, *Çanakkale Cephesi Vncu Cilt*, 474.
37. However, there are several historians who dispute this view, these are: Stanford Shaw, Bernard Lewis, and Jay Winter.
38. For excellent summaries of the Armenian situation in 1915, see J. Stanford and Ezel K. Shaw, *History of the Ottoman Empire and Modern Turkey*, vol.2 (Cambridge: Cambridge University Press, 1977); W. E. D. Allen and Paul Muratoff, *Caucasian Battlefields: A History of the Wars on the Turco-Caucasian Border, 1828-1921* (Cambridge: Cambridge University Press, 1953).
39. Turkish General Staff, *Belgelerle Ermeni Sorumu* (Ankara: GK Basimevi, 1992), 342-343.
40. Stanford J. and Ezel K. Shaw, *History of the Ottoman Empire and Modern Turkey*, vol. 2, 287.
41. Muammer Demirel, *Birinci Dünya Harbinde Erzurum ve Cevresinde Ermeni Hareketleri (1914-1918)* (Ankara: GK Basimevi, 1996), 17.
42. Ibid., 17.
43. ATASE, Headquarters Third Army, Report on Criminal Activity, October 8, 1914. Archive 4/3671, Cabinet 163, Drawer 2, File 2828, Section 59, Index 2-85.
44. ATASE, Report from Hudut Battalion to Headquarters, IX Corps, October 22, 1914, Archive 4/3671, Cabinet 163, Drawer 2, File 2818, Section 59, Index 2-39.
45. ATASE, Headquarters, Third Army Report to Acting Commander in Chief, October 23, 1914, Archive 4/3671, Cabinet 163, Drawer 2, File 2818, Section 59, Index 1-41, 1-42.
46. Kamuran Gurun, *Ermeni Dosyasi* (Ankara: GK Basimevi, 1983) Included in this book are numerous reports sent to the Turkish General Staff and the Ministry of Defense from the Third and Fourth Army commanders.
47. ATASE, Headqaurters, V Corps Report, February 25, 1915, on the bombing incident in Ankara. Archive 1/131 Cabinet 149, Drawer 4, File 2287, Section 32, Index F8.
48. ATASE, First Division, Turkish General Staff cable, February 25, 1915. Archive 1/31, Cabinet D149, Drawer 4, File 2287, Section D32, Index F9.

49. ATASE, Special ciphered correspondence No. 2086, Chief, Second Division, Ministry of the Interior to Chief, Second Division, Turkish General Staff, January 31, 1915. Archive 1/2, Cabinet 113, Drawer D3, File S21, Section 2029, Index 2.

50. See Winston S. Churchill, *The World Crisis* (New York: Charles Scribners, Sons, 1931); Vahakn N. Dadrian, *Warrant for Genocide: Key Elements of Turko-Armenian Conflict* (New Brunswick, N.J.: Transaction Publishers, 1999); Richard G. Hovannisian, ed. *Remembrance and Denial* (Detroit: Wayne State University Press, 1998); Alan Moorehead, *Gallipoli* (New York: Harper & Row, 1956); and Henry Morgenthau, *Ambassador Morgenthau's Story* (Garden City, N.Y.: Doubleday Press, 1918) for varied commentary.

51. Allen and Muratoff, *Caucasian Battlefields,* 299-301.

52. Demirel, *Birinci Dünya Harbinde Erzurum ve Cevresinde Ermeni Harekatleri*, 40-48.

53. Rafael De Nogales, *Four Years beneath the Crescent* (New York: Charles Scribner's Sons, 1926), 60.

54. ATASE, Cipher, Ministry of Defense to Headquarters Third Army, April 20, 1915. Archive 4/3671, Cabinet 163, Drawer D2, File 2820, Section 100, Index I2.

55. ATASE, Cipher to the Turkish General Staff from Governor of Sivas, April 22-23 1915. Archive 4/3641, Cabinet C163, Drawer D2, File 2820, Section 69, Index 3-45, 3-46.

56. ATASE, Chief of the Turkish General Staff Directive, April 24, 1915. Archive 1/1, File 44, Section 207, Index F 2-3.

57. ATASE, Cipher from the Acting Commanding General to the Office of the Undersecretary of the Ministry of Defense, April 24, 1915. Archive 1/131, Cabinet 101-149, Drawer 14-4, File 2287, Section 32-12, Index 12-1. Enver never identified what he had in mind when he used the phrase "more suitable location." However, the author believes that he had prison or concentration camps in mind.

58. ATASE, Message from the Operations Division, Office of the Acting Commanding General to the Ministry of the Interior, May 2, 1915. Archive 1 /1, Cabinet 102, Drawer 1, File 44, Section 207, Index 2-1,2-1.

59. Sinasi Orel and Sureyya Yuca, *The Talat Paşa Telegrams* (Nicosia: K. Rustem & Brother, 1983), 116. A complete copy of the May 27, 1915, Provisional Law may be found in this book.

60. ATASE, Ministry of the Interior Regulation from the Department of Tribes and Immigrants, May 30, 1915. Archive 1 /2, Cabinet 109, Drawer 4, File 361, Section 1445, Index 1.

61. Yair Auron, "The Forty Days of Musa Dagh," in *Remembrance and Denial*, ed. Richard G. Hovannisian (Detroit: Wayne State University Press, 1998), 147-164.

62. ATASE, Ministry of the Interior Regulations Concerning the Management of the Land and Properties belonging to Armenians who have been sent elsewhere as a result of the State of War and the Extraordinary Political Situation, June 10, 1915. Archive 1 /2, Cabinet 109, Drawer 4, File 361, Section 1445, Index 1-3.

63. Allen and Muratoff, *Caucasian Battlefields*, 299-301.

64. De Nogales, *Four Years beneath the Crescent*, chaps. 7, 10.

65. ATASE, Memorandum from Jandarma Headquarters to the Ministry of War, September 26, 1915. The subject and title of this memo was a "Delicate Matter." The Jandarma notified the ministry that it was sending a commission of three officers from the Fourth Directorate of the Symrna Headquarters to the Anatolian *vilayets* to investigate charges that the movement of the Armenians was in violation of the law. Archive 1-131, Cabinet 219, Drawer 2, File 2287, Section 13, Index 3.

66. Allen and Muratoff, *Caucasian Battlefields*, 289.
67. Ibid., 291.
68. Ibid., 303.
69. Allen and Muratoff, *Caucasian Battlefields*, 311. The authors based the Malazgirt and Right Wing operations on the detailed Turkish staff study done by Colonel R. Balkan (see *Caucasian Battlefields*, 548).
70. Turkish General Staff, *3ncu Ordu Harekati*, Kroki (Map) 64.
71. Allen and Muratoff, *Caucasian Battlefields*, 319. The authors used the source noted in endnote 69 for their summary of the Elişkirt valley operation.
72. Larcher, *La Guerre Turque*, 327.
73. Turkish General Staff, *Birinci Dünya Harbinde Turk Harbi IIIncu Cilt Irak-Iran Cephesi 1914-1918 Incu Kisim*, (Ankara: GK Basimevi, 1979), 201.
74. Ronald Millar, *Death of an Army, The Siege of Kut 1915–1916* (Boston: Houghton Mifflin Co., 1970), 16.
75. For an interesting capsule biography of Townshend, see Millar, *Death of an Army*, 20-22.
76. Ibid., 31.

Mehmetçik, Gallipoli, 1915

Turkish trenches at Gallipoli, 1915

Turkish trenches at Gallipoli, 1915

Mustafa Kemal Paşa (Postwar)

Esat Paşa and his staff, Gallipoli, 1915

Ottoman Army machine-gun detachment

Turkish Mountain Troops (ski troops), Caucasian Front

Fortress Guns at Erzurum, Caucasian Front

Turkish Light Artillery, Caucasian Front

Enver Paşa Inspecting Troops in Palestine

Ottoman Infantry (Arab) on the March in Syria

Turkish Cavalry on the March in Syria

5
High Tide, January–December 1916

1916

1916 proved to be the high tide of the Turkish Army in the First World War. It was a year of triumph and of defeat as the Turks attempted to regain the strategic initiative that they had lost in 1915. By the end of 1916, Turkish soldiers were engaged in Mesopotamia, in the Sinai, in Galicia, in Romania, in Macedonia, in the Caucasus, in Persia, and in Arabia. They defeated the Anglo-French invasion at Gallipoli and forced the Allies to withdraw. They captured Townshend's force at Kut in Mesopotamia. In Europe, they fought well on the eastern front and on the Romanian front. They launched another attack on Egypt. Turkish soldiers were deep in Persia. Although they had sustained massive casualties in the Caucasus, that front now appeared stabilized and, at the very least, was now held by two reorganized armies. Munitions, supplies, and support from Germany and Austria-Hungary were beginning to appear and further aid appeared to be forthcoming. Successful battlefield commanders, who seemed to be capable of dealing with crisis, were emerging, and for a time the Ottoman Empire had military heroes again. In spite of the catastrophic loss of Erzurum, Trabzon, and Erzincan, 1916 was a year of triumph.

Turkey entered 1916 with a surplus of forces concentrated at Gallipoli and in Turkish Thrace. These forces were initially large in January 1915 and, over the course of the nine month Gallipoli campaign, had grown even larger. It was impossible to redeploy this force rapidly over the antique and crumbling Ottoman lines of communications. The strategic question facing Enver Paşa and the Turkish General Staff in January 1916 was quite simply how to get the bulk of the Gallipoli Army moved to a front where it could do some good. Certainly there must have been some conservative staff officers, who would have preferred that Turkey conserve its strength and use this time to reconstitute the battered infantry divisions of the Fifth Army. When these formations could be rehabilitated and brought back to fighting trim, then they could be sent off at regular intervals to active fronts requiring reinforcements. It made excellent military sense, but it did not fit into the aggressive and ambitious plans of Enver Paşa. Enver wanted to get the Turkish Army back into the fight quickly and in numbers which would contribute to decisive results.

Part of Enver's solution was to send troops northward, in response to German requests, to Hungary, Romania, and Macedonia, using the excellent European rail system. Although the seven infantry divisions involved in these operations performed valuable service for the Central Powers, the operations were very costly for Turkey. Furthermore, these operations dispersed a powerful portion of the army's strength instead of concentrating it for decisive operations.

Enver's principal strategic concept, for 1916, was to assemble a large army in Caucasia that, in conjunction with the Third Army, would inflict a massive defeat on the Russians. Unfortunately for the Turks, preparations for this deployment proceeded at an astoundingly slow pace, which was compounded by an even slower deployment schedule. Once in the Caucasus, these troops (the Second Army) were withheld from battle while the adjacent Third Army literally collapsed, losing Erzurum, Trabzon, and Erzincan. This sad misuse of available forces places the Third Army debacle of 1916 into the category of a preventable disaster.

If there is criticism to be leveled at the Turkish high command in 1916, it is for their failure to understand and to remedy the strategic transportation deficiencies so glaringly brought to light by the 1914 mobilization and the redeployment of combat forces in 1915. In particular, the Turks might have accelerated the construction work aimed at closing the uncompleted gaps in the railway system. They might also, perhaps, have constructed additional rail lines and sidings aimed at compressing the turnaround time of rail assets. In particular need of improvement was the low operational rate of Turkish locomotives and rail stock, which had already been partially remedied with German and Austrian assistance. At sea, the Turks might have established an intercoastal convoy or steamer system to run on a routine basis troops to Trabzon and Sinop. Certainly the Russian Black Sea Fleet was a distinct threat, but perhaps with mines and submarines, that could have been negated. Finally, although the Turkish General Staff had a strategic railroad staff division, additional German expertise might have substantially increased its efficiency earlier in the war.

Because of these deficiencies, the Turks were unable to take advantage of surprise opportunities, such as the unexpected victory at Kut, or the great weakness of the Russian southern flank in 1916. Given the geography of the Ottoman Empire, adequate interior lines of communications could have meant the difference between victory and defeat.

CAUCASIAN OFFENSIVES

January began as a quiet month in the Turkish Third Army sector and its commander looked forward to a continuing lull in the tempo of operations. Likewise, the Turkish General Staff in Constantinople also thought that the area would remain quiet throughout the winter. Accordingly, the Third Army commander, Mirliva Mahmut Kamil Paşa was in the capital on leave, and the army's chief of staff, Major Guse, was in Germany recovering from a bout of typhus.[1] The army itself remained in winter defensive positions, which along most of the front, were a series of fortified strong points. The Caucasus, unlike the heavily fortified and entrenched western front, was not held with an unbroken line of trenches, but was garrisoned mostly by forces concentrated along critical avenues of advance. In these particular areas, however, entrenchments were elaborate and continuous, and often in depth.

The Third Army was substantially under strength. The chronically weak state of its three army corps continued, as losses from the summer battles were never made up. The 1st and the 5th Expeditionary Forces were detached from the Third Army and were sent on to their original destinations in Mesopotamia. No new formations arrived to take their place. This was due to the ongoing Gallipoli campaign, which after the second Allied invasion at Suvla Bay in August 1915 had lengthened the front, requiring even more Turkish divisions. The more or less stable Caucasus front apparently had lapsed into a stalemate and the Turkish General Staff did not believe that the situation was threatening enough to strip totally the few remaining First and Second Army divisions in Thrace for service in the east. As long as the Russian Black Sea Fleet remained a powerful force capable of amphibious operations, the Turkish General Staff retained at least a corps-equivalent force in the immediate vicinity of Constantinople. The Third Army, therefore, continued to remain weak and monthly grew less capable, as sickness, desertions, and causalities eroded its manpower. The total strength of the Third Army in January 1916 was 126,000 men, of which 50,539 were infantrymen assigned to mobile units. The average strength of the IX, X, and XI Corps was approximately 11,500 men in each corps. The army had a field strength, including the Erzurum Fortress, of 74,057 rifles, 77 machine guns, and 180 field artillery pieces.[2]

The bulk of the fighting strength of the IX, X, and XI Corps guarded the approaches to Erzurum and lay concentrated in a strong series of defensive lines at Köprüköy. In an economy of force mission, the long southern sector to the north of Lake Van was thinly held by the indomitable 3rd Reserve Cavalry Division, the 2nd Regular Cavalry Division, and the 36th Infantry Division. The northern approaches to Trabzon were lightly held by improvised detachments of infantry. In the end, it was a defensive strategy that depended on the enemy not to attack. Opposing the Turkish Third Army were approximately 200,000 Russian soldiers and 380 cannons. It was a dangerous deployment and the Turks were doubly disadvantaged because they had almost no reserves to speak of. The Russians, on the other hand (if they decided to attack), could concentrate their forces at will to achieve a decisive superiority at the point of attack.

The Third Army, as well as the Turkish General Staff, was completely taken by surprise when on January 10, 1916, General Yudenich began a major winter offensive. This attack was directly into the heart of the Turkish concentration in the lines of Köprüköy and was aimed at the sudden seizure of the key city and fortress of Erzurum. Although the Turks had concentrated most of their combat strength in this area, the Turkish lines were really only a series of strongly fortified positions on the high ground dominating the avenues of approach, rather than a solid line of continuous entrenchments. Unlike the continuously entrenched Gallipoli front, this strongpoint system of tactical deployment (forced on the Turks by their acute shortage of infantrymen) proved exceedingly vulnerable to determined attack. The initial Russian attack fell squarely of the divisions of the XI Corps (the 18th, 33rd, and 34th Infantry Divisions). The Turks committed their scant reserves in attempts to hold the Russians. The Turkish Third Army headquarters moved forward from Erzurum to Hasankale to control the battle more effectively. Regiments from the adjacent IX Corps were sent to the growing fight in the XI Corps sector. By January 14, the Russians had shattered the XI Corps defenses. Over the next three days, the Turks were driven off the Köprüköy lines, and by January 18 the Russians were approaching Hasankale, halfway to Erzurum. The next morning the four-battalion Turkish rear guard was annihilated. In only a week, the Turkish strategic posture on the Caucasus rapidly destabilized to the point of imminent disaster.

Turkish divisions found themselves continuously outflanked and forced to retreat in disarray.[3] Because of poor and uncoordinated operations at corps level, the Turks were unable to plug the gaps that the Russians seemed to find in their lines. This series of regimental and divisional defeats in detail came to be known as the Battle of Köprüköy and it ended badly for the Turks. The entire front before the Erzurum Fortress lay broken and the Turkish Third Army itself lay shattered and defeated. Even if the Turks had maintained theater-level reserves, unfavorable winter weather and the poor condition of the Turkish lines of communications probably would have prevented their expeditious use.

The errant Turkish Third Army commander, Mirliva Mahmut Kamil Paşa was still in Constantinople on January 19 and the acting commander was Mirliva Abdül Kerim Paşa. It is unknown whether the absence of the actual Third Army commander adversely affected that army's performance. During the Turkish fall offensives at Eleşkirt, Enver Paşa demonstrably had more shown confidence in Abdül Karim than in Mahmut Kamil and Abdül's performance at Malazgirt had been exemplary. Kamil's subsequent performance, however, would prove inept and it is likely that the Turk's were better off with Abdül Karim. Unquestionably, the absence of a strong and well-trained German General Staff officer serving as the Third Army's Chief of Staff certainly had a negative effect on the army's tactical dispositions and reactive ability.

In the opening January battles, the Turkish Third Army lost about ten thousand men who were killed, wounded, or frozen. Fortunately, only about sixteen cannons were lost and the forty thousand defeated troops were able to take refuge in the Erzurum Fortress.[4] The Russians took five thousand Turkish soldiers prisoners and, according to Russian estimates, an equal number deserted. Losses were mostly concentrated in the XI Corps, which lost as much as 70 percent of its strength. However, losses in the X Corps were slight.[5] Although the Turks had been savagely mauled and badly defeated, they managed to fall back in fair order, which prohibited the Russians from exploiting this victory. Unknown to the Turks, the Russians now began to make plans for the seizure of Erzurum itself.

In Constantinople, the news of the defeat at Köprüköy did not seem to be particularly ominous. The Turkish Fortress of Erzurum was highly regarded; thought to be well armed, it had withstood Russian siege in the past. Although the losses from Köprüköy were serious and were not locally replaceable, they were, in comparison to the recent slaughter of Gallipoli, relatively light. The mood in Constantinople was, in fact, almost euphoric. By January 1916, the Allies had been forced to evacuate completely their beachheads on the Gallipoli Peninsula and had abandoned a veritable mountain of valuable war material and supplies. Additionally, the occupation of Serbia by the German and Austro-Hungarian armies provided, at long last, a continuous and reliable line of communications between the members of the Central Alliance. Encouraged by these developments, Enver Paşa had conversations with the chief of the German General Staff, General Erich von Falkenhayn, to determine how Turkey could best use the surplus of forces available, which were coming available after the victory at Gallipoli. At least four Turkish infantry divisions were immediately available in early January 1916. With German encouragement, Enver and the Turkish General Staff decided to redeploy thirteen Turkish infantry divisions to sectors threatened by allied successes. The staff determined that two divisions would deploy to Mesopotamia, two would go to Syria and Palestine (which had been drained of first class units for Gallipoli), two would go to garrison the Levant coast, and seven infantry divisions would deploy to the Caucasus. Overall, it was sound strategic thinking.

Unfortunately for the Turkish Army, the deployment planning of the critical seven infantry divisions bound for the Caucasus was based on three flawed assumptions. Firstly, the Turks assumed that the exhausted Russians would not be able to renew their winter Caucasian offensive until well into the early summer 1916. Therefore, the battle-hardened and well-trained Gallipoli divisions bound for the east did not even begin to entrain for the east until February. The second flawed assumption was that the Turkish rail and road system could deliver large forces to the east in an expeditious manner. After the experiences with the 1st and the 5th Expeditionary Forces, it is difficult to understand Turkish thinking on this matter in early 1916. The final flawed assumption, and perhaps the most damaging of all, was that the Erzurum Fortified Area could withstand a determined Russian siege for some unspecified and extended period of months. Indeed, in this regard, the Turks had a splendid history of holding out in difficult circumstances, dating back to Plevna in 1877, Erzurum itself in 1878, Adrianople and Çatalca in 1912 and 1913, and most recently, at Gallipoli in 1915. The combination of these assumptions suggested that Turkey had some degree of breathing space within which to redeploy these forces.

The Erzurum Fortress had been redesignated as the Erzurum Fortified Area in 1914 and it had been a major Ottoman Army fortress for several centuries. After the disastrous defeat of 1878, British army engineers began to upgrade the fortress to modern standards, in particular by moving the outer works farther from the center of the city. By 1888, the fortress was considered by the Russians to be in excellent condition and was believed to possess a strong fighting capability. German technical advisors replaced the British in the 1890s. By 1914, the primary defenses of Erzurum consisted of a central group of sixteen forts and two flanking groups of two forts each. Although some histories suggest that the forts were laid out in two concentric rings,[6] the bulk of the forts were echeloned in three lines blocking the valley access from Hasankale to the northeast. The two flanking groups of forts lay twelve kilometers to the north and five kilometers to the south from the center of Erzurum, respectively. There was a final concentric ring of entrenchments directly around the city itself. The city ranked second in the strength of its fortifications to the concentrically fortified city of Adrianople. The fortress was extremely well equipped with artillery with a total of 235 artillery pieces available for the defense of the city[7] (Table 5.1).

Table 5.1
Artillery Strength-Erzurum Fortified Zone, January 1916

Type	Number
150 mm guns	4
150 mm short howitzers	20
120 mm howitzers	18
87 mm field guns	102
80 mm field guns	34
90 mm quick firing Krupp	39
75 mm field guns	18
TOTAL	235

Note: These numbers reflect only the fixed and semifixed artillery assigned to the fortress garrison itself (divisional and corps field artilleries are not included).

Source: Turkish General Staff, *Birinci Dünya Harbinde Kafkas Cephesi 3ncu Ordu Harakati. Cilt II.* (Ankara: GK Basimevi, 1986), 54.

The Third Army commander returned to his headquarters from Constantinople on January 29 to find the tactical situation somewhat stabilized. However, there were ominous signs that the Russians intended to renew the offensive not only at Erzurum but near Lake Van as well. Russian probes continued. Mahmut Kamil began to strengthen his tactical dispositions. The IX Corps held the southern flank with its northern corps boundary as the Erzurum-Hasenkale road. The XI Corps held the center and the X Corps held the northern approaches. The X Corps sector fronted a large Russian salient that flanked the northern side of Erzurum. In effect, the fortress was vulnerable from two directions, from the north and from the east. Each Turkish corps maintained a regimental equivalent as a reserve, but to achieve this, the lines were dangerously thin. The Russians soon took advantage of this weakness.

On the night of January 27-28, an unusual incident occurred. Russian soldiers, who spoke excellent Turkish, penetrated the lines near the village of Kornes. In a brilliant feat of arms, the Russians captured the 38th Infantry Division commander, eight staff officers, the division veterinarian, the division artillery commander and three of his staff, and several others. On the way home the Russians seized three cannons and two hundred Turkish soldiers.[8] The scale and success of this raid indicated that extremely large gaps existed in the front; events of this nature were unheard of at Gallipoli or on the Gaza line.

In Lazistan on the Black Sea, the Russians pushed forward about eight kilometers in the first week of February 1916. In the southern reaches of the Third Army area, Russian attacks from Malazgirt pushed toward Hinis. These attacks were opposed by the 36th Infantry Division and the 2nd Regular Cavalry Division, however, the Turks could not hold back the corps-sized Russian attacks. Table 5.2 presents the army as of the end of January 1916.

At noon on February 11, 1916, the Russians began intense preparatory artillery fires, which lasted until 8 P.M. These fires were concentrated mainly on the first line of center forts at Çobandede and Dalangöz, and the Russians had massed over 250 guns to achieve fire superiority. Russian infantry attacked later that evening as darkness descended over the mountains. In infantry, the Russians had three to one superiority in fighting men.[9] Turkish infantry battalions of 350 men were confronted by full strength Russian battalions of 1,000 men. The fighting was reminiscent of the fighting for the French forts surrounding Verdun; hand-to-hand, deadly, isolated, ending with battered bands of survivors holding individual bunkers and tunnels. Casualties on both sides were high. Overhead, the Turks were waging an intense counterfire battle with the Russian artillery. The situation was especially critical in the X Corps sector and the Mirliva released regimental-sized reserves in its support. By February 12 the Russians were in possession of a salient, which bit deeply into the first line of Turkish forts. The Turks committed what few reserves that they had available in an effort to stem the Russian onslaught. In other areas of the Third Army front, Russian supporting attacks began in Lazistan and at Çoruh.

The subsequent Russian assault of five regimental columns on different avenues of approach was irresistible and the Turkish defenses began to crumble. In the middle of the offensive, the weather turned to blizzards, particularly effecting the exposed Russians.[10] Despite the adverse weather and determined Turkish efforts, the forts could not be held in the face of the overwhelming Russian attacks.

By the evening of February 14, the lead elements of the Russian divisions stood overlooking the plain of Erzurum. A supporting Russian attack on the northern group of Turkish forts had been equally successful. It was apparent to the Third Army staff that Erzurum could not be held and the Turks made a decision to conduct a fighting retreat and to withdraw as many troops and as much material as they could before the fortress fell to the Russians. The following day began with the Turkish front line regiments abandoning the first line forts that they still held and with the rear elements of the Third Army pulling out of the city itself. As the Turks attempted to withdraw, the tempo of the Russian assault intensified, especially to the north of the city.

Table 5.2
Disposition of Turkish Forces, January 1916

THRACE
First Army
1 In.f. Div.
20 Inf. Div.
1 Cav. Bde.
Second Army
VI Corps: 16, 24, 26 Inf. Div.
Forming: 43, 44, 47, 48 Inf. Div.

GALLIPOLI
Fifth Army
I Corps: 2, 3 Inf. Div.
II Corps: **4, 5, 6** *Inf. Div.*
III Corps: 7, 8, **9, 19** *Inf. Div.*
IV Corps: 10, 11, **12** *Inf. Div.*
V Corps: **13, 14, 15** *Inf. Div.*
25 Inf. Div.

SYRIA-PALESTINE
Fourth Army VIII Corps: 23, 24, 27 Inf. Div.
XII Corps: 41, 42, 46 Inf. Div.

CAUCASIA
Third Army
IX Corps: 17, 28, 29 *Inf. Div.*
X Corps: 30, 31, 32 *Inf. Div.*
XI Corps: 18, 33, 34 *Inf. Div.*
2 Regular Cav. Div.
3 Reserve Cav. Div.
Van Reserve Cav. Bde.
Van Jandarma (Inf) Div.
36th Inf. Div.

MESOPOTAMIA
Sixth Army
XIII Corps: **35**, 52 *Inf. Div.*
XVIII Corps: 45, 51 Inf. Div.

ARABIA-YEMEN
VII Corps: 21, 22, 39, 40 Inf. Div.

Note: Units in boldface type indicate new formations; units underlined indicate units redeployed since summer 1915; units in bold italic type indicate seriously understrength units. Units Inactivated: 38 Inf. Div.

The Russians entered the city of Erzurum about 7:30 A.M. on February 16. As the city fell, rapid Russian successes in the north created conditions for envelopment and it was only by the thinnest of margins that the Turks held the western exits from the fortress. The Turks managed to conduct a fighting retreat and extracted most of their infantry from the Russian envelopment, but many service support elements of the Third Army were captured including 250 wounded Turks in the Erzurum military hospital. The battered X and XI Corps reestablished a defensive line about eight kilometers to the west of the city.

Artillery losses for the Turks were particularly heavy, with the Russians capturing 327 Turkish guns, or almost all of the artillery present in and around the fortress. In infantry, the Third Army lost over ten thousand men were killed or wounded; a further five thousand men were taken prisoner.[11] Although most of the Turkish infantry losses were concentrated in the X Corps; in the XI Corps, the 34th Infantry Division was literally annihilated. The Russians expected the Third Army to disintegrate as a consequence of the fall of Erzurum and began to make preparations for a pursuit. In his after action report,[12] Mahmut Kamil Paşa attributed the loss of Erzurum to the extended length of his front in comparison to the troops that he had available. He noted that at Gallipoli on the Cape Helles front, Turkish corps held five to six kilometers, and that on the Anafarta front, not more than ten kilometers. At Erzurum, the Third Army corps were responsible for frontages of thirty kilometers or more in length.

These unfolding events found a thoroughly alarmed Enver Paşa then in Aleppo, where he immediately accelerated the deployment tempo of reinforcements to the east. The Turkish V Corps, consisting of the 10th and the 13th Infantry Divisions, was ordered to begin immediate movement to the east. Other news from the Lake Van area and from the Lazistan front on the Black Sea was equally disturbing and indicated serious Russian offensives were in the offing at those locations. The heady exuberance which had resulted from the great victory at Gallipoli was gone and was replaced by a gathering sense of despair. However, the irrepressible Enver promptly sent an encouraging message to the V Corps, stating that although the morale of the Third Army had been destroyed, he knew that the veteran infantry of the V Corps would act as stiffeners in the defense.[13]

In addition to accelerating the reinforcement flow to the Third Army, on February 23 Enver determined to change the defeated leadership of the Third Army. On February 27, 1916, Enver relieved Mirliva Mahmut Kamil Paşa of command and appointed XI Corps Commander Abdül Karim Paşa as interim Third Army Commander. Second Army Commander and Gallipoli veteran, Mirliva Mehmet Vehip Paşa was ordered to depart Thrace immediately and assume command of the Third Army. Vehip Paşa's primary mission was to turn around the deteriorating situation in the Third Army. The German chief of staff, the recently promoted Colonel Guse, remained in his position. The departing commander exited the theater via ship from Trabzon. The situation facing the interim commander was bleak. The Third Army rolls on February 23 showed a strength of only 25,500 riflemen, 76 machine guns, and 84 artillery pieces ready for action. Additionally, the loss of the Erzurum Fortress with its hospitals and logistical support placed a great strain on service support for the Third Army. In particular, there were between eight thousand and ten thousand men sick and wounded, for whom there was little medical aid available. To compound matters, the Third Army headquarters itself was forced to displace to the city of Erzincan where it had to reestablish communications under very austere conditions. Vehip Paşa arrived in that city on March 16.

The fall of Erzurum had a decisive effect on the strategic direction of the Turkish war effort. It was now apparent to Enver and the Turkish General Staff that the strategic and operational situation in the Caucasus resembled a house of cards, which could collapse at any time. It was also apparent that the ever-increasing length of the eastern front was rapidly eclipsing the command and control capability of the Third Army. The addition of the V Corps, and an incoming seven infantry divisions would place an unmanageable strain on the existing Third Army headquarters. Therefore on March 1 Enver decided to deploy the Turkish Second Army headquarters, under the command of Ahmet Izzet Paşa, from Thrace to Diyarbakir. Once there, the Second Army would assume responsibility for the eastern portion of the Third Army's front. Enver envisioned that this powerful army would strike a decisive flanking blow on the Russians and recover the territory lost in the recent Russian offensives. By March 22 the lead elements of the army headquarters were bound for the east. The Turkish General Staff hoped to have the Second Army in place and ready for operations by early June 1916.[14] Further reinforcements, in the way of Colonel Mustafa Kemal's newly formed XVI Corps and the veteran 5th Infantry Division, were ordered east to join the Second Army on March 10. By August the Second Army would grow to a strength of four corps and ten infantry divisions. Unfortunately for the Third Army, this redirection of Turkish strategic priorities was too little too late and further disasters awaited their thinly stretched forces.

The Russians were bent on maintaining the momentum and advantage that they had won at Erzurum. Pushing hard in Lazistan, the Russians took the port of Rize on the Black Sea coast in March 1916 in an amphibious assault. The Russians continued to push and on April 16 captured the key port of Trabzon. This was a critical loss for the Turks, since Trabzon was the largest port in the Third Army area and was serviced by paved roads leading into the Anatolian highlands. Logistically, this was a disaster for the Third Army. Visiting the Third Army in early May, Enver found that although the Mirliva Fezi Paşa's V Corps had arrived in the operational theater, Russian pressure along the Black Sea coast dissipated the effect of this badly needed reinforcement. In fact, one entire infantry division of the V Corps had already been diverted to the collapsing Trabzon sector.

Unfortunately also for the Third Army, the Turkish General Staff had given rail and transportation priority in March and April to the Turkish divisions bound for Mesopotamia.[15] This fateful decision was in response to the developing situation at Kut and the serious British attempts to relieve the Imperial forces encircled there. Because of the scarcity of Turkish rail transportation, this inevitably forced further delays in the eastward deployment of the Second Army, since both theaters competed for the same rail lines from European Thrace to Adana. As a temporary solution to the growing command and control problem, Vehip Paşa decided on April 13 to divide his front into three operational regions. The First Region was the southeast front north of Diyarbakir, which would fall under the command of Mustafa Kemal Paşa and his XVI Corps headquarters, with two infantry divisions. The Second Region, in the center, was under the command of X Corps Commander Yusuf Ziya Paşa, who would also control the IX Corps, the XI Corps, and the 2nd Regular Cavalry Division. Along the Black Sea coast, in the north, Fevzi Paşa and the V Corps assumed control of the Third Region. Fevzi Paşa had two divisions and the remnants of the Lazistan and coastal defense detachments. This operational grouping of formations was similar to those that the Turks had used during the Gallipoli battles. In total combat strength, the Third Army was at last beginning to grow (Table 5.3).

Table 5.3
Third Army Strength, April 28, 1916

Region	Soldiers	Rifles	Machine Guns	Artillery
First	13,741	9,970	7	19
Second	23,444	19,046	59	52
Third	29,601	16,119	25	37
TOTAL	66,786	45,135	91	108

Source: Turkish General Staff, *Birinci Dünya Harbinde Kafkas Cephesi 3ncu Ordu Harakati. Cilt II.* (Ankara: GK Basimevi, 1986), 165.

Encouraged by their gathering strength and by the exhortations of Enver Paşa, the Turks felt strong enough to launch limited attacks in the center and in the south. The first of these attacks in late May 1916 was aimed at securing favorable positions from which to launch a subsequent major offensive to retake Erzurum. This attack was moderately successful. Enver and Vehip were also concerned about the potential Russian advantage in seaborne reinforcements now gained by the capture of the port of Trabzon and ordered even more attacks in the north. On June 26 the V Corps attacked into the Pontic Alps, trying to recapture Trabzon. Although this attack met with initial success, like many battles in the First World War, the Turks did not have adequate forces available to exploit their success. The offensive ground to a halt without securing its objective and exhausting the V Corps.

In the meantime, the slowly arriving Second Army was building its strength. The movements consumed considerable time even under the best circumstances. In the best case, infantry divisions departed Constantinople by train for the east and either went to Ergli or southeast to Pozanti. For example, the last elements of the 8th Infantry Division left Constantinople on April 5 and arrived at Pozanti on April 7, where it foot marched for four days over the uncompleted railroad gap in the Taurus Mountains. After a one-day train ride, the division arrived at the Osmaniye railroad gap on April 12. Here it detrained and foot marched five days to the railroad spur at Katma for another one-day train ride. Beginning its final foot march on April 20, the division arrived at Diyarbakir on April 30. As the first elements of the division had departed Constantinople previously on March 20, the total time spent moving this division into its eastern tactical assembly area was forty-one days.[16] Divisions deploying directly east took even longer since the distance requiring foot marches were longer. The 9th Infantry Division, for example, took fifty-three days to reach its final tactical assembly area. Needless to say, sickness and attrition took a severe toll on the troops and animals moved by these methods. Formations thus moved required a recuperation period in rear area tactical assembly areas in the new operational sector before being further deployed into active combat. Often the commanders and the divisional staffs were moved separately and more quickly so that advanced planning might occur in the new area. Sometimes this had an adverse effect on the movements as well since the commanders were physically removed from insuring the care and welfare of their men enroute.

Both the 5th and 8th Infantry Divisions of the XVI Corps had arrived at Diyarbakir and Bitlis, respectively. By May 15, the veteran III Corps, now consisting of the experienced 1st, 7th, 14th, and the newly raised 53rd Infantry Divisions was entrained for the east. The independent 9th Infantry Division, detrained at Ergli, was road marching toward Sivas, and the 3rd Regular Cavalry Division was detraining at Adana. The independent 12th Infantry Division, escorted by the former SMS *Breslau*, now renamed the *Midilli*, was dispatched by sea to the Black Sea port of Samsun. The IV Corps, in Symrna, was alerted for deployment and by May 30, this corps and its 47th and 48th Infantry Divisions, was en route east too. However, as this huge force slowly made its way east, disaster again struck the Third Army.

Hoping to cut off the forward Russian elements at Trabzon, the Turkish V Corps launched yet another offensive. This attack, employing the 9th and the 13th Infantry Divisions, was aimed north toward the Black Sea coast. By June 28, the Turks stood within ten kilometers of the sea, but an aggressive Russian defense held them firm and the attack collapsed on July 2. In Constantinople, the Turkish General Staff alerted another infantry division for service in the east and ordered the new 49th Infantry Division to entrain at once. Cumulatively these Turkish counterattacks drained vital combat power from the Third Army again leaving it in a dangerously under strength condition. The Turk's geographic position had not improved either, leaving them in an unfavorable strategic posture.

Throughout the late spring and early summer of 1916, the Russians had been conserving their strength and preparing to launch a massive offensive toward Erzincan. Success here would threaten the Turkish city of Sivaş and would remove the threat posed by the Turkish V Corps against the newly won port of Trabzon. The Russians launched their attack on July 2 and concentrated the bulk of their strength against the city of Bayburt, which lies in a bend of the Çoruh River. Within a week they were on the outskirts of the city of Bayburt. Holding this threatened sector of the Turkish lines was the X Corps. Although the X Corps had a hardened cadre of experienced combat veterans, it had repeatedly been subjected to Russian attacks over the past year. Fighting heroically, it was unable to hold its ground. By July17, Bayburt fell. Russian attacks on the adjacent Turkish IX Corps were equally successful. The Turks pulled back and established strong successive defensive positions.

The Russians renewed the offensive on July 19, with strong attacks out of the Bayburt bridgehead. Attacking across the Karasu River, the Russians again hammered the IX and X Corps. Once across this river, the Russians broke into the Erzincan plain. There were no natural obstacles remaining upon which the weakened Turks could build a defensive line and the Russians converged on Erzincan. Advance Russian elements sweeping down from the northeast entered Erzincan on July 25 and Vehip Paşa decided that he would attempt to hold the western exits into the Anatolian heartland rather than attempt to defend the city. The Russian offensive ended on July 28. In the Bayburt, Karasu, and Erzincan battles, the Third Army lost an estimated seventeen thousand killed and wounded and lost an additional seventeen thousand men taken prisoner.[17] This was the worst loss of men taken as prisoners of war that the Turks suffered up until this point in the war. The Turks called this series of battles the "Çoruh campaign."

Overall, these battles were a disaster for Turkish arms. Enver's intent had been to launch a massive flanking attack with the newly deployed Second Army, while the Third Army fixed the Russian Army in place. Ultimately, Enver hoped to retake Erzurum and Trabzon, while destroying the Russians. This would open the way for an offensive to retake Kars, lost to the Russians since 1878. The Çoruh campaign had totally destroyed these ambitious plans by reducing the Third Army to an ineffective shambles and by eliminating its forward positions at Bayburt. Now both the Third Army and Enver's grandiose plans lay in ruins; however, the front soon erupted in renewed fighting.

The long-awaited Second Army offensive began on August 2, 1916 (Map 5.1 shows the general area of the Second Army's offensive). Ahmet Izzet Paşa had resisted all of Vehip Paşa's pleas for both assistance and for diversionary attacks on the Russian flank during the desperate days of July. Now, a week after the conclusion of the Russian offensive, Ahmet Izzet Paşa chose to attack. As in earlier Turkish offensives on the southern flank of the Caucasian front, the immediate objective was Malazgirt and the final objective was the fertile Eleşkirt Valley. The Second Army Commander had assembled a powerful force consisting of the III Corps with the 1st, 7th, 14th, and 53rd Infantry Divisions, the II Corps with the 11th and 12th Infantry Divisions, the IV Corps with the 47th Infantry Division (reinforced by the 48th Infantry Division just now arriving in theater), and the XVI Corps with the 5th and 8th Infantry Divisions. The Second Army also had the 3rd Regular Cavalry Division assigned as well as five heavy artillery battalions. Concentrated and launched a month earlier, this formidable force might have had a dramatic effect on the Russian army. It might have even

Map 5.1
General Situation, Turkish Land Forces, 1916

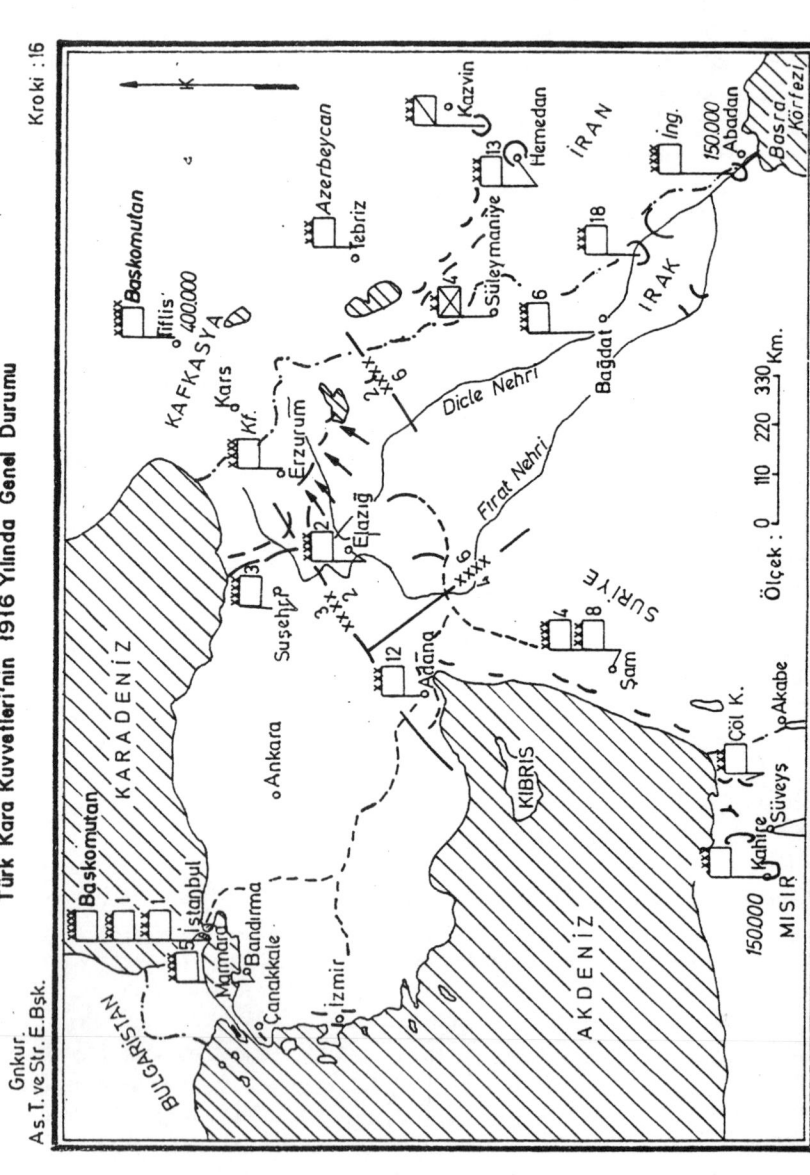

Source: Turkish General Staff, *Turk Silahli Kuvvetleri Tarihi Osmanli Devri Birinci Dünya Harbi İdari Faaliyetler ve Lojistik Xncu Cilt* (Ankara: Basimevi, 1985), Kroki (Map) 15.

saved the Third Army from destruction and Erzincan from capture. However, now, in the aftermath of the Erzincan offensive, the Russians were free to move their reserves to the southeast to confront the Second Army's attack.

In the Second Army's attack, Ahmet Izzet Paşa failed to concentrate his forces, preferring instead to form his forces into three corps-sized groups. Each of these groups attacked on a different axis and none were close enough to support another. It was a recipe for failure. The XVI Corps attacked in the Bingöl area, the III Corps attacked in the Oğnot area, and the IV Corps attacked toward Kığı. Mustafa Kemal's hard driving XVI Corps took both Bitlis and Muş early in the campaign, however, these victories were on the flank of the main Turkish attack. In the center, it was slow going for the Turkish *askers* as they struggled forward. Locally, in many cases, the Turks had numerical superiority, a condition rare on the Caucasian front at any time in the war. But the terrain in this area of the front was extremely difficult and this served to negate the combat effectiveness of both the experienced and veteran III Corps infantry divisions, and the new but well-trained IV Corps infantry divisions. Operating on interior lines of communications, the Russians rushed experienced mountain units to stem the Turkish attacks. Unfriendly Kurds helped the Russians find uncharted tracks across the mountains. By August 18 the Russians had finished reinforcing this front and were able to launch corp-sized counterattacks. The Turkish offensive ground to a slow halt in early September, and by the time snow fell on September 26, 1916, the attack was finished. In the final days of September, the XVI Corps pulled out of Muş. Although the Turks had gained some ground, they lost heavily in irreplacable infantry strength. Out of one hundred thousand men engaged, thirty thousand were killed or wounded.[18] Because of the high spirit and magnificant elan of these experienced Gallipoli formations, the Russians took very few prisoners. Several Turkish infantry divisions were reduced to cadre strength, and at the end of September 1916 the effective rifle strength of the Second Army had been reduced to about sixty thousand men.

Coming fast on the heels of the Third Army's July debacle, the defeat of the Second Army was a disaster of enormous magnitude. Eight out of the ten Second Army infantry divisions were Gallipoli veterans and had both combat experience and high morale. This magnificant fighting force, augmented by two newly raised top quality infantry divisions was Turkey's last strategic reserve in 1916. Table 5.4 vividly shows the emptying of the Thracian manpower pool by August 1916. Carefully husbanded, while its sister Third Army was destroyed in the hard fighting of the summer of 1916, the Second Army was carelessly flung at the Russians. Instead of these two armies fighting simultaneously against the Russians, they fought sequentially, and as such were destroyed in detail by the numerically superior Russians. The Second Army attack was to become the last major Turkish Army offensive launched against the Allies in the First World War.

It might have been possible to coordinate operations between the Second and Third Armies, even as early as late June or early July 1916. Certainly, the seven

Table 5.4
Disposition of Turkish Forces, August 1916

GALICIA
XV Corps: 19, 20 Inf. Div.

ROMANIA
VI Corps: 15, 25 Inf. Div.
26 Inf. Div.

MACEDONIA
50 Inf. Div.

THRACE
First Army
1 Cav. Bde.
49 Inf. Div.

GALLIPOLI
Fifth Army
I Corps: *14, 16 Inf. Div.*

SYRIA-PALESTINE
Fourth Army
VIII Corps: 3, 23, 24, 27 Inf. Div.
XII Corps: 41, 42, 43, 46 Inf. Div.

ARABIA-YEMEN
VII Corps: 21, 22, 39, 40 Inf. Div.

CAUCASIA
Third Army
V Corps: 9, 10, 13 Div
IX Corps: *17, 28, 29 Inf. Div.*
X Corps. *30, 31, 32 Inf. Div.*
XI Corps: *18, 33, 34 Inf. Div.*
2 Regular Cav. Div.
Van Cav. Bde.
Van Jandarma (Inf) Div.
36th Inf. Div.
Second Army
III Corps: 1, 7, 14, 53 Inf. Div.
II Corps: 11, 12 Inf. Div.
IV Corps: 47, 48 Inf. Div.
XVI Corps: *5, 8 Inf. Div.*
3 Reserve Cav. Div.

MESOPOTAMIA
Sixth Army
XIII Corps: 2, 4, 6 Inf. Div.
XVIII Corps: 35, 45, 51, 52 Inf. Div.

Note: Units in boldface italic type indicate new formations; units underlined indicate units redeployed since January 1916; units in bold italic type indicate seriously understrength units. Units inactivated: 38 Inf. Div.

infantry divisions available to Ahmet Izzet Paşa in July, might have executed supporting attacks against the flanks of the Russians then engaged in the capture of Erzincan. Unfortunately for the Turks, there was no theater or front commander authorized to coordinate the operations of these two armies. Apparently, Ahmet Izzet Paşa, in spite of urgent pleas for help from Vehip Paşa, felt that his mission was to assemble his army first and then attack. It was entirely possible that rapid intervention by the Second Army in the summer of 1916 might have prevented the collapse of the Third Army and the loss of Erzincan. Instead, the Turkish Army lost, in the Caucasus, in the summer of 1916, a total of almost one hundred thousand men. These massive losses of trained men could never be replaced at this point in the war.

In the face of these calamities, the Turkish Army began a massive and long overdue reorganization of its forces in the Caucasus. Painfully aware that the lack of an army group-level headquarters had effectively crippled coordinated operations between the Second and Third Armies, the Turks belatedly formed an Anatolian Army Group. Ahmet Izzet Paşa moved up to command this group and Mustafa Kemal Paşa moved up to replace him at the Second Army. Kemal had performed brilliantly as a divisional and group commander at Gallipoli. His stellar performance in command of the XVI Corps further marked him for high command. Now he was promoted to command the Turkish Second Army.

Other changes soon followed. On paper, the Third Army had a strength of thirteen infantry and one cavalry division. With supporting arms and services, this force at full strength would have numbered about two hundred thousand men. However, in a situation where divisions had the strength of regiments, and regiments had the strength of battalions or even companies, the Third Army only numbered about thirty thousand effectives. There were no reinforcements available and furthermore, there were perhaps fifty thousand deserters roaming around in the Third Army area. It was an intolerable situation. Because of this, the Turkish General Staff desired to reorganize the Third Army completely by eliminating entire corps and divisions and consolidating their assets into new formations which could be maintained at nearly full strength. It was a radical and visionary solution to an ever worsening problem. Accordingly, on September 4, Enver Paşa approved the concept of reorganizing the Third Army along these lines. By September 13 Vehip Paşa had developed an idea, which he hoped would galvanize the tired Turkish troops. While eliminating some formations, Vehip decided to rename the new units as "Caucasian" formations. It was hoped that this new designation would wipe away the stigma of defeat and add luster to newly renamed formations. On September 23 the Third Army began to reorganize.

At corps level, the V, IX, X, and XI Corps headquarters were simply eliminated from the Turkish force structure. In their place and using their staff offficers, Vehip formed the 1st and 2nd Caucasian Corps. This consolidation enabled the two new corps staffs to operate at full strength and with greater efficiency. At divisional level, Vehip converted the 13th Infantry Division to the 5th Caucasian Infantry Division, the 28th Infantry Division became the new 9th Caucasian Infantry Division, the 30th and 33rd Infantry Divisions formed the new

10th and 11th Caucasian Infantry Divisions, respectively. Vehip retained the 36th Infantry Division and converted it to the 36th Caucasian Infantry Division. He formed the new 49th Caucasian Infantry Division from independent infantry regiments. Finally, the new 37th Caucasian Infantry Divisions was formed from the coastal detachments. These new Caucasian infantry divisions were smaller than ordinary peacetime Turkish infantry divisons and their infantry strength was set at six thousand men.[19] Vehip then completely dissolved the 9th, 10th, 17th, 18th, 29th, 31st, 32nd, and the 34th Infantry Divisions. Thus eight entire infantry divisions vanished from the Turkish Army's order of battle. The officers, men, animals, and equipment of these divisions were transferred to flesh out the seven remaining Third Army Caucasian infantry divisions. It was a dramatic organizational change and restored a great deal of efficiency to the Third Army.

Almost overnight, the surviving Third Army infantry divisions went to almost full strength in infantry effectives. The field artillery was also reorganized with each new division receiving twelve to eighteen field or mountain howitzers. Mirliva Yusuf Izzet Paşa received command of the 1st Caucasian Corps and Merliva Fevzi Paşa received command of the 2nd Caucasian Corps. The cavalry was not forgotten and was consolidated into the new 2nd Caucasian Cavalry Brigade. Fortunately, the Russians remained quiet while these sweeping organizational changes were accomodated by the Third Army command structure.

In addition to these organizational changes, there were operational changes, as well. The three operational regions of the Third Army were examined and by October 19, 1916 the following tactical changes had taken place. In the south, the 2nd Region was divided into three zones, the 1st Zone held by the 36th Caucasian Infantry Division, the 2nd Zone by the 9th Caucasian Infantry Division, and the 3rd Zone by the 10th Caucasian Infantry Division. The 3rd Region in the north was likewise divided into the 4th Zone with the 5th Caucasian Infantry Division, the 5th Zone with the 11th Caucasian Infantry Division, and the 6th Zone with the 37th Caucasian Infantry Division. The 1st Region was eliminated. In army reserve, within the 3rd Region area, was the 49th Caucasian Infantry Division. The Third Army headquarters remained at Suşehri, while the headquarters of the 2nd Caucasian Corps set up at Alucra and the 1st Caucasian Corps went to Refahiye. In the middle of December 1916, the Third Army had an effective rifle strength of 36,382 men. Divisional strength varied between five thousand and eight thousand men.[20]

As at Gallipoli in 1915 and as during the Malazgirt offensive in 1915, the Turkish command appeared more comfortable with creating operational groups, which were task-organized without regard to existing formal corps command relationships. This showed a greater flexibility in operational thinking than the Turkish Army possessed when it went to war in 1914. This new found flexibility would have long term benefits later in the war when the Russians collapsed in 1918 and opened the way for the Turks to drive to the Caspian Sea.

Significant changes were also afoot in the Second Army area. Although Ahmet Izzet Paşa had suffered far less casualties in the Second Army, numerous formations were reduced to ineffective remnants of fighting units. In October 1916 the Second Army had sixty-four thousand effectives on its rolls. Compounding Ahmet Izzet Paşa's difficulties were increasing problems with hostile Kurds in his rear areas.[21] Therefore, Ahmet Izzet Paşa withdrew his forces from the Dersim and Bingöl-dağ area in order to straighten out his lines and to create reserves, then badly needed to rein in the Kurds in the rear areas. Following this, he dissolved the gallant and experienced III Corps. Thus passed into history one of the premier fighting corps in the Turkish Army, which had survived the Balkan Wars intact and which had done so much valuable work at Gallipoli. The divisions of the III Corps (the 7th and 14th Infantry Divisions) were retained and were redeployed to Syria and Mesopotamia, respectively. The Second Army thereupon reorganized itself into three corps; the IV Corps of the 11th and 12th Infantry Divisions, the II Corps of the 1st and the 47th Infantry Divisions, and the XVI Corps of the 5th and 8th Infantry Divisions. Additionally, the 53rd Infantry Division was sent to Syria, as was the newly arrived 48th Infantry Division. So, by the end of December 1916, the formerly powerful Second Army was reduced to only six infantry divisions.[22]

The year 1916 ended badly for the Turks in the Caucasus. In manpower, the Turkish forces on the Caucasian front remained the same, but the total number of Turkish divisions engaged on this front dropped from a September high of twenty-five to a December total of thirteen. They had lost the mighty fortress city of Erzurum, the critical port of Trabzon, and the important city of Erzincan. They had come close to losing Diyarbakir. They had lost well over one hundred thousand men and had seen the Third Army all but destroyed and the Second Army literally thrown away. Fortunately, events in other parts of their empire forced the Russians into a lull, which perhaps saved the day for the Second and Third Armies and the Turkish position in Caucasia.

GALICIA

During the first three days of the Brusilov Offensive, on the eastern front in early June 1916, the Russian Army took two hundred thosuand Austro-Hungarian soldiers as prisoners of war. By the end of the offensive later that summer, the Hapsburg Army had officially lost 464,382 men and 10,756 officers; however, unofficial and modern estimates range as high as 750,000 soldiers, of which 380,000 were taken prisoners.[23] In his definitive study of the Austro-Hungarian war effort, Holger Herwig states that these losses were a blow from which the Hapsburg Army never recovered. That the Russians lost a million men was immaterial, the Austro-Hungarian losses from the Brusilov offensive, combined with the crippling losses suffered in 1914 and 1915, emptied the Hapsburg manpower pool. There were several consequences for Austria-Hungary from this, but chief among them was irrevocable loss of control of the strategic direction on the eastern front to Germany. Another consequence was the huge, and from a Hapsburg perspective, unrepairable hole torn in the defensive fabric of the front. For this, there was no solution except for a massive infusion of German assistance and troops. However, in the summer of 1916, Germany was heavily engaged on the Somme in France, on the northern portions of the Eastern Front, and on the newly opened front against Rumania, and had little aid to give. This was the situation that drew Turkish soldiers to the far reaches of Hungary for the first time since the seventeenth century.

At the suggestion of General Falkenhayn, the chief of the German General Staff, an urgent request was made to Turkey to provide combat troops to help Germany plug the gaps in the Eastern Front. The Austrian High Command was uneasy with this idea and required both time and persuasive arguments in order to be convinced to accept Turkish troops on the Galician front.[24] In the meantime, on June 4, 1916, Enver Paşa approved Falkenhayn's request and ordered that Turkish troops be dispatched to the eastern front. This was the first step in a series of European diversions in 1916, which would ultimately involve three Turkish corps headquarters and seven Turkish infantry divisions. Liman von Sanders considered this diversion of Turkish troops to the eastern front to be a serious mistake.[25] His thinking on the matter was that Turkey could barely protect its frontiers and could ill afford to dissipate its strength. In Liman von Sanders's judgment, the increasingly large British forces forming in Egypt and Mesopotamia posed an imminent threat to the Turks. Also by the summer of 1916, both the Fortress of Erzurum and the key Black Sea port of Trabzon had fallen to the Russians, and the Turkish Third Army was largely destroyed. This deteriorating strategic situation in the Caucasus was a dangerous and pressing threat, which required immediate attention. Belatedly, the Turkish General Staff was redeploying the Second Army from Çorlu to the east to rectify this problem, but the perennially weak Turkish rail system delayed the timely movement of forces to the Caucasus. The situation in the east was critical. Liman von Sanders felt that the Turks should maintain a strong central strategic reserve against the day when the empire would inevitably have to deal with the increasing Russian and British threats. His advice and warnings were ignored.

From Berlin, it looked as if Turkey had a surplus of available divisions. Von Falkenhayn felt that of the currently active Turkish fronts, apart from Armenia, that the situation was "still sufficiently secure for no alarm to be felt."[26] Concentrated in Thrace, Constantinople, and on the Gallipoli Peninsula, Liman von Sanders alone had a total of twenty-two Turkish infantry divisions. Although many were worn and bloodied from the savage Gallipoli fighting from the previous year, all were reasonably well rested and fresh. Many of these divisions were considered to be superb in quality by the British and had excellent fighting reputations. Moreover, from the German viewpoint, the rail network running north into the Balkans could sustain greater traffic, whereas the Turkish lines running south could not. It mattered little what the Turks wanted to do, given their abysmal lines of communications. Left to their own devices, the Turkish divisions in Thrace probably would have remained there for some time. In this regard, and certainly from an alliance perspective, getting more Turks back into action in 1916 was a major accomplishment for Germany.

After the Gallipoli campaign, Mustafa Kemal's famous but now battle-worn 19th Infantry Division was moved northward to Keşan and Şarkoy, where on January 9, 1916, it was combined with the 20th Infantry Division to form the new XV Corps.[27] On July 10, 1916, the XV Corps was ordered to make ready for movement to the eastern front. At the expense of other First Army regiments, the XV Corps infantry divisions received an influx of artillery, technical, and logistical detachments, which brought them up to authorized strength. To fill the depeleted ranks of the infantry regiments, Liman von Sanders was ordered to strip other First Army divisions of fit men for transfer to the XV Corps. He was very unhappy about this and he was especially concerned about the long-term effect that this would have on the units remaining behind in Thrace.[28] Nevertheless, by early July the corps had thirty thousand men assigned on its rolls. These soldiers were the last fully trained and fit replacements that the XV Corps would see for many months.[29] The two divisional artillery regiments were given an additional three hundred draft horses. The corps headquarters, under the command of Colonel Yakup Şevki, departed from Uzunköprü on July 17 by rail, for destinations in Hungary. The route traveled through Sofia and through Nis and Belgrade in newly conquered Serbia. The 20th Infantry Division, under the command of Lieutenant Colonel Yasin Hilmi, departed for Hungary on July 22 and the 19th Infantry Division, under the command of Lieutenant Colonel Şefik, followed on July 24. The movement went smoothly and the lead elements of the XV Corps began to arrive in Hungary on August 5, 1916. The corps was assigned to Army South, commanded by Lieutenant General Graf von Bothmer, and was assigned a section of the line on the west bank of the Zlotalipa River.

German divisions stood on both flanks of the corps' twenty-eight-kilometer front and at noon on August 22, the Turks established liaison with the German 55th Infantry Division on their left flank and with the Bavarian 1st Reserve Infantry Division on their right flank. The XV Corps headquarters sent its first written report to Graf von Bothmer the same day. By August 28 the corps was in line with its two infantry divisions and three artillery regiments ready for action. In sector, opposite the Turks, were elements of three Russian divisions--the 47th, the 113th, and the 3rd Turkistan. The Turks were now in contact with the Russian Army, in Europe, for the first time since 1878 and the Turkish soldiers manning the trenches had not long to wait for action.

The XV Corps was, by Turkish standards, very well equipped.[30] For artillery, the corps had twenty-four 90 mm, four 120 mm, two 220 mm, two 105 mm howitzers, and 8 mine throwers. Once there, the Turks received additional twelve 90 mm and four 120 mm howitzers. Since they were, as usual, weak in machine guns, the Germans transferred thirty captured Russian machine guns to them. Additionally, the Germans sent eight German machine gun detachments to reinforce the Turkish infantry regiments. Later in the campaign, more captured Russian machine guns would be sent to the Turks.

The corps headquarters received an intelligence estimate on the morning of August 31 warning of an expected Russian attack, which would be preceded by a heavy artillery bombardment. The Turks had not long to wait and the Russian offensive began on September 2. By noon, several Turkish regiments were heavily engaged. Fighting was heaviest in the southern sector, held by the 20th Infantry Division, and over the next several days, the Turks launched several counterattacks. By September 7 both the Turkish 20th Infantry Division and the Bavarian 1st Reserve Division had been pushed out of their entrenchments along the west bank of the Zlotalipa River and had fallen back about ten kilometers.[31] However, contact between the Turks and the Bavarians remained intact and the line remained unbroken. Casualties were extremely heavy and the Russians apparently lost about fifteen thousand men killed or wounded in these early attacks on the XV Corps.

On September 15 the Russians launched a major attack on the 61st Infantry Regiment, which held the far right of the Turkish line and which was the link to the adjacent Bavarian regiment. This was a serious enemy attempt to rupture the vital seam between the Turkish and the German corps. The 61st Infantry Regiment tenaciously clung to its positions but was steadily forced back. The situation was dangerous because, after several weeks of intensive combat, the Turks had no tactical reserves left with which to stem the onslaught. However, in a typical display of German tactical initiative, the German 185th Infantry Regiment was dispatched to assist the Turks by conducting a counterattack. This regiment entered the Turkish sector and began an immediate counterattack, which drove the Russians back to their starting line. It was a very close encounter with disaster for the XV Corps. As the Russian offensive ground to a halt several days later, it was apparent that the Turks had taken a severe pounding and, in their first encounter on the Galician front had lost ninty-five officers and seven thousand men.[32] Additionally, the Turks had lost six battalion commanders and twenty-two company commanders. Most of the casualties were concentrated in the 20th Infantry Division. This battered division now held a front of only five kilometers, while the stronger 19th Infantry Division held the remaining ten kilometers of XV Corps front.

The front was stabilized for the remainder of September, with both sides conducting local counterattacks. In the Turkish 20th Infantry Division sector, the 61st Regiment was pulled back into reserve. A German infantry regiment, a German cavalry regiment, and several batteries of German artillery were also put in reserve in the XV Corps sector to backstop the Turks in the event of a subsequent Russian attack. On October 8, 1916, the Corp Commander, Colonel Yakup Şevki was promoted to brigadier general.

October 1916 was marked by continuous Russian pressure along the Turkish corps front. To relieve the pressure on the 19th Infantry Division, which had all three of its infantry regiments in the line, the XV Corps formed the *Ledabor Müfrezesi* (detachment) composed of the German 228th Reserve Infantry Regiment (one of the German reserve regiments in the Turkish sector). On the night of October 12-13 the Ledabor detachment went into the line at the far left flank of the corps enabling the 19th Division to pull one of its regiments off the line and into reserve.[33] By mid-October, Graf von Bothmer shortened the length of the XV Corps sector by ten kilometers by stationing the German 36th Infantry Division in the southern sector, which had been formerly occupied by the

Turkish 20th Division. The XV Corps now had a corps sector with a total frontage of about ten kilometers. This was a much need respite for the Turks and provided them an opportunity to rotate the exhausted front line Turkish infantry into reserve areas for rest and rehabilitation.

In early November, the tactical situation was so favorable that, despite constant Russian attacks, the German Ledabor detachment was dissolved and withdrawn from the Turkish sector. Although the Turks were by now completely off the defensible Zlotalipa River line, the tactical situation was favorable. On November 10, 1916, Brigadier General Şevki returned to Turkey to command the XIV Corps, and the commander of that corps, Brigadier General Cevat assumed command of the XV Corps in Galicia.[34] Large-scale Russian attacks continued throughout December 1916, but the Turks were able to repulse these without further loss of ground.

The year 1917 began auspiciously for the Turkish XV Corps. The corps was significantly reinforced with units which enhanced its fighting efficiency. Among these units were independent artillery batteries, intelligence and labor detachments, an aircraft company, a balloon detachment, a field bakery company, and a veterinary hospital. The two infantry divisions had also received much needed infantry replacements and the divisions were able to form assault companies.[35] The strength of the XV Corps, in January 1917 rose to 27,031 men assigned to units and 5,668 men training in regimental depots. As a result of these reinforcements and the favorable tactical situation, moral in the Turkish units in Galicia was very high.[36] Russian attacks continued throughout January and February.

At 8 P.M. on March 5, 1917, the XV Corps came under heavy machine gun, hand grenade, and artillery attack. This signaled the start of yet another major Russian attack by three Russian infantry divisions against the Turkish sector. Fortunately for the Turks, the XV Corps occupied the very defensible high ground overlooking the Zlotalipa River valley and was able to repulse these attacks without assistance from their allies. With great determination, the Russians repeated these attacks in April 1917 and were again repulsed with heavy losses.

May was a quiet month in the Turkish sector, but in June the Russians renewed the offensive. These attacks were no more successful than previous endeavors, but continued without respite throughout the remainder of the month. In this intense battle, the twenty-four artillery batteries in the Turkish 20th Infantry Division sector expended forty-three thousand artillery shells. The fighting intensified even more and on July 1 the Turks came under gas attack from Russian artillery shelling. This was a new experience for the soldiers of the XV Corps, but the lines continued to hold. The front-line trenches were subjected to three days of continuous shelling. The Russians, reinforced by fresh Siberian and Finnish troops, continued to attack. Russians losses were thought to number about thirteen thousand men. By July 11 the Russian attacks began to subside, giving the sorely pressed Turkish regiments a respite, and at the end of July the front was relatively quiet once again. As an indicator of the severity of the summer fighting, according to Turkish reports during the period June 29 through July 2, 1917, the XV Corps lost 6 officers; in addition, two hundred forty-two soldiers were killed, 15 officers and 1,012 soldiers were wounded, and 1,275 men were missing.[37]

In early August 1917 the Turkish General Staff decided to withdraw the XV Corps from Galicia and return it to Turkey where it was desperately needed for operations against Allied offensives in Palestine and Mesopotamia. Units of the Turkish corps began to be replaced in the line by German units on August 5. The infantry divisions were brought back to staging areas which were behind the lines and adjacent to rail terminals. While preparing for departure in these staging areas, the Turkish commanders held ceremonies and parades and awarded war medals to their soldiers.[38] The artillery entrained for Constantinople and Thrace on August 16. Shortly thereafter, on August 22 the infantry regiments also departed the eastern front forever. By September 26, 1917, the final units of the XV Corps had all returned to Constantinople, but the fighting divisions of the corps would not linger there for long.

In retrospect, it is apparent from the scale and continuous nature of the Russian Army's attacks that the Russians intended to make a decisive breakthrough in the Turkish Galician sector on at least five separate occasions--and failed. Although it cannot be ignored that the Germans gave the Turks considerable assistance, especially in the fall of 1916, it also cannot be ignored that, under similar circumstances, the Austro-Hungarians frequently broke completely before the Russian steamroller. That the Turks held their ground speaks to the heroism and tenacity of the *Mehmetçik* when he was well led and adequately supplied. In his memoirs, General Erich von Falkenhayn claims that the Turks were an "uncommonly valuable asset to the Southern Army."[39] The overall losses sustained by the XV Corps are not available in contemporary sources; however, they must have been considerable--perhaps as high as twenty-five thousand men. It cannot be argued that these Turkish soldiers did not make a valuable contribution to the ability of the Central Powers to hold the line in Russia in 1916 and 1917. However, it must be borne in mind that this campaign was essentially an economy of force mission, which allowed the Germans to mass troops elsewhere for decisive operations. In the meantime, the Turks lost Erzincan in the Caucasus, Kut and Baghdad in Mesopotamia, and Gaza in Palestine. Certainly a case can be made, as Liman von Sanders thought, that these troops could have been used with greater effect in other theaters, which were more strategically significant to the Ottoman Empire.

ROMANIA

Romania entered the war on August 27, 1916. She had been alternately courted by both the entente and by the Central Powers over a two-year period. In finally choosing the entente, the Romanians expected to receive Transylvania, the Banat, and the Dobruja as payment for their efforts. The Romanian Army numbered about five hundred thousand men and was organized into ten regular and thirteen reserve infantry divisions. Although it was poorly led and poorly equipped, the entente, and the Russians especially, expected a substantial contribution to the war effort from the Romanian Army. The Russians had recommended to the Romanian General Staff that they stand fast in the easily defensible Carpathian Mountains overlooking the Transylvanian plain and to conduct instead a limited offensive aimed at seizing the Dobruja (the land between the lower Danube River and the Black Sea).[40] Unimpressed with the condition of crumbling Austro-Hungarian Army, the ambitious Romanians decided to initiate a large-scale offensive into Transylvania with the idea of seizing that territory. They divided their army into four field armies, the three best of which were oriented for an attack into Transylvania, there to link up with the advancing Russians. The weak Romanian Third Army, consisting of six divisions, was spread thinly along the southern frontier with Bulgaria.

The Romanians opened the war with a night attack on their neighbor, Austria-Hungary. In several weeks time, they had advanced about fifty miles into Transylvania. The Romanians followed up this success by developing logistical lines into the forward areas and they anticipated renewing the offensive in mid-September. In the meantime, the Central Powers had not been inactive. To the contrary; not content to simply defend Austro-Hungarian territory, the German high command saw an opportunity to destroy Romania and rapidly developed an alliance plan to do so. The Germans planned a double envelopment, which would crush the exposed Romanian armies in a battle of annihilation. The Austro-Hungarian Fourth Army would fix the Romanians in the north, while the German Ninth Army would attack south toward Bucharest. A newly formed Danube Army, comprising Bulgarians, Germans, and Turks would drive northward into the Dobruja and act as the anvil for the Ninth Army's hammer. German infantry divisions were entrained through Hungary in early September 1916. As finally configured, General Erich von Falkenhayn commanded the Ninth Army of three German and two Austrian divisions, and Field Marshal August von Mackensen commanded the polyglot Danube Army comprising the Third Bulgarian Army, the Turkish VI Corps, and a handful of small German units. Perhaps unhappy with his secondary role and with the seemingly uneven quality of his army, Mackensen's Danube Army attacked early on September 1. Falkenhayn's Ninth Army would attack later in mid-September. Nevertheless, this coordinated offensive was a remarkable logistical achievement for the Central Powers.

Obviously, the decision to provide Turkish forces for a combined offensive into Romania did not occur overnight, nor did the movement of Turkish forces into Bulgaria happen quickly. As with the deployment of Turkish troops to Galacia, Enver Paşa was determined that Turkey would be a full participant in the Balkan war effort. The surplus of forces generated by the Gallipoli victory provided him with the vehicle to accomplish this. During conversations with von Falkenhayn in the early summer of 1916, the subject of Turkish troops on the eastern front had come up and resulted in the deployment of the XV Corps to Hungary. About the same time, the VI Corps was also alerted for service in the Balkans. This corps was commanded by Brigadier General Hilmi. On July 20, 1916, the Fifth Army Commander was ordered to prepare the 15th Infantry

Division, commanded by Lieutenant Colonel Hamdi, and the 25th Infantry Division, commanded by Colonel Şükrü Ali, for service in the Balkans. These divisions came from the XVII and the XIV Corps, respectively. One of the infantry regiments of the 25th Infantry Division was mainly composed of Arabs, who did not speak Turkish very well; therefore the division commander requested permission to trade this Arab regiment for a Turkish regiment. This request was approved and upon deployment, the strength of the 25th Infantry Division stood at 192 officers and 12,501 men.[41] Several artillery units and machinegun companies were added to each division. As the infantry divisions and corps headquarters moved forward to the vicinity of Adrianople, the corps and division commanders met for the first time on August 2, where the commanders learned that they would move against Romania. The formations continued to mass throughout August 1916. Meanwhile, the Turkish General Staff sent a General Staff officer, Major Hüseyin Hüsnü to Sofia to act as liaison officer at Mackensen's headquarters.[42] However, moving the 15th Infantry Division from Manisa, near Symrna, was not an easy task. The 25th Infantry Division was projected to be ready at Uzunköprü on September 7, but the 15th Infantry Division would not completely arrive until September 26. This did not fit with Mackensen's aggressive timetable, which called for an offensive on September 1. The chief of the Turkish General Staff's Railroad Directorate worked tirelessly and coordinated with the Bulgarians to speed up deployment. However, the deployment was seriously delayed and these forces missed the opening attacks.

The combined railroad directorates programmed the 25th Infantry Division to proceed to Pravade and the 15th Infantry Division to the port city of Varna. From there, these two divisions would road march by foot to the VI Corps assembly area at Dokuzağaç. This area was in the center of the Dobruja front and was about fifty kilometers north of the Romanian-Bulgarian frontier. Once there, the Turkish infantry divisions would conduct a relief in place and take over the sector held by the Bulgarian 6th Infantry Division.

By September 17 the 25th Infantry Division was concentrated in the corps assembly area. Instead of simply taking over the Bulgarian lines, it vigorously attacked the Romanians for several days, in an attempt to move the front forward. These attacks failed, as did similar Bulgarian attacks on the flanks. By the September 21 the 25th Infantry Division was solidly in the line. On its right flank was the Bulgarian 1st Cavalry Division and on its left was the Bulgarian 6th Infantry Division. Attacking through the day of September 24, the Turkish division gained about six kilometers of ground. On October 1 and 2 the Romanians conducted a major counteroffensive designed to envelop the Third Bulgarian Army and the 25th Infantry Division came under heavy attack. These Gallipoli veterans held their ground against repeated Romanian attacks. Fortunately, the leading regiment of the 15th Infantry Division arrived on October 2 and went immediately into action on the flanks of the Turkish sector. The Romanian attacks continued for six days. Additional units of the 15th Infantry Division arriving in sector provided a welcome reserve. During these battles, the 25th Infantry Division fought with three regiments abreast (from left to right: the 56th Infantry regiment, the 59th Infantry Regiment, and the 75th Infantry Regiment) on a ten kilometer front. The divisional artillery was broken into three groups so that each regiment had direct support artillery. The intensity of the fighting was reflected in the casualties in the 25th Infantry Division with 18 officers and 794 men killed, 39 officers and 2,854 men wounded, and 8 officers and 944 men missing.[43] This totaled 4,657 men out of a beginning roll call of about twelve thousand men.

Over the next two weeks the remainder of the 15th Infantry Division arrived and gradually assumed control of the left flank of the VI Corps sector, which had extended to a width of ten kilometers. With the entire corps in position, it was time to attack. At 6:30 A.M. on the morning of September 19 the Turkish divisional and corps artillery began to register its fires (a practice the XV Corps artillerymen learned from German artillery experts in which accurate firing data is found by shooting at predesignated targets of known location) and at 8 A.M. began its artillery preparation fires. Then, at 10:00, the artillery fires ceased and the Turkish infantry went over the top. The initial objective was a hill mass about eight kilometers beyond the frontlines. By 1916 standards, this constituted a very deep objective for a corps in any nation's army. The fighting was hard and lasted for three days. The Turks broke through and advanced over twenty kilometers.

At 7 A.M. on the morning of September 24th, the Bulgarians telephoned the VI Corps commander and revised the operations order. The Turkish VI Corps was to turn on its axis and attack west towards Cernovoda on the Danube River. This altered the VI Corps direction of advance 90 degrees from north to west! With some difficulty the corps adjusted its orientation, and by nightfall both infantry divisions were reoriented and advancing west. At 11 A.M. on September 25 the Turkish 75th Infantry Regiment reached the Danube, thereby cutting off several Romanian formations. The attack ended on the 27, with the Turks deep inside Romanian territory and, with the Bulgarians, holding the narrowest part of the Dobruja, between the Black Sea and the Danube River. The total casualties for the VI Corps were heavy: 1,864 killed, 7,720 wounded, and 2,020 missing.[44] Proportionately, these were massive casualties for a corps of less than thirty thousand men. Following the heavy losses earlier in the 25th Infantry Division, casualties on this scale were devastating to combat effectiveness.

The battered Romanians were in even worse shape, and Mackensen sensed that it was time to push relentlessly forward. The VI Corps attacked again on November 1, 1916, with assigned objectives that lay over twenty kilometers to the north. The Turkish 15th Infantry Division met with immediate and astounding success, literally breaking through the Romanian lines. In a single day, the division swept almost to its assigned objectives. The 25th Infantry Division was switched to follow in train and quickly came forward.

At this time, a dramatic development occurred; the Turks received reports that Russian formations were entering Romania in strength to honor the political and military agreements that had brought Romania into the war. The advance was halted and the Turks and Bulgarians worked feverishly to prepare a defensive position. Between November 9 and 15 a covering force of two Bulgarian divisions was thrown sixteen kilometers out in front of the main line of defense to slow the advancing Russian Army. Holding fine defensive positions on high ground, the VI Corps dug in to await the Russians. They had not long to wait, and on November 17 the Russians broke through the covering force and assaulted the main defensive positions throughout the following week. These attacks failed, as did the Russian follow-on attacks on December 1 through 3. The rock-solid VI Corps held its ground.

Believing that the Russians had exhausted themselves, Mackensen decided to resume the offensive and ordered the Third Army and the VI Corps to plan attacks. On December 8, 1916, the Turks again pushed north, breaking through the Russian lines. By December 15 their forward elements were eighteen kilometers from their starting trenches. The attacks routed the Russians and the Turks began a relentless pursuit of the demoralized and retreating enemy. In the next five days, the hard-marching Turkish infantry divisions covered over fifty kilometers, and on December 22 they reached the high ground overlooking the Danube River delta. Within two days, the infantry division headquarters closed to within eight kilometers of the river and the corps cavalry squadron seized the town of Isaccea on the Danube itself. It was a magnificent achievement.

Mackensen was not yet finished with his Turks. Intending to complete the gigantic encirclement of the Romanian forces, begun earlier, Mackensen ordered the VI Corps to reverse itself and turn south. The entire corps reoriented and began a rapid foot march toward the town of Harsova, fifty kilometers to the southwest and rear of the corps, on the banks of the Danube River. Turning over their hard-won positions on the lower Danube to the Bulgarians, the corps began its march down a single road south. The leading 15th Infantry Division and the VI Corps headquarters reached the river on December 30, and on January 1, 1917, began crossing. The 25th Infantry Division arrived on January 11 and made the crossing a week later. In a fifteen-day period, in the winter, the VI Corps had marched by foot over two hundred kilometers. Clearly Mackensen was growing to appreciate the capabilities of the Turks.

In fact, Field Marshal Mackensen had earlier requested an additional Turkish corps to help him finish off the Romanians. Eager to get into more Turkish troops into a campaign that was promising to become a great victory, Enver Paşa and the Turkish General Staff, decided to provide an additional infantry division. Enver immediately alerted the 26th Infantry Division, then stationed in the Gallipoli area, for service in the Balkans. Alerted on September 29, this division reached the rail terminal at Uzunköprü on November 19. The three regiment 26th Infantry Division was commanded by Lieutenant Colonel Mahit Fahri, who ordered his division to entrain for Bulgaria at once. Detraining and subsequently crossing the Danube at Zistrovi, the 26th Infantry Division was in contact with the Romanian Army on November 25. Turkey now had a total of three divisions fighting against Romania. Mackensen pushed these Turks as hard as he could and the division began a series of attacks toward the Romanian capital of Bucharest. Attacking relentlessly, the 26th Infantry Division advanced over one hundred kilometers by December 1. Counterattacked by the Romanian

9th Infantry Division, the 26th held its ground and on the following day, the leading division of Falkenhayn's 9th Army made contact with the Turks. On December 4 the combined armies of Falkenhayn and Mackensen began their assault on the city of Bucharest, which fell four days later. Determined to drive the Romanian Army physically out of its own country, Mackensen continued his pursuit. Advancing an average of twenty-five kilometers a day, the 26th Infantry Division marched north. One hundred fifty kilometers farther, on January 5, 1917, the 26th Infantry Division made contact with units of the Turkish VI Corps, at last coming under the command that corps. At 1 A.M., the next day, VI Corps Commander Mustafa Hilmi published his first operations order for his new three-division corps. On January 7, 1917, the VI Corps deployed 26th Infantry Division and the 15th Infantry Division to attack toward the banks of the Sered River, north of the city of Ibrail. The attacks secured the high ground overlooking the river and by early February, the corps deployed the 26th, the 15th, and the 25th Infantry Divisions, from left to right across a twenty-kilometer corps front. The Romanian campaign had ended.

The VI Corps would remain along the Danube River until April 1918, when it was withdrawn for deployment to the Caucasus. On May 13 of that year, the corps headquarters deployed by ship from Costanza, bound for the newly captured Black Sea port of Batum. The 15th Infantry Division accompanied it, ending Turkish involvement on the Romanian front, both the 25th and the 26th Infantry Division having departed previously in the fall of 1917 for other more active theaters of war. Although the Romanian campaign was relatively brief, for the Turks—only about five months of actual hard combat—it was very costly and wore down three excellent infantry divisions. Perhaps as many as twenty thousand Turkish soldiers became casualties in this campaign. In combat against the Romanians and the Russians, the Turkish infantry divisions had proven themselves to be reliable and courageous formations. Of particular value to Field Marshal Mackensen was the remarkable ability of the Turkish soldiers to endure hard foot marches under adverse weather conditions. In the latter stages of the Romanian campaign, the daily marches by the VI Corps and the 26th Infantry Division were truly remarkable. Overall, the Turks made a valuable contribution to the conquest of Romania and added luster to their reputation as relentless adversaries.

MACEDONIA

A combination of events served to bring the Turkish Army back to Salonika in Macedonia, from which they had been driven in 1912. Although located in neutral Greece, an Anglo-French Expeditionary Force had landed there on October 3, 1915. This small force of two divisions was put ashore in the vain hopes of aiding the Serbs, then engaged in the final and hopeless battle for the defense of their country. The Allies hoped that the Serbian Army could, at least, retreat to the safety of the Greek port city if forced out of their homeland. Unfortunately, because of the intervention of the Bulgarians, the Serbs were unable to do this, and were forced instead into the Albanian ports of Durazzo and Valona. From there, they were evacuated and brought by sea to Salonika. About 150,000 Serbian soldiers thus made their way to join the Allied force in Greece. By the summer of 1916, this force grew to over a quarter of a million men. Although this army had limited logistical support, and even more limited political support (Greece was neutral), it represented a serious threat to the Vardar Valley and to the newly established railway lines linking Germany and Austria-Hungary with Bulgaria and Turkey. Therefore the Allied Salonika Army acted as a kind of a magnet for substantial numbers of German and Bulgarian forces. By the summer of 1916, the Allies had about 350,000 men in the Salonika bridgehead and their commander, French General Sarrail, was anxious to expand his perimeter.

On September 12, 1916, the German General Staff again asked Enver Paşa to provide additional Turkish troops for the Balkan theater, this time to help contain or reduce Salonika. In a typically flamboyant gesture Enver promised to send troops that very day.[45] Enver decided to send the 50th Infantry Division, then resting near Izmit in Asia Minor, fifty kilometers east of Constantinople, and alerted them for deployment at 3:00 P.M. that same day. It was a fast reaction and the Germans must have been surprised. Enver planned to bring the division to Scutari by train and then by boat across the Bosphorus to Bakirkoy on the European side. The division began preparations for movement on the next day.

The 50th Infantry Division was commanded by Staff Lieutenant Colonel Şükrü Naili and had 11,979 men and 1241 animals assigned to the division. The division had a total of 11,320 rifles, 12 machine guns, 16 cannons, and 190 wagons as its weaponry.[46] At nearly full strength, the division entrained from Bakirkoy for the Greek city of Drama and the Bulgarian Army's front at Salonika. Arriving in early October 1916, the 50th Infantry Division was assigned a sector at the mouth of the Struma River directly on the Aegean Sea. With its left flank firmly against the sea, the division's right flank neighbor was the Bulgarian 10th Infantry Division. The division deployed two regiments forward and retained one in reserve. Because of the overwhelming British naval presence in the Aegean, the division also had to deploy an entire infantry battalion to guard its vulnerable coastal flank. It had not long to wait for action. Probing attacks by British troops were turned back within the week, as was a major attack on October 31. Stalemate then set in along the divisional sector.

Stretched thin for troops by the ongoing Romanian campaign, the Bulgarians and Germans asked for further Turkish assistance at the beginning of November 1916. The Turkish General Staff responded positively to this request on November 9, and ordered the headquarters of the new XX Corps and the 46th Infantry Division to prepare for Balkan service. Brigadier General Abdülkerim, the commander of the XX Corps reported to the Turkish General Staff for orders and learned that his corps would join the Bulgarian Second Army in Greece. By November 27, units of the corps were moving. Like the 50th Infantry Division, the 46th Infantry Division was at full strength, with 12,609 men, 9,858 rifles, 12 heavy machine guns, 16 cannons, and 2,150 animals.[47] A replacement regiment, with which the corps could train incoming draftees, was also ordered to accompany the force. The corps headquarters reached Drama on December 6 and made contact with the 50th Infantry Division, then already holding a portion of the line. By mid-December, the corps was in the line defending a front of about thirty kilometers, in the middle of which was a ten-kilometer long lake, which effectively split the sector into two disconnected halves. There was much snow that winter in the high mountains and service in Greece was arduous but there was little combat action on the front. For the next three months, the XX Corps enjoyed a period of relative quiet, although there were periods of regimental level fighting. In the corps' last major engagement, the Turkish 177th Infantry Regiment was involved in heavy fighting against the French during March 1917.

Because of the low level of activity in Macedonia and because of pressing operational requirements in other theaters, the Turkish General Staff decided to withdraw the XX Corps in late March 1917. By April, the corps headquarters and both infantry divisions were withdrawn from combat and were moving back to Turkish Thrace. From there, the 46th Infantry Division would deploy to Mesopotamia and the 50th Infantry Division would deploy to Palestine. The Turks left a small detachment in Macedonia, comprising an infantry regiment, which would remain there for almost another year. This ended the Turkish contribution to containing the Salonika bridgehead and, unusually for such endeavors, it cost them very little in human terms.

THE SIEGE OF KUT AL AMARA

January 1916 seemed to offer brighter prospects for the Turkish Army in Mesopotamia than had hitherto been possible in that distant theater of war. Nurettin had driven off the British at Ctesiphon and had encircled General Townshend's 6th Infantry Division at Kut Al Amara. Some reinforcements had arrived from the Third Army and within the Turkish Sixth Army the situation seemed favorable. On the negative side of the balance sheet, however, the 38th Infantry Division was disbanded in late December 1915 for want of replacements and there was an Imperial relief force poised to relieve Kut. Townshend appeared solidly entrenched and, oddly enough, there was both river and telegraph traffic between the encircled Townshend and the relief force under General Aylmer.

Nurettin had divided his army into two parts. The XVIII Corps, composed of the 45th and 51st Infantry Division encircled Kut and the XIII Corps with the 35th and 52nd Infantry Divisions, blocked the British relief force about thirty kilometers downstream. On January 6 and 7 the British began to probe the Turkish lines and began to extend their cavalry around both flanks of the Turkish position.[48] These probes were speedily repulsed. The British launched a stronger attack on January 8, 1916, which also failed. Concerned about the British cavalry presence on their right flank, a Turkish cavalry regiment was brought forward. On January 12 Aylmer attempted to break through the lines of the Turkish 52nd Infantry Division in a night attack. His leading brigade was discovered by the alert Turks and was badly handled before abandoning the attack. Strong British attacks continued to hammer the 52nd Infantry Division from January 16 through 21. The Turkish line was buttressed on the right by the river and on the left by a salt marsh prohibiting movement. It was an unassailable position against which the British repeatedly conducted frontal assaults. The XVIII Corps was strongly dug in along the Wadi-Nakhailat and the relief force was discouraged from further attacks. This news was relayed to an astonished Townshend in Kut.

Despite his victories and despite the current favorable tactical situation, Enver Paşa decided to replace Nurettin with Colonel Halil Bey. Technically, German Field Marshal von der Goltz was in command of this army and the entire Mesopotamian and Persian Theater as well, but he left the daily conduct of tactical operations to the Turkish commanders. The change of command occurred on January 20, but Halil Bey did not change the basic tactical dispositions already made by Nurettin. By late January Townshend began to consider the option of surrendering his force. Seeing the deteriorating condition of the beleaguered British and Indian troops in Kut, Halil Bey determined to starve them out. Additionally, the Turks continuously lobbed shells into the town, which served to keep everyone inside the British lines on edge. In the meantime, the Turks repeatedly conducted feint attacks, which further exhausted the British, who were forced to respond as if these were real attacks. In February, as the encircled force at Kut went on half rations, the Turks received the 2nd Infantry Division as a reinforcement. In March the Turks intensified their artillery barrage and kept aircraft over the town on a more or less continuous basis.[49] Conditions within Kut worsened by the day.

Aylmer made several subsequent relief attempts, the first on March 8 which failed. This attack occurred on the south bank of the Tigris River. The newly arrived 2nd Infantry Division was assigned to the XIII Corps and with the 35th Infantry Division had established a very strong defensive line about ten kilometers east of Kut. This line was well backed by artillery and there were several infantry battalions in reserve in each Turkish infantry division sector. By this time, the Kut garrison was so weak that the 51st Infantry Division was brought forward to reinforce the 2nd and the 35th. As the British attacks failed, the Turks vigorously pushed forward.

April 6 brought renewed British attacks on the 51st Infantry Division which had constructed a solid defensive line including minefields.[50] Although the division repelled these attacks it withdrew to a fallback position three kilometers to the rear. Repeating an assault in a right-left sequence, the British launched a large three-division offensive on the XVIII Corps holding the south bank on the Tigris position on 17-18 April 1916. These attacks gained no ground and the Turkish counterattacks punished the British severely. Turkish casualties during the period 17-19 April included 619 killed, 1,585 wounded, and 1,337 captured or missing. Since these southern attacks occurred within ten to fifteen kilometers of the center of the town of Kut the noise, smoke, and explosions must have been heard or seen by the beleaguered British.

The British relief force continued to probe the Turkish defenses throughout the following week with no success. Thus, the Turkish Sixth Army weathered many serious attempts to relieve Kut during the first four months of 1916. All were beaten back. By April 22 it was apparent to Townshend that further resistance was useless and that he must surrender. On April 27 Townshend asked for terms of surrender, hoping for generous conditions from Halil Bey. In particular, Townshend was completely out of food and both his troops and the local population were on the verge of starving. Townshend asked therefore, above all, for immediate assistance in rationing his force. There was much confusion as blindfolded staff officers were passed between the two armies and further confusion concerning the exact terms of surrender. Finally, Townshend himself met with Halil Bey, von der Goltz having died of cholera on April 19. Townshend attempted to buy his army out of captivity with a promise of a one-million-pound payment.[51] He also attempted to secure some sort of a parole. However, in the end, Halil Bey demanded an unconditional surrender, which Townshend was forced to accept. Over the next two days, the British and Indians destroyed their howitzers, ammunition stocks, and other military equipment. At 1:00 P.M., on April 29, 1916, a Turkish infantry regiment marched into Kut to receive the surrender.

The surrender of Townshend's 6th "Poona" Division was the largest mass surrender of Imperial troops between Yorktown in 1783 and Singapore in 1942. It was a horrible embarrassment for British arms, although the total number of soldiers lost was hardly a day's worth of cannon fodder in the big battles raging in Flanders. Overall, Townshend surrendered 13,309 men, including 272 British and 204 Indian officers, 2,592 British and 6,988 Indian soldiers, and 3,248 noncombatant troops.[52] Over four thousand of these men subsequently died in Turkish captivity. Seventy percent of the British men taken prisoner died. Halil Bey exchanged 1,136 sick and wounded British and Indian soldiers for an approximately equal number of unfit Turks (10 officers and 1,085 enlisted men). The Turks also recorded capturing forty artillery pieces, three aircraft, two river steamers, and forty automobiles.[53] The first Turkish food supplies arrived by relief boat on May 1, 1916. Townshend and his aides were sent to Baghdad on May 3, and the Turks began to evacuate their prisoners the following day. The first British out of Kut after Townshend were 4 generals, 160 officers, and 180 of their helpers[54] (or "batmen" as they were called in the British Army). To date, the British had lost forty thousand men in the Mesopotamian campaign. Colonel Halil Bey became an overnight hero and received the honorific "Paşa." It was a magnificent achievement for Turkish arms.

With the surrender of the Imperial forces at Kut Al Amara, the campaign in Mesopotamia stalemated. The fighting had exhausted both sides and without Townshend to rescue, there seemed no be good reason for the British to hurry up river. Halil Bey began to redeploy slowly his forces downstream, carefully fortifying both banks of the Tigris and finally finding enough surplus forces to fortify the Euphrates as well. There was little activity in Mesopotamia for the remainder of 1916 until December, when a renewed and greatly reinforced Imperial force under General Maude again began the slow march up river.

SECOND INVASION OF PERSIA

In early May 1916 Enver Paşa journeyed to Baghdad to confer with Halil Paşa and Colonel von Lossow about the possibilities of a renewed offensive against Persia. Enver already had troops in motion coming to Mesopotamia; however, the surrender of Kut in April made their use in the Tigris-Euphrates valley redundant. Enver was eager to use them in an offensive capacity and had hatched a plan to invade Persia. The 2nd Infantry Division, from the II Corps had already reached Mosul and its sister divisions, the 4th and the 6th Infantry Divisions, were due in theater by the end of May.[55]

Enver's plan was ambitious. The XIII Corps would detach the 35th and the 52nd Infantry Divisions to its Sixth Army sister, the XVIII Corps. In place of these tired and understrength formations, the XIII Corps would assume command of the fresh and rested 2nd, 4th, and 6th Infantry Divisions. Additionally, an independent cavalry brigade, some irregular units, and Persian nationalist volunteers would swell the ranks of the XIII Corps. The Germans promised artillery (which never came). Altogether, the force would total approximately twenty-five thousand men. Opposing them in Persia was a mixed Russian force equivalent to several Russian divisions, but this force was not concentrated.

The commander of the XIII Corps, Ali Insan Paşa, began his advance in late May after concentrating his corps near the frontier. The aggressive Russians soon attacked the 6th Infantry Division and attempted to encircle both the division and the headquarters of the XIII Corps at the border town of Hankin on June 3, 1916. The Russians came close to succeeding, but their thinly spread infantry battalions were held in check while the centrally positioned Turks crushed the encircling Russian cavalry. Threatened with defeat in detail, the Russians withdrew. Turkish loses were light, 85 killed, 276 wounded, and 68 missing.[56] After the ill-advised Russian preemptive attack on the Turkish 6th Infantry Division, Ali Insan Paşa crossed the Persian frontier on June 8. The terrain in this area consisted of fairly rugged mountains with narrow valleys which made the defense easier. The Russians, under Baratov, skillfully conducted a fighting retreat. The main Turkish force comprised the 2nd and the 6th Infantry Divisions, which advanced through the mountains along the main road to Kermansah. On the Turkish left (northern) flank, the 4th Infantry Division crossed the frontier from Süleymaniye and pushed east toward Sine and Kurve. This division was reinforced with some Persian volunteer battalions and was now styled the Mosul Group.[57] The main force found a strong Russian defensive position near Karind and halted to prepare an attack.

The Turks attacked on June 28 and carried Karind two days later. By now Ali Insan Paşa was over one hundred fifty kilometers beyond the frontier and he proceeded slowly eastward. The Russians continued to retreat and concentrated for a stand at Hamadan. The XIII Corps closed on Hamadan on August 1 and after a brief reorganization fought a six-day battle, taking the town on August 9, 1916. Baratov pulled back some one hundred kilometers and sat in blocking positions at key mountain passes to await reinforcements. The Turkish campaign came to a stuttering halt. The actual combat casualties of the XIII Corps had been very light, but disease had ravaged the force. Perhaps as many as several thousand Turks died of diseases such as cholera and typhus on the march to Hamadan. The XIII Corps was now split into two distinct elements; the main body of the corps at Hamadan (2nd and 6th Infantry Divisions) and the Mosul Group (4th Infantry Division), which was screening well forward of the frontier in front of Süleymaniye. This meant that the three infantry divisions of the corps were not mutually supporting each other because of the distances between the formations. Additionally, the large numbers of Persian volunteers predicted to join the Turks had not materialized. For these reasons, the ever cautious Ali Insan Paşa decided that his force was insufficient to continue the conquest of Persia. The Turkish Second Invasion of Persia now firmly stalled, and the XIII Corps settled in to await developments and limited its activities to a series of patrols to the north and east of Hamadan.[58] Table 5.5 shows the disposition of Turkish forces in December 1916.

SINAI/SECOND SUEZ CANAL INVASION

In Syria, Palestine, and in the Sinai, after the failed expedition against the Suez Canal, the remainder of 1915 proved to be a very uneventful year. Cemal Paşa's Fourth Army continued to command both the VIII and the XII Corps, but his army was continually stripped of experienced units and personnel. Fortunately, the British were quiet throughout this time and contented themselves with running rail lines and logistical lines out into the Sinai to facilitate future operations. In the absence of fighting, Cemal contented himself with organizational matters concerning his army.[59]

Cemal decided to create the "Desert Force Headquarters," which would command and control the forces in the Sinai. This headquarters was located at Beersheba and Cemal placed German Colonel Von Kress in command. The headquarters was organized into two components; the GHQ Desert Force, which was charged with operational and tactical matters, and the Desert Lines of Communications Inspectorate, which was charged with logistics and communications. Slowly, over 1915, most of Cemal's experienced divisions were ordered north for the meatgrinder at Gallipoli: he lost the 8th, 10th, and 25th Infantry Divisions. He also lost machine guns and field howitzers. Many of his remaining battalions were composed of Arab conscripts who spoke no Turkish. Additionally, in 1915 Cemal faced Armenian insurrections in Urfa and Leitun.

The year 1916 began uneventfully for Cemal and the Fourth Army. Enver Paşa came for a visit in February 1916 and made an extended tour of the army area. Enver and Cemal met with Sherif Faisal, who was then on friendly terms with the Turks. However, Sherif Hussein was then in the early stages of raising his rebellion against the Turkish yoke. This worried both Enver and Cemal. In April, German and Austro-Hungarian help began to arrive in the form of German aircraft and Austro-Hungarian howitzer batteries. The aircraft were put to immediate work scouting the British positions along the canal.

Table 5.5
Disposition of Turkish Forces, December 1916

GALICIA
XV Corps: 19, 20 Inf. Div.

ROMANIA
VI Corps: 15, 25, 26 Inf. Div.

MACEDONIA
XX Corps: <u>49</u>, 50 Inf. Div.

THRACE
First Army
I Corps: 14, 16 Inf. Div.
1 Cav. Bde.

GALLIPOLI
Fifth Army
XIV Corps: 57, 59 Inf. Div.

SYRIA-PALESTINE
Fourth Army
VIII Corps: 3, 23, 24, 27 Inf. Div.
XII Corps: 41, 42, 43, 46 Inf. Div.

CAUCASIA
Third Army
1st Cauc. Corps: 9, 10, 36 Cauc. Inf. Div.
2nd Cauc. Corps: 5, 11, 37 Cauc. Inf. Div.
V Corps: Coastal Detachments
49 Inf. Div.
2 Regular Cav. Div.
Van Cav. Bde.
Van Jandarma (Inf) Div.
Second Army
II Corps: 1, 47 Inf. Div.
IV Corps: 11, 12 Inf. Div.
XVI Corps: 5, 8 Inf. Div.
3 Reserve Cav. Div.

ARABIA-YEMEN
VII Corps: 21, 22, 39, 40 Inf. Div.

MESOPOTAMIA
Sixth Army
XIII Corps: 2, 4, 6 Inf. Div.
XVIII Corps: 45, 51, 52 Inf. Div.

Note: Units in boldface type indicate new formations; units underlined indicate units redeployed since August 1916; units in bold italic type indicate seriously understrength units. Units inactivated: 9, 10, 17, 18, 29, 31, 32, 34, 35, 38 Inf. Div.; units redesignated: 13, 28, 30, 33 Inf. Div.

All was not totally quiet. When Sherif Hussein's revolt broke out that spring, Cemal appointed Fahri Paşa to command at Medina and to maintain control of the Hedjaz railway. With a handful of Turkish battalions, this officer performed outstanding service in keeping lines of communications open. For the remainder of 1916, the Turks managed to keep the railway open on a more or less regular basis.

Conventional combat action renewed itself in this theater when the Turks pushed forward towards the British outpost at Katia. On April 23, 1916, von Kress sent his cavalry forward to pin the British reserves near Kantara. Meanwhile, a small infantry force of two battalions supported by a four gun artillery battery successfully encircled a British cavalry unit at Katia.[60] In this action von Kress and his Ottoman soldiers captured the better part of a British cavalry regiment and its commander.

In late April, the first reinforcement from the victorious Gallipoli Army arrived in Palestine. This was the experienced 3rd Infantry Division, full of hardened and disciplined combat veterans. Concerned about elaborate British offensive preparations along the canal, Cemal and von Kress decided to launch a second expedition against the British defenses. This limited attack was intended to keep the British off balance and to spoil their plans. The attack force was built around the 3rd Infantry Division and additionally contained four batteries of German and Austrian artillery, a machine gun battalion, and two antiaircraft gun sections. It totaled 11,873 men armed with 3,293 rifles, 56 machine guns, and 30 artillery pieces.[61] At the beginning of July 1916 this force closed with the British at Katia and Bir Romani. On the evening of July 16, 1916, the Turks pressed forward with a force of about an infantry regiment and began to prepare their attack. Von Kress planned to pin the British 52nd Infantry Division in its defenses forward of Bir Romani and then to swing a left hook around it in hopes of cutting it off. The British were spread out along their newly built railroad and were deployed in vulnerable divisional clusters stretching back into Egypt. He began his attack at 5:15 A.M. on the morning of August 4, 1916. As the 31st Infantry Regiment went forward to pin the British, von Kress swung the 32nd and the 39th Infantry Regiments around the left and into the British rear.[62] At 2 P.M., the British counterattacked halting the Turkish attacks. The Turkish attacks stalled later that day and on the following day British reserves hammered the Turkish to a halt. Von Kress realized that his attack had failed and on August 7 began to pull back his forces. The Turkish losses were again light; about a thousand were killed or wounded. Thereafter the Sinai front lapsed into a period of stasis and inaction.

NOTES

1. W. E. D. Allen and Paul Muratoff, *Caucasian Battlefields, A History of the Wars on the Turco-Caucasian Border 1828-1921* (Cambridge: Cambridge University Press, 1952), 331.

2. Turkish General Staff, *Birinci Dünya Harbinde Kafkas Cephesi 3 ncü Ordu Harekati. Cilt II*. (Ankara: GK Basimevi, 1986), 4.
3. Allen and Muratoff, *Caucasian Battlefields*, 342.
4. Turkish General Staff, *3 ncü Ord Harekati*, 51.
5. Allen and Muratoff, *Caucasian Battlefields*, 342.
6. Ibid., 351.
7. Turkish General Staff, *3 ncü Ordu Harekati*, 54.
8. Ibid., 79.
9. Ibid., 90. The Turks estimated Russian infantry strength at 110,000 to their own 38,000.
10. Allen and Muratoff, *Caucasian Battlefields*, 361.
11. Ibid., 363.
12. Turkish General Staff, *3 ncü Ordu Harekati*, 120.
13. Ibid., 136. Enver's message equated the veteran Gallipoli divisions to laundry starch in shirt collars.
14. Ibid., 148.
15. Allen and Muratoff, *Caucasian Battlefields*, 399.
16. General Fahri Belen, *Birinci Cihan Harbında Turk Harbi 1916 Yili Hareketleri* (Ankara: Basimevi, 1965), chart after page 74.
17. Allen and Muratoff, *Caucasian Battlefields*, 411.
18. Turkish General Staff, *3 ncü Ordu Harekati*, 380.
19. Ibid., 437.
20. Turkish General Staff, *3ncü Ordu Harekati*, 404.
21. Allen and Muratoff, *Caucasian Battlefields*, 437.
22. Belen, *1916 Yili Hareketleri*, Kuruluş (Chart): 5.
23. Holger W. Herwig, *The First World War Germany and Austria-Hungary 1914–1918* (London: Arnold, 1997), 208-210.
24. General Erich von Falkenhayn, *General Headquarters, 1914-1916, and Its Critical Decisions* (London: Hutchinson, n.d.), 273.
25. Otto Liman von Sanders, *Five Years in Turkey* (London: Bailliere, Tindall & Cox, 1928), 120-125.
26. Von Falkenhayn, *General Headquarters*, 259.
27. Turkish General Staff, *Birinci Dünya Harbinde Türk Harbi Avrupa Cepheleri (özet)* (Ankara: Genelkurmay Basım Evi, 1996), 14.
28. Liman von Sanders, *Five Years in Turkey*, 121.
29. Turkish General Staff, *Avrupa Cepheleri*, 63. Replacements received in September would be as young as fourteen to fifteen years old, and as old as fifty to sixty years old. Most of these men were completely untrained, and 20 percent were unable to speak Turkish.
30. Ibid., 61.
31. Ibid., Kroki (Map) 4.
32. Ibid., 32-36.
33. Ibid., Kroki (Map) 8.
34. Ibid., 64.
35. Ibid., 63. On December 12, 1916, the corps received 2,685 trained soldiers as combat replacements and 6,700 untrained soldiers for the regimental depots.
36. Turkish General Staff, *Avrupa Cepheleri*, 64-68.
37. Ibid., 64.
38. Ibid., 59-60.
39. Von Falkenhayn, *General Headquarters*, 273.

40. Cyril Falls, *The Great War* (G. P. Putnam's: New York, 1959).
41. Turkish General Staff, *Avrupa Cepheleri*, 91.
42. Ibid., 92.
43. Ibid., 130.
44. Ibid., 151.
45. Ibid., 219.
46. Ibid., 220.
47. Ibid., 229-230.
48. Turkish General Staff, *Birinci Dünya Harbinde Turk Harbi IIIncu Cilt Irak-Iran Cephesi, 1914-1918, Inci Kisim* (Ankara: GK Basimevi, 1979), Kroki (Map) 47.
49. Ronald Millar, *Death of an Army: The Siege of Kut, 1915-1916* (Boston: Houghton Mifflin, 1970), 194.
50. Turkish General Staff, *Irak-Iran Cephesi*, 761.
51. Millar, *Death of an Army*, 256.
52. Turkish General Staff, *Irak-Iran Cephesi*, 780.
53. Millar, *Death of an Army*, 284.
54. Turkish General Staff, *Irak-Iran Cephesi*, 781.
55. It was the movement of these formations to Mesopotamia, which delayed the movement of the Second Army to Diyarbakir.
56. Belen, *1916 Yili Hareketleri*, 176-177.
57. Ibid., Kuruluş (Chart) 15.
58. Ibid., 194-195.
59. Cemal Pasa, *Memories of a Turkish Statesman, 1913-1919* (London: Hutchinson, n.d.), 164.
60. Belen, *1916 Yili Hareketleri,* 208.
61. Ibid., 211.
62. Ibid., 214.

6
Strategic Pause, January–December 1917

1917

The year 1917 was characterized by few pitched battles and proved to be a year of respite for the Turks. It was a year of strategic pause in which the Turks gained time and strategic breathing space at minimal cost. After two brutal years of combat, this respite was badly needed but it allowed Enver, once again, to dream grand dreams. The strategic situation facing Turkey in early 1917 was both promising and worrisome at the same time. Turkish divisions were returning home from successful campaigns in the Balkans and in Hungary, the situation in the Caucasus appeared to have stabilized, Turkish soldiers threatened Persia, and increased German and Austrian assistance was finally making itself felt. It appeared possible, yet again, to seize the initiative. Set against this positive backdrop was a rapidly eroding balance of forces in Mesopotamia and in Palestine. The fundamental military question for Enver Paşa and for the Turkish General Staff was where and how to establish strategic priorities. The options were fairly simple; defensively reinforce Palestine, Mesopotamia, or the Caucasus or take the offensive with the last strategic reserve that Turkey would accumulate in the war. Turkish and German military opinion on this subject was not unified, which added to Enver's dilemma. The final solution was almost a compromise of these options. First, a newly formed army group was to be employed in Palestine, sent there to render a knock-out blow to the British and send them reeling back to the Suez Canal. Enver called this force the Yildirim or Thunderbolt Army Group.[1] Then, the Yildirim force would be sent to retake Baghdad, Mesopotamia, and Persia. Although there was a certain amount of strategic beauty in this concept, it hinged upon nonexistent interior lines of communications.

Optimistically, this was exactly what Enver and von Falkenhayn intended to do and they set the wheels in motion to accomplish these ends. However, the chronic shortfalls in strategic transportation once again crippled their plans. The Yildirim Army Group arrived in Palestine too late to conduct offensive operations but just in the nick of time to prevent a major disaster. Once there, the Yildirim Army Group was irrevocably committed to the defense of Palestine. Indeed, the timely arrival of the Yildirim infantry and cavalry divisions provided just enough reserve forces to provide the thinnest of margins necessary for a competent defense. Without these troops, it is doubtful that Cemal Paşa's Fourth Army, alone, could have held back the British. Thus, as in the 1914 deployment of forces to Thrace and the subsequent Gallipoli campaign, the deployment of the Yildirim Army Group to Palestine had an unintended and fortunate consequence in the Turk's favor.

The Allies were again relearning the bitter lesson of Gallipoli that it took superior forces and material to turn the Turks out of their trenches. They were also relearning the tactical equation that to do so would cost many lives. It is not at all surprising, given the political repercussions arising in Great Britain with large casualty lists in 1917, that both Maude's and Allenby's offensives ground to a halt after only three months of combat operations.

Overall, the Turks fought well in 1917. The Turks attempted once again to take the initiative with the Yildirim Army. In concept, this army was extremely powerful and Enver had, at last, apparently understood the principle of mass and concentration at a decisive point. However, once again the means were insufficient to accomplish the ends and the operations planned for the Yildirim Army were overcome by rapidly changing events. In Mesopotamia and in Palestine, the Turks were greatly outnumbered, outgunned, and overmatched in resources. Yet they managed to fight successful delaying retreats, losing the politically important cities of Baghdad and Jerusalem, but maintaining their armies in the field. Although there were no great victories, as there had been in 1916, there were no catastrophic defeats either. In other countries, such as France and Russia, the field armies were beginning to show signs of war weariness, internal rot and mutiny, and strategic stagnation. The Turks, on the other hand, proved as aggressive and as confident as ever. Despite huge losses, Enver Paşa and the Turkish General Staff maintained a dedication to the offensive that was remarkable at that late stage of the war.

THE CAUCASIAN FRONT

The Turkish General Staff's official history of the Third Army in the First World War composes a total of 1,660 pages of narrative text. One of the most striking features of this massive two-volume set is the total number of pages that cover the entire year of 1917–only twenty, or less than 1.5 percent of the total text.[2] Commandant Larcher spends proportionately even less on the subject–two pages out of 582 pages of narrative text.[3] Allen and Muratoff devote about the same emphasis to the year 1917, and attribute it to the weaknesses of both the Turkish and the Russian Armies in the Caucasian theater.[4]

The winter of 1916-1917 in the Caucasus was especially severe and this brought combat operations to a halt. The spring thaw brought no change to this situation. This de facto cosponsored lull in this hitherto active theater amounted to an armistice of a sort and allowed both sides to focus their attentions in other regions. During 1917 the Turkish Second and Third Armies enjoyed a much-needed respite from over two years of continuous and brutal combat. On the other side of the trenches, beginning in the summer of 1917, the Russian Army began the slow process of disintegration. The Russians began thinning the lines and conducting local withdrawals, evacuating Muş in May. Fortunately for the Russians, the Turks were in no position to take advantage of their rapidly deteriorating combat capability. The year 1917 ended, in the Caucasus, with no major battles and without any great changes in the front lines themselves.

FIRST AND SECOND GAZA

The British Imperial force in Egypt grew substantially in 1916, first by the return of the defeated Gallipoli divisions and later as territorial and cavalry formations were deployed to the area. In the late fall of 1916, this force began to push its railheads rapidly farther east toward El Arish. This forced the Turks to abandon El Arish on December 16, 1916, and retire to the Hans Yonus-El Hafir line on the old frontier.[5] However, after conferring with Enver Paşa and von Kress, Cemal Paşa decided to retire even farther and to establish a defensive line between Gaza and Beersheba.[6] Beginning the withdrawal in February, the Turkish Fourth Army was in position in its new defensive line by mid-March 1917. Cemal Paşa had received additional reinforcements that spring also: the 3rd Cavalry Division (from the Caucasus region) and the 16th Infantry Division (from Thrace). Guarding both politically sensitive Jerusalem and the long coastline, Cemal had a further three infantry divisions. Altogether, along the thirty-kilometer-long Gaza–Beersheba line, the Fourth Army had about eighteen thousand effectives. The general military situation of the late spring 1917 is shown in Map 6.1.

The British attacked on the morning of March 26, 1917, by hitting Gaza with infantry and by sending their cavalry on a short flanking movement designed to envelop the town. They nearly succeeded. By the end of the day, Gaza was almost completely encircled. However, the well dug-in Turks held in the face of repeated British assaults, and refused to retreat. The Fourth Army launched counterattacks with the 3rd and the 16th Infantry Divisions. The 3rd Cavalry Division arrived also and was ordered to Beersheba. The next day, the British began to retire. It was a very close call for the Turks and victory was achieved, once again, by a steadfast defense and by furious counterattacks. According to Cemal, the Turks lost less than 300 men killed, 750 wounded and 600 missing. The British lost about four thousand. Having won the day, von Kress wanted to launch a counteroffensive, but Cemal decided against such action.

The Turkish victory at the First Battle of Gaza, as the March 26 battle came to be called, was locally decisive in this particular theater. The battle represented

Map 6.1
General Military Situation, 1917

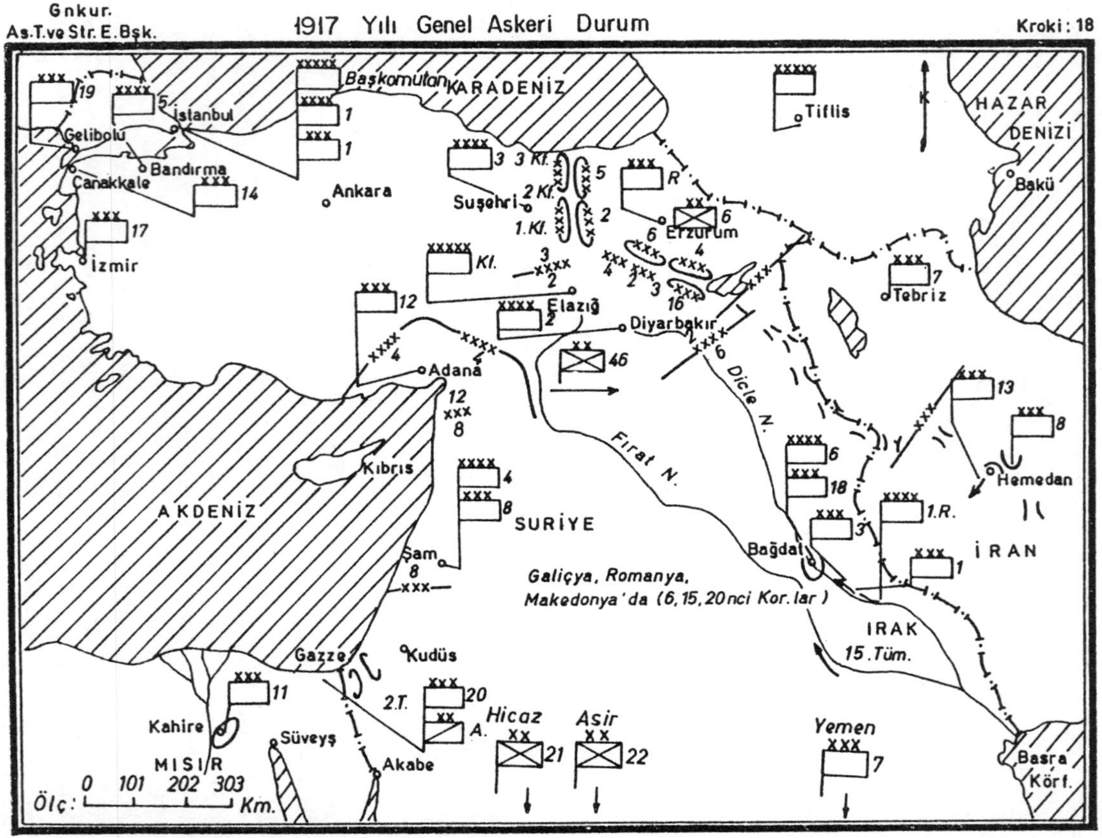

Source: General Fahri Belen, *Birinci Cihan Harbinde Turk Harbi 1917 Yili Hareketleri Incu Cilt* (Ankara: GK Basimevi, 1985), Kroki (Map) 18.

the best chance that the British had to break the Turkish line without committing major forces to the region. The Gaza-Beersheba line was the finest natural defense line between the frontier and Jerusalem. The city of Gaza rested on the Mediterranean Sea and Beersheba sat at the foot of the rugged Judean Hills. The line itself was similar in importance and geography to the El Alamein line in the Second World War. In the First Battle of Gaza, three full strength British infantry divisions and two full strength Imperial cavalry divisions were stopped cold by three understrength Turkish infantry divisions. It was a magnificent achievement for the Turks and bought them enough time to reinforce the Fourth Army. The British would eventually commit seven infantry divisions and four cavalry divisions to Palestine.

The Second Battle of Gaza began on April 17, 1917, and lasted three days. In the intervening twenty-fours days, Cemal Paşa had brought forward the 53rd Infantry Division.[7] This division was sadly understrength but contributed about two thousand rifles to the defense. The British had also, in the meantime, brought up an additional infantry division and additional mounted formations. The British even deployed a few tanks and gas shells[8] here in the desert for the first time in history and brought additional artillery forward as well. The scales of combat potential still remained tipped in the British favor; however, the Turks had not sat idle and had increased the width and the depth of their lines. This time, supported by naval gunfire, the British launched frontal attacks directly into the Turkish front near Gaza. Two days later, after sustaining about sixty-five hundred casualties, the British called off the attack. Turkish casualties were heavier in this battle--about two thousand men altogether[9]--but the Turks still held Gaza. The British generals were relieved of command. Cemal recounted that the British left three of their eight tanks within the Turkish trench lines. April ended with the Turkish lines intact and with an increased sense of optimism in the Fourth Army.

In May 1917 the Fourth Army was organized into five army corps, two of which garrisoned the Gaza-Beersheba line. The overall personnel and material situation in the Fourth Army was as follows: 174,908 men, 36,225 animals, 5,351 camels, 145,840 rifles, 187 machine guns, and 282 artillery pieces.[10] Of course, substantial portions of this strength were scattered along the coast and garrisoned Arabia. Facing the British on the Gaza line were the XXII Corps, comprising the 3rd, 7th, and 53rd Infantry Divisions, and the XX Corps, containing the 16th and 54th Infantry Divisions. Also facing the British and under army-level control were the 3rd Cavalry Division and the 178th Infantry Regiment. With these troops, the Turks continued to improve their defensive lines. By July, the Fourth Army had grown to 151,742 rifles, 354 machine guns, and 330 artillery pieces (its highest recorded strength). However, the defensive lines had also been extended, now almost encircling the oasis town of Beersheba, and stretching continuously for almost fifty kilometers. Although the opposing Imperial force was greatly increasing its strength as well, the Turks were optimistic (Enver, in particular).[11]

There was one important addition to the Imperial force, which must be mentioned as significant, and that was the assignment of General Edmund Allenby as the new British commander in June 1917. Allenby would prove to be as relentless and as tenacious as the American General U. S. Grant, once he began his attacks later that year. Allenby would spend the summer of 1917 preparing his great offensive aimed at breaking the Gaza-Beersheba line.

SECOND KUT AND BAGHDAD

After a dismal showing in the first half of 1916, the British made several important changes in their army in Mesopotamia. The first change was to send the aggressive General Sir Stanley Maude to assume theater command. The second change in the Imperial force in the Tigris and Euphrates valleys was greatly to increase its strength, by sending two additional infantry divisions to reinforce Maude. During the summer and fall of 1916, Maude began to make serious preparations to advance up river and break the Turkish hold on the gateway to Baghdad. Maude now had a huge force available at his command, with a total of five infantry divisions, well supported by cavalry, artillery, and aircraft. Additionally, he built up a large and capable riverine fleet of fighting steamers and supply vessels. Maude had a fighting strength of 166,000 men, of whom 107,000 were men of the Indian Army.[12] In spite of this huge number of men and equipment, Maude was determined not to advance until he was ready.

Because of pressing strategic commitments elsewhere and because of problems with rail communications, the Turkish General Staff did not augment the Turkish Sixth Army's strength in the final nine months of 1916. Additionally, Halil Paşa received very few replacements to fill his ever depleting ranks. Slow attrition from disease, from desertion, and from occasional British activity, continually wore away at his army. Thus, whereas General Maude's army was growing exponentially, Halil's was steadily growing weaker. In the fall of 1916, the Sixth Army was still organized into two corps, the XVIII Corps of the 46th and 51st Infantry Divisions, and the XIII Corps of the 35th and 52nd Infantry Divisions. Additionally, the XIII Corps maintained a separate infantry brigade. In the summer of 1916, the shattered 38th Infantry Division was inactivated and its soldiers reassigned to one of the Sixth Army's remaining four infantry divisions.

The operational and tactical situation facing the Sixth Army was dismal. Unfortunately, it was compounded by the geography of the Tigris and Euphrates River system. There were two avenues of approach into Mesopotamia available to General Maude. The primary route was along the Tigris River, along which lay Kut Al Amara, Baghdad, and Mosul. The second route was along the Euphrates River, via the ruins of Babylon, to a point about thirty kilometers west of Baghdad. Unfortunately for Halil, by the summer of 1916, the British remained in possession of forward positions located at approximately the widest distance between the two rivers. This meant that Halil had to hold two different defensive positions separated by almost one hundred kilometers of desert. This invited defeat in detail, since Maude could choose his point of attack and mass greatly superior forces there. Consequently, the strategic posture and operational situation facing the Sixth Army appeared hopeless to all but the most optimistic Turk.

In December 1916, Maude began his long awaited drive up river. The Turks were anxious to identify which river approach the British would take as their primary axis of advance. Maude chose the Tigris and advanced with a full-strength corps on either side of the river. Rains slowed his advance, but by February 17, 1917, Maude had advanced to Sannaiyat, about twenty kilometers downstream from Kut. The plodding progress of the British made it possible for Halil Paşa to shift some of his meager forces to reinforce the XVIII Corps, which guarded the Tigris approach. Thus, by mid-February 1917, the XVIII Corps, commanded by Colonel Kazim Bey, contained the 45th, 51st, and 52nd Infantry Divisions. Kazim Bey also commanded the River Group, which contained four infantry regiments, a cavalry regiment, an artillery regiment, and supporting services. This made the River Group literally a divisional equivalent in combat power. As a percentage of available strength, Halil was able to mass over 75 percent of his small army to oppose the British.

Colonel Kazim Bey deployed almost all of his corps on the north bank of the Tigris in an attempt to guard the well-trodden path to Kut. However, Maude shifted both of his corps to the south bank and began to mass on the Turkish right flank just up river from the town of Kut. Halil was unaware of the true situation and sat tight waiting for the British to move. The British attacks began on February 17, 1917. On the morning of February 22 the British began demonstrations at Sannaiyat and at Kut. The following day, the British began divisional-sized assault crossing of the Tigris upriver from Kut and by the end of the day had a pontoon bridge across the river. Local Turkish counterattacks were unsuccessful in dislodging the bridgehead. Most of Halil's strength and his reserves lay to the south of Kut, and by nightfall he realized that the XVIII Corps was in danger of encirclement from the north. He reacted promptly and ordered an immediate withdrawal. The XVIII Corps began to pull out of its defensive positions that very night. Desperate rear guard actions bought enough time for the Turks to evacuate most of their infantry; however, losses in material, artillery, and supplies were heavy. Halil withdrew up river for the final defense of Baghdad.

The Turkish line was along the Diyala River, a tributary entering the Tigris about fifteen kilometers below Baghdad. There the XVII Corps made its stand. The shattered 45th Infantry Division was inactivated and its survivors combined with the newly arriving 3rd and 64th Infantry Regiments to build a reformed 14th Infantry Division. This division was assigned to the XVIII Corps to assist in the defense of Baghdad. The British resumed their march up river on March 4 and began to press the tired and dispirited Turkish troops along the Diyala. After several days of hard fighting, it was apparent to Halil that he could not hold the Diyala or Baghdad itself. Although reluctant to surrender this city with its great political, cultural, and religious significance, Halil made the bitter decision to abandon Baghdad and to continue his retreat up river. On March 11, 1917,

General Maude entered Baghdad. It was a new low point in the Mesopotamian theater for the Turkish Army.

Halil took his army about sixty kilometers up the Tigris. His battered Sixth Army now rested its right flank at Ramadiye on the Euphrates River and rested its left flank in Persia. Halil moved his army headquarters to Mosul. His total force, at this time, amounted to not over thirty thousand men in total, and was spread over a front of about three hundred kilometers. In April 1917, the 2nd Infantry Division arrived as a much needed reinforcement; however, this was a small addition to Halil's total strategic requirements. For the Turks, the overall strategic situation in Mesopotamia, in the late spring of 1917, continued to appear quite hopeless.

Then one of the great windfalls of the First World War occurred for the Turks; General Stanley Maude stopped advancing. Maude felt that because his supply lines were inadequate and since the summer season of disease was upon the region, prospects for an offensive were low.[13] There were other reasons too, dealing mostly with the question of when the Russians would begin a supporting attack on Mosul. Maude may also have been worried over intelligence that the Turks were preparing a massive counter offensive with new armies aimed at the recapture of Baghdad. For this eventuality, he had requested and had been denied reinforcements. In any case, the British were content to rest on their laurels and to sit tight at Baghdad, waiting out the long hot summer. This was a godsend for Halil Paşa, for the Turkish Sixth Army, and for the Turkish General Staff as well. In retrospect, it is doubtful that the Sixth Army could have prevented further British attacks, or have held Mosul, had Maude continued his advance. Furthermore, given the huge disparity in combat forces and in logistics, it is remarkable that Halil's Sixth Army held the British back for as long as they did. Thus, the situation in Mesopotamia stabilized by late March 1917, with the British in possession of Baghdad. This would have important consequences for the future strategic direction of the war by the Turkish General Staff.

THE YILDIRIM ARMY GROUP

It is unclear when and where the idea of forming the Yildirim Army originated. Although it certainly actualized in the fertile and aggressive mind of Enver Paşa, it is unknown exactly how much the Germans had to do with it. In the first two and one half years of war, there had been much profitable discussion and cooperation between Turkey and her Central Powers partners, and especially with Germany. The idea of a large Turkish-German Army Group may have originated in the mind of German General Erich von Falkenhayn, the victor of the Romanian Campaign. In any case, sometime after the fall of Baghdad and before the arrival of von Falkenhayn in Turkey for staff discussions on May 7, 1917, Enver was seized with the idea of retaking Baghdad. He intended to accomplish this by forming the Yildirim Ordular Grubunu, or the Thunderbolt Army Group. Enver envisioned this force concentrating in upper Mesopotamia, perhaps centered on Mosul. From there, the Yildirim Army Group would conduct a grand offensive to retake Baghdad. From there it would either complete the reconquest of lower Mesopotamia or perhaps invade Persia. It was strategy on a grand scale and it appealed to Enver's grandiose sense of high drama. In Enver's grand scheme, Halil's Sixth Turkish Army would form one component of the Yildirim Group. The second component would be a newly formed Seventh Army. Together with German assistance, these two Turkish armies would take the offensive. Troops for the new Seventh Army would come from the divisions returning to Turkey from Galicia, Romania, and from Macedonia. In the First World War, these combat hardened divisions represented Turkey's last strategic reserve. They could never be replaced. With the Caucasus, Palestine, and Mesopotamia apparently stabilized for the summer of 1917, the Turks now had a bit of strategic breathing space and time, with which to regain the initiative at least in one theater of war.

The possibilities of retaking the offensive excited Enver Paşa and he visited the Palestine front in June. There he told Cemal Paşa that he was contemplating an offensive to retake Baghdad and that he intended to form an army group called the "Yildirim Group."[14] Enver also told Cemal that he had decided which divisions would be assigned to this force and that General von Falkenhayn would command it. On June 24, 1917, Enver convened a meeting in Aleppo to discuss his plans. Attending this meeting were Ahmet Izzet Paşa, commanding the Caucasus Army Group, Mustafa Kemal Paşa, commanding the Second Army, Cemal Paşa, commanding the Fourth Army, and Halil Paşa, commanding the Sixth Army. Also attending the meeting were Bronsart von Schellendorf of the Turkish General Staff, staff officers from the Turkish General Staff and Caucasus Army Group staff, and the chiefs of staff of the Third and the Fourth Armies. At this meeting, Enver unveiled his plan to create a new Seventh Army on the upper reaches of the Euphrates River using the divisions made available by the conclusion of the European operations. Enver explained that Halil's Sixth Army would attack south along the Tigris River while the Seventh Army attacked east along the Euphrates River. The British, at Baghdad, would be caught in a pincers and would be destroyed.[15]

Cemal Paşa was not at happy with this plan and pressed for a revision.[16] Cemal felt that instead of aiming to retake Baghdad, the Turks should concentrate their dwindling number of fresh divisions in the vicinity of Aleppo. At Aleppo, Cemal reasoned, this force could act as a centrally positioned strategic reserve and would be able to respond to threats in the Caucasus, Palestine, or Mesopotamia. He also put forth the idea of maintaining troops in the Adana region as insurance against an amphibious landing by the entente. Cemal concluded his summary of the strategic situation by stating that an all-out offensive against Baghdad was dangerous for the Turks. Once expended, it became problematic whether this last Turkish strategic reserve could ever be reconstituted. Enver replied that the Turkish General Staff had already decided upon this course of action and had already provided the "best German General" for it.[17] Enver then told Cemal that the Germans would also provide a light division of six infantry battalions, with a large number of machine guns. Izzet Paşa, likewise, was uncomfortable with the plan and recommended that Enver leave a division at Aleppo to act as a reserve contingency force. His appeals also went unheeded. From that day forward, all priority of effort in the Caucasian, Palestinian, and Mesopotamian theaters went towards the activation of the Yildirim Army Group.

Later, Cemal Paşa, who was a member of the inner circle of Young Turks, cabled the grand vizier directly to express his concerns over this adventure. He received replies which said that the decision had already been made in the Council of Ministers, and that the grand vizier, personally, had requested the services of von Falkenhayn from the Germans.

Cemal was apparently so incensed about the Yildirim idea that he journeyed to Constantinople in mid-August 1917 to argue against the concept. Erich von Falkenhayn was also having doubts about the feasibility of an offensive strategy and expressed them in a memorandum to the German General Staff.[18] Another Council of War was held, at which Cemal, Enver, von Falkenhayn, Bronsart von Schellendorf, and Cemal's chief of staff, Colonel Ali Fuad Bey, were present. Cemal and his chief of staff presented their appreciation of the weakness of the Fourth Army, then holding the Gaza-Beersheba line and concluded that the retention of a theater reserve was vital to a successful defense. Cemal related[19] that at this point in the meeting Enver and von Falkenhayn began conversing in fluent German and began an animated discussion at the map boards. It was apparent to Cemal that he had lost the argument. Afterwards, much to Cemal's surprise, Enver explained that von Falkenhayn agreed with Cemal about the vulnerable condition of the Fourth Army. Furthermore, von Falkenhayn now advocated using the Yildirim Group to throw the British back across the Suez Canal, before attempting to retake Baghdad. Cemal was uncomfortable with this new proposal, preferring instead to simply abandon the Baghdad scheme and maintain a theater reserve. If and when troops were needed to reinforce the defense of Palestine, they would be readily available. Cemal was also very uncomfortable that the Yildirim staff and the new Seventh Army staff would deploy into his own strategic backyard. This would inevitably supercede his authority and autonomy as commander in Palestine.

This strategic dispute at the highest levels continued until Cemal received an invitation from Kaiser Wilhelm to visit Germany, which he promptly accepted. Cemal went to Germany and visited the fleet at Kiel, the Krupp works, and the headquarters at Bad Kreuznach. Everywhere he went, he was feted. However, when he arrived at Bad Kreuznach, a cable from Enver reached him. This cable informed Cemal that he was relieved of command in Palestine and that von Falkenhayn would take over the war effort there. Cemal fired back a cable predicting catastrophe and then made his way back to Constantinople. However, he was too late to affect events. Cemal returned to Syria, taking the title of commander of the armies in Syria and western Arabia and was reduced to providing logistical support to von Falkenhayn.[20] Unhappy with this turn of events but willing to continue to serve in a diminished capacity, Cemal settled in to a new headquarters in Damascus. There he observed the destruction of von Falkenhayn's army during the next year. Cemal noted later in his memoirs that there were continuous disputes between Mustafa Kemal and von Falkenhayn over command and policy issues in the Yildirim Group. Cemal further went on record in stating that, were it not for von Falkenhayn, the Turks could have held the Gaza-Beersheba line for years.[21]

The Germans came to refer to the Yildirim Army Group as Army Group F, and von Falkenhayn arrived at the end of July 1917 to command it. As originally configured, the staff of the Army Group would consist of sixty-five German and nine Turkish staff officers. This scheme was presented to the Turks as being easier for von Falkenhayn because the staff would not have to depend as much on translators.[22] It is doubtful that von Falkenhayn, who expressed the highest admiration for the Turkish asker, ever trusted Turkish officers to carry out general staff work to German standards. However, the Turks were not fooled by this charade and, in any case, were not assigned important staff work, which further cut them out of the decision cycle. The Germans also sent the "German Asia Corps", which was in reality only a brigade-sized force, to help the new Army Group. The Turks had expected to see some kind of light German infantry divisions, and instead, received three infantry battalions, three machinegun detachments, and three cavalry detachments. However, it was not in combat troops that the Asia Corps proved most useful. Also accompanying the Asia Corps were an artillery battalion, a squadron of aircraft for artillery spotting, two heavy artillery sections, an infantry/artillery coordination section, communications, and motor transport. Of particular value was a small air component made up of four detachments of eight aircraft each.[23]

The disposition of Turkish forces in August 1917 is shown on Table 6.1. The Turks began to funnel forces to Aleppo and by the month of September, substantial forces were assembling there. In July the XV Corps headquarters arrived from Galicia. Coming by train from Hungary, the divisions arrived in Constantinople, where they staged for deployment south. Each day, for almost one hundred days, a train carrying elements of the XV Corps departed for Aleppo. By the end of August, the 19th Infantry Division had arrived, and its sister division, the 20th Infantry Division arrived in September. A new III Corps was activated and deployed, as were its subordinate units, the 50th Infantry Division from Macedonia and the 59th Infantry Division from Aydin. Four or five trains a day ran south to bring these formations into Syria. However, there were severe problems beginning to appear indicating a gradually weakening Turkish Army. In a report to the Yildirim Army headquarters in September 1917, von Kress noted that the 24th Infantry Division from Gallipoli had departed from Hyderpaşa train station with 10,000 men and that only 4,634 arrived fit for duty.[24] In this division 19 percent were sick, 24 percent had gone missing, and 3 percent were given permission to return home on leave. The German Asia Corps was the last major unit to arrive in Syria, having come all the way from its staging area in Neu Hammer in Silesia. Considering the poor state of the Turkish railroads, the staging of the Seventh Army to Aleppo was a considerable achievement. Once there, the Turkish General Staff planned to move the army east by rail to the end of the railhead. From there, the 400 trucks of the Asia Corps would transport the infantry divisions the last 160 kilometers to assembly areas south of Mosul. It was a very ambitious undertaking.[25]

Table 6.1
Disposition of Turkish Forces, August 1917

ROMANIA
VI Corps: 15, 25, 26 Inf. Div.

THRACE
First Army
I Corps: 42 Inf. Div.
1 Cav. Bde.

GALLIPOLI
Fifth Army
XIV Corps: 57 Inf. Div.
XIX Corps: 59 Inf. Div.
XXI Corps: 49 Inf. Div.

WESTERN ANATOLIA
58 Inf. Div.

CAUCASIA
Third Army
1st Cauc. Corps: 9, 10, 36 Cauc. Inf. Div.
2nd Cauc. Corps: 5, 11, 37 Cauc. Inf. Div.
V Corps: Coastal Detachments

SYRIA-PALESTINE
Fourth Army
VIII Corps: 48 Inf. Div.
XII Corps: 23, 44 Inf. Div.
XV Corps: 43 Inf. Div.
XX Corps: 16, 54 Inf. Div.
XXII Corps: 3, 7, 53 Inf. Div.
3 Cav. Div.

Second Army
II Corps: 1, 42 Inf. Div.
IV Corps: 11, 12, 48 Inf. Div.
XVI Corps: 5, 8 Inf. Div.
2 Regular Cav. Div.
Van Jandarma (Inf) Div.

Yildirim Army Group (SYRIA)
Seventh Army (SYRIA)
III Corps: 24, 50 Inf. Div.
XV Corps: 19, 20 Inf. Div.
Asia Corps (German)
Sixth Army (MESOPOTAMIA)
XIII Corps: 2, 6 Inf. Div.
XVIII Corps: 14, 51, 52 Inf. Div.
46 Inf. Div.

ARABIA-YEMEN
VII Corps: 21, 22, 39, 40 Inf. Div.

Note: Units in boldface type indicate new formations, units underlined indicate units redeployed since December 1916; units in bold italic type indicate seriously understrength units.
Units inactivated: 4, 9, 10, 17, 18, 29, 31, 32, 34, 35, 38 Inf. Div.; units redesignated: 13, 28, 30, 33 Inf. Div.

The Hayderpaşa train station explosion of September 6, 1917, which supposedly blew up large quantities of supplies necessary to sustain the operations of the Yildirim Army, is not mentioned in any of the Turkish official histories. Likewise any damage which may have been sustained by the railroad infrastructure itself is not mentioned and apparently had no long term effect on the eastward flow of supplies.

But by the middle of September 1917 the ambitious plan to retake Baghdad was consigned to the scrap heap. Enver Paşa had, at last, made up his mind to take von Falkenhayn's advice and send the Yildirim Army to Palestine first. He may also have been spurred on by disturbing reports from von Kress concerning the massive British offensive preparations then being observed opposite the Gaza – Beersheba line. Furthermore, Enver was apparently uncomfortable with the lingering influence of Cemal Pasa in Palestine and decided to do something about that too. As a result, on September 26, 1917, Enver moved the Fourth Army Headquarters north to Damascus.[26] In the same order, he split the old Fourth Army area, giving Cemal both Syria and West Arabia. He also ordered the Yildirim Army Group and the Seventh Army to Palestine. In subsequent orders, given on October 2, Enver changed the organization of the Palestine command and activated the new Eighth Army, appointing von Kress to command it. He then assigned both the Seventh and the Eighth Armies to Falkenhayn's Yildirim Army Group. Falkenhayn also retained command and control of the Sixth Army in Mesopotamia.

The Seventh Army was now commanded by Mustafa Kemal who was not at all happy with the new command arrangements. In a long and strongly worded letter sent directly to Enver Paşa in late September 1917, Kemal advocated a return to a defensive military policy within which every reserve unit was to be guarded and carefully committed.[27] He based this on the premise that superior British lines of communications (ship and rail) would ensure their continued numerical superiority in any theater that the Turks wished to contest. Therefore it would be impossible for the Turks to gain the initiative with the Yildirim Army anywhere. He also advocated the merging of the Seventh and the Eighth Armies and offered to step down in favor of von Kress. Mustafa Kemal also stressed the importance of strengthening the internal administration of the country so that the army would have the people and the economy solidly behind it.

In an emotional but rather poorly thought out conclusion to his letter, Kemal bitterly condemned German influence in Turkish strategy and expressed his concern that Turkey was becoming a "German colony." This letter led to the resignation of Mustafa Kemal several weeks later, after which Fevzi Paşa took command of the Seventh Army.

The headquarters and the infantry divisions near Aleppo began to move south on September 30. Not all went south to Palestine. Recognizing the need to reinforce Halil Paşa with additional troops, the 50th Infantry Division was sent eastward to Ramadiye in Mesopotamia. The 59th Infantry Division was then inactivated and its troops used to fill out the other divisions departing the Aleppo staging area. To make up for these lost forces, the Fifth Army was ordered to send the 42nd Infantry Division to Syria, the Second Army was ordered to send the 1st Infantry Division to Damascus, and the Third Army was ordered to send the 2nd Caucasian Cavalry Division. However, it would be quite sometime before these formations arrived in the Syria-Palestine area of operations. Near the end of October, only the headquarters of the Seventh and Eighth Armies would actually be in position to participate in combat operations in Palestine. Time would run out for von Falkenhayn at dawn on October 31, 1917, when Allenby's long awaited offensive began.

THIRD GAZA

In its final prebattle deployment, the Yildirim Army Group held the Gaza-Beersheba line with two field armies abreast. On the right flank, holding Gaza, was the Eighth Army, commanded by von Kress, composed of the XXII Corps (with the 3rd and 53rd Infantry Divisions in a strongly fortified position around Gaza) and the XX Corps (with the 26th and 54th Infantry Divisions holding the line east, out into the desert). The Seventh Army held the Turkish left and the decisive oasis town of Beersheba. This army, commanded by Mustafa Kemal Paşa, held the line with the 16th Infantry Division and held Beersheba itself with the III Corps (comprising the 27th Infantry Division and the 3rd Cavalry Division). By October 28 the 24th Infantry Division had arrived and was in reserve behind the 16th Infantry Division, and the 19th Infantry Division was detraining in an assembly area twenty kilometers behind the lines. The Turks had expected an attack for some time and were well aware of the British preparations. In terms of planning the defense, the Yildirim Army Group simply took over the old Fourth Army plans in situ.[28] The defense rested on a well-sited defensive layout and relied on dug-in Turkish soldiers and counterattacks. The keys to the defense were the towns of Gaza and Beersheba. Both were ringed by entrenchments presenting an almost all-around defense. Defending the lynchpin of Beersheba were just 4,400 riflemen, 60 machine guns, and 28 artillery pieces. In British terms, this force amounted to about a brigade.

Allenby's attack began at dawn on October 31, 1917, and, at the tactical level at least, caught some Turkish front-line troops by surprise. Two entire British corps executed a massive attack on the well town of Beersheba. The British Twentieth Corps attacked from the west and the Cavalry Corps enveloped and attacked the Turkish III Corps in Beersheba from the east. In the concentric battle, fighting lasted all day and finally the Australian Light Horse mounted a successful charge directly into the Turkish defenses. It was a magnificent hour for British and Imperial cavalry. With this, the defense of Beersheba crumbled and the Turks began to pull back. The flow of reports coming from the front so disturbed the army chief of staff that he personally went forward to verify the bad news. The loss of Beersheba, in a single day, stunned the Yildirim Army Group Commander and his staff. Nevertheless, he immediately ordered the reconstitution of a defensive line just to the north of Beersheba and ordered the famous 19th Infantry Division forward to hold the line once again.

The next day, Allenby's army hit the Turkish right flank at Gaza, with a heavy attack by a corps of three British infantry divisions. Defending Gaza, the Turks had but 8,000 riflemen, but they were well supported by 116 cannons. The British began with a coordinated bombardment from artillery on land and from naval gunfire from the sea. The Turks were pounded mercilessly. On November 1 and 2 the Turkish 53rd and 7th Infantry Divisions were able to hold most of the line and to conduct locally successful counterattacks. Remarkably, the British only made limited progress on the extreme right flank (adjacent to the sea) of the well-entrenched Turks.

After successfully drawing most of the Turkish reserves to the flanks, on November 6 Allenby shifted his forces and attacked in the center. He made startling progress and ordered his cavalry through the broken Turkish lines to envelop Gaza. Allenby expected that the outnumbered and outgunned Turks would fold completely and that his cavalry divisions would pursue them to destruction. He was wrong.

Falkenhayn realized that the Yildirim Army Group would be destroyed if it attempted to retrieve the tactical situation which was already lost. Instead, he ordered the Eighth and the Seventh Armies to conduct a fighting withdrawal to a new defensive line about ten kilometers to their rear. It was a dangerous maneuver under any circumstances. Very skillfully, von Kress and Mustafa Kemal began to disengage their forces, leaving small rear guards when necessary. Many Turks died holding the line while larger forces withdrew and much of the movement was done at night. In these extreme circumstances, many Turks were taken prisoner. The Turkish 3rd Cavalry Division screened the left flank of the Seventh Army. The British main effort was now clearly identified in the center and along the coast, and the Eighth Army had great difficulty maintaining control and cohesion in the face of the massive British pursuit. By November 9 the Eighth Army had been driven back twenty kilometers, but the Seventh Army had lost hardly any ground and was conducting a masterfully deliberate withdrawal. The headquarters of the Yildirim Group retired to Jerusalem and the Seventh Army's headquarters retired to Bethlehem.

JERUSALEM

Allenby relentlessly continued his attack driving von Kress's Eighth Army back even more on November 11. The attacks continued along the coast and had the effect of making the forward position of the Seventh Army, now commanded by Fevzi Paşa, vulnerable to a flanking attack. Fearing encirclement, Fevzi was forced to withdraw. Maintaining his cavalry as a screen, he pulled his scattered infantry formations tighter around Jerusalem. Between November 19 and 21, 1917, the British wheeled again and attacked east toward Jerusalem. On November 25th 1917, von Kress executed a counteroffensive with the 3rd and the 7th Infantry Divisions, driving the British back and restoring the tactical situation along the coast. During the next week, the British shifted their main effort towards the capture of Jerusalem, but Fevzi's Seventh Army fought them to a standstill. The 53rd and the 27th Infantry Divisions of the XX Corps absorbed punishing blows and took heavy casualties. For the first seven days of 1918, Fevzi's XX Corps held out. Nevertheless, by dusk on January 8 the British were in the outskirts of the Holy City. That night, the battered but intact XX Corps withdrew to new defensive positions four kilometers to the east of Jerusalem. On December 8 Allenby entered the city.

Between October 31 and December 1, 1917, in the Eighth Army 59 officers and 1,336 men were killed, 158 officers and 2,823 men were wounded, 81 officers and 5,694 men were taken prisoner, and 89 officers and 1,281 men were missing. About 674 animals had been killed, 120 wounded, and a further 2,377 were lost. In late November, the army returns showed a total of 310 officers and 11,380 men remaining on the rolls.[29] On December 1 the Eighth Army lost its fighting commander Freiherr von Kress, who had been in Palestine since September 27, 1914. The faithful Von Kress, now a brigadier general, was finally relieved of his duties and was replaced by Turkish Brigadier General Cevat Bey.

British attacks continued from December 13 through 17. The 2nd Caucasian Cavalry Division arrived in Palestine on December 15 and went into reserve positions behind the XXII Corps. The 3rd Cavalry Division was also pulled out of the line and put into reserve behind the 54th Infantry Division on December 16. The 1st Infantry Division arrived from the Caucasus and remained in reserve at Nablus. The British continued to attack, making small gains along the coast, where they could employ naval gunfire from the Royal Navy. By December 26 the British were fifteen kilometers north of Jaffa on the coast, and there was a dangerous gap developing between the Eighth and the Seventh Armies, Fortunately, the 3rd Cavalry Division screened this gap and maintained contact between the two armies. On December 27th, the 2nd Caucasian Cavalry Division conducted a determined counterattack, which successfully restored the situation along the coast. The new year found the Turks battered, but holding a solid line anchored in the east on the Dead Sea and in the west on the Mediterranean Sea. Every Turkish infantry division, which had begun the fight on October 31 on the Gaza-Beersheba line, was intact and still fighting (although some were reduced to cadre strength).

Screened by the Dead Sea and the Jordan River, the Turks still held the railway from Dera to Medina, although this line was constantly being harassed and cut by insurgent Arab bands. To the north, Cemal's VIII and XII Corps still guarded the Levent coast with four infantry divisions. As 1917 came to an end, so too did Allenby's offensive. Exhausted and living on lean logistical support, his army ceased offensive operations. The battered Turks earned yet another respite.

Casualties had been severe during the period from October 31 through December 31, 1917, for both Yildirim armies. In the Seventh Army a grand total of 110 officers and 1,886 men were killed, 213 officers and 5,488 men were wounded, 79 officers and 393 men were captured, and 183 officers and 4,233 men were missing. Also lost were 1,762 animals, 7,305 rifles, 22 light and 73 heavy machine guns, and 29 artillery pieces. The Eighth Army was harder hit by the British and reported 70 officers and 1,474 men killed, 118 officers and 3,163 men wounded, 95 officers and 5,868 men captured, and 97 officers and 4,877 men missing. The army also reported 700 animals lost and 2,384 wounded.[30] The total casualties for the Yildirim Army Group were 25,337 men killed, wounded, captured, or missing. Although this number seems high, Allenby lost about eighteen thousand men. In the eloquent words of British historian Cyril Falls, "Considering that he [Allenby] had odds of well over two to one in infantry and eight to one in cavalry, his achievement may not seem so remarkable. In fact, it was hard and costly to turn Turkish troops out of defensive positions in this hilly, rocky, country."[31] Falls's tribute does not include the massive artillery superiority that Allenby enjoyed, or the huge logistical support that he amassed, nor does it attribute any advantage to the Royal Navy. Considering all of these factors in combination, it is remarkable that any Turks survived the onslaught at all. Indeed, not only did they survive, but the fighting divisions of the Turkish Army retired in fair order to continue the fight. All in all, the Turkish fighting withdrawal under intense British pressure may be seen as a great accomplishment.

SYRIA AND WEST ARABIA

By 1917 the Arab Revolt was in full swing, financed and aided by the British. There were four principal bands of armed Arabs, which operated mainly against the Dera-Medina railway. In the north, Prince Faisal, operating out of Akaba, conducted large-scale raids on January 25 and on July 23, 1917, against the garrison towns of Tafile and Fulye, respectively. Farther south, the Emir Ali operated against Tebuk, Abdullah operated against El Ala, and Sheriff Hussein attacked the fortified city of Medina itself. Most of these Arab bands numbered about three thousand to four thousand men. While these Arabs could not (and would not) hold ground, they were capable of repeatedly cutting both the rail and the telegraph lines extending south. While these raids were bothersome, they were not militarily significant. Nevertheless, larger and larger numbers of Turkish soldiers were called upon to guard the lines of communications south to Medina.

After losing control of the Palestine front, Cemal Paşa's Fourth Army retained control of Syria and West Arabia. This caused the Fourth Army's operational area to become shaped like a large inverted "L," encompassing Syria in the north and then running to the east of the Dead Sea and the Jordan River, and finally south to Medina. The Fourth Army's headquarters was in the ancient city of Damascus.

Cemal assigned the VIII Corps, headquartered in Dera, the responsibility to protect this giant and sprawling sector of over seven hundred kilometers of rail line. The VIII Corps had substantial forces at its disposal, however, with which to accomplish this mission. The corps disposed an infantry brigade near Dera itself, the 48th Infantry Division in Amman, the 1st and the 2nd Provisional Forces (which were infantry division equivalents) strung out along the railway, and the

58th Infantry Division guarding the southern portions at El Ala and at Hedye. Medina was garrisoned by the Hijaz Expeditionary Force, which had strongly fortified the city.

Cemal's other formation was the XII Corps, which had the responsibility to protect the long Levant coastline and to provide security for the vital lines of communications leading south from Anatolia into Syria. The XII Corps deployed the 43rd Infantry Division around Beirut, the 41st Infantry Division around Antioch and Alexandretta, the 44th Infantry Division guarded the Osmaniye Gap, and the 23rd Infantry Division garrisoned Adana and Mersin. It was a substantial force, which could not really be spared simply to watch for an invasion that never came. However, the Turks had little choice in the matter and maintained strong forces in these locations until the end of the war.

PERSIA

There had been a lull in the Persian theater from August 1916, which lasted the remainder of the year. The Turkish XIII Corps, with the 2nd, 4th, and 6th Infantry Divisions, held the town of Hamadan and the surrounding frontier area through the winter of 1916 to 1917. Although urged by Enver Paşa and by Halil Paşa to advance on Teheran, XIII Corps Commander, General Ali Insan, did not feel strong enough to accomplish this task. The XIII Corps did receive some meager reinforcements in the form of an Austrian 105 mm howitzer battery and three battalions of Muslim ex-prisoners from French North African units.[32] However, disease and desertions eroded Ali Insan's strength faster than the incoming reinforcements could maintain it.

In spring 1917 events in Mesopotamia took a turn for the worse for the Turks, as Halil's defense of Kut and Baghdad failed. The deteriorating situation along the Tigris forced Halil to recall the XIII Corps from Persia and by mid-February 1917, the XIII Corps was ordered to retreat toward Baghdad. Ali Insan began to withdraw his corps about February 22 and he withdrew it over a preplanned route of retreat. Marching hard, the XIII Corps covered over four hundred kilometers of extremely rough terrain in just three weeks. The Russians and the British were hot on the Turk's heels but failed to pin the XIII Corps so that it could be brought to ground and destroyed. Persia was now left to the Russians and to the British.

By March 15 forward elements of the XIII Corps arrived on the upper Diyala River. Baghdad having fallen, Halil Paşa planned to deploy the corps on his left flank against any Russian incursion into the Mesopotamian territory of the Ottoman Empire. In late April 1917 the XIII Corps was concentrated on the upper Tigris, with the 2nd and the 4th Infantry Divisions colocated with the corps headquarters. The 6th Infantry Division occupied a froward position on the west bank of the upper Diyala River, where it confronted both the Russians and the English. The Turkish Persian adventure was finally over.

NOTES

1. The correct modern Turkish spelling of this word is *Yıldırım*–the nearest English equivalent is Yildirim. This is also the spelling used in the Turkish official histories for the Turco-German army group. Early histories of the First World War, particularly German and British, written prior to the implementation of the modern Turkish alphabet, incorrectly transliterated the word from Ottoman script as Yilderim. This error has been carried forward by many western historians into the present day. Sometimes the word is translated as lightning, however, a more appropriate usage is thunderbolt, which implies a powerful force hurled with purpose and direction rather than a random act of nature.
2. Turkish General Staff, *Birinci Dünya Harbinde Turk Kafkas Cephesi 3ncu Ordu Harekati Cilt II* (Ankara: GK Basimevi, 1993), 413- 432.
3. Commandant M. Larcher, *La Guerre Turque Dans La Guerre Mondiale* (Paris: Chiron & Berger-Levrault, 1926), 413.
4. W. E. D. Allen and Paul Muratoff, *Caucasian Battlefields: A History of the Wars on the Turco-Caucasian Border 1828-1921* (Cambridge: Cambridge University Press,1953). 436-441. For additional vivid analysis of potential combined operations that the Russians and the British might have enjoyed in the region in 1917, see Larcher, *La Guerre Turque*, 448-456.
5. Cemal Paşa, *Memories of a Turkish Statesman–1913-1919* (London: Hutchinson, n.d.), 171.
6. Ibid., 171.
7. Ibid., 180.
8. General Fahri Belen, *Birinci Cihan Harbinde Turk Harbi 1917 Yili Hareketleri, IV Ncu Cilt* (Ankara: Gnkur. Basimevi, 1966), 111. There were no apparent effects from the British gas attack. Dr. Yigal Sheffy suspects that adverse climatic conditions dissipated the gas.
9. Ibid., 112. Actual reported Turkish casualties for the battle were 82 killed, 1,336 wounded, and 242 missing.
10. Turkish General Staff, *Birinci Dünya Harbiinde Türk Harbi, Sina-Filistin Cephesi, IV ncü Cilt 2nci Kasım* (Ankara: Gnkur. Basımevi, 1986), 18.
11. Cemal, *Memories of a Turkish Statesman-1913-1919*, 184.
12. Cyril Falls, *The Great War* (New York: G. P. Putnam's Sons, 1959), 250.
13. Brigadier General F. J. Moberly, *History of the Great War, based on Official Documents, The Campaign in Mesopotamia 1914-1918*, vol. 4 (London: HMSO, 1923), 1-8.
14. Cemal, *Memories of a Turkish Statesman-1913-1919*, 183.
15. Belen, *1917 Yili Hareketleri*, 114, 115.
16. Cemal, *Memories of a Turkish Statesman-1913-1919*, 183.
17. Ibid., 184.
18. Moberly, *Campaign in Mesopotamia*, vol. 4, 65.
19. Cemal, *Memories of a Turkish Statesman-1913-1919*, 188.
20. Ibid., 190-192.
21. Ibid., 195.
22. Belen, *1917 Yili Harekatleri*, 115.
23. Ibid., 116.
24. Ibid., 125.
25. Ibid., 117.
26. Turkish General Staff, *Sina-Filistin Cephesi*, 114, 115.

27. Letter from Commander, Seventh Army to Acting Commanding General, Belen, *1917 Yili Harckctlori*, Document 2; Moberly, *Campaign in Mesopotamia*, vol. 4, Appendix 42, 348-351. Belen gives the date of this letter as September 20, 1917, and Moberly gives the date as September 30, 1917. It is possible that Belen used the Ottoman date instead of the western date.
28. Turkish General Staff, *Sina-Filistin Cephesi*, 128.
29. Ibid., 389.
30. Ibid., 509.
31. Falls, *The Great War*, 326.
32. Larcher, *La Guerre Turque*, 444.

7

End of Empire, January–November 1918

1918

Until late September 1918, the strategic situation for the Turks appeared hopeful. There was an expectation that Liman von Sanders would repeat his famous Gallipoli defense in Palestine and once again stem the British onslaught. Mesopotamia was holding fast and in Caucasia the Turks were relentlessly pushing forward toward the Caspian Sea. In comparison to their failing alliance partners—Germany, Austria-Hungary, and Bulgaria—the Turks seemed to be doing well. All of this changed in a matter of weeks with Allenby's final offensives at Meggido and in Syria and with the collapse of the Salonika front and Bulgaria. Although the Turks appeared able to accept the loss of Palestine and Syria, they were unable to attempt a large-scale defense of Turkish Thrace in late 1918.

For once, Enver's grandiose Caucasian expeditions met with success. However, this success had more to do with the absence of the Russian Army than it did with sound strategic planning and well executed operations. While much territory was taken including Armenia, Azerbaijan, and much of Georgia, the very success of these conquests inflamed Enver Paşa's imagination and distracted him from more compelling strategic priorities.

The suddenness of the final realization that the war, at long last and at such cost, was lost did not seem to demoralize the Turkish army. There were no mass desertions nor did any units simply throw down their arms and come apart at the seams. In fact, the Turkish high command began immediately to plan for returning the defeated but proud army to a peacetime configuration.

ARMENIA

There had been a sort of an informal truce between the Turks and the Russians along the Caucasian front since May 1917. On the Russian side, there was a continual deterioration of the Russian Army because of the deleterious effect of the revolution on troop morale. However, by the end of 1917 the Russians still had four army corps guarding their conquests in Anatolia, none of which were in any mood to fight. As W. E. D. Allen and Paul Muratoff put it[1], the Russian Army in the Caucasus "self-demobilized." Left behind to face the Turks, as the Russians withdrew the remnants of their army, was the loosely organized Trans-Caucasian Federation composed of the newly independent states of Armenia, Azerbaijan, and Georgia. Unfortunately for these peoples, the beleaguered Russians were focused on salvaging their nation from the grasping German negotiators at the ongoing peace talks at Brest Litovsk. None of these new countries were represented at the peace table nor did the Russians evince any interest in safeguarding their future. Therefore, when the Treaty of Brest Litovsk was signed, the continued existence of these states was not guaranteed in the treaty by any major power and the Turks were not treaty bound to honor their territorial integrity. This situation would create a serious power vacuum in the Caucasus. Although these small states had armies of a sort, they could not hope to withstand the power of the Turkish Army.

As the Russian threat to Central Anatolia dissipated, the Turks were able to draw down their Caucasian military assets also. The Caucasian Army Group was dissolved on December 16, 1917, and the Turkish Second Army was inactivated as well on February 4, 1918. The IV Corps, with the 5th and the 12th Infantry Divisions, were subsumed into the Third Army, which assumed the frontage and the responsibilities of the inactivated Second Army. Table 7.1 shows the disposition of Turkish Forces in January 1918. Vehip Paşa had been carefully husbanding the strength of his Third Army for more than a year. His carefully crafted reorganization of the army into Caucasian corps and divisions was successfully completed during the previous year, and the rebuilt formations were rested and combat-ready. However, he had not received any reinforcements or many replacements either, because the Mesopotamian, Persian, and Palestinian fronts had received strategic priority during 1917. In fact, Vehip Paşa actually had to fend off requests from the Turkish General Staff to send some of his infantry divisions to more active fronts. He was fairly successful in this endeavor, losing only the 2nd Caucasian Cavalry Division to the Yildirim Army Group. The depleted state of his army was reflected in the strength returns of the 1st Caucasian Corps on February 11, 1918, which reported 498 officers and 11,390 men present for duty.[2] Additionally, the corps returns showed a total of only 98 machine guns and 46 artillery pieces present on the same date. Indeed, the total combined strength of both the 1st and the 2nd Caucasian Corps on New Year's Day 1918, was 20,026 men, 186 machine guns, and 151 artillery pieces. The total barely exceeded the combat strength of a single British infantry division fighting on the western front. Under most circumstances, the Turkish Third Army would be considered incapable of offensive action.

Table 7.1
Disposition of Turkish Forces, January 1918

THRACE
First Army
1 Corps: 42 Inf. Div.
1 Cav. Bde.
<u>15, 25 Inf. Div.</u>

ANATOLIA
Second Army
XV Corps: None
58 Inf. Div.

CAUCASIA
Third Army
1st Cauc. Corps: 9, 10, 36 Cauc. Inf. Div.
2nd Cauc. Corps: 5, 11, 37 Cauc. Inf. Div.
IV Corps: 5, 8, 12 Inf. Div.

PALESTINE
Yildirim Army Group
Seventh Army
III Corps: 1, 19, 24 Inf. Div.
XX Corps: 26, 53 Inf. Div.
3 Cav. Div.
Asia Corps (German)
Eighth Army
XXII Corps: 3, 7, 20 Inf. Div.
16, 54 Inf. Div.
2 Cauc. Cav. Div.

GALLIPOLI
Fifth Army
XIV Corps: 57 Inf. Div.
XIX Corps: 59 Inf. Div.
XXI Corps: 49 Inf. Div.

SYRIA-WEST ARABIA
Fourth Army
VIII Corps: 43, 48 Inf. Div.
XII Corps: 23, 41, 44 Inf. Div.
Hicaz Group: 58 Inf. Div. and
three Provisional Inf. Div.

MESOPOTAMIA
Sixth Army
XIII Corps: 2, 6 Div.
XVIII Corps: 14, 51, 52 Inf. Div.
46 Inf. Div.

ARABIA-YEMEN
VII Corps: 21, 22, 39, 40 Inf. Div.

Note: Units in boldface type indicate new formations; units underlined indicate units redeployed since August 1917; units in boldface italic type indicate seriously understrength units. Units inactivated: 4, 9, 10, 17, 18, 29, 31, 32, 34, 35, 38 Inf. Div.; units redesignated: 13, 28, 30, 33 Inf. Div.

However, the fertile and aggressive mind of Enver Paşa was always at work, and he had been watching the situation in the Caucasus over the course of 1917. In a December 1917 report from the Third Army, Captain Hüsamettin wrote that the Russians were incapable of maintaining the front for very much longer.[3] The Third Army also noted reports of British and French involvement in the Tiflis region and the formation of large Armenian and Greek military units. Furthermore, there was mention of massacres of Muslim Azerbaijanis by Armenians. Finally, the report concluded with the information that Armenian Taşnak committees were preparing to establish a breakaway republic in the eastern Turkish *vilayets*.

After receiving the Third Army report on the Caucasian situation, Enver invited the refugee leaders of the Azeri Muslim Assembly to Constantinople for discussions on eastward expansion.[4] Not content with simply maintaining the status quo in a remarkably quiet sector, Enver Paşa and the Turkish General Staff began to consider the possibilities of a renewed offensive in the Caucasus. Somewhere around New Year's Day 1918, Enver was seized with the idea of taking the offensive to reclaim not the just the 1914 frontier but also the frontiers lost in 1877, and he decided to reinforce Vehip's army. Enver issued official orders to the Third Army on January 23, 1918, to begin planning and preparations for offensive operations.[5] The 15th Infantry Division, recently returned from operations in Romania, 120 motor driven trucks, three Jandarma battalions, and the 3,000-man 123rd Infantry Regiment were earmarked for service with the Third Army. These forces were put on fast steamers on February 9, and they began to arrive in the small Black Sea port of Giresun on February 12, 1918 (the Russian Navy, by now, being reduced to inactivity). The Turkish General Staff was now ably assisted in these endeavors by German Major General Hans von Seeckt, who had replaced Bronsart von Schellendorf on January 3, 1918 as the first assistant chief of the Turkish General Staff.

The Third Army was being brought to a condition of combat readiness. The 1st and the 2nd Caucasian Corps received orders assigning them objectives deep within the territory occupied by both the Russians and the Armenians. In concept, the plan envisioned a three pronged drive into Russian held territory. The 2nd Caucasian Corps would drive along the northern Black Sea coast, with the 37th Infantry Division, to reclaim Trabzond. The 1st Caucasian Corps would seize Erzincan and then drive on toward Erzurum. The IV Corps received orders to seize Malazgirt. The Caucasian front was about to explode into a renewal of the contest for Eastern Anatolia.

Opposing the Third Army was the Armenian National Army, equipped with cast-off Russian equipment. The Turks estimated that the Armenians could field one rifle division, three infantry brigades, and three cavalry regiments. They also estimated that the Armenians could field fifty thousand men.[6] Post-war Russian sources put the Armenian's strength as two rifle divisions, three brigades of Armenian volunteers, and a cavalry brigade.[7] The rifle divisions were made up of veteran soldiers from the Druzhiny units, which had fought alongside the Russians for almost four years. These were augmented by volunteers from the local Armenian populations of Erzurum, Van, and the Elişkırt Valley. Contrary to the Turkish opinion, the Armenian National Army was rather well equipped, since it was allowed to recover the best of the equipment left behind by the decaying Russian Army. Allen and Muratoff state that the strength of the Armenian National Army did not exceed sixteen thousand infantry, one thousand cavalry, and four thousand volunteers. In any event, this small Armenian force could not hope to stand against the power of the Turkish Third Army.

On the morning of February 12, 1918, Vehip's troops went forward. Erzincan was seized in short order and with it the Turks took tons of supplies, three howitzers, twenty-five mortars, and substantial quantities of munitions. The Armenian population in the area began immediately to flee toward the east. The Third Army made rapid progress as the Armenian National Army began a delaying retreat toward the rear. Concurrently with the Turkish offensive, peace negotiations were being conducted between the Russians, the Trans-Caucasian Federation, and the Turks. These highly political discussions added to the drama and to the confusion, particularly for the Armenians and the Georgians. Ultimately, the Turks gave up on negotiations when it became apparent in March 1918 that there was no force, Russian, Armenian or otherwise, which could hold the Caucasus against them. The important Black Sea port of Trabzond fell on February 25. Incoming Turkish sea-borne reinforcements immediately began to debark in this newly reacquired port.

Despite adverse weather and occasional Armenian resistance, Vehip Paşa urged his troops forward. The Armenians attempted to hold the fortress of Erzurum, but after several days of fighting, the 1st Caucasian Corps reclaimed the city on March 12. Upon investigating Erzurum and the surrounding hinterland, the Turks discovered numerous Muslim villages in which either the Russians or the retreating Armenian National Army had massacred the inhabitants.[8] By March 25 the Turks were crossing the 1914 frontier. Malazgirt fell to the 5th and the 12th Infantry Divisions on March 23. Meanwhile, the 37th Infantry Division continued to advance along the Black Sea coast. By the end of March, the Turks estimated that the Armenian National Army had been worn down to about fifteen thousand effectives. Vehip Paşa sent congratulatory messages to Enver Paşa and the Turkish General Staff and prepared to continue the campaign eastwards to the 1877 frontier. But as the Turks pressed eagerly forward they expected to encounter tough resistance from the Armenians.[9]

To accomplish what he believed would become a fast moving pursuit of disintegrating Armenian forces, Vehip Paşa decided to reorganize his army once again. Vehip formed what would be called in modern terminology an "operational maneuver group," and transformed the headquarters of Yakup Şevki Paşa's 2nd Caucasian Corps into a group command, appropriately called the Şevki Paşa Group. Under this new command, Vehip assigned the entire 1st Caucasian Corps and the 5th Caucasian Infantry Division. Vehip Paşa retained the 11th Caucasian Infantry Division as an army reserve. The IV Corps remained unaltered. In addition to the forces on hand, the commander and the staff of the VI Corps were brought by fast steamer for assignment to the Third Army. The VI Corps, commanded by Staff Colonel Kazim, received the 10th and the 37th Caucasian Infantry Divisions. In the center the new Şevki Paşa Group would drive on Kars, lost in 1878, and the VI Corps would drive on the left toward Batum. On the right flank the IV Corps would liberate Van and Bayazit. The concept of operations was hugely ambitious and it was a remarkable undertaking to reorganize the entire command structure on such a short and unannounced basis. In spite of potential problems, the Turkish commanders moved ahead and made it work. In the middle of all of this success, Enver Paşa sent a message scolding Vehip for failing to take Batum quickly enough.[10] Vehip was mildly surprised but quickly turned to the business at hand. On April 3 Vehip replied to Enver saying that "today we took Sarikamiş and tomorrow we'll begin operations along the coast,"[11] perhaps intending to remind Enver that he had succeeded where Enver had failed in 1914. Vehip added that he intended to liberate the Caucasus and help the Muslim peoples living there. Significantly, Vehip also mentioned that he thought that the Caspian port of Baku, then held by Armenians, was obtainable as well. The entire message was drenched with optimism. Enver replied immediately on the same day, saying that the difficulties and bloodletting of the preceding three years would be wiped away like old wounds, and that he looked forward to the fact that Batum, Kars, and Ardahan would soon be liberated. Actually, Vehip's troops were a little behind schedule and finally took the city of Sarikamiş on April 5 and then began advancing on Kars. The memory of the bitter defeat of the winter of 1914 and 1915 had been avenged. The long-held city of Van was liberated on April 6 and Dogubeyazit on April 14. The IV Corps maintained the tempo of its attack and took the frontier town of Saray. However, it did not stop and drove into Persia, taking Kotur (last held in the spring of 1915 by the Van Jandarma Division) on April 20, 1918.

Along the coast, Armenians and local Greeks attempted to defend Batum, but the VI Corps attacked with its two Turkish infantry divisions. The VI Corps had about ten thousand to twelve thousand men to put into the fight and Batum fell on April 14, 1918. Again, the Turks captured quantities of war material, particularly much needed transport including two locomotives, automobiles, and wagons. In the coastal regions, the Turks also discovered many Muslim villages that were reduced to piles of burnt debris and their residents reduced to dismembered corpses. The Turks attributed these atrocities to the local Christian inhabitants rather than to the Russians.[12] From Batum, the Turks fanned out to the north taking Ozurgeli and to the south taking Ardahan by mid-April.

In the center, the Armenians attempted to hold the fortress city of Kars. The Russian Army had heavily fortified Kars, captured from the Turks in 1878, in the intervening fifty years. The Russians turned over the defenses intact to the Armenians, and so Kars was potentially a place where the Third Army could expect to encounter serious resistance. Kars was defended by ten thousand Armenians; Table 7.2 breaks down the weapons available for the defense of the fortress.[13]

Table 7.2
The Fortress of Kars, April 30, 1918

Weapons	Number on Hand
Fixed artillery	154
Machine guns	46
Reserve artillery	66
Reserve machine guns	20

Source: Turkish General Staff, *Birinci Dünya Harbinde Turk Harbi Kafkas Cephesi 3ncu Ordu Harekati, Cilt II* (Ankara: GK Basimevi, 1993), Kroki (Map) 79.

The Şevki Group advanced on this heavily fortified city in early April 1918. The Armenians tried to delay the Turks by establishing defensive lines in depth, but Yakup Şevki Paşa hammered them back. By April 24 the Turks had almost encircled Kars and laid siege to the city. It was clear to all concerned that the Turks had the means and the determination to take the city. The Armenians frantically tried to negotiate their way out of having to fight for the city. Vehip Paşa demanded the surrender of the fortress intact as the price for a peaceful withdrawal. The Armenians had no choice but to accept. The next day at 9 A.M., the Turks entered the intact fortress of Kars with its abundant storehouse of supplies and large quantities of weapons. The artillery park was captured in its entirety and added significant combat power to the Turkish Army. Vehip's men continued eastward and near the end of April 1918, the Third Army had swept to the old 1877 frontier.

Turkish offensive operations continued into May of 1918. In the IV Corps area of responsibility, the 5th Infantry Division advanced over fifty kilometers into northern Persia and captured the city of Hoy on May 2. From there the division moved south and by May 18 had reached the vicinity of Dilman. The IV Corps pushed east into Persia from Dogubeyazit as well, taking the city of Moko. The Şevki Paşa Group pushed beyond the 1877 frontier on a broad front, conducting offensive operations along the railway line toward the Caucasian city of Tiflis. The local Armenian population continued to flee to the east and to the north. By the end of May 1918 the Şevki Paşa Group had taken Gumru and Karakilis. The leading elements of the group were now about fifty kilometers from Tiflis itself. It was a magnificent achievement, but it reenergized Enver Paşa's grand idea of a Pan-Turanic empire stretching beyond the Caspian Sea.

The political situation continued to deteriorate and became very confusing. The Turks, Russians, and delegates from the Trans-Caucasian Federation had been trying to reach some sort of an agreement since February 23 at a conference in the port city of Trabzond. The Russians were hoping for an end to Turkish expansion into the Caucasus and the Georgians, Azeris, and Armenians sought to gain legitimacy for their fledgling national states. In the middle of these negotiations, Georgian nationalists in Tiflis proclaimed the complete independence of the Trancaucasian Federative Republic.[14] Soon afterwards, the

Diet of the new state proclaimed its commitment to a continued state of war with the Ottoman Empire. The talks at Trabzond collapsed.

Peace discussions were resumed in Batum on May 11, 1918. This time, the Turks held all of the cards and rather than to become involved in time consuming negotiations, Vehip Paşa simply issued an ultimatum. Vehip demanded the occupation of the Georgian regions around the cities of Akhaltzikhe and Aleksandropol, the transfer of control of the Aleksandropol–Nahcivan railway to the Turks, and the free use of all Transcaucasian railways as long as the war against Britain continued. While the delegates bickered, the Third Army continued its relentless advance. On May 15 Vehip was able to issue further ultimatums, this time demanding full rail access to the Caspian port of Baku.

The German delegate to the conference, General Otto von Lossow, who had formerly played an active part in the negotiations, was stunned by the Turkish demands. The Germans were not at all happy with the continuing Turkish drive into the former Russian Empire, and regarded the Turkish acquisition of the Caucasus as bordering on a serious violation of the Treaty of Brest Litovsk. At the highest diplomatic levels, the Germans were unable to dissuade Enver Paşa from attempting to realize his dream of a Pan Turanic Empire. Unfortunately for the Germans, alliance politics required the maintenance of effective relations with Enver Paşa. Therefore the Germans resorted to creatively devious methods by which to halt the Turkish incursion into the Caucasus. Colonel Kress von Kressenstein, having been released from his assignment commanding the Turkish Eighth Army, was sent to Tiflis, along with German diplomat von Schulenberg. These two Germans hastily conferred with the alarmed leaders of the Transcaucasian Federated Republic to arrive at an odd, yet enormously creative solution to the problem.

On May 27 the Georgian members of the federated republic announced the creation of a separate Georgian state. Simultaneously, von Kress and von Schulenberg announced the creation of a German protectorate for the newly independent Georgian state. The Turks were furious, Vehip calling for an immediate invasion of Georgia. Von Lossow departed the Batum Conference for Berlin, cutting off debate. Almost immediately signs of German influence appeared in Georgia, with German and Georgian flags flying everywhere together. The German Army transported companies of infantry by sea from the Crimea to the Georgian port of Poti. Additionally, Berlin recalled German troops in Syria and from the Ukraine for service in Georgia. The survival of the Georgian Republic appeared to be a fait accompli. Alarmed by the growing rift between allies, Enver Paşa and his new first assistant chief of staff, General Hans von Seeckt went to Batum on June 5 for discussions with the Germans. While there, Vehip's troops came directly into contact with a combined German and Georgian force on the main road to Tiflis. The Turks attacked and took many prisoners.[15] This incident resulted in Berlin officially threatening to withdraw its troops and support from the Ottoman Empire! Tensions between the Germans and the Turks were at an all-time high.

In a moment unusual for the hot tempered Enver Paşa, he and von Seeckt decided to attempt to reduce tensions. Conceding to German pressure, the northward expansion of the Turks into Georgia was, for the moment, finished. However, Enver refused to relinquish his cherished dream of a Pan Turanic Empire and almost overnight revised the command arrangements and the mission of the Third Army. On June 7 Enver decided once again to reform his Caucasian forces. From the units of the Third Army, Enver formed a new Ninth Army, the headquarters of which would be provided by the Şevki Paşa Group staff made up of personnel from the 2nd Caucasian Corps, which he now officially dissolved. To coordinate the activities of these two armies, Enver formed the new Eastern Army Group. Vehip Paşa moved up to command the new Eastern Army Group, Lieutenant General Esat Paşa moved up to command the Third Army, and Yakup Şevki Paşa was appointed to command the new Ninth Army.[16] The Third Army retained the VI Corps (the 3rd and the 36th Caucasian Infantry Divisions) and the 5th and the 37th Caucasian Infantry Divisions. The new Ninth Army commanded the 1st Caucasian Corps (the 9th and the 10th Caucasian Infantry Divisions, and the 15th Infantry Division), the IV Corps (the 11th Caucasian Infantry Division and the 5th and the 12th Infantry Divisions), and an independent cavalry brigade. Contrary to some histories of the war, very few additional Ottoman forces were diverted to the Caucasus in support of these operations (about one and a half infantry divisions altogether). Table 7.3 shows the disposition of Turkish Forces in June 1918.

In orders issued to all formations on June 8, Enver's plan went into effect on June 9. This was an incredible revision of the command arrangements on the Caucasian front and reflected Enver's new strategic concept for eastern expansion. Halted from northward movement into Georgia, Enver Paşa now reoriented the strategic direction of his Caucasian forces to the east and to the south, or toward Azerbaijan and Persia. The new command structure of the Eastern Army Group accommodated that change in strategic direction by establishing separate two armies, which could operate on a wide front.[17] Along with the new command arrangements came new missions and objectives. The Ninth Army was directed to attack into Persia and to seize Tabriz. The Third Army was directed to continue the drive eastwards towards the Caspian Sea. The Third Army staff hurried to move troops and equipment around the theater to support the new command structure and the new missions.

In the wake of the ill feelings built up between the Turks and the Germans over the Batum crisis in early June, Enver also determined to replace Vehip Paşa. On June 29 Enver ordered Vehip home to Constantinople, and ordered Halil Paşa, the Sixth Army commander, up from Mosul to replace Vehip Paşa as the commander of the Eastern Army Group. Enver hoped that the change in command in the Turkish Caucasian forces would end any lingering animosity between the Germans and the Turks.

By mid-June 1918, the Third Army was well under way with a renewed advance eastward. This advance proceeded along a twin axis of approach toward Baku. The 5th Infantry Division led the way and relentlessly pushed east along the Akstafa–Baku road, and along the railroad leading to Alyat on the Caspian

Table 7.3
Disposition of Turkish Forces, June 1918

THRACE
1 Corps: 42 Inf. Div.
1 Cav. Bde.
25 Inf. Div.

ANATOLIA
Second Army
XV Corps: None
58 Inf. Div.

CAUCASIA
Eastern Army Group
Third Army
VI Corps: 3, 36 *Cauc. Inf. Div.*
5, 37 *Cauc. Inf. Div.*
Ninth Army
1st Cauc. Corps: 9, 10 *Cauc. Inf. Div.*
and 15 Inf. Div.
IV Corps: 5, 11, 12 *Inf. Div.*
Independent Cav. Bde.

PALESTINE
Yildirim Army Group
Seventh Army
III Corps: 1, 24 *Inf. Div.*,
and 3 Cav. Div.
XX Corps: 26, 53 *Inf. Div.*
19 *Inf. Div.*
Asia Corps (German)
Eighth Army
XXII Corps: 3, 7, 20 *Inf. Div.*
16, 54 *Inf. Div.*
2 *Cauc. Cav. Div.*

MESOPOTAMIA
Sixth Army
XIII Corps: 2, 6 *Inf. Div.*
XVIII Corps: 14, 51, 52 *Inf. Div.*
46 *Inf. Div.*

GALLIPOLI
Fifth Army
XIV Corps: 57 Inf. Div.
XIX Corps: None
XXI Corps: 49 Inf. Div.

SYRIA-WEST ARABIA
Fourth Army
VIII Corps: 43, 48 Inf. Div.
XII Corps: 23, 41, 44 Inf. Div.
Hicaz Group: 58 Inf. Div. and
three Provisional Inf. Div.

ARABIA-YEMEN
VII Corps: 21, 22, 39, 40 Inf. Div.

Note: Units in boldface type indicate new formations;
units underlined indicate units redeployed since January 1918;
Units in boldface italic type indicate seriously understrength units.
Units inactivated: 4, 9, 10, 17, 18, 27, 29, 31, 32,
34, 35, 38, 54, 59 Inf. Div.;
units redesignated: 13, 28, 30, 33 Inf. Div.

coast south of Baku. The Armenians and Azeris counterattacked the advancing Turkish columns and attempted to establish a defensive line in the vicinity of Kurdamir. However, the 5th Infantry Division drove through all opposition and pushed onward towards Baku. On many days the Turks advanced fifteen kilometers or more and by the 27 of July had advanced to the high ground overlooking the city of Baku.

The rest of the Third Army labored to catch up with the 5th Infantry Division's swift movements and there was a temporary lull in the tempo of operations. The VI Corps, having been left far behind, was dissolved and its divisions assigned directly to the Third Army. Other organizational developments were also in the making. Enver Paşa could not resist the psychological lure of Pan-Turanism and conceived yet another idea supporting his dreams of empire. In July 1918, he began to put together the idea of an "Army of Islam."[18] This Islamic army, with a hard core of Turkish divisions, would mobilize Islamic supporters in the Trans-Caspian and Caucasian regions, and would sweep down through Persia and retake the Shaat Al Arab. There it would block and entrap the British forces in Mesopotamia. From there, the establishment of a Pan-Turanic Empire was just a short step away. Enver's agents went to work to establish ties with and support from the Pahlevi family in Persia. On July 10, 1918, Enver ordered his ideas into action and activated the new Army of Islam. The nucleus of this new army was small–only the 5th Caucasian Infantry Division and the 15th Infantry Division, plus an independent brigade and an independent regiment. Command of the Army of Islam was given to Mirliva Fahri Ferik Nuri Paşa. To maintain the strength of both the Ninth Army and the Army of Islam, the Third Army was reduced in strength and was sent to garrison the coast at Batum and the Georgian frontier. The Ninth Army headquarters maintained itself in Kars and now assumed the theater responsibilities from Baku to Tebriz and on to Saray inside the Ottoman Empire. The headquarters of the new Army of Islam began to deploy toward the city of Baku, where it could pick up control of the offensive there. Map 7.1 shows Turkish operations in the this region in the summer of 1918.

Meanwhile, along the roads in Georgia, and in the Balkans and Black Sea ports as well, Turkish soldiers who had been Russian prisoners of war (POWs) began to appear in the Turkish lines. By July 21, 1918, the Ottoman government knew that 1,457 officers and 17,715 soldiers who had been captured by the Russians had been reported alive in Russian POW camps.[19] That summer these men began to make their way by train, and then by foot or boat, home to Turkey. Some of these POWs had been mixed in with German POWs in camps near Moscow. Of these known prisoners, only 2,260 returned to Turkey. However, an additional 6,750 unaccounted for prisoners and 2,250 civilians returned from Russian camps. These returnees reported that 15 percent of their number had been massacred while in convoy en route.[20] The fate of the others remains unknown.

Map 7.1
Third Army Operations, 1918

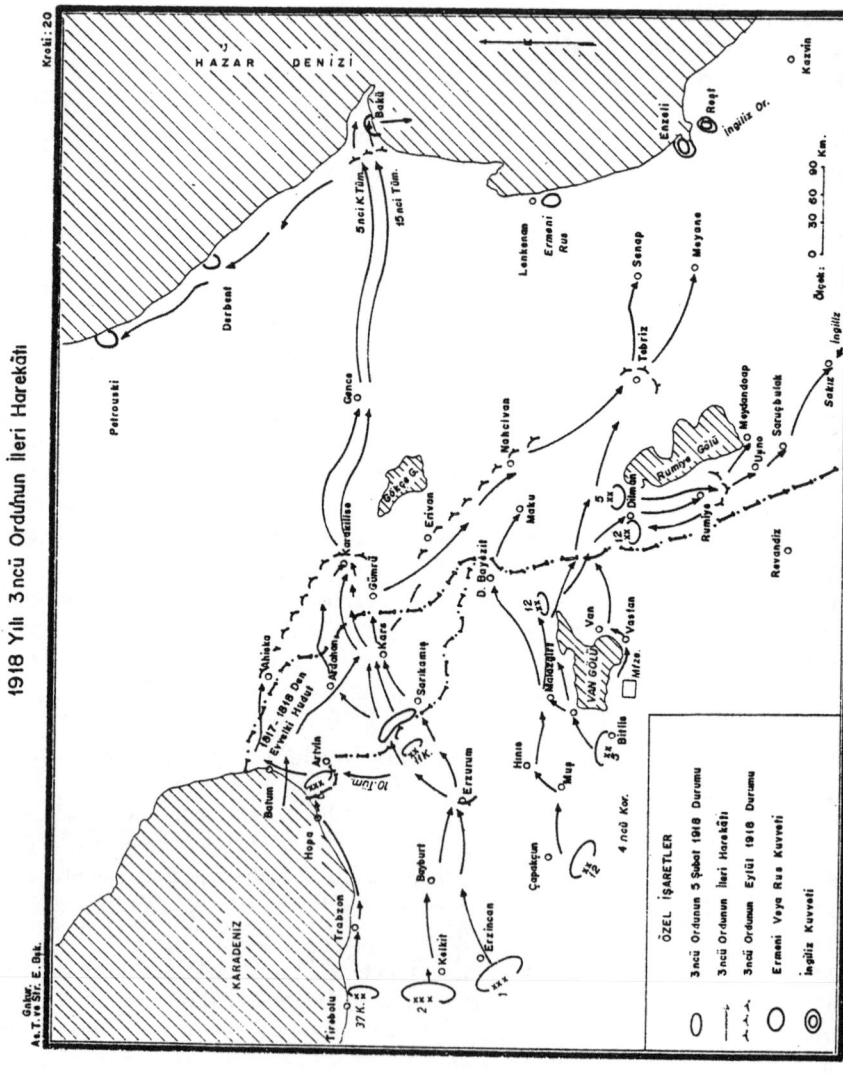

Source: Turkish General Staff, *Birinci Dünya Harbinde Turk Harbi Kafkas Cephesi 3ncu Ordu Harekati, Cilt II* (Ankara: GK Basimevi, 1993), Kroki (Map) 20.

AZERBAIJAN

One of the more interesting vignettes of the First World War occurred as the Turks conquered Azerbaijan and approached Baku. In early January 1918, the British became quite concerned about Turkish inroads into the Caucasuses and, in particular, were concerned about a possible threat to British interests in Persia. Major General L. C. Dunsterville, who was a boyhood friend of Rudyard Kipling and the model for "Stalky" of Kipling's *Stalky and Co.* was appointed as the Chief of the Military Mission to the Caucasus. Dunsterville began to organize his expedition, now called "Dunsterforce" at Baghdad in the spring of 1918. Dunsterville had a rather fuzzy mission, which was to proceed into Persia and enter the Caucasus via the Caspian Sea. Typically, Dunsterville was well supplied with money and advice. Dunsterville reached Enzeli, on the Caspian coast, in mid-February, and there formed a small army of Cossacks, Russians, and Azeris. He narrowly escaped ambush several times and retired to Hamadan. There, Dunsterville began training his force with his British officers and noncommissioned officers and awaited events as they unfolded in Enzeli. Worried by the developing Turkish threat to the Baku oil fields, the British began to send reinforcements to Dunsterville in June 1918. Dunsterforce then had to fight its way back to Enzeli, where Dunsterville coordinated future combined operations with Bicherakov's Cossacks. In early July, the Cossacks landed at Alyat and the main body of Dunsterforce began to debark in Baku on August 20.

In the meantime, the Army of Islam had begun its attack on Baku. At 3:30 A.M. July 31, the Turks attacked Hill 905, to the northwest of Baku. The attack continued until August 2, when the Turks called it to halt. Turkish reinforcements, in the form of the 10th Caucasian Infantry Division, joined the 5th Infantry Division, as well as several batteries of artillery and a cavalry regiment. Halil Paşa prepared a second assault and on August 5 this attack was launched, again aimed at Hill 905. The attack also failed, with the Turks losing a total of 547 officers and men killed and wounded. The commander of the Army of Islam attributed his failure to a well-organized defense and to the fact that his soldiers were tired.[21] The 10th Caucasian Infantry Division was pulled off the line and the 15th Infantry Division, which had seen little fighting since its deployment to the Caucasus, arrived to take its place.

Compounding the problem for the Turks were the first reports that three hundred British soldiers had arrived in Baku on August 5 and that a further five thousand were awaiting transportation in Enzeli. To compensate for this, the Ninth Army was directed to threaten Enzeli and Hamadan with the hopes that the British troops would be retained in Persia. The worried staff of the Army of Islam now considered that they would need an additional five thousand fresh troops and several batteries of heavy artillery to take Baku. By August 17 Dunsterforce had three battalions of British infantry, some field artillery, and three armored cars in Baku. However, Dunsterville was becoming more discouraged every day as the Azeri and Armenian defense force began to fall apart from the lack of dynamic leadership. The Turks began to plan for the final assault on Baku, with the 15th Infantry Division coming in from the north and the 5th Caucasian Infantry Division attacking from the west. The main attack would be made on the northwest corner of the Baku defenses. The Army of Islam began its attacks at 1:00 A.M. on September 14, 1918, and the Turks made rapid progress against crumbling defenses. Dunsterforce, in withdrawal planning reminiscent of the Gallipoli evacuation, had its transport ready. Dunsterville realized that the defense was failing and decided about 11:00 A.M. that he must withdraw his forces. While his rear guards protected the evacuation, Dunsterforce loaded its personnel and equipment, and by 10:00 P.M. on September 14 they set sail for Enzeli.

With the withdrawal of the British, chaos broke out amongst the Azeris, the Cossacks, and the refugee Armenians. Throughout the night, as the Turks drove in the remaining defenses, fires, pillaging and massacre broke out in Baku. The Turks continued their artillery bombardment of the town throughout the night. By the next day, perhaps as many as six thousand Armenians were dead, many of them refugee civilians, slaughtered by the Azeris.[22] The Turks took the town on September 15, 1918.

In the final assault on Baku, the Turks lost about a thousand casualties. Halil Paşa telegraphed Enver Paşa on September 16 to announce the capture of Baku. The Turks were stunned by the internecine massacre of the Armenians, but many regarded it as just punishment for the massacres of Turks in the Erzurum *vilayet*, which had happened when the Armenian National Army pulled out in March 1918.[23]

After a period of reorganization, the Army of Islam pushed the 15th Infantry Division northwards along the Caspian Sea to the town of Derbent, where on October 7 the advance was halted by determined resistance. Under heavy naval gunfire by Russian fleet units, the Turks continued their attacks on October 20, the running battle lasting until October 26, when the Turks shattered all remaining resistance. The 15th Infantry Division then continued to drive northwards along the Caspian coast, arriving at Petrovsk on October 28. The division launched several attacks in early November, finally taking the city on November 8, 1918. The 15th Infantry Division had the honor of conducting the last Turkish offensive operation in the First World War. This operation was successful and it also marked the northernmost point of the Turkish advance into the Caucasus Mountains.

PERSIA

Yakub Şevki Paşa's Ninth Army initially had six infantry divisions assigned to its rolls when it received the mission to invade Persia and to take Tabriz. By the end of June 1918, two divisions had been taken away for other theater requirements. Nevertheless, Şevki Paşa attacked with his remaining forces. His

12th Infantry Division attacked south, taking Dilman on June 18. By July 27 the division had beaten its way down to Rumiye, and a month later it had taken the southern shore of the Rumiye lake. To the north, Şevki Paşa began a two-division attack, which bypassed Erivan and went straight toward Nahcivan. That city fell on July 19, 1918. Continuing down the railway toward Tabriz, the 11th Infantry Division took Tabriz on August 23.[24] Confronting an increasing British presence in Persia, the Ninth Army's offensive now ground to a halt. In September, the Turks had consolidated their hold on Northern Persia and held a line reaching from Astara on the Caspian Sea to Miane in Persia (about sixty kilometers southeast of Tabriz) and on into the Ottoman Empire near Süleymaniye. The Turks held this territory until the Armistice.

MEGGIDO

In Palestine, torrential rainstorms in the last week of 1917 and an ever-hardening Turkish defense brought Allenby's offensive to a halt north of Jerusalem. Entering 1918, the Yildirim Army Group enjoyed a period of relative calm after the storm of the British offensive. The Turks used this time to reinforce the 1st and the 24th Infantry Divisions with additional infantry battalions and to consolidate their defensive lines.

In February 1918 Allenby renewed his offensive by ordering an attack on Jericho. The British hoped to force the Turkish XX Corps back across the Jordan River. The attack began on February 19 and hit hard the 26th and the 53rd Infantry Divisions. In just two days, the British broke into the Turkish defensive system. The Turks ordered a withdrawal to the east bank of the Jordan River, where the Seventh Army reestablished a solid defense.

February 1918 also brought an important change in the command structure of the Yildirim Army Group–the relief of von Falkenhayn. Over the preceding four months, the Turks, at all levels, had become increasingly dissatisfied with the advice and command of General von Falkenhayn. His direction and dispositions were thought to have resulted in the debacles at Gaza and Beersheba. Part of von Falkenhayn's troubles were caused by his high-handed contempt for Turkish officers and by his refusal to allow Turkish staff officers to participate in planning combat operations. The reputation for success and credibility in multinational combat operations that von Falkenhayn had built in Romania was proving to be a disappointment in the eyes of Enver Paşa and the Turkish General Staff. The Yildirim Army Commander found himself remembered for his direction of Verdun and for his failure to hold the Gaza-Beersheba line, rather than for his success in Romania. First assistant chief of staff von Seeckt had visited von Falkenhayn's headquarters on February 6 and had come away disappointed. Because of this loss of confidence, Enver Paşa, in consultation with von Seeckt, was determined to relieve von Falkenhayn.[25] As potential replacements, there were several possibilities available in Constantinople, particularly General von Lossow, Chief of the Military Mission and Liman von Sanders Paşa (having been awarded this honorific after the successful Gallipoli campaign), then commanding the Turkish First Army. In spite of their great differences in opinion about Turkey's strategic direction of the war, Enver retained great respect for the fighting abilities of Liman von Sanders (hereafter called by his Turkish title of Liman Paşa). On February 19 Enver approached Liman Paşa with an offer to command the Yildirim Army Group. Liman Paşa, tired of being sidelined in Turkish Thrace, eagerly accepted Enver's offer. On February 24, 1918, the Turkish General Staff issued orders stating the following:

1. By order of the German General Staff, Marshal von Falkenhayn is recalled and is assigned to other duties. Marshal Liman von Sanders is assigned as Commander of the Yildirim Army Group.
2. The officers of the First Army headquarters will embark from Bandirma (for departure with Liman Paşa) and the Fifth Army will reorganize itself to assume the responsibilities of the First Army.
3. The First Army is hereby inactivated and all assets and units will herewith fall under the control of the Fifth Army.
4. The Second and Sixth Armies are reassigned to the control of the Turkish General Staff.
5. The Second and Sixth Armies, and the Euphrates Group are relieved from assignment to the Yildirim Army Group.
6. The Fourth Army will insure that it coordinates operations with the Seventh and the Eighth Armies (author's note: effectively subordinating the Fourth Army to the control of the Yildirim Army Group).
7. Under the authority of paragraph 1, Marshal Liman von Sanders will report when he has assumed command. Paragraphs 2 through 4 will take effect on March 1, 1918. [26]

This order had several far-reaching consequences. First, by dissolving the First Army staff and by sending these officers with Liman Paşa, Enver ensured that the composition of the Yildirim Army Group staff would become predominately Turkish. Second, the wording in paragraph one of the order transferred the onus of Falkenhayn's relief to the German General Staff, which would assuage any residual bad feelings resulting from von Falkenhayn's relief. Third, the order decoupled the Mesopotamian Theater from the Yildirim Army Group, which would streamline and simplify its responsibilities. Finally, the order directed Cemal's Fourth Army to coordinate its operations with Liman's forces. Cemal would shortly thereafter give up command of the Fourth Army, thus clearing the way for the full control of that army by Liman Paşa. This insured that the Palestine front was finally brought under the control of a single commander. Overall, these revisions were very carefully orchestrated and put to rest several organizational problems which had afflicted the defense of Palestine.

Liman Paşa turned over his responsibilities for the defense of Thrace to the Commander of Fifth Army and departed immediately for his new posting. He arrived in Syria with his staff on March 8 and immediately assumed command of the Yildirim Army Group. There he consulted with von Falkenhayn about the defensive strategy for Palestine. Von Falkenhayn was an advocate of the active defense[27] and had set up a flexible defense, which allowed for both retreat and for the surrender of ground. Liman Paşa, based on his unyielding defense of the Gallipoli Peninsula, held to an opposite theory of tactical defense—that of refusing to give up an inch of ground by compelling formations to defend terrain at all costs. Unhappy with von Falkenhayn's plans and tactical instructions, Liman Paşa began immediately to reverse the operational and tactical direction of the Yildirim Army Group. This would have serious consequences in the fall of 1918.

Shortly after Liman Paşa's arrival, the British conducted another offensive, aimed again at establishing a bridgehead on the east bank of the Jordan. This offensive was coordinated with large scale Arab raids on the Dera-Hejaz railway and was preceded by diversionary attacks across the entire front. On March 21, the British launched a major attack with two infantry divisions and two cavalry divisions, which broke through the Jordan River line. The British advanced against the Turkish 48th Infantry Division. By March 30, in a stunning advance, the British had pushed the 48th Division back into the city of Amman, on the Hejaz railway. For reasons not clearly explained either in the British official campaign history or by Field Marshall Wavell in his biography of Allenby, the British decided to withdraw on March 31. Certainly, the stated reason that the Turks had brought up substantial reserves, which offset the numerical advantage of the British, was not at all true. Possession of Amman would cut, once and for all, the Dera-Hejaz railway and also outflanked the strong Turkish main defensive lines. It was an important objective for the British and the abandonment of their attack, and subsequent withdrawal, is not easily explained. The Turks pursued the withdrawing British and continued to compress them into the Jordan River valley. After a bloody repulse on April 11, the Turks halted their counterattacks and began to dig in. The Turks called this the First Battle of the Jordan.

The Second Battle of the Jordan began on April 30, with the British again launching an attack from their bridgehead across the Jordan toward Amman. In the intervening two weeks, the Turks had finally brought up strong forces (the 24th Infantry Division and the 3rd Cavalry Division), which were available to conduct a flank attack on the advancing British. Counterattacks by these Turkish divisions were executed between May 2 and May 4 and brought the British offensive to a quick termination. Further fighting broke out in this area in mid-July 1918, but it was costly and failed to give either side any significant advantage.

With the exception of these operations on the far-left flank of the Turkish line, the Palestine theater was relatively quiet during the spring and summer of 1918. The principal reason was that the gigantic Ludendorff Offensives in France during the spring of 1918 forced the Imperial General Staff to tap Allenby's Army for vitally needed reinforcements. Allenby was forced to send to France, beginning in March, two infantry divisions, nine yeomanry (cavalry) regiments, twenty-four British infantry battalions, five heavy artillery batteries and five machine gun companies.[28] In return, he received several Indian Army infantry divisions from Mesopotamia, and a number of Indian cavalry regiments and infantry battalions. Thus gutted, Allenby lost a significant portion of his trained and experienced British Army combat power, and in return received less welltrained Indian Army troops. This turn of events forced Allenby to spend the summer engaged in a complete reorganization and retraining of his army. The British were still left with seven full infantry divisions in Palestine, but the national character of these formations had changed significantly. Only a single all-British infantry division remained, four others being two-thirds Indian, and the final two were entirely Indian Army infantry divisions. Only in mounted strength did Allenby's situation actually improve, gaining one division, for a total of four mounted divisions. Allenby still commanded a large and well-equipped army with which to renew the offensive against the Yildirim Army Group. Turkish intelligence estimated Allenby's effective and mobile combat strength at 56,000 riflemen, 11,000 cavalry, and 552 artillery pieces.[29]

To oppose this collection of Imperial strength, in August 1918, the Yildirim Army Group disposed 40,598 front line infantrymen, who were armed with 19,819 rifles, 273 light and 696 heavy machine guns.[30] The number of Turkish machine guns available to the Yildirim Army Group, in comparison with other campaigns, seems unusually high and probably includes the assets of the German Asia Corps. For the ninety-plus kilometer-wide front, the Turks had twelve understrength divisions available for the defense. Cevat's Eighth Army defended the coast with the XXII Corps (7th and 20th Infantry Divisions) and the Left Wing Group, a corps-sized formation commanded by German Colonel von Oppen (16th and 19th Infantry Divisions, and the German Asia Corps). The line continued with Mustafa Kemal Paşa's Seventh Army of the III Corps (1st and 11th Infantry Divisions) and the XX Corps (26th and 53rd Infantry Division). Cemal's Fourth Army hooked south with the VIII Corps (the 48th Infantry Division, a provisional division, and the division-sized Şerştal Group), the Şeria Group or Jordan Group (3rd Cavalry and 24th Infantry Divisions), and the II Corps (62nd Infantry Division). A significant asset for the Turks returned in the person of Mustafa Kemal when he took command of the Seventh Army on August 17. Liman Paşa and his subordinate commanders worked feverishly to prepare the defense to receive what was expected to be a major British offensive. In early September 1918, the signs of an impending British offensive were undeniable, but Liman and the Turks were unable to pinpoint the exact area where Allenby would strike. This was due to the superb tactical deception measures which Allenby used. Consequently, the Yildirim Army Group remained spread along the entire front in static defensive positions. The only divisional formations available for reserve duty at the operational level were the 2nd Caucasian Cavalry Division in the Eighth Army area and the 3rd Cavalry Division in the Fourth Army area. In the event of a major British breakthrough, Liman Paşa had few reserves and even fewer options. However, Liman's faith in the fighting qualities of his well-dug-in Turkish infantry remained high. Table 7.4 shows the disposition of Turkish forces in September 1918.

Allenby's plan was the reverse of the Gaza-Beersheba plan of 1917. Instead of feinting near the sea and then attacking inland at Beersheba, in 1918 Allenby

Table 7.4
Disposition of Turkish Forces, September 1918

THRACE
First Army
I Corps: 42 Inf. Div.
1 Cav. Bde.

ANATOLIA
Second Army
XII Corps: 23 Inf. Div.
XV Corps: 41, 44 Inf. Div.

GALLIPOLI
Fifth Army
XIV Corps: 57 Inf. Div.
XIX Corps: None
XXI Corps: 49 Inf. Div.

PALESTINE
Yildirim Army Group
Fourth Army
II Corps: *62 Inf. Div.*
<u>+ three Provisional Inf. Divs.</u>
Jordan Group: 24 Div., 3 Cav. Div.
VIII Corps: 48 Div., *Provisional Inf. Div.*
Seventh Army
III Corps: 1, 11 Inf. Div.
XX Corps: 26, 53 Inf. Div.
Eighth Army
XXII Corps: 7, 20 Inf. Div.
Left Wing Corps: 16, 19 Inf. Div.
  + Asia Corps
2 Caucasian Cav. Div.

CAUCASIA
Eastern Army Group
Third Army
3, 10, 36 *Caucasian Inf. Div.*
Ninth Army
9, 11 *Caucasian Inf. Div.*
12 Inf. Div.
Independent Cav. Bde.
Army of Islam
5 *Caucasian Inf. Div.*
15 Inf. Div.

MESOPOTAMIA
Sixth Army
XIII Corps: 2, 6 Inf. Div.
XVIII Corps: 14, 46 Inf. Div.

ARABIA-YEMEN
VII Corps: 21, 22, 39, 40 Inf. Div.

Note: Units in boldface type indicate new formations; units underlined indicate units redeployed since August 1918; units in bold italic type indicate seriously understrength units. Units inactivated: 3, 4, 8, 9, 10, 11, 17, 18, 25, 27, 29, 31, 32, 34, 35, 38, 50, 51, 52, 54, 59 Infantry Divisions; 37 Caucasian Infantry Division; units redesignated: 13, 28, 30, 33 Infantry Divisions.

chose to feint near the Jordan River (scene of his spring and summer offensives) and then to smash his way through the Turkish defenses on a narrow avenue next to the sea. Achieving a breakthrough, Allenby intended to pass his cavalry corps through the breach and rupture the Turk's lines of communications. This being accomplished, Allenby sought to envelop the remaining Turkish forces. It was strategy on a grand scale.

The British offensive began with the Arabs and Colonel T. E. Lawrence conducting railway cutting raids between Dera and Amman on September 16. On September 17 and 18 the British Twentieth Corps began a diversionary attack in the center of the Turkish front. These operations were designed to fix the Turks in place and to deceive them as to the true location of the main attack. The Turks were not deceived but their attention remained fixed on the hills near Jerusalem where Liman von Sanders thought Allenby would strike.[31] This was reinforced by supporting Arab activity (primarily rail and bridge interdiction) near Amman and by the aerial bombing of the Dera railroad station.[32] Because of allied air superiority, the Turks were unable to conduct air reconnaissance to confirm Allenby's true intentions. By the evening of October 18, in reaction to the British plan the reserves of the Yildirim Army Group were beginning to shift to the east. At 4:30 A.M. on the morning of September 19 Allenby attacked with a reinforced corps on a narrow twenty-kilometer-wide sector adjacent to the sea. Here he massed 35,000 infantry, 9,000 cavalry, and 400 guns against the 8,000 infantry and 120 guns[33] of the Turkish 7th and the 20th Infantry Divisions. What the British would call the Battle of Meggido and the Turks would call the Battle of the Nablus Plain had begun.

Because of Liman Paşa's tactical guidance, the Turks were prepared to fight to the finish for their positions. Initially, very heavy British artillery fires pounded the frontline positions of the regiments of the 7th and the 20th Infantry Divisions. At 4:50 A.M., the British artillery firing had ceased. Allenby did not believe in extended bombardments and the assaulting infantry came forward almost immediately on the heels of the incoming artillery. By 5:45 A.M. the Turk's telephone lines to the front were cut and by 5:50 A.M. all local Turkish reserves had been committed to the fight.[34] Modern Turkish military histories report that there was very little barbed wire available on the Palestine front at this time and indicate that the absence of heavy defensive wiring had a significant effect on the rapidity of the British onslaught.[35] Reports indicating an imminent collapse poured into the Turkish XXII Corps Headquarters. By 7:00 A.M., the British had broken cleanly through the Turkish defenses and were about to pass the waiting cavalry through the breach into the Turkish rear. The first real reports about the conditions in the breakthrough area reached Liman Paşa at 8:50 A.M. from the Eighth Army. These reports said that the 7th Infantry Division was all but destroyed and the situation was very bad. Additionally, the XXII Corps artillery had been lost. The army also reported that the adjacent 19th Infantry Division was now under heavy attack. The report ended with an urgent request for assistance.[36] Two small rear guards, comprised of one hundred men, two machine guns, and seventeen artillery pieces in the 7th Infantry Divisions sector; and of 300 men, four machine guns, and seven artillery pieces in the 20th

Infantry Division's sector, were desperately trying to keep the British from breaking into the Turkish rear areas.[37] To make matters worse, an Arab regiment threw down their arms and deserted. Liman Paşa responded immediately sending his only available large reserve, the 110th Infantry Regiment, forward to help the Eighth Army. It was too little too late. By 10:00 A.M., the British had passed two entire cavalry divisions through the huge hole blown open in the Turkish defenses. These cavalry divisions were instructed to ride hard and straight towards the Turkish rear. Deep objectives were chosen, including the town of Nazareth, containing Liman Paşa's headquarters, Meggido, and the northern exits of the Plain of Esdraelon. It was hoped that the cavalry would be able to capture Liman Paşa himself. One of the last great cavalry operations in the history of warfare was about to begin.

Disturbing reports from the center and the left wing began arriving at Liman Paşa's headquarters throughout the day. Tire fell at 11:00 A.M. that day as well. He quickly interpreted the devastating news correctly; his right wing was destroyed and his flank exposed. He reacted promptly and ordered the Seventh Army to begin withdrawing to the north in order to prevent the British from conducting a short envelopment to the Jordan River. He also ordered the newly arrived 46th Infantry Division forward towards Tire. Liman hoped that the Fourth Army could hold firm and provide a solid anchor for his rapidly disappearing army. By September 20, the British cavalry had taken Nazareth, almost capturing the surprised Liman Paşa at 4:30 A.M. that morning. Reports indicated that the XXII Corps had been reduced to one thousand to fifteen hundred riflemen and three batteries (about twelve guns). The following day the enemy had reached the shores of the Sea of Galilee and the upper Jordan River. The Eighth Army headquarters had survived, but all contact with the remnants of the 7th and 19th Infantry Divisions had been lost. For all practical purposes, the Turkish XXII Corps was destroyed.

Under Mustafa Kemal Paşa's sure grip, the Seventh Army was retiring towards the Jordan River in fair order and the Fourth Army was holding firm on the left flank. The remnants of the shattered Eighth Army were slowly retreating but were now in danger of encirclement. However, the Yildirim Army Group had absolutely no combat formations available to prevent Allenby's army from advancing north along the coast. It was an impossible strategic and operational situation for Liman Paşa. On September 21 through 23, the famous III Corps fought a gallant rear guard action from Tubas to the Jordan River. This allowed the retreating elements of the Eighth Army to block the developing British encirclement. Together, these units bought enough time for the Turks to pull back behind the Jordan River. By September 25, the great coastal cities of Haifa and Acre fell, as did Meggido. Under these chaotic conditions, huge numbers of prisoners were captured as the Allied cavalry swept up the beaten remnants of many proud Turkish regiments. The operation was the swan song of the British cavalry and went down in history as one of the great cavalry campaigns of history. The slow marching British and Indian infantry struggled to catch up. By September 27 the cavalry had broken the Jordan River line and pushed the Turks back toward Dera. The British had now entered Syria. The Battle of Meggido, which was really a series of battles within a campaign, had finally ended.

The Battle of the Nablus Plain ranks with Ludendorff's "Black Days" of the German Army in the effect that it had on the consciousness of the Turkish General Staff. It was now apparent to all but the most diehard nationalists that the Turks were finished in the war. In spite of the great victories in Armenia and in Azerbaijan, Turkey was now in an indefensible condition, which could not be remedied with the resources on hand. It was also apparent that the disintegration of the Bulgarian Army at Salonika and the dissolution of the Austro-Hungarian Army spelled disaster and defeat for the Central Powers. From now until the Armistice, the focus of Turkish strategy would be to retain as much Ottoman territory as possible.

Why had Liman von Sanders's front collapsed so quickly? He had, after all, the highest ratio of artillery and machine guns yet seen by a Turkish army available to support his entrenched infantry. Additionally, his flanks were solidly anchored on the sea and on the Jordan River heights. There were three basic reasons, none of which had anything to do with the fighting attributes of the Turkish soldiers themselves. First, at the strategic level, the terrain was favorable for the attack, at least in comparison with Gallipoli or Caucasia. Second, there was scope at the operational level for Allenby to shift corps-sized formations around the battlefield for deception and concentration. Third, the British Army had made mighty improvements in its tactical techniques at the lower battlefield level in 1917 and 1918. Falkenhayn grasped these changes to a greater degree than did Liman von Sanders. This was quite likely due to Falkenhayn's greater and more recent European combat experience, when compared with Liman von Sanders's rather limited Gallipoli experience, which had occurred very early in the war against a tactically unsophisticated British Army. Falkenhayn's ideas reflected contemporary German tactical thinking about ceding ground followed by immediate and powerful counterattacks, rather than holding every square inch at whatever the cost.

Whether the outcome of these battles would have been different had Falkenhayn's ideas prevailed will never be known. However, it is likely that a more flexible Turkish defense would not have resulted in the uniquely decisive and rapid British breakthrough. A subsequent orderly fighting withdrawal, as at Gaza, might have avoided the total destruction of division-level Turkish formations. Although surely the British would have advanced in any case, the survival of the infantry divisions on the Turkish right flank might have prevented the ruptured lines that enabled the great British cavalry breakthrough leading to the Meggido disaster.

SYRIA

Liman Paşa and his subordinate Turkish officers fought valiantly to keep the armies intact and in being, Allenby maintained relentless pressure and ordered his fast-moving, powerful cavalry to seize Damascus. Liman Paşa shifted some of his few remaining combat formations northwards to deal with this threat and assembled the 24th, 26th, and the 53rd Infantry Divisions and the 3rd Cavalry Division under the command of the III Corps for the defense of the city. However, these units were badly worn down by combat and by retreat and could not hold Damascus, which fell on October 1, 1918. The 3rd Cavalry Division fought a heroic rear guard action, which allowed the remainder of the Turkish forces to escape northward. Liman's headquarters retired to Baalbek.

The strategic situation confronting Liman Paşa on October 6, 1918, was grim to say the least. The Eighth Army had been destroyed and its headquarters dissolved. The III Corps, with the 1st and the 11th Infantry Divisions was still intact and conducting a fighting retreat, as was the XX Corps, and the 48th Infantry Division. In addition to the lost divisions of infantry, the Yildirim Army Group had lost most of its artillery. In early October the 43rd Infantry Division arrived and was immediately committed to the defense of Beirut. The situation appeared hopeless.

Allenby's pressure never stopped, and the British took Beirut on October and kept driving northward. On October 16 the Fourth Army headquarters was encircled and destroyed in the city of Humus. The 48th Infantry Division attempted to set up blocking positions at Hama, south of Aleppo, but was thrown out of them on October 19. On October 25 Allenby's amy entered Aleppo. The campaign for Syria was over.

On October 26, 1918, the headquarters of the Yildirim Army Group had fallen back to the Anatolian city of Adana, where it was collocated with the Second Army, XII Corps headquarters, and the headquarters of the 23rd Infantry Division which had its main body at Tarsus. The XV Corps was in Osmaniye (41st and 44th Infantry Divisions). The Seventh Army was located in Raco and maintained the III Corps at Alexandretta (11th and 24th Infantry Divisions), and the XX Corps near Katma (1st and 43rd Infantry Divisions).

On October 30 the newly installed Turkish minister of war, Ahmet Izzet Paşa recalled Liman Paşa to Constantinople. Mustafa Kemal Paşa was appointed to command the Yildirim Army Group in his place and reported to the headquarters at Adana the next day. Liman Paşa's farewell message to his armies praised their performance at Ariburnu, Anafarta, and at subsequent locations. He expressed how proud he was to command Turkish forces from the first time he set foot in Turkey and he thanked the Turks for their hospitality.[38] The tireless Mustafa Kemal went immediately to work planning for the defense of the Anatolian homeland. Table 7.5 shows the disposition of Turkish Forces in November 1918. The Turkish Official History of the Sinai-Palestine campaign does not list the cost or the casualties that Turkey sustained in these campaigns. General Wavell, in his biography of Allenby, states that the British took 75,000 prisoners and 360 guns in the six weeks campaign from September 18 through October 31. Indeed, the Turkish official history of the campaign quotes these British figures, possibly as a result of the loss of records caused by the destruction of the Fourth and the Eighth Army headquarters. The cost to the British was about six thousand men. Allenby's lopsided victory seemed near complete; however, it must be pointed out that the Turkish Army was still in the

Table 7.5
Disposition of Turkish Forces, November 1918

THRACE
Third Army HQS
<u>10 Cauc. Inf. Div</u> (moving)
XXV Corps: None

GALLIPOLI
Fifth Army
I Corps: 55 Inf. Div.
XIV Corps: 49, 60, 61 Inf. Div.

SYMRNA-WEST ANATOLIA
Eighth Army (reforming)
XVII: 58 Inf. Div.
XXI Corps: 57 Inf. Div.

SYRIA
Yildirim Army Group
Asia Corps (German)
Second Army
XII Corps: *23 Inf. Div.*
XV Corps: *41, 44 Inf. Div.*
Seventh Army
III Corps: *11, 24 Inf. Div.*
XX Corps: *1, 43 Inf. Div.*

CAUCASIA
Eastern Army Group
Ninth Army
3, 9, 11 Cauc. Inf. Div., 12 Inf. Div.
Independent Cav. Bde.
Army of Islam
5 Cauc. Inf. Div., 15 Inf. Div.

MESOPOTAMIA
Sixth Army
XIII Corps: *2, 6 Inf. Div.*

ARABIA-YEMEN
VII Corps: 21, 22, 39, 40 Inf. Div.

Note: Units in boldface type indicate new formations; units underlined indicate units redeployed since September 1918; units in boldface italic indicate seriously understrength units. Units Inactivated: 3, 4, 8, 9, 10, 11, 17, 18, 25, 27, 29, 31, 32, 34, 35, 38, 50, 51, 52, 54, 59 Inf. Div; 36, 37 Cauc. Inf Div.; units redesignated: 13, 28, 30, 33 Inf. Div.

field and actively preparing its defense of the Anatolian heartland when the Armistice was signed.

MESOPOTAMIA

For most of 1918 Mesopotamia remained a quiet backwater for both the British and the Turks. The British stripped the theater in the spring of 1918 in order to backfill troops to replace forces that Allenby had to send to France. The Dunsterforce adventure further drained valuable resources from the theater. On the Turkish side, the theater received no replacements and their forces slowly wore away because of disease, desertions, and some small combat losses. The British attacked in March 1918, attempting to outflank the XVIII Corps' line on the Euphrates at Khan Baghdad. However, except for severe Turkish losses of about five thousand men, the results were inconclusive. Then, beset by the requirement to send reinforcements to Allenby, the British settled in to endure the long Mesopotamian summer.

Nothing of importance happened in the theater until late September, when suddenly, the War Cabinet directed General Marshall to advance up river. It was apparent to London that the Turkish War would soon end and there was belatedly great interest in the seizure of Mosul, with its oil resources. The British began to prepare and outfit an expeditionary force to attack Mosul. On October 2 General Marshall was "put on notice" to gain as much ground as possible in the event of an armistice with Turkey. This acted as a stimulant to the lethargic British command in Mesopotamia. The British began to advance up-river and they met the XVIII Corps' 14th and 46th Infantry Divisions at their defensive positions along the Tigris. The British attacked on October 23 and forced the Turks to fall back to the Little Zab River. A British cavalry brigade found a ford upstream and began a flanking maneuver, which forced the Turks back once again. The Turkish Commander, Ismail Hakki Bey, retreated to a position north of Sharqat, where he dug in. British cavalry again swept in from behind and cut off the Turkish force. Hakki Bey was aware of the ongoing Mudros peace talks and was in no mood to either fight or attempt to break out. He, therefore, decided to surrender his force and at 7:30 A.M. on October 30, 1918, the Tigris Group surrendered. The British counted 11,322 prisoners and 51 guns taken. The British cavalry brigade made for the now totally undefended city of Mosul and occupied it on November 1, 1918, in violation of the terms of the armistice agreement. The Turkish Sixth Army and portions of the XIII Corps remained in being, although possessing very little combat capability. The war in Mesopotamia was over.

ARMISTICE AT MUDROS

It was not Allenby's success in Palestine and in Syria that convinced the Turks to quit the war. Rather, it was the advance of General Milne's army from

Bulgaria, which threatened Thrace and Constantinople, that convinced them of the empire's untenable position.[39] The force pool which had been maintained so carefully throughout the war in European Thrace had long been emptied to support the compelling requirements of Palestine, Caucasia, and Mesopotamia, leaving Constantinople almost undefended. The breakout of the Allies from the Salonika beachhead created a strategic crisis for which there was no answer. On October 5, 1918, Talat Paşa's cabinet decided to explore the possibility of an armistice.

On October 13, 1918, the Turkish charge d'affaires in Madrid sought Spanish assistance in requesting President Wilson's help in taking Turkey out of the war. The Turks were impressed with Wilson's Fourteen Points and also by his apparent magnanimity towards Turkey. When this failed to achieve the desired results, the Turks sent out their highest-ranking British prisoner, Major General Townshend, the defeated commander of Kut, to the island of Lesbos to announce their intention to seek an armistice. This act galvanized the British and provoked the French. Turkey and the Allies then entered into negotiations, which took place on the island of Mudros at the mouth of the Dardanelles. There was much dissension and rivalry between the victors. Ultimately, conditions favored by the British were agreed to by the Turkish delegation and an armistice was signed on the deck of the battleship *Agamemnon* on October 30, 1918.[40] Turkey was out of the war.

But what of the Turkish Army? Although battered and ground down, the Turkish Army was still in the field on October 31, 1918. It counted on its rolls twenty-five numbered infantry divisions, four fortress commands, and three provisional infantry divisions. The command and control structure of the Turkish Army was still intact and remained capable of conducting combat operations with approximately one million men still under arms. Although it was bloodied, the Turkish Army still retained possession of the Anatolian heartland and most of the Russian Caucasian provinces. The British felt that the Turkish Army was on the verge of collapse, but there is almost no question that the army would have continued to fight until the very end.[41]

NOTES

1. W. E. D. Allen and Paul Muratoff, *Caucasian Battlefields: A History of the Wars on the Turco-Caucasian Border 1828-1921* (Cambridge: Cambridge University Press, 1953), 457.

2. Turkish General Staff, *Birinci Dünya Harbinde Turk Harbi Kafkas Cephesi 3ncu Ordu Harekati, Cilt II* (Ankara: GK Basimevi, 1993), 441.

3. General Fahri Belen, *Birinci Cihan Harbinde Turk Harbi 1918 Yili Hareketleri, V Cilt* (Ankara: GK Basimevi, 1967), 149-150.

4. Ibid., 150.

5. Ibid., 151.

6. Turkish General Staff, *3ncu Ordu Harekati*, 442.
7. W. E D. Allen and Paul Muratoff, *Caucasian Battlefields*, p. 458.
8. ATASE, Commander, Ciphered Report, Operations of 13-14 March, from Third Army Commander to Acting Commanding General, March 21, 1918. Numerous dead Muslim Turks were discovered in the area between Erzincan and Erzurum, including children. However, the Third Army troops had not gotten off the main roads and into the villages yet, and larger numbers of the dead were expected to turn up. Archive 4/3671, Cabinet 163, Drawer 5, File 2947, Section 628, Index 31-, 3-3.

ATASE, Cipher to Fourth Army, April 1, 1918. In the city of Erzurum 2,127 dead Muslim Turkish males were found. The only people there at the time were the Armenians (the Russians having previously departed). Archive 4/3671, Cabinet 163, Drawer 5, File 2947, Section 628, Index 3-4.

9. ATASE, Ciphered message from the Operations Division, Headquarters, Third Army to the 1st and 2nd Caucasian Corps Commanders, March 25, 1918. "Prepare to move onwards to Oltu and Kars. You can expect to find armed resistance in the villages from Armenians and Greeks, including artillery and machine guns." Archive 4/3671, Cabinet 161, Drawer 1, File 2914, Section 477, Index 67-2, 67-3.

10. Turkish General Staff, *3ncu Ordu Harekati,*477.
11. Ibid., 478.
12. ATASE, Ciphered message from the 2nd Division (Intelligence), Headquarters, Third Army to the Turkish General Staff, May 1, 1918. This report identifies villages between Trabzon and Erzincan. It also noted that in Erzincan that Muslims were not only slaughtered but that they had been dismembered into pieces. Archive 1 /2, Cabinet 109, Drawer 4, File 359, Section 1023, Index 3-36.
13. Turkish General Staff, *3ncu Ordu Hareketleri*, Kroki (Map) 79.
14. Allen and Muratoff, *Caucasian Battlefields*, 466.
15. Ibid., 478.
16. Contrary to the information presented by Allen and Muratoff, Vehip Paşa was not immediately fired and replaced by Halil Paşa.
17. Turkish General Staff, *3ncu Ordu Harekati*, 526.
18. Ibid., 544.
19. Turkish General Staff, *Turk Silahli Kuvvetleri Tarihi Osmanli Devri Birinci Dünya Harbi Idari Faaliyetler ve Lojistik, Xncu Cilt*, (Ankara: Gnkur Basimevi, 1985), 507.
20. Ibid., 507.
21. Turkish General staff, *3ncu Ordu Harekati*, 580, 581.
22. Allen and Muratoff, *Caucasian Battlefields*, 495.
23. Turkish General Staff, *3ncu Ordu Harekati*, 592.
24. Ibid., 544.
25. Turkish General Staff, *Birinci Dünya Harbinde Turk Harbi Sina-Filistin Cephesi IV Cilt 2ncu Kisim* (Ankara: GK Basimevi, 1986), 536.
26. Ibid., 538.
27. Ibid., 540.
28. General Sir Arcihbald Wavell, *Allenby: A Study in Greatness* (New York: Oxford University Press, 1941), 249-250.
29. Turkish General Staff, *Sina-Filistin Cephesi,* 615.
30. Ibid., 617.
31. Belen, *1918 Yili Hareketleri*, 69.
32. Belen, *1918 Yili Hareketleri*, 71.
33. Wavell, *Allenby: A Study in Greatness*, 269.
34. Turkish General Staff, *Sina-Filistin Cephesi,* 626.

35. Belen, *1918 Yili Hareketleri*, 72.
36. Turkish General Staff, *Sina-Filistin Cephesi*, 627.
37. Belen, *1918 Yili Hareketleri*, 72.
38. Turkish General Staff, *Sina-Filistin Cephesi*, 731.
39. Belen, *1918 Yili Hareketleri*, 206.
40. Busch, Briton Cooper. *Mudros to Lausanne*: Britain's Frontier in West Asia, 1918-1923 (Albany: State University of New York Press, 1976), 10-20.
41. Turkish General Staff, *Turk Istiklal Harbi I, Mondros Mütarekesi ve Tatbikati* (Ankara: Genelkurmay Basimevi, 1999), 11-20. At the tactical level, the Turkish armies in the field were preparing to continue the fight into the winter of 1918-1919.

8
Conclusion

AFTER MUDROS

The armistice found the Turkish Army in the midst of three important actions: (1) the Yildirim Army was preparing for a determined defense of the Anatolian heartland immediately to the north of Aleppo, (2) the Ninth Army was withdrawing forces from the Caucasian front for service in Thrace, and (3) a re-created Third Army was working on plans to establish a defense of Constantinople.[1] The armistice ended these endeavors and the Turkish General Staff went immediately to work to return the army to a peacetime environment. As planned, the new postwar Turkish Army would have just twenty infantry divisions (down from a 1914 peacetime total of thirty-six infantry divisions).[2] Instead of renumbering or reconstructing the entire force structure, the Turks simply maintained the surviving divisional base. Most of the surviving infantry divisions were comprised of ethnic Turks from the Anatolian heartland and the divisions which did not meet this criteria were dissolved. Although this left the Turks with a rather untidy lot of unconsecutively numbered infantry divisions, it left them with their hard core of tough combat infantry divisions intact. Mirroring their prewar military policies, the Turks immediately began to downsize their formations by going back to a cadre structure of undermanned infantry divisions. Within these infantry divisions, every infantry regiment would maintain one battalion at 50 percent strength and two battalions at 25 percent strength. The divisions would also maintain four artillery batteries each and keep thirty-six machine guns operational (or 33 percent of their normal wartime authorizations).

By January 27, 1919, the Turks were well into the implementation of this plan, much to the discomfort of the British commanders trying to occupy Constantinople and its surrounding environs.[3] Under this cadre plan the Turkish Army planned to maintain about 40,000 infantrymen under arms supported at divisional level by 240 cannons. There were more men assigned to the Jandarma and to the supply services. This force had 48,000 rifles on hand and an additional 791,000 stored in depots. Additionally, there were about 4,000 machine guns and 945 artillery pieces stored in depots in the Anatolian heartland.[4]

The postwar army was garrisoned more or less evenly throughout what is now the modern Republic of Turkey. Table 8.2 shows the disposition of Turkish Forces in January 1919. As the regiments reoccupied their garrison homes, the British occupied the Dardanelles and Constantinople, the Italians occupied enclaves around the southern Mediterranean littoral, the French occupied the southeast, the Armenians reclaimed Kars, and the Greeks occupied Smyrna and the central hinterland. There were confrontations and tension in these areas as the victorious allies sought to impose further restrictions on the Turkish Army. However, the tough core of emergent Turkish leadership seasoned in the cauldron of war held the army together until it was needed again.

THE COST

The cost of defeat in the First World War for Turkey remains hard to calculate. In spite of meticulous records keeping by the wartime Turkish staffs, none of Turkey's official histories contain consolidated casualty statistics for the entire war.[5] Contradictory figures abound, especially concerning the number of civilian casualties. Generally, a total count of 325,000 Ottoman military dead is the number most commonly used for the past seventy-five years. This number seems to have originated in Commandant Larcher's book written in 1926 and from early Turkish General Staff accounts (Table 8.1 shows casualty statistics typical of the Turkish official histories compared to Larcher's casualty statistics). Early twentieth-century *Encyclopaedia Britannica*'s list the same figures and attributes them to a U.S. War Department estimate. These numbers vastly understate the true number of Ottoman casualties.

Table 8.1
The Cost of Defeat—Commonly Used Figures

Category	Turkish Histories	Larcher
Number of men mobilized	2,608,000	2,850,000
Killed	50,000	50,000
Died of wounds	35,000	35,000
Died of diseases	240,000	240,000
Wounded	400,000	not available
Wounded, permanently disabled	not available	400,000
Sick, Deserters, Missing, or POW	1,565,000	1,560,000

Sources: Turkish General Staff, *Turk Silahli Kuvvetleri Tarihi Osmanli Devri Birinci Dünya Harbi Idari Faaliyetler ve Lojistik*, (Ankara: Gnkur. Basimevi, 1985), 509, and Commandant M. Larcher, *La Guerre Turque Dans La Guerre Mondiale* (Paris: Mondiale. Chiron/Berger-Levrault & Co. 1926), 602–604.

Table 8.2
Disposition of Turkish Forces, January 1919

THRACE
I Corps: 49, 60 Inf. Div.
XXV Corps: 1 Div., 10 Cauc. Inf. Div.

GALLIPOLI
XIV Corps: 55, 61 Inf. Div.

ANATOLIA
XX Corps: 23, 24 Inf. Div.
III Corps: 15 Inf. Div., 5 Cauc. Inf. Div.
XII Corps: 11, 41 Inf. Div. and 7, 20 Cav. Regt.
XVII Corps: 56, 57 Inf. Div.

CAUCASIA
XV Corps: 3, 12 Inf. Div. and 8, 11 Cauc. Inf. Div.

SYRIAN BORDER
XIII Corps: 2, 5 Inf. Div. and 12 Cav. Regt.

If Larcher's figures are accurate, every fourth male mobilized died or became a permanent casualty. However, more modern writers such as Niall Ferguson suggest far larger numbers of Ottoman dead. In his recent *The Pity of War*, Ferguson calculates that Turkey lost 804,000 dead, 400,000 wounded, and 250,000 prisoners.[6] He also states that this total of 1,454,000 is the best modern estimate, and that a maximum (maxima) Turkish total may be as high as 2,290,000 and a minimum (minima) Turkish total to be as low as 970,000. Furthermore, Ferguson concluded that Turkish total killed as a percentage of men mobilized was 26.8 percent[7] and his ratio of Turkish dead to wounded was two dead to one wounded.

The truth probably lies somewhere in the middle. Obviously the Turk's and Larcher's figures for the dead are too low (the dead of Gallipoli alone numbered around fifty-five thousand) and Ferguson's figures are probably too high. Since the Turks never published postwar statistics, most estimates of their casualties are based on supposition and flawed perceptions of Turkish losses. Sarikamiş, in particular, stands out as an example in this regard. The Turkish General Staff's official campaign histories list definite numbers of killed for the following campaigns, Sarakamiş, Sinai 1915, Gallipoli, Ctesiphon, Second Kut, First/Third Gaza, Jerusalem, and Second Jordan. They list combined figures of killed and wounded for Tortum/Van/Malazgirt, the Elişkirt valley, Shaiba, First Kut, the seige of Kut, Koprukoy, Erzurum, Bayburt, Erzincan, the 1916 Second Army offensive, Sinai 1916, and Second Gaza. Other campaigns can only be estimated, with the high loss leaders: Meggido and Galicia, and others with few casualties: the early Mesopotamian campaign, Macedonia, Persia, and 1st and 2nd Gaza. In very few cases did the total number of killed exceed the number of wounded by a substantial margin. The author's estimates of Turkish casualties appear in Table 8.3 and a fuller explanation of the methodology and data may be found in Appendix F.

Regardless of the method of calculation, Turkey suffered enormously in the First World War. Using the author's estimates, the Ottoman Empire suffered a death rate of 10.6 percent (as a percentage of men mobilized) of men who were either killed or missing in action, or who died of combat wounds. This rate is plausible and reflects the known loss rates suffered on the Ottoman fronts, which were lower than on the European fronts due to the lower intensity of combat operations. However, when the horrific numbers of men who died of disease are considered, the death rate skyrockets to confirm Ferguson's astounding 26.9 percent of men mobilized. When the wounded whom suffered permanent injury are considered, every third man mobilized died or became crippled. The Ottoman wounded outnumbered the dead and missing in a ratio of two to one (reversing Ferguson's ratio) and mirroring casualty ratios experienced by other combatants. Of course these figures only present military losses. To the military losses must be added the huge loss of life and productivity of the Muslim, Armenian, and other Ottoman civilians killed or injured during the war.

Table 8.3
Ottoman Casualties (Author's Estimates)

Category	Number	Remarks
Number of men mobilized	2,873,000	includes Jandarma and navy
Combat dead	243,598	includes died of wounds
Missing in action	61,487	
Died of diseases	466,759	
Seriously wounded	303,150	permanent loss
Total wounded	763,753	includes the seriously wounded plus all others
POW's	145,104	does not include 1918 returnees from Russia
Estimated Deserters	500,000	based on Yalman
Total dead or missing	771,844	

Sources: See Appendix F for detailed notes on sources.

In geographic terms, the Turks began the war with 2,410,000 square kilometers of territory inhabited by about 22 million people, and after Mudros, they retained 1,283,000 square kilometers of territory inhabited by about 10 million people. The heavily fought over eastern provinces in Caucasia were devastated in physical and human terms and the local infrastructure was almost completely destroyed. Hundreds of thousands of deserters roamed the hinterlands. The empire's productive Armenian population was largely gone. Substantial parts of the most productive area of the empire were occupied by foreign powers. The economy was ruined and coal production had fallen to almost nothing. Moreover, Turkey's former enemies were bent on carving even more territory from her, particularly the Greeks. By any standard, Turkey was absolutely crushed by the First World War.

TURKISH MILITARY PERFORMANCE

Is there a standard by which to measure Turkish military performance during the First World War? Certainly when compared against the collapse of the Russian and Bulgarian Armies, and perhaps against the 1917 mutinies in the French Army, the Turkish Army fares well. Even in the end, at the time of the Mudros Armistice, the Turkish Army remained in the field and under competent command authority. It was, in spite of horrific losses, still a fighting army. What then, could be said about the army's performance over the four years of war? On the positive side of the military ledger appear the following points

First, without doubt, the Turkish Army almost invariably fought at a numerical disadvantage in every theater and campaign in which it engaged. This disadvantage usually included men, artillery, munitions, and logistical support. Although there were times when the Turks were able to achieve local superiority for temporary periods, this quantitative inferiority persisted throughout the entire war. Despite this, the Turks often won battles. Therefore, the combat-effectiveness of the Turkish Army must be judged with this in mind and consequently must be judged as fairly high.

Second, the combat formations comprising primarily ethnic Turks were notable for their superb fighting spirit, high morale, and tactical capability. Dr. Yigal Sheffy found that the British Army's intelligence assessments of the Ottoman Army in Palestine in the early days of the war characterized Anatolian infantry divisions as "elite" or "crack."[8] However, in the case of non-Turkish formations, particularly after 1916, the weaknesses and indiscipline frequently demonstrated by these units tended to become a liability at the tactical and operational level. Increasingly as the war went on, the Turks came to rely on a hard core of Anatolian ethnically Turkish combat infantry divisions. Among the best of the Turkish infantry divisions were the 1st, 3rd, 5th, 7th, 8th, 9th, 10th, 19th, 51st, and 52nd.

Third, the Turkish Army displayed a remarkable ability to sustain itself under extremely adverse conditions. Furthermore, its soldiers proved resilient and capable of great feats of endurance. When allowed to dig-in and entrench themselves, the army proved almost impossible to force out of its lines. The cost of defeating the Turkish Army was usually high. The hard-fighting *Askers* needed very little of the service support that western armies viewed as essential military requirements. As a result, the Turkish Army was never "top heavy" with support units and was able to put more soldiers into the front lines as a result. The army was also able to conduct offensive operations on a shoestring of support and the marching capacity of the Turkish infantry was astounding. The Sarikamiş, the Romanian, and the Azerbaijan Campaigns standout in this regard.

Fourth, at the strategic and operational level, the Turkish Army proved capable of rapid reorganization and demonstrated a great ability to task organize combat groups at the operational level. At Gallipoli in 1915, in Mesopotamia in 1916, in the Caucasian campaigns of 1916 and 1918, and in Palestine in the spring of 1918, this ability greatly increased combat effectiveness. This was combined with a great recuperative capability to reorganize the army tactically and under combat conditions. The Yildirim Army, as late as October 1918, showcases this capacity.

Fifth, the Turkish Army produced many great combat commanders throughout the war. Among these were Mustafa Kemal Paşa, Esat Paşa, Şevki Paşa, Izzet Paşa, Halil Paşa, Fevzi Paşa, and Vehip Paşa. As a group, they were aggressive and well trained. They possessed active imaginations and the will to act. They were superb organizers and also worked well with their German comrades-in-arms when the situation required. The ability of these men to use the instruments at their command significantly increased the effectiveness of the Turkish Army. Stacked against this line-up of outstanding high commanders are the inept Mahmut Kamil Paşa, who lost Erzurum and Erzincan, the indolent Cemal Paşa, and Cevit Paşa, who allowed the British to gain an easy foothold in Mesopotamia. The remainder of senior Turkish commanders were generally competent, especially while on the defense.

Sixth, the Turks displayed a great willingness to conduct alliance warfare, even when their national interests were clearly not at stake. Often, as was the case in the initial Caucasian campaigns, in the European campaigns of 1916, and in the planning of the Yildirim Army operations, the Turks put their interests second to the needs of their allies. There was continuous dialogue and cooperation between Turks and Germans, at all levels, throughout the war. The Turks remained loyal partners of the Germans and the Austrians far beyond any prospect of a reasonable conclusion of peace on favorable terms.

On the negative side of the balance sheet, there were also tally marks. First, the decision to bring the Ottoman Empire into a position risking war with the Great Powers was a tremendous mistake. The empire was exhausted from the Balkan Wars and was unprepared to engage in a World War. The mobilization effort and concentration plan delivered ill-prepared forces to locations where the Ottoman Army was incapable achieving of decisive results. Compounding this mistake was the flawed campaign plan demanding simultaneous offensives on widely separated fronts.

Second, the emergence of Enver Paşa as the directing force behind Turkey's war strategy greatly impaired the war effort. Enver's amateurish strategic vision led to his continual insistence on offensive operations and wildly optimistic plans. Beginning with Sarikamiş in 1914 and lasting until the Islam Army's operations in 1918, Enver consistently overestimated the military means necessary to accomplish the tasks he assigned. Perhaps his plans for the Yildirim Army and the Army of Islam are the best examples of this tendency. This forced Turkey to dissipate its strategic reserves in many ill-advised operations.

Third, Enver and the Turkish General Staff failed to prioritize particular strategic theaters and consequently failed to mass adequate forces at decisive points. This led to the failure to maintain the initiative when favorable conditions would have permitted offensive operations. In particular, the weak opening attacks in 1914, the Third Army's attacks in 1915, and the Second Army's attacks in 1916 stand out as evidence of this problem. Additionally, the overestimation of troops-to-task ensured that many operations were launched with forces insufficient to guarantee success.

Fourth, the Turks consistently overestimated of the ability of the Turkish lines of communications to support strategic movements. Beginning with the abysmally slow concentration of the army in 1914 the transportation problem continued until the end of the war. The failure of the Turkish General Staff to move rapidly the Second Army east in 1916 was one of the worst mistakes made during the war. While continuous efforts were made to improve the railroads by both the Turks and the Germans, this remained a problem throughout the war. Improvements to the empire's infrastructure (as suggested by Mustafa Kemal in September 1917) would have significantly improved Turkey's ability to conduct the war.

There are many myths about the Turks and their army, which should be laid to rest. These were generally created over time as a result of inaccuracies and exaggerations.

Myth 1: The Germans commanded or planned most of the Ottoman Army's operations. With the exception of the Fifth Army at Gallipoli (Liman von Sanders) and the Yildirim Army in Palestine (von Falkenhayn and von Kress), but discounting von der Goltz, who had little real impact in Mesopotamia, Germans rarely commanded large-scale Turkish forces in combat. At corps level and below, command and staff was almost an exclusively Turkish affair, although again there were exceptions: von Sodernstern at Gallipoli and von Oppen in Palestine. At division level and below, Stange, Nicolai, and Willmer must receive praise for their determined tactical leadership of Turkish soldiers. As is sometimes presented, Bronsart von Schellendorf and von Seeckt never served as the Chief of the Turkish General Staff, although a strong case can be made that they functioned as de facto chiefs. Although many armies had German chiefs of staff like the Third Army's Colonel Guse, most of the planning work was done by highly trained Turkish General Staff officers.

Myth 2: The Turks kept poor records. In fact, the exact opposite is true, the Ottomans literally invented bureaucracy and red tape, and they kept most of their records no matter how trivial. The Turkish General Staff Archives alone contain 1.5 million documents on the First World War (out of total holdings of over 8 million documents). The other Turkish national archives contain many millions more. However, the vast bulk of these records, particularly those dealing with sensitive political and military issues, are unavailable to researchers.

Myth 3: Ottoman units were prone to desertion and disintegration under the pressure of combat. There may be some grain of truth to this if the Meggido and Syrian campaigns are used as a model. However, Megiddo was an envelopment battle followed by a pursuit, ideal conditions for the gathering of large numbers of prisoners. These two battles were unique and do not characterize the nature of combat on the Ottoman fronts. Although there were minor instances of collapse, these were rare and, in any case, were not unique to the Ottoman Army and none involved the wholesale rupture of a particular battle zone. The Turkish Army was far more characterized by its ability to conduct skillful fighting withdrawals successfully under intense enemy pressure. The units, which did suffer mass disintegration, were generally non-Turkish formations of regimental strength and below. Desertions occurred primarily during unit movements across the empire, during lulls in action, and from hospitals in the rear areas.

Myth 4: Enver Paşa and the CUP sought to regain Ottoman territory lost in previous wars, especially areas occupied by fellow Turkic peoples. Unquestionably Pan-Turanism was a dominant theme in the thinking of Enver Paşa, but it is equally clear this idea was never an initial war aim nor did it ever really dominate Turkish strategic thinking. This is illustrated by the fact that the recovery of irredentist territory in Caucasia or in the former Turkey-in-Europe never appeared in the prewar campaign planning process. The startling advance to Baku in 1918 was more of a unique opportunity to seize a momentary advantage rather than the conclusion of Pan-Turanic strategic objectives. That the Russian collapse happened to open the door to the Caucasus for Enver was coincidence more than a preconceived Turkish strategy to reclaim the area.

Subsequent planning for Yildirim Army operations were likewise opportunistic and dwelt mainly with the recovery of territory actually lost during the war itself.

Myth 5: The Ottoman Army suffered unusually large casualties in combat. This argument stems mainly from erroneously high Russian estimates from the Sarikamiş campaign, including abnormally high loss rates from exposure and frostbite. The Gallipoli campaign also contributed to this idea as the Allies struggled to rationalize their horrific casualties. It is important to remember that the tempo of combat operations on the Ottoman fronts was generally lower than on the European fronts. There were some exceptions like Gallipoli, however, most of the battles in this theater were not of long duration nor did they involve sustained artillery bombardments. Very importantly, the levels of combat intensity in these campaigns were lower than in Europe, primarily due to the lower ratios of artillery and machineguns (the real killers of the First World War battlefields). Likewise, gas was literally unknown on these fronts. Finally, much of the campaigning was done on a seasonal basis; thereby cutting down on the continuous nature of combat operations commonly experienced in Europe. The actual combat related loss rate (10.6 percent) was similar to that of other combatants. Disease was the great killer of men, particularly in Mesopotamia and in Caucasia.

ORDERED TO DIE

Overall, the story of the Turkish Army in the First World War is a remarkable saga. Given its exhausted condition in 1913, its lack of resources, its poor lines of communications, and the fact that it faced powerful enemies on multiple fronts, it is a story of success against great odds. Incredibly, the Turks were still on their feet at the end of the war.

Time and again Turkish commanders and staffs sent the army into combat on operations doomed to defeat. In many cases the army was literally ordered to die–in deep snows, in arid deserts, in malarial swamps, and in rugged terrain. The staggering overall casualty statistics, including disease, insured that the army was bled white over the course of the war.

Could Turkey have done better? Perhaps, but only by the accidental or intentional exit of Enver Paşa. The active presence of this aggressive and opportunistic nationalist in the master planning of Turkey's wartime strategy doomed her to defeat. Time and again, Enver forced his excessively optimistic ideas on the Turkish General Staff, and time and again, these ideas brought disaster to Turkish arms. Remarkably, the empire and its army weathered these disasters and sustained its will to victory. At the highest levels, the Turks never seemed to become infected with defeatism. In Enver, the Turks enjoyed a perpetual optimist who continually attempted to seize the strategic initiative when the opportunity presented itself. They might have done worse.

Consistently underestimated by their enemies, the Turks fought on until the bitter end of the war. After the Armistice at Mudros, Turkey's enemies would attempt to dismember the country forever. However, once again, the underestimated leaders and soldiers of the Turkish Army would arise from the ashes of disaster to astound and defeat their enemies.

NOTES

1. General Fahri Belen, *Birinci Cihan Harbinde Turk Harbi 1918 Yili Hareketleri Vnci Cilt* (Ankara: GK Basimevi, 1967), 217-236.
2. Ibid., 237.
3. Ibid. 238.
4. Turkish General Staff, *Turk Silahli Kuvvetleri Tarihi Osmanli Devri Birinci Dünya Harbi Idari Faaliyetler ve Lojistik* (Ankara: Gnkur. Basimevi, 1985), 583.
5. The massive five volume set of books called *Sehitlerimiz* (Our Dead), published by T. C. Milli Savunma Baskanligi, Ankara, 1998, contains comprehensive lists of war casualties. The books start with the Russo-Turkish War of 1877 to 1878 and runs through 1998 with security operations against the PKK. Unfortunately for researchers, these books list the dead individually by name and by province and village, and the total numbers are never tallied.
6. Niall Ferguson, *The Pity of War* (New York: Basic Books, 1999), 295.
7. Ibid., 299.
8. Yigal Sheffy, *British Intelligence in the Palestine Campaign 1914-1918* (London: Frank Cass, 1998), 47-51. Dr. Sheffy noted that the 8th and 10th Infantry Divisions were made up of Anatolian troops were regarded as higher quality infantry divisions than the locally recruited 23rd, 25th, and 27th Infantry Divisions (made up mostly Arabs).

Appendix A
Commanders' Biographies

Parentheses indicate the acquisition of a last name during the postwar period

CEMAL 1881-1922

Late 1890's-Served in the Operations Division, Turkish General Staff
1899-Served in Salonika with Talat
1910-Promoted to General Staff major
1908-CUP member (Young Turk)
1912-Served as commander of a reserve infantry division and fought at Çatalca
January 23, 1914-Appointed as the minister of the marine
August 2, 1914-Served as commander, Fourth Army, Syria-Palestine
1918-Resigned command of the Fourth Army
1922-Killed in Tiflis by Armenian terrorists

Remarks: Cemal was neither particularly aggressive nor professionally competent. He tended to leave command issues up to his German chief of staff except when his position as an army commander was threatened by intrigues from Constantinople. Essentially, he was more of a political animal than a soldier. Cemal stands accused of conducting an extensive campaign of genocide against the Armenians.

ENVER 1881-1922

1899-Commissioned as a lieutenant
1903-Graduated from the War Academy
1908-Served in Salonika, CUP member (Young Turk)
1909-Served as military attaché in Berlin
1911-Served in Libyan War
1913-Served in First Balkan Wars as chief of staff, X Corps, Şarkoy amphibious operation

January 23, 1913-Participated in the raid on the Sublime Porte
July 21, 1913-Orchestrated the seizure of Adrianople
January 1914-Appointed as the minister of war and chief of the Turkish General Staff
October 1918-Resigned
1922-Killed while leading a cavalry charge in Southern Russia

Remarks: Enver was an extremely aggressive nationalist, who was prone to making hasty and ill-advised decisions with incomplete information. His personality was flamboyant, volitile, and charismatic. He consistently overestimated both his own abilities and the capabilities of the forces under his command, although it could be argued that he matured considerably during the course of the war in his understanding and application of strategy. He was extremely cordial with his German allies and maintained excellent alliance relations with all of the Central Powers throughout the course of the war. Enver, with Talat and Cemal, also stands accused as one of the principal architects of the Armenian genocide.

ESAT (BÜLKANT) 1862-1938

1890s-Graduated from the War Academy and aide-de-camp to General Colmar von der Goltz
1897-Served as corps commander, Turkish-Greek War
1899-Served as instructor, Military School
1907-Served as chief of staff, III Corps, Çorlu
1911-Served as commander 5th Infantry Division, Gallipoli
1912/1913-Served in the First Balkan War as commander, Yanya Corps, Jannina, Greece
1914-Served as commander, III Corps, Gallipoli
1916-Served as commander, First Army, Thrace
1917-Served as commander, Second Army, Caucasia
Postwar-cabinet minister

Remarks: Esat was the brother of Vehip (Kaçı). He was the product of the Ottoman General Staff system and had progressively important assignments. His outstanding performance in Greece during the First Balkan War earned him promotion and honors. Esat's performance as a corps commander and group commander at Gallipoli was brilliant. He was extremely hard working, professional, and was highly regarded by the Germans. Sidelined for the remainder of the war, Esat never had the opportunity to show what he could do in command of larger forces.

MUSTAFA FEVZI (ÇAKMAK) 1876-1950

December 1898-Graduated from the War Academy
1912-Served as commander, 21st Infantry Division
1913-Served in the First Balkan War as commander, Ankara Reserve Infantry Division, Çatalca

March 2, 1914-Promoted to major general
December 22, 1914-Served as commmander, V Corps, eastern Marmara region
December 6, 1915-Served as commander, Anafarta Group, Gallipoli
April 1916-Served as wing commander, Third Army, Caucasia
September 7, 1916-Served as commander, 2nd Caucasian Corps, Caucasia
July 5, 1917 – Served as commander, Second Army, Caucasia
October 9, 1917-Served as commander, Seventh Army, Palestine
July 28, 1918-Promoted to lieutenant general
December 24, 1918-Appointed chief of the Turkish General Staff
Postwar-Served as army commander in the War of Independence

Remarks: Fevzi was a solid peformer who commanded successfully at all levels during the war. He was very highly regarded by the Turks themselves and was appointed as the chief of the Turkish General Staff in 1918. Much of his fighting reputation rests on laurals earned in later campaigns against the Greeks in the War of Independence.

HALIL (KUT) 1882-1957

1905-Graduated from the War Academy
1909-Served in Libya
1912-Served in the Balkan Wars
1914-Served in First Army as commander, Constantinople Area Command
1915-Served as commander, 5st Expeditionary Force, Caucasia
1915-Served as commander, XVIII Corps, Mesopotamia
1915-Served as commander, Sixth Army, Mesopotamia
1917-Served as commander, Eastern Army, Caucasia
1918-Served as commander, Caucasus Army Group
1918-Returned to Constantinople
Postwar-Served in the War of Independence

Remarks: Halil was the uncle of Enver Paşa and a genuine military hero to the Turkish people. He later claimed the surname *Kut* to commerate his victory over the British at Kut al Amara. One of the few Turks who was successful while on the offense, his performance in Mesopotamia and in the offensive Caucasian campaigns in 1918 was excellent. He was later accused of war crimes and genocide against the Armenians during operations around the city of Van during the spring of 1915.

AHMET IZZET (FURGAÇ) 1864-1937

Early 1890s-Served in Guards Cavalry Regiment and aide de camp for General Colmar von der Goltz
Mid-1890s-Sent to Germany for two years and served with troops in Palestine
1897-Plans & preparations officer, Çatalca Fortified Zone staff
1902-Served in Yemen
1903-Promoted to Mirliva and served an additional three and one half years in Yemen

1909-CUP member (Young Turk)
1912-Served as commander, Second Army, Balkans
1916-Served as commander, Second Army, Caucasia
October 4, 1918-Appointed as the minister of war and chief of the Turkish General Staff
Postwar-Served as commander in the War of Independence

Remarks: Izzet was generally a competent commander but shares the responsibility for the disastrous 1916 campaigns in Caucasia. He withheld the Second Army while its sister army, the Third, was destroyed. His subsequent counteroffensive was badly planned and poorly executed. He was, however, highly regarded by the Turks but much of his reputation rests on his performance in the War of Independence.

MUSTAFA KEMAL (ATATÜRK) 1881-1938

1902-lieutenant
1905-Graduated from the War Academy
1908-Served with "Action Army," CUP member (Young Turk),
1912-Served in the Libyan War
1913-Served in Balkan Wars as chief of operations, Gallipoli Army (Bulair front)
1914-Served as military attaché in Belgrade
March 1, 1914-Promoted to lieutenant colonel
January 20, 1915-Served as commander, 19th Infantry Division, Tekirdag
April 25, 1915-Led counterattacks at Gallipoli
June 1, 1915-Promoted to colonel
July 28, 1915-Served as commander, XV Corps, Gallipoli
August 8, 1915-Served as commander, Anafarta Group and XVI Corps, Gallipoli
January 27, 1916-Assigned to Adrianople Fortress
August 1916-Served as commander, XVI Corps, Second Army offensive, Caucasia
March 7, 1917-Served as commander, Second Army, Caucasia
July 5, 1917-Served as commander, Seventh Army, Palestine
November 7, 1917-Assigned to the Turkish General Staff
December 20, 1917-Sent to Germany
August 7, 1918-Reassigned to and served as commander, Seventh Army, Palestine
October 31, 1918-Served as commander, Yildirim Army Group
November 7, 1918-Yildirim Army Group dissolved, returned to Constantinople
Postwar-Commander of Turkish Forces during the War of Independence, and later as president of the Turkish Republic

Remarks: Without question the finest commander produced by the Ottoman Empire in the First World War. He was an ardent nationalist and spoke German and French. Kemal was personally fearless in combat and relentless in his ability to drive his troops to victory. His savage counterattacks on the Anzac beach head on April 25, 1915 catapulted him to international fame. However, his successful fighting withdrawal under intense enemy pressure in Palestine in 1918 was arguably his finest military achievement. He performed well at all levels. Kemal was a soldier's soldier with the instincts of a political infighter. A competitor for the political leadership of the CUP with Enver, Cemal, and Talat, he was ambitious and continually had to avoid being marginalized in unimportant assignments. Kemal continuously advocated a rational strategic posture for the empire based on a defense backed by substantial reserves.

YAKUP ŞEVKİ (SÜBAŞI) 1876-1939

1900-Graduated from the War Academy
1912-Served as staff officer, Second Army, Balkans
1912-Promoted to lieutenant colonel
1913-Served as chief of staff, Çatalca Fortified Zone Artillery
1914-Served as commander, Bosphorus Fortified Zone
August 31, 1915-Served as commander, 19th Infantry Division, Gallipoli
November 15, 1915-Served as commander, III Corps, Gallipoli
March 1916-Served as commander, XV Corps, Galicia
November 5, 1916-Promoted to colonel
August 10, 1917-Served as commander, 2nd Caucasian Corps, Caucasia
October 17, 1917-Served as commander, Second Army, Caucasia
June 8, 1918-Served as commander, Ninth Army, Azerbaijan and Georgia
Postwar-Served in the War of Independence

Remarks: Yakup Şevki was an unusually bright man who spoke French, English, German, Russian, Pharsee, Arabic, Syrian, Kurdish, and Serbo-Croatian. He was highly regarded as one of the "brains" of the Turkish Army. He performed very well at all levels and was hand picked to lead Turkish troops against the Russians in Galicia. His performance in command of the Ninth Army in 1918 proved him to be an aggressive and relentless commander. He was one of the few Turkish commanders to be successful on both the offensive and the defensive.

MEHMET VEHİP (KAÇI) 1877-1940

1890s-Graduated from the War Academy
Early 1900s-Served as chief of staff, Diyirbakir Infantry Division and as commander, Erzincan Military School
1909-Promoted to General Staff major
1913-Served as corps commander, Balkan Wars
1914-Served as commander, 22nd Infantry Division, Hicaz
Spring 1915-Served as chief of staff, Second Army, eastern Marmara region
July 1915-Served as commander, Southern Group (Cape Helles), Gallipoli
September 1915-Served as commander, Second Army, eastern Marmara region
1917-Served as commander, Third Army, Caucasia
June 7, 1918-Served as commander, Eastern Army Group, Caucasia
June 29, 1918-Reassigned to Constantinople
Postwar – Served as front commander, War of Independence

Remarks: Vehip was a well-balanced and professional officer, who performed well as both a commander and as a chief of staff. After a long and distinguished career in the Ottoman and Republican Armies, Vehip ended his military career by travelling to Africa to advise the Ethiopians against the Italians in 1936.

Appendix B

The Ottoman General Staff, Summer 1914

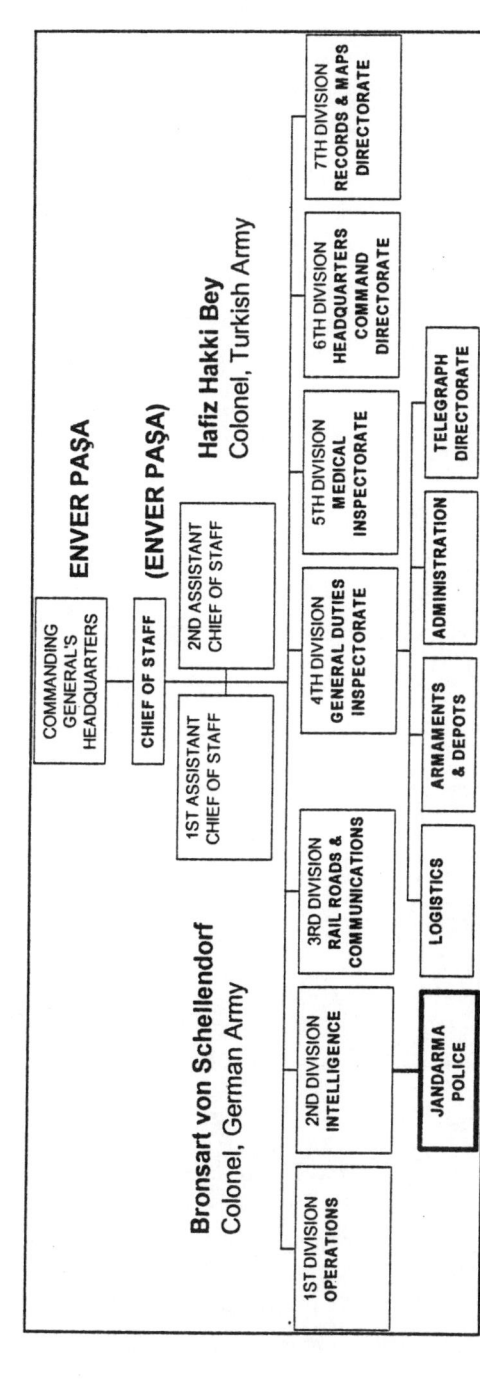

(After mobilization)

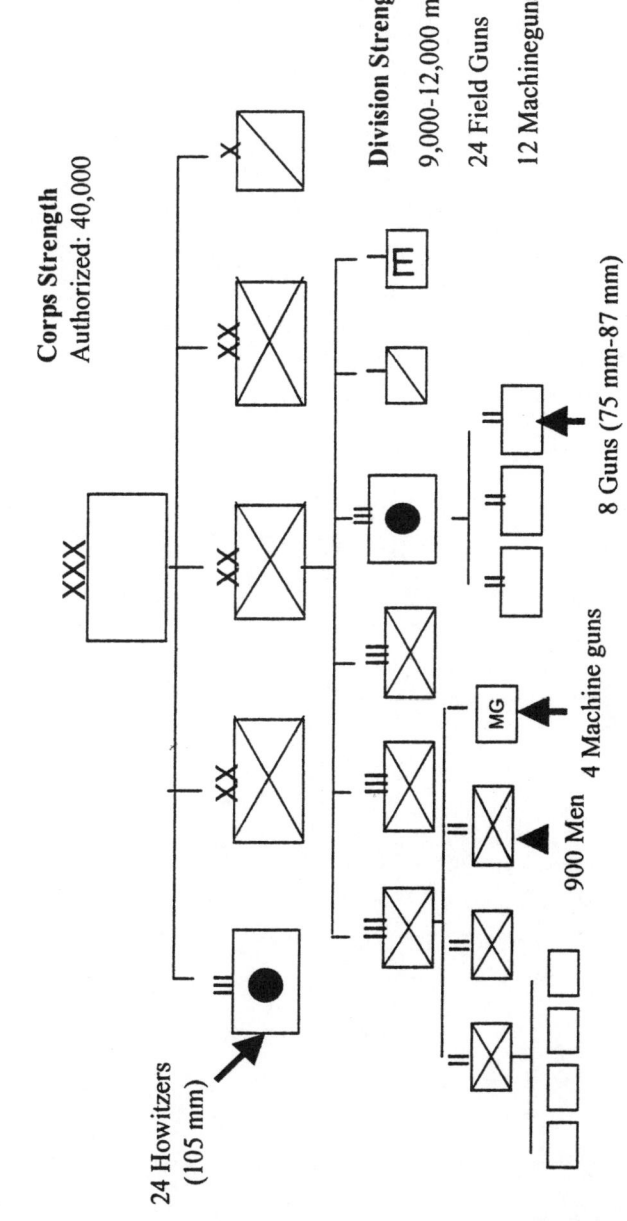

Appendix D
The Ottoman Aviation Inspectorate and Aviation Squadrons

At the war's beginning, the Ottoman Air Force was simply known as the Yeşilkoy Tayyare Mektebi (Aviation School) and was under the direct control of the Başkomutanlik Vekaleti (Office of the Supreme Military Command). Upon mobilization in August 1914, the Turkish military had a total of eight airplanes assigned to operational units and a further four assigned to the flying school in Yeşilkoy (San Stefano on the outskirts of Constantinople). Of these aircraft, only six were operational; two were sent to eastern Turkey and four remained at Yeşilkoy. Although the Turks had used aircraft for several years and had seen them used in for military purposes in the Libyan and Balkan Wars, the cost of aircraft acquisition prohibited expansion.

The military aviation structure of the Ottoman Army was largely decentralized. The Ottoman aviation units were organized into formations called Tayyare Boluğu (flying detachments or the rough equivalent of European aviation squadrons). Each Tayyare Boluğu normally had between two to eight aircraft assigned, as this was the maximum that the primitive logistics system could support. When deployed, the Tayyare Boluğu did not come under any system of centralized control but were under the tactical command of the army or corps responsible for a tactical area. Later fighter squadrons (Av Boluğu) were established under the same system.

The lack of a centralized air command greatly hampered Ottoman air operations since the fighting units fell under the tactical command of the local commander, were controlled operationally by the area army commander, and finally were responsible to the staffs in Constantinople for administrative and logistical matters. In essence, the aviation arm of the Turkish Army was always a branch of the general staff structure and it never matured into an independent arm or corps as it did in other countries. Indeed, the very term Ottoman Air Force is a gross exaggeration and the term Osmanli Havakuvvetleri (Ottoman Air Force) unfortunately is often repeated in contemporary Turkish sources.

In January 1915, Oberleutnant Erich Serno arrived with a staff of twelve German aviation personnel to organize an air force. In order to make up pilot and observer shortfalls in Ottoman squadrons, Serno's men were rapidly sent out and assigned directly to Ottoman squadrons. Early operations were conducted mostly in the west and south where favorable weather conditions generally favored flying. In the spring and summer of 1915 most Turkish air operations consisted of reconnaissance flights. In particular, during the Gallipoli campaign, the Turks frequently flew over the British naval bases on Limnos and Imroz Islands. These sorties were flown to support Liman von Sanders' urgent requests to investigate British preparations and amphibious landing capabilities. By late 1915 there were a total of seven flying squadrons in the Turkish Air Force at the following stations:

Table D.1
Aviation Squadrons, late 1915

Squadron Number	Location
1 and 6	Gallipoli
2	Mesopotamia
3	Uzunkopru (Western Thrace)
4	Adana
5	Second Army (Constantinople area)
7	Third Army, Caucasia

To man these squadrons, the Turks had seven army pilots, three navy pilots, and three civilian pilots. There were also eleven Ottoman observers on duty and twenty-three Ottoman personnel receiving training at Yesilkoy. To make up the desperately shortage of Ottoman aviation personnel, the squadrons at Gallipoli grew decidedly heavy with German flyers. For example, the 6nci Av Boluğu was composed solely of German personnel and the 1nci Tayyare Boluk had only one Ottoman (an observer) among its personnel. All German aviators at this time wore Ottoman uniforms when on duty.

At the end of 1915, an office, the 9ncu Şube (9th Branch) was established and attached to the Harbiye Dairesi (Office of the Minister of War) to administer aviation matters. In parallel, the 13ncu Şube-Umuru Havaiye (13th Branch - Aviation Affairs), a staff division of the Karargahi Umumi (Turkish General Staff headquarters) was organized to coordinate training, acquisition, operations, meteorological support, and repair work. Serno was appointed as the commander of the Umuru Havaiye Mufettisligi (Inspectorate of Aviation Affairs). Although the 13th Branch was organizationally higher in the chain of command, many of its duties and responsibilities overlapped and conflicted with the 9th Branch.

By 1916 the Turkish Air Force had grown to eighty-one pilots and observers, and about ninety aircraft, as German military assistance began to provide increasing numbers of aircraft and technical assistance. In use at this time were Albatross B.I, C.I, C.III; Rumpler B.I; LVG B.I; Fokker E.I, E.III; Gotha LD.2, WD.I, WD.2; Pfalz AII and a variety of captured types. The total number of operational Turkish squadrons had grown to twelve in 1916 (including one naval aviation unit) as well. By this time, tactical air operations in the mountainous Third Army area were being carried out on a routine basis.

Also, in March 1916, the German aviation detachment Fliegerabteilung (FA) 300 was established and became fully operational the following month. The detachment had twelve pilots and six observers. Initially FA 300 had six aircraft initially assigned to it, but grew to twelve operational aircraft in 1917. However, the addition of German aircraft and pilots failed to solve the growing organizational dilemma caused by the complex command relationships embedded in the Ottoman air hierarchy. As a result of the conflicts between the 13th Branch and the 9th Branch, new regulations were announced on December 31, 1916, which separated the authorities and duties of the two branches. Effectively, the 13th Branch of the Ottoman General Staff won the organizational battle and now managed aviation affairs. Concurrently, Serno was elevated in authority equal to that of a divisional commander (major general).

On April 22, 1917, the Turks had five aircraft in the First Army, five aircraft in the Second Army, six aircraft in the Third Army, five aircraft in the Fourth Army, nine aircraft in the Fifth Army, and thirteen aircraft in the Sixth Army (these totals reflect operational aircraft only). The German FA 300 squadron also deployed sixteen operational aircraft in the Fourth Army area at this time. Numerically, the emphasis in the air in 1917 was predominately against the British in Palestine (Fourth Army) and in Mesopotamia (Sixth Army), and against possible British operations in Gallipoli (Fifth Army).

As a result of the ongoing Turco-German military cooperation agreements aimed at establishing the Yildirim Army Group, an additional four German squadrons were organized in Germany in July and August of 1917 for service in the Ottoman Empire. These detachments were FA 301 - 304 and they became operational in the Middle East in November 1917. Collectively, these four FA were referred to as the Yildirim Abteilungen, and the previously deployed FA 300 became known as the Paşa Abteilung.

By 1918, the Turks had received substantial numbers of German aircraft: thirty-seven in 1915, seventy-two in 1916, one hundred eight in 1917, and seventy-nine in 1918 (figures for 1917 and 1918 include aircraft handed over directly from German to Ottoman aviation units). In July 1918, Serno's office was renamed as Kuva-i Havaiye Mufettisi Umumiligi (General Inspectorate of the Air Force). The title reflects the fact that Serno achieved the authority of an air force inspector, however, he did not enjoy operational command of the individual Tayyare Boluğu.

Additionally, the German Navy belatedly sent six seaplanes (LVG SF5s and a single Hansa Brandenburg NM-1) to Turkey in 1918. Air operations in the Turkish theaters would remain lowkey when compared with the western front and most of the Turk's air operations revolved around reconnaissance and some limited bombing. On January 20, 1918, the battlecruiser *Yavuz* (ex-S.M.S.Goeben) enjoyed air support for its ill-fated sortie from the Dardanelles.

Of particular note was the loss of air parity on the Palestine front in late summer 1918. During Allenby's great offensives at Meggido and in Syria, the British paid special attention to denying the Turks the capability to conduct aerial reconnaissance. This greatly damaged Liman von Sanders's ability to accurately gauge Allenby's deception operations of September 17 and 18, 1918. Unable to observe, the Yildirim aerial squadrons were likewise unable to protect the army from Allied air attacks. Consequently, retreating Ottoman forces were hammered mercilessly from the air.

Throughout the course of the war, the Turks flew primarily LVGB.1s; Albatross B.I, C.I, C.III, D.II, D.III, D.V, D.Va types; Rumpler B.I and C.I types; Halberstadt D.Vs; Fokker E.Is and E.IIIs, Fokker D.Is and D.VIIs; Pfalz A.IIs; Gotha LD.2, WD.1, WD.2 types; and AEG C.IVs. The Turks captured and flew one Farman MF.73, three Caudron G.3 and one Caudron G.4, one Bristol Bullet, two Voisin, one Morane-Saulnier Parasol, two Nieuport 17, two DeHavilland DH.4, and one Gregorivitch G.5. At the end of the war the Turks had approximately two hundred aircraft in varying conditions of operability. Although no Ottoman pilots became aces, both pilots and observers did shoot down numerous enemy aircraft throughout the war.

Appendix E
German Military Assistance

German military assistance to the Ottoman Empire began after the Russo-Turkish War and grew slowly over the years. By 1914 German influence was substantial as a result of the presence of the German Military Mission, however material assistance was minimal. This changed as Germany sought to bring Turkey into the Central Alliance. In September the Germans attempted to influence Enver Paşa and sent him a large payment of gold. Later in the fall, the Germans sent several hundred coastal defense specialists to help with the upgrading of the Dardanelles and Bosphorus defenses. Immediately after the outbreak of the war, the lack of continuous lines of communications with Germany reduced assistance to a trickle until the conquest of Serbia in November 1915. German aid then resumed as howitzers and ammunition were rushed south to support the Gallipoli campaign. As the war progressed, German aid would continue to increase.

The Turks had never been particularly comfortable with the terms of the Secret Treaty of Alliance with Germany and on January 11, 1915, they renegotiated another treaty with the Germans. The new treaty obligated Germany to help defend the empire against the British, French, and Balkan powers (the original treaty being more or less operative against only the Russians). Subsequent diplomatic treaties would continue to develop this relationship substantially in the Turk's favor.

In August 1916, there were approximately 640 German officers and 5,900 German soldiers in Ottoman territory. About a thousand of these were permanently assigned duties at the Dardanelles defenses. Actual German combat strength was minimal: there were eight machine gun detachments, one artillery training detachment, seven heavy artillery batteries, six air detachments, and one light artillery battery assigned to assist the Turkish Army. By far the most valuable contribution that Germany made to the Turkish war effort was in its continued willingness to provide highly trained General Staff officers to assist the Turkish staffs. Of special importance were two Special Railroad Companies and two Special Railroad Communications Detachments, which the Germans sent to help the Turks streamline their inefficient railway operations. Included in this railway package were personnel, equipment, and funding to complete the Taurus and Amanus tunnel complexes.

By late September 1916 German presence and influence had grown to such proportions that both sides felt the need to once again renegotiate the diplomatic agreement. On September 23, 1916, Halil Bey and Ambassador von Jagow signed a Turco-German Agreement which had two major provisions. First, both parties agreed to establish joint conditions to end the war. Second, both pledged to maintain the strength and harmony of cooperative relationship that the two countries had developed. This agreement was also the result of a gathering consciousness in both Germany and in Turkey that the war was going to drag out for a long time and that the eventual peace agreement would necessarily be a joint alliance document.

German aid began to pour into the empire as 1916 and 1917 progressed. Advocates of greater cooperation ensured that as Turks went north to serve in Europe, more and more German and Austrian equipment flowed south. There were two subsequent Turco-German Agreements in 1917. The first on January 11, 1917 was another secret agreement which formally ended the much-despised capitulations. This agreement used the previous (September 28, 1916) treaty's recognition of the Ottoman Empire as an equal war partner as the legal basis for this action. A subsequent and wide-ranging Turkish-German Military Cooperation Agreement was signed on October 18, 1917. This agreement had ten clauses, the most important of which pledged the two powers to jointly plan strategy and the associated disposition of military forces. In particular, both sides committed themselves to the formation of joint large-scale combat groups. The Germans also promised to provide an additional five years of training assistance. Provisions were also made for the military punishment of soldiers committing crimes in each other's countries, operations management, and mandatory consultations. Finally, both parties pledged secrecy. The importance of this treaty was that it opened the way for the establishment and the integration of German and Turkish forces into the Yildirim Army Group. Generally, cooperation between the Turks and the Germans remained excellent throughout the war, except for brief periods in 1918.

In the late summer and early fall of 1917, units of the German Army made their way from Germany to Palestine to support the commitments made by the German General Staff. The principal units involved were the so-called 701, 702, and 703 Paşa Infantry Battalions. Later, these units were consolidated under the grandiose title of the "German Asia Corps" (the composition and the deployment of this force is detailed in Chapter 6). The Turks had expected to see several German light infantry divisions of some sort and received instead a brigade group. Although this force was extremely useful, it was never an army corps, nor did it contain the command elements of an army corps headquarters. In modern doctrinal military terms, the German Asia Corps would be called a "corps force multiplier task-force." It was never designed to fight independently, rather it was designed to augment and rectify the deficiencies of the Turkish

Army, most notably in communications, in transportation, and in machine guns. Properly employed, the German Asia Corps greatly enhanced (or multiplied) the effectiveness of the Turkish Army in Palestine. Occasionally, and erroneously, the German Asia Corps is shown in modern histories as an actual army corps headquarters controlling Turkish infantry divisions. Additionally, in November 1917, the 146th Infantry Regiment in Macedonia received orders to reorganize for shipment to Palestine. The regiment arrived in May and June 1918, and participated in the Megiddo and Syrian campaigns. Altogether, including the 701-703 Paşa Infantry Battalions, the 146th Infantry Regiment, and assorted field artillery batteries, the total German ground combat strength in the Ottoman Empire amounted to about two thirds of a normal German infantry division.

A German expeditionary force was sent to the Caucasus in the summer of 1918. Its purpose was not to assist the Turks, but rather to oppose their conquest of Georgia. This small force was composed of the 29th Bavarian Infantry Regiment (7th and 9th Jaeger Battalions), the 10th Strum Battalion, 1 machine-gun detachment, and the 176th Mortar Company.

Belatedly in 1918, significant German aid dedicated towards the revitalization of the Turkish railway system arrived in the empire. Thus by midyear, there were twenty-five railroad staff officer specialists, there were five Military Railway Groups, three Special Railway Companies, eleven Special Railway Commands, and four German railway equipment repair workshops actively working in the empire. These staff officers and units specialized in the planning of railway operations and the rapid switching of assets to ensure continuous and efficient operations. Additionally, work on closing the Pozanti Gap and the Osmaniye Gap was progressing steadily as the Germans and the Turks worked to complete the Taurus and the Amanus tunnels. The thirty-six-kilometer Amanus Tunnel complex had been completed in February 1917 and the more difficult fifty-four-kilometer Taurus Tunnel complex finally completed eighteen months later at the beginning of October 1918.

By the end of the war, total German aid had been substantial. The Germans provided 559 cannons, 557,000 rifles, 100,000 carbines, 1,570 light and 30 heavy machine guns, 200,000 shrapnel shells with 500,000 fuses, 930 million rifle cartridges, almost 300 aircraft, and 30 flame-throwers. The total numbers of nonlethal equipment sent to the Turks had also been substantial as well; 1,000 vehicles, 16,000 gasmasks, 244 field telephones, 20 military telephone switchboards, surveying equipment, and a host of other kinds of gear. Germany also sent 120 railroad steam engines to alleviate the crippling shortage of operational Turkish rolling stock. At the end of the war, there may have been as many as twenty thousand Germans in the empire; however, this number included military and thousands of civilians and their families who had been brought in to increase the efficiency of the empire's economy and infrastructure.

A further major source of equipment although non-German, which must also be considered as significant, was that of captured enemy equipment. During the successful campaigns in Romania in 1916 and in the Trans-Caucasus's regions in 1918, the Turks captured large amounts of enemy equipment. A case in point is artillery. The official Turkish logistical history of the war lists 1,314 pieces of artillery ranging in caliber from 57 mm quick-firing guns to 253 mm howitzers (most are in the 87 mm to 122 mm range) as captured inventory. Accompanying this large number of cannons were approximately 360,000 shells of various calibers. Most of this material was Russian, but some Romanian, German, and Japanese models were also included. This was a significant addition to the Turkish army's combat power, especially when considered that large numbers of machine-guns, communications equipment, and other supplies were obviously captured as well.

The importance of the assignment of German general officers to command positions within the Ottoman Army has often been overstated. Certainly Liman von Sanders played a vital role at Gallipoli, but his subsequent performance at Megiddo left much to be desired. Additionally, he twice refused command of the Third Army which was probably the front where the Turks needed him the most. Von der Goltz died before accomplishing anything of substance in Mesopotamia. Von Falkenhayn's performance in Palestine was, arguably, less than brilliant. At corps level and below, German commanders tended to do very well, however no more so than many of the better Turkish commanders. The most effective use of the highly trained Germans seems to have been in their assignment as general staff, army, and corps chiefs of staff. It was here that their finely tuned staff skills seemed to provide the most return on investment.

Overall, German assistance was a substantial asset to the Turk's ability to prosecute the war. Taken as a total percentage of the actual German wartime production and military strength, the levels of German assistance were small. Unquestionably, the German military aid and equipment packages enabled the Turks to sustain themselves for a much longer period that they could have without such assistance. However, the greatest benefit that the Ottoman Empire received from the Germans was in the area of military and industrial technical assistance. This ranged from highly trained German General Staff officers working on high-level Turkish military staffs to German railway engineering officials specializing in the repair of rolling stock. This German expertise enabled the Turks to gain greater efficiency out of their own thin military, infrastructure, and industrial assets. It was in this area that Germany made its weight felt by enabling the Turks to prolong the war.

The relationship between Germany and the Ottoman Empire proved to be very effective. It was difficult for the Germans to logistically support combat operations deep within the Ottoman Empire. Therefore, most German assistance was in the form of technical support and equipment rather than in German combat forces. Germany achieved its objective of keeping the Turks in the war for as long as possible and with minimal investment. On their part, the Turks effectively used the German aid to multiply and sustain their own combat power. Once in the war, the Turks were very careful in managing their treaty obligations with Germany. After the initial secret treaty in 1914, diplomatic treaties negotiated between the Germans and the Turks tended to favor the Ottoman Empire. These treaties advanced the Turk's economic and political agendas as the Ottoman Empire moved to end the capitulations and edged towards establishing itself as an equal partner in the alliance. Clearly this relationship was not dominated by Germany and could be characterized as complementary rather than as one-sided.

Appendix F
Ottoman Casualties

The purpose of this appendix is to attempt a reconciliation of Ottoman casualties from the First World War using known points of reported information from Turkish sources to build tabular data. This appendix is not meant to be a definitive statement of Ottoman casualties but rather is intended to be holistic view of when, where, and how Ottoman soldiers became casualties.

Table F.1
Ottoman Battle Casualties

Campaign/Battle	Total reported KIA/WIA	KIA	WIA	MIA	POW	Text Pages
NE Frontiers 1914 (defensive)		**1,983**	**6,170**		3,070	72
Basra 1914 (defensive)		{100}	{200}		1,200	67
Qurna 1914 (defensive)		{150}	{300}		1,045	68
Sarikamis 1915 (offensive)		**23,000**	**10,000**			59-60
1st Persia 1915 (offensive)		{200}	{400}	7,000		71
Sinai 1915 (offensive)		**192**	**381**			71
Gallipoli 1915/16 (defensive)		**56,643**	**97,007**	11,178	[—727—]{400}	94-95
Tortum/Van/Malazgirt 1915 (defensive)	58,000	(19,000)	(39,000)			107
Eliskirt Valley 1915 (offensive)	10,000	(4,000)	(6,000)		6,000	108
Shaiba 1915 (offensive)	6,000	(2,000)	(4,000)		700	110
1st Kut 1915 (defensive)	4,000	(1,600)	(2,400)		1,200	112

Campaign	Total KIA/WIA	KIA	WIA	MIA	POW	Text Pages
Ctesiphon 1915 (defensive)		**4,500**	**9,000**		1,200	113
Siege of Kut 1915/16 (offensive)	**4,000**	(1,600)	(2,400)			113
Koprukoy 1916 (defensive)	**10,000**	(4,000)	(6,000)		5,000 [a]	122
Erzurum 1916 (defensive)	**10,000**	(4,000)	(6,000)		5,000	127
Trabzon/Lazistan 1916 (offensive)		{3,000}	{6,000}			131
Bayburt/Erzincan 1916 (defensive)	**17,000**	(5,600)	(11,400)		17,000	133
2nd Army Offensive 1916 (offensive)	**30,000**	(10,000)	(20,000)			
Galicia 1916 (defensive)		{5,000}	{10,000}		{3,000}	
Romania 1916 (offensive)		2,676	10,613	2,972		145
Macedonia 1916/17 (defensive)		{600}	{1,200}			150
Relief of Kut 1916 (defensive)		619	1,585		1,337	152
2nd Invasion Persia 1916 (offensive)		85	276	68		155
Sinai 1916 (offensive)	**1,000**	(250)	(750)			
1st Gaza 1917 (defensive)		300	750	600		161
2nd Gaza 1917 (defensive)		82	1,336	242		163
2nd Kut/Baghdad 1917 (defensive)		{2,000}	{4,000}			
3rd Gaza/Jerusalem 1917 (defensive)		3,540	8,982	9,100	6,435	174
2nd Jordan 1918 (defensive)		{1,000}	{2,000}			
Armenia/Azerbaijan 1918 (offensive)		{1,500}	{3,000}			
Persia 1918 (defensive)		{500}	{1,000}			
Megiddo/Syria 1918 (defensive)		**10,000** [a]	{20,000}		71,300	201
Mesopotamia 1918 (defensive)		{500}	{1,000}		11,322	203
Yemen/Asir/Hedjaz 1914-1918 (defensive)		{5,000}	{10,000}			
Unreported missing				{30,000} [b]		
Unreported POWs					{20,000} [c]	
Returned POWs from Kut, 1916					+ 1,095	151
Returned POW's from Russia 1918					+ 9,010	189
TOTAL		175,220	303,150 [d]	61,487	145,104	

KEY   Total KIA/WIA: Total combined killed and wounded (permanently disabled) in action
       KIA: Killed in Action
       WIA: Wounded in Action (permanently disabled)
       MIA: Missing in Action
       POW: Prisoners of War
       Text Pages: Information on sources may be found on these pages of the main text

Notes: Methodology--Ottoman casualties are reported in about two thirds of contemporary official Turkish campaign histories. These numbers provided the baseline and also became the known points of information. General estimates were then established based on the trends of campaigns and battles selected as representative of combat conditions in various theaters. Numbers in boldface type reflect published Turkish historical data (or data taken from Turkish sources) and the sources may be found in the text. Numbers shown in brackets (XXX) are the author's estimated breakdowns of casualties reported solely as totals, calculated in a ratio of .4 KIA/ .6 WIA. Numbers shown in italicized brackets {XXX} are the author's own estimates based on the number of troops involved, the intensity and duration of combat, and the offensive or defensive posture of the forces involved.

a. POW figures from Koprukoy 1916 are found in W. E. D. Allen & Paul Muratoff, *Caucasian Battlefields*, page 342. The KIA figures from Megiddo/Syria are found in Charles F. Horne, *The Great Events of the Great War*, vol. 4, 1918, "The Fall of Turkey" by W.T. Massey, page 334. Both sources closely follow Turkish sources for these particular periods, and the author believes these numbers to be congruent with Turkish data.
b. Rather than estimate the amount of missing by campaign, the number of unreported missing is a cumulative total estimated by the author to be an amount equal to the number of accurately reported missing.
c. Like the number of estimated missing in note b, the author estimates the number of unreported POW's to be an amount equal to the number of accurately reported POWs during ordinary campaigning. The Palestine and Mesopotamian campaigns of 1918 and the Erzurum campaign of 1916 were aberrations and do not reflect the army's POW rates from other theaters. By deleting these particular campaigns and battles, the author is left with about 20,000 POWs lost during ordinary campaigning, which is used as the number of unreported POWs.
d. These totals are the reported wounded (yaraly). The author interprets this to mean permanently disabled or otherwise seriously incapacitated (as opposed to lightly wounded and returned to duty).

Table F.2
Other Ottoman Casualty Figures

Total sick	3,515,471
Total died of disease	466,759
Total wounded	763,753
Total died of wounds	68,378

Notes: Dr. Yalman's numbers were based on direct access to an unpublished official source. Yalman's unpublished primary source, the Turkish Ministry of War's *The Sanitary History of the War* was apparently never published. Yalman's total of wounded is approximately twice the author's estimated number of dead and missing. Although Yalman's total number of wounded conflicts with the author's estimate, Yalman's figures very likely include all categories of wounded, including the lightly wounded and injured in non-combat accidents.

Source: Emin Ahmed Yalman, *Turkey in the World War*, (New Haven: Yale University Press, 1930), 252-254.

Table F.3
Consolidated Summary of Ottoman Losses in the First World War (Author's Estimates)

Category	Total	Source
Killed	175,220	Table F.1
Missing	61,487	Table F.1
Total died of wounds	68,378	Table F.2
Total combat dead and missing	305,085	Table F.1
Total wounded	763,753	Table F.2
Total wounded, permanent loss	303,150	Table F.1
Total sick	3,515,471	Table F.2
Total died of disease	466,759	Table F.2
Prisoners of war	145,104	Table F.1

Table F.4
Consolidated Ottoman Losses By Year of the War (Author's Estimates)

Year	KIA	MIA	Died/wounds	Died/disease	POW	WIA (perm)	WIA (all)
1st Year	112,850	25,000	22,441	77,667	20,464	174,858	234,532
2nd Year	37,430	12,927	31,110	155,757	32,891	72,413	351,112
3rd Year	6,440	9,534	8,180	137,889	12,084	18,943	50,635
4th Year	18,500	14,026	7,647	95,446	79,665	36,936	127,475
Total	175,220	61,487	68,378	466,759	145,104	303,150	763,753

Notes: These estimates consolidate the author's campaign estimates (Table F.1) and Dr. Yalman's annual army losses (pages 252-253 of *Turkey in the World War*). Author's conclusions based these numbers:

(1) The first year of the war was by far the worst year for actual battlefield combat losses, however, some prewar medical capacity or stockages of medicine obviously reduced the number of Ottoman soldiers dying of disease.

(2) Acute medical shortages in the second year of the war probably increased the number of men dying of disease. Thereafter, increasing amounts of German aid probably caused the reduction of this number seen in the last two years of the war.

(3) 1917 was a year of badly needed respite on the battlefield caused by inactivity on the Caucasian front and by lower levels of combat on the fronts facing the British.

(4) The worst year for POW losses was 1918 due to the massive British envelopment operations in Palestine.

Table F.5
Ottoman Army Strength 1918

Army	January 1, 1918 Assigned Strength	Rifles	MG	Artillery	September 1, 1918 Assigned Strength
First Army	237,300	52,918	0	284	*50,000* [a]
Second Army	140,016 [b]	67,250	79	64	249,730
Third Army	147,390	46,925	24	180	*70,000*
Fourth Army	190,898	94,815	138	179	*190,000*
Fifth Army	220,286	126,811	511	548	*200,000*
Sixth Army	79,360	32,216	135	122	54,109
Seventh Army	35,065	11,099	279	86	*40,000*
Eighth Army	32,000	12,799	338	126	39,783
Ninth Army - June 1918	80,000	21,791	307	136	*120,000* [c]
Other Areas	14,000	not reported			14,000
TOTAL	1,096,315 [d]	466,624 [d]	1,504 [d]	1,589 [d]	1,027,622

Notes: Numbers in *Italics* are the author's estimates.

a. Although the First Army was inactivated in the spring of 1918, the capital garrison and surrounding fortresses are included in this number.
b. The Second, Fourth, and Fifth Armies had substantial numbers of labor troops (amele) supporting the empire's lines of communications. The only army reporting such troops as a separate line included in total assigned strength was the Second Army which reported 41,931 labor troops. It highly likely that the Second and Fourth Armies had similar numbers of labor troops.
c. Ninth Army totals include the Army of Islam.
d. The total does not include the Ninth Army- June 1918 totals (because this army was organized in the summer of 1918).
e. In January 1918, the Yildirim Army had an additional 172,591 rifles stored in depots.
f. At the armistice, the Ottoman Army probably had about 930,000 men on its rolls, the Ottoman Navy probably had about 15,000 men on its rolls (1908 strength: 5,451 officers, 7,419 seamen), the Ottoman Jandarma probably had about 150,000 men on its rolls (1914 strength: 250,000 men of which 40,000 were in mobile regiments and battalions). Therefore, the author's estimate of total armed forces at Armistice is 1,095,000 men.

Source: Turkish General Staff, *Turk Silahli Kuvvetleri Tarihi Osmanli Devri Birinci Dünya Harbi Idari Faaliyetler ve Lojistik, Xncu Cilt* (Ankara: Basimevi, 1985), 544-550.

Table F.6
Consolidated Ottoman Battle and Non-Battle Losses (Author's Estimates)

Category	Total	Source
Combat dead or missing	305,085	Table F.3
Died of disease	466,759	Table F.2
POWs	145,104	Table F.1
Wounded - permanent loss	303,150	Table F.1
Deserters	500,000	Yalman, page 255, see note b.
Total Wartime Losses	**1,720,098**	Author's estimate
Total men under arms at armistice	1,095,000	Table F.5, note f.
Men mobilized, Army	2,608,000	Table F.5, note f.
Jandarma	250,000	Table F.5, note f.
Navy	15,000	Table F.5, note f.
Men Mobilized, Total	2,873,000	Author's estimate, see note a.

Men unaccounted for: 57,902
Percent of men unaccounted for: 2%

Notes:

a. Yalman claimed that the empire mobilized a total of 2,998,321 men and Commandant Larcher used a figure of 2,850,000 men mobilized during the war.

b. Liman von Sanders estimated that in 1916, there were 300,000 deserters at large in the Ottoman Empire. Yalman cited a similar number for 1916, and furthermore claimed that the number of deserters in 1918 was 500,000.

c. Some POW estimates for the Ottoman Army in the First World War range as high as 220,000 to 250,000 men, although the author found no reliable data to suggest such high figures. The total British POW count was probably about 100,000 Turks and the total Russian POW count was probably about 50,000 Turks (returnees would reduce these totals somewhat).

d. The "unaccounted for" men are most likely distributed across the data fields in various battles and campaigns as yet unreported by the Turks.

243

Appendix G
Turkey in the First World War–Chronology

DATE	CAUCASUS / EASTERN ANATOLIA	EUROPE AND THE BALKANS	PALESTINE	MESOPOTAMIA
AUG 1914 (2) *Turco-German Secret Treaty of Alliance*		(10) *Goeben & Breslau enter Dardanelles*		
SEP				
OCT	(28) *Black Sea Raids*			
NOV	Russian Offensive at Koprukoy	(3) *Initial Naval Bombardment of Gallipoli*	Defense behind Suez Canal	(6) *Initial Landing & Bridgehead* (17) *Turks routed*
DEC	(22) *Third Army Offensive in Caucasia* (9) *Third Army defeat at Sarikamiş*			(9) Al Quirna occupied
JAN 1915 (11) *2nd Turco-German Treaty*			*1st Turkish attack on canal*	*1st Turkish Invasion of Persia*
FEB		(19) 1st Naval Attack	British defense of canal & minor raids	

MAR			1st British Advance
APR	(14) Van Rebellion Armenian Rebellion	(18) 2d Naval Attack (25) GALLIPOLI Landing at Cape Helles and Anzac (28) 1st Krithia	Turks withdraw from Persia (12) Battle of Shaiba
MAY	(6) Russian Offensive at Tortum & Erzurum Armenian Rebellion	(1) *Turkish Counterattack* (2) Baby 700 (6-8) 2d Krithia (19) *Turkish Counterattack at Anzac*	British occupy Amara
JUN	Armenian Rebellion Armenian deportations begin	(4) 3d Krithia (28/29) British attack at Anzac	
JUL	(10) Russian Offensive northwest of Lake Van	(12/13) British offensive at Helles	
AUG	(5) *Turkish Counter-Offensive -Eliskirt valley* (22) Russian Offensive halted at Malzgirt	(2) British Offensive (6) 2d British Landing at Suvla Bay (6) Lone Pine (7) Sari Bair (10) *Turkish counterattack*	

SEP			
OCT			(28) 1st Battle of Kut
NOV			(21) Battle of Ctesiphon
DEC	(18-20) Evacuation of Suvla & Anzac		(7) *Siege of Kut*
JAN 1916	Russian Offensive at Koprukoy	(8/9) Evacuation of Cape Helles	*Siege of Kut*
FEB	Russians storm Erzurum		*Siege of Kut*
MAR	*Second Army forms at Bitlis*		*Siege of Kut*
APR	(18) Trabzon falls		(23) *Battle of Katia*	(28) Surrender of Kut
MAY	(29) Russian offensive from Erzurum		British Advance	
JUN	*Turks attack in Pontic Alps*		Clearing of Sinai	2nd Turkish Invasion of Persia
JUL	(2) Yudenich Offensive at Bayburt (25) Russians capture Erzincan	ROMANIA *VI Corps deploys* GALICIA *XV Corps deploys*	Clearing of Sinai	

247

AUG	*(2) Second Army Offensive* *Ataturk captures Mus & Bitlis*	*Romanian Offensive*	(4) *Turkish attack at Bir Romani*	
SEP (23) *Turco-German Military Agreement*	*Restructuring of the Third Army*	(1) *Danube Army Offensive into Dobruja*		2nd British Advance
OCT				2nd British Advance
NOV				2nd British Advance
DEC		(5) *Bucharest falls* (6) *Ploesti falls* MACEDONIA (6) XX *Corps deploys to Drama*	(23) British attack El Arish	
JAN **1917** (11) *Turco-German Treaty ending capitulations*		(7) ROMANIA *Turks closed on Isman on the Danube River*	(9) British arrive at Turkish frontier	
FEB				(22) 2nd Battle of Kut
MAR	Russian Revolution		(26) 1st Battle of Gaza	(11) Capture of Baghdad Turks retreat from Persia
APR			(17) 2d Battle of Gaza	

MAY				
JUN				
JUL				
AUG		*Yildirim Army Group formed*		
SEP			(22) GALICIA *XX Corps returns*	
OCT	(18) *Joint Turco-German Military Cooperation Agreement*	(31) 3d Battle of Gaza & Beersheba		
NOV				British advance to Tikrit
DEC		(11) Capture of Jerusalem (26) *Turkish counterattacks*	Russian Armistice	
JAN 1918				
FEB			*Third Army Offensive*	
MAR			Treaty of Brest-Litovsk Turks retake Trabzon	
APR		(30) 2nd Battle of the Jordan	*Turkish Recovery of Armenia, Batum and Kars*	

MAY			
JUN	(4) *Turkish Azerbajian Offensive*		*Turks take Tabriz in Persia*
JUL	*Siege of Baku*		
AUG	*Siege of Baku*		(4) British take Enzeli (20) British arrive in Baku
SEP	(17) *Turks seize Baku*	(19) Battle of Meggido/Mt Carmel Pursuit (27) Dera falls	
OCT		(10) Capture of Damascus & Beirut (16) Capture of Homs (25) Capture of Aleppo	
NOV 1918 (1) Armistice at Mudros			(1) Advance to Mosul

Note:

a. Italics indicate Turkish actions.
b. Numbers in parentheses indicate day of the month.

Selected Bibliography

ARCHIVAL SOURCES

Ankara: Askeri Tarıhı ve Stratejik Etut Başkanlığı (ATASE) - Turkish General Staff Archives
   1 /2 Headquarters, Ministry of the Interior
   1 /1 Office of the Acting Commanding General
   1/131 Jandarma Headquarters, Constantinople (Istanbul)
   1/131 Operations Division, Headquarters, Turkish General Staff
   4/3671 Headquarters, Turkish Third Army
   4/8749 Headquarters, Turkish Fifth Army
   1/65 Headquarters, Şevki Group

OFFICIAL DOCUMENTS AND HISTORIES

Akbay, Cemal. *Birinci Dünya Harbinde Turk Harbi, 1nci Cilt, Osmanli Imparatorlugu'nun Siyasi ve Askeri Hazirliklari ve Harbe Girisi*. Ankara: Genelkurmay Basimevi, 1991.
Ari, Kemal, *Birinci Dünya Savasi Kronolojisi*. Ankara: Genelkurmay Basimevi, 1997.
Aspinall-Oglander, Brig.-Gen. C. F. *History of the Great War, based on Official Documents: Military Operations Gallipoli*, vol. 1-2. London: HMSO, 1924-1930.
Bean, C. E. W. *Official History of Australia in the War of 1914-1918: The Story of ANZAC,* vol. 1-2. Queensland: University of Queensland Press, 1981 (reprint of 1942 edition).
Belen, General Fahri. *Birinci Cihan Harbinde Turk Harbi 1914, 1915, 1916, 1916, 1918 Yili Hareketleri, I-V Cilt.* (five volumes) Ankara: Genelkurmay Basimevi, 1965-1967.
Demirel, Muammer. *Birinci Dünya Harbinde Erzurum ve Cevresinde Ermeni Harekatleri (1814-1918)*. Ankara: Genelkurmay Basimevi, 1996.
Falls, Captain Cyril. *History of the Great War, based on Official Documents, Military Operations Egypt and Palestine, 1914-1918*, vol. 1. London: HMSO, 1930.
Gooch, G. P. and Harold Temperley, eds. *British Documents on the Origins of the War, 1898-1914*, vol. 11. London: HMSO, 1926.
Hurewitz, J. C. *Diplomacy in the Near and Middle East: A Documentary Record: 1535-1914*, vol. 1 and *1914-1956,* vol. 2. Princeton, NJ: Van Nostrand Company, 1956.

Intelligence Section, Cairo, British Army, *Handbook of the Turkish Army*. 8th Provisional ed., February 1916, Nashville: Battery Press, (reprint).

Moberly, Brig.-Gen. F. J. *History of the Great War, Based on Official Documents, The Campaign in Mesopotamia 1914-1918*, vol. 1. London: HMSO, 1923.

Sukru, Mahmut Nedim, *Filistin Savasi (1914-1918)*. Ankara: Genelkurmay Basimevi, 1995.

Thomazi, Albay A., *Çanakkale Deniz Savasi*. Ankara: Genelkurmay Basimevi, 1997.

Turkish Air Force, *Turk Havacilik Tarihi 1912-1914 (Birinci Kitap)*, Eskisehir: Ucus Okullari Basimevi, 1950.

Turkish Air Force. *Turk Havacilik Tarihi 1914-1916 (Ikinci Kitap)*, Eskisehir: Ucus Okkullari Basimevi, 1951.

Turkish Air Force. *Turk Havacilik Tarihi 1917-1918 (Ikinci Kitap Ikinci Cilt)*, Eskisehir: Ucus Okkullari Basimevi, 1951.

Turkish Air Force. *Istiklal Harbi, 1918-1923 (III Cilt Ikinci Kitap)*, Eskisehir, Ucus Okkullari Basimevi, 1953.

Turkish Air Force. *Havacilik Tarihi Turkler I*, Etimisgut: Hava Kuvvetleri Basimevi, 1971.

Turkish General Staff. *Turk Istiklal Harbi I Mondros Mutarekesi ve Tatbikati*. Ankara: Genelkurmay Basimevi, 1962.

Turkish General Staff. *Birinci Dünya Harbi IXncu Cilt Turk Hava Harekati*, Ankara, Genelkurmay Basimevi, 1969.

Turkish General Staff. *Turk Silahli Kuvvetleri Tarihi IIIncu Cilt 6nci Kisim (1908-1920) Inci Kitap*. Ankara: Genelkurmay Basimevi, 1971.

Turkish General Staff. *Birinci Dünya Harbinde Turk Harbi Vncu Cilt Çanakkale Cephesi, 2nci Kitap*. Ankara: Genelkurmay Basimevi, 1978.

Turkish General Staff. *Birinci Dünya Harbinde Turk Harbi IIIncu Cilt Irak-Iran Cephesi, 1914-1918, Inci Kisim*. Ankara: Genelkurmay Basimevi, 1979.

Turkish General Staff. *Turk Silahi Kuvvetleri Tarihi Osmanli Devri Birinci Dunya Harbinde Turk Harbi Vncu Cilt 3ncu Kitap Canakkale Cephesi Harekati (Haziran 1915-Ocak 1916)*, Ankara: Genelkurmay Basimevi, 1980.

Turkish General Staff. *Askeri Tarih Yayinlari Belgelerle Ermeni Sorunu*. Ankara: Genelkurmay Basimevi, 1983.

Turkish General Staff. *Turk Silahli Kuvvetleri Tarihi Osmanli Devri Birinci Dunya Harbi Idari Faaliyetler ve Lojistik Xncu Cilt*. Ankara, Genelkurmay Basimevi, 1985.

Turkish General Staff. *Turk Silahi Kuvvetleri Tarihi Osmanli Devri Birinci Dunya Harbinde Turk Harbi Vncu Cilt 3ncu Kitap Canakkale Cephesi Harekati (Haziran*

Turkish General Staff. *Turk Istiklal Harbi'ne Kalilan Tumen ve Daha Ust Kademelerdeki Komutanlarin Biyografileri*. Ankara: Genelkurmay Basimevi, 1989.

Turkish General Staff. *Balkan Harbi (1912-1913)*. Ankara: Genelkurmay Basimevi, 1993.

Turkish General Staff. *Birinci Dünya Harbinde Turk Harbi Kafkas Cephesi 3ncu Ordu Harekati, Cilt I and II*. Ankara: Genelkurmay Basimevi, 1993.

Turkish General Staff. *Birinci Dünya Harbinde Turk Harbi, Vnvi Cilt, Çanakkale Cephesi Harekati, Inci Kitap (Haziran 1914- 25 Nisan 1915)*. Ankara: Genelkurmay Basimevi, 1993.

Turkish General Staff. *Turk Silahli Kuvvetleri Tarihi, Balkan Harbi (1912-1913), II Cilt, Edirne Kalesi Etrafindaki Muharebeler*. Ankara: Genelkurmay Basimevi, 1993.

Turkish General Staff. *Turk Silahli Kuvvetleri Tarihi, Balkan Harbi (1912-1913), III Cilt, Garp Ordusu Vardar Ordusu ve Ustruma Kolordusu*. Ankara: Genelkurmay Basimevi, 1993.

Turkish General Staff. *Birinci Dünya Harbinde Turk Harbi Avrupa Cepheleri (Ozet)*. Ankara: Generalkurmay Basimevi, 1996.
Turkish General Staff. *Birinci Dünya Harbinde Turk Harbi V. Cilt Çanakkale Cephesi Harekati 1nci, 2nci, ve 2ncu Kitaplarin Ozetlenmis Tarihi (Haziran 1914-9 Ocak 1916)*. Ankara: Generalkurmay Basimevi, 1997.
Turkish General Staff. *Birinci Dünya ve Istiklal Harbinde Sehit Olan Subay, Askeri Memur, ve Astsubaylarin Kunye Kayitlari*, Ankara: Genelkurmay Basimevi, 1997.
Turkish General Staff, *Turk Istiklal Harbi I, Mondros Mütarekesi ve Tatbikati*, Ankara: Genelkurmay Basimevi, 1999.
Turkish Military Museum, *Askeri Muze Resim Koleksiyonu*, Istanbul: Harbiye, Askeri Muze ve Kultur Sitesi Komutanligi, 1995.
Turkish Ministry of Culture. *Cephelerden Kurtulus Savasina Imparatorluktari Cumhurriyet'e*. Instabul: Cenk Offset, 1992.
Turkish Ministry of Defense. *Sehitlerimiz 1-5 Cilt*, Ankara: TC Milli Savunma Bakanligi, 1998.
Yuceer, Nasir. *Birinci Dünya Savas'inda Osmanli Ordusu'nun Azerbaycan ve Dagistan Harekati, Azerbaycan ve Dagistan Bagimsizligini Kazanmasi 1918*. Ankara: Genelkurmay Basimevi, 1996.

MEMOIRS

DeNogales, Rafael. *Four Years beneath the Crescent*. New York: Charles Scribner's Sons, 1926.
Djemal Pasha. *Memories of a Turkish Statesman-1913-1919*. London: Hutchinson, n.d.
Lawrence, T. E. *Revolt in the Desert*. Garden City, N.Y.: Doubleday, 1927.
Lawrence, T. E. *Seven Pillars of Wisdom: a Triumph*. Stockholm: Alb. Bonniers, 1946.
Liman von Sanders, General of Cavalry. *Five Years in Turkey*. London: Bailliere, Tindall & Cox, 1928.
Morgenthau, Henry. *Ambassador Morgenthau's Story*. Garden City, N.Y.: Doubleday Press, 1918.
Von Falkenhayn, Erich. *General Headquarters 1914-1916 and its Critical Decisions*. London: Hutchinson, n.d.

BOOKS

Albertini, Luigi. *The Origins of the War of 1914*. Oxford: Oxford University Press, 1952.
Allen, W. E. D., and Paul Muratoff. *Caucasian Battlefields: A History of the Wars on the Turco-Caucasian Border, 1828-1921*. Cambridge: Cambridge University Press, 1953.
Atasu, Remzi, *Demiryollarinin Askeri Rolleri ve Yarina Hazirlanislari*, Istanbul: Askeri Matbaa, 1939.
Busch, Briton Cooper. *Mudros to Lausanne: Britain's Frontier in West Asia, 1918-1923*. Albany: State University of New York Press, 1976.
Churchill, Winston S. *The World Crisis*. New York: Charles Scribners, Sons, 1931.
Dadrian, Vakhakn N. *Warrant for Genocide: Key Elements of the Turko-Armenian Conflict*. New Brunswick, N.J.: Transaction Publishers, 1999.
Esposito, Brig. General Vincent J., ed. *The West Point Atlas of American Wars, vol 2: 1900-1953*. New York: Praeger, 1964.
Falls, Cyril. *The Great War*. New York: G. P. Putnam's Sons, 1959.

Ferguson, Niall. *The Pity of War*. New York: Basic Books, 1999.
Freyberg, Paul. *Bernard Freyberg V.C.: Soldier of Two Nations*. London: Hodder and Stoughton, 1991.
Haythornthwaite. Phillip J. *Gallipoli 1915*. London: Ospry Press, n.d.
Herwig, Holger H. *The First World War, Germany and Austria-Hungary, 1914-1918*. London: Arnold, 1997.
Hovannisian, Richard G., ed. *Rememberance and Denial*. Detroit: Wayne State Press, 1998.
Hovannisian, Richard G. *The Armenian Holocaust: A Bibliography Relating to the Deportations, Massacres, and the Dispersion of the Armenian People, 1915-1923* 2d ed. Cambridge, Mass: Armenian Heritage Press, 1980.
Hickey, Michael. *Gallipoli*. London: John Murray, 1995.
James, Robert Rhodes. *Gallipoli*, New York: Macmillan, 1965.
Johnstone, Tom. *Orange, Green and Khaki, The Story of the Irish Regiments in the Great War, 1914-1918*. Dublin: Gill and Macmillan, 1992.
Keegan, John, *The First World War*. New York: Alfred A. Knopf, 1999.
Kent, Marian, ed. *The Great Powers and the End of the Ottoman Empire*. London: George Allen & Unwin, 1984.
Kiraly, Bela K., and Nandor F. Dreisziger, eds. *East Central European Society in World War I*. New York: Columbia University Press, 1985.
Langensiepen, Bernd, and Ahmet Guleryuz. *The Ottoman Steam Navy*. Annapolis Md.; Naval Institute Press, 1995.
Larcher, Commandant M. *La Guerre Turque Dans La Guerre Mondiale*. Paris: Chiron & Berger-Levrault, 1926.
Macfie, A. L. *The End of the Ottoman Empire 1908-1923*. London: Longman, 1998.
McCarthy, Justin. *Muslims and Minorities, The Population of Ottoman Anatolia and the End of the Empire*. New York: London Press, 1983.
Millar, Ronald. *Death of an Army, The Siege of Kut 1915-1916*. Boston: Houghton Mifflin, 1970.
Miller, Geoffrey. *Straits: British policy towards the Ottoman Empire and the origins of the Dardanelles Campaign*. Hull: University of Hull Press, 1997.
Miller, Geoffrey. *Superior Force: the conspiracy behind the escape of the Goeben and Breslau*. Hull: University of Hull Press, 1996.
Moorehead, Alan. *Gallipoli*. New York: Harper & Row, 1956.
Moorhouse, Geoffrey. *Hell's Foundations: A Town, Its Myths & Gallipoli,* Bury St. Edmund: Hodder and Stoughton, 1992.
Nicolle, David. *The Ottoman Army 1914-1918*. London: Reed International Books, 1996.
Nicolle, David. *Lawrence and the Arab Revolts*. Oxford: Osprey, 1998
Perrett, Bryan. *Megiddo 1918: The Last Great Cavalry Victory*. Oxford: Osprey Publishing, 1999.
Shaw, Stanford J. *History of the Ottoman Empire and Modern Turkey*, vol. 1. Cambridge: Cambridge University Press, 1976.
Shaw, Stanford J. and Ezel Kural Shaw. *History of the Ottoman Empire and Modern Turkey*, vol. 2. Cambridge: Cambridge University Press, 1977.
Sheffy, Yigal. *British Military Intelligence in the Palestine Campaign, 1914-1918*. London: Frank Cass, 1998.
Steel, Nigel, and Peter Hart. *Defeat at Gallipoli*. London: Macmillan, 1994.
Stevenson, David. *Armaments and the Coming of War: Europe, 1904-1914*. Oxford: Clarendon Press, 1996.
Stone, Norman. *The Eastern Front, 1914-1917*. New York: Charles Scribner's Sons, 1975

Taylor, Phil, and Pam Cupper. *Gallipoli:A Battlefield Guide*. Kenthurst, Australia: Kangaroo Press, 1989.
Trumpener, Ulrich. *Germany and the Ottoman Empire*. Princeton, N.J.: Princeton University Press, 1968.
Wavell, General Sir Archibald. *Allenby: A Study in Greatness*. New York: Oxford University Press, 1941.
Weber, Frank G. *Eagles on the Crescent: Germany Austria, and the Diplomacy of the Turkish Alliance, 1914-1918*. Ithaca, N.Y.: Cornell University Press, 1970.
Westlake, Ray. *British Regiments at Gallipoli*. London: Leo Cooper, 1996.
World Press. *The World Almanac and Encyclopedia 1914*. New York: Press Publishing, 1913.
Yalman, Ahmed Emin. *Turkey in the World War*. New Haven, Conn.: Yale University Press, 1930.
Yilmaz, Veli. *Birinci Dünya Harbinde Turk-Alman Ittifaki ve Askeri Yardimlari*. Istanbul: Gem Offset, 1993.

ARTICLES

Doyle, Peter and Matthew R. Bennett. "Military Geography: the influence of terrain in the outcome of the Gallipoli Campaign, 1915. " *The Geographical Journal*, 165 (1999): 12-36.
Dyer, Gwynne. "The Origins of the 'Nationalist' group of officers in Turkey 1908-1918." *Journal of Contemporary History*, 8 (1973): 121-164.
Kocabaş, Süleyman. "Birinci Dünya Harbi'nde Bogazlar Meselesi." *Askeri Tarih Bülteni*, 39 (1995): 90-97.
Kurkcuoglu, Omer. "An Evaluation of the Ottoman Empire's Entry into the World War." *Ankara Universitesi Siyasal Bilgiler Fakeultesi*, 38 (1983): 227-243.
Seyhun, Mehmet Arif. "Yemen Savaş Anilari (5 May 1914-5 March 1919)." *Askeri Tarih Bülteni*, 42 (1997): 1-51.
Wolf, John B. "The Diplomatic History of the Bagdad Railroad." *The University of Missouri Studies: A Quarterly of Research*, 11 (2) (1936): 1-107.

Index

Abdülkerim, Brigadier General, 148
Abdul Karim Paşa, 107, 108, 122, 127
Acre, 199
Action Army, 2
Adana, 99, 129, 130, 167, 176, 201
Adrianople, 3, 5-7, 9, 10, 23, 37, 45, 79, 80, 124, 144
Afghanistan, 39
Ağri, 105
Ahmet Fevzi, 53, 55, 128-129, 136
Ahmet Izzet Paşa, 5, 128, 131-133, 135, 137, 167, 201; biography 219-220
Akaba, 175
Alaaddin, Colonel, 53
Albania, 148
Albertini, Luigi, *The Origins of the War of 1914*, 31
Aleppo, 63, 98, 99, 167, 169, 171, 201
Alexandretta, 201
Ali, Captain, 79
Ali Fuad Bey, 168
Ali Insan Paşa, 55, 59, 152, 176
Ali Remzi, 93
Allen, W. E. D. and Paul Muratoff, *Caucasian Battlefields: A History of the Wars on the Turco-Russian Border 1828-1921*, 22, 32, 105, 107, 160, 180
Allenby, General Edmund, 160, 164, 172-174, 193, 195, 196, 198-203
Amman, 175, 195, 198
Anzac, 69, 83, 87, 89, 91; withdrawal 93,
Arabia, 9, 32, 119, 168, 175-176
Arab Revolt, 175-176

Aras River valley, 107-108
Ardahan, 54, 65, 184
Ari Burnu, 83
Armenian National Army, 182-183, 184, 192
Armenian Rebellion, 95-104, 153
Armenians, 52, 62, 80, 107, 153, 184, 192; Daşnaks, 96, 101; deportation orders 100, 102; Druzhiny, 99, 102; Erzurum Congress, 97; Hunçaks, 101; Patriarch, 98; population, 96; reports of abuses 104; Taşnaks, 97, 182; weapons, 96, 100
Australian cavalry 172, 198
Austria-Hungary, 39, 119, 120, 137-138, 143
Austro-Hungarian Army, 91, 93, 137, 143, 153, 155, 176
Aylmer, General, 149
Azerbaijan, 39, 62, 180, 182, 187, 191-192; Azeri Muslim Assembly 182

Baghdad, 66, 101, 111-112, 114, 152, 159-160, 164-168, 171, 176
Baku, 186-189, 191-192; battle of, 191-192
Balkan League, 2
Balkan Wars, 2-4, 7, 9-10, 41, 45, 96, 101; defense of the Dardanelles, 82; First Balkan War, 2; Second Balkan War, 3, 33-23, 32-33
Baratov, General, 152
Basra, 45, 63, 66-67, 100, 114
Batum, 55, 147, 184-186
Bayburt, 131

Beersheba, 70, 153, 161, 163-164, 168, 172-173; loss of, 172
Beyazit, 99, 184
Bingöl, 133
Bir Romani, 155; battle of, 155
Bitlis, 97-98, 131
Black Sea, 34, 55, 128, 130, 182; Black Sea raids, 35-36
Bosphorus, 5, 7, 42, 80
Breslau SMS, (Midilli), 27, 33, 35, 130
British Army, 69-71, 91, 110, 124, 147, 149-151, 153, 155, 161-167, 171-174, 191-203; use of tanks, 163; use of gas, 163
Bronsart von Schellendorf, 12, 29, 32, 35-36, 39, 44, 45, 55, 59, 68, 167-168
Brusilov offensive, 137
Bucharest, 143, 146
Bulgaria, 31-32, 37, 39-40, 78, 91, 143
Bulgarian Army, 142-148
   Second Army, 148
   Third Army, 143, 146
   6th Infantry Division, 144
   10th Infantry Division, 148
   1st Cavalry Division, 144

Cape Helles, 82, 85, 89, 89, 93; Ay Tepe/Gozubaba Tepe, 84; Krithia, 85, 87; Mal Tepe, 84; V Beach, 84; withdrawal 93
Capitulations, 27
Caspian Sea, 186-187, 191, 192
Casualties, Ottoman, 208, 210-211
Caucasia (Caucasus Mountains), 9-10, 37, 39, 42, 45, 52, 66, 101, 103-108, 119-138, 147, 159-161, 167-168, 179-189, 191; Second Army offensive (1916), 131-136; Turkish offensive (1918) 182-190
Cemal Paşa, 1, 3, 28-30, 34-35, 52, 69, 71, 95, 153, 155, 161, 163, 167-171, 174-176, 194; biography, 217
Cevat Paşa, 5, 65, 78, 81, 94, 141, 174, 196
Cevid Bey, 1, 28, 36, 65-66, 93, 113
Churchill, Winston, 33
Committee of Union and Progress (CUP), 1, 3-4, 29, 96. *See also* Young Turks
Constantinople, 5, 8-9, 12, 37, 42, 45, 63, 80, 121, 130, 138, 169, 182, 203
Costanza, 147
Cost of the war, 207-211
Ctesiphon, 112-115, 149; battle of 112-115

Çatalca, 2, 5, 7, 10, 37, 42, 45, 80, 82
Çorlu, 138
Çoruh, 55, 125, 131

Damascus, 171, 200
Dardanelles, 5, 33, 42, 76, 78-80, 85, 94; Bulair, 81-84; Ecabet, 81-82; Erenkoy minefeld, 79, Kum Kale, 78-79, 82-84; Seddelbahir, 78-79, 89, 91
Danube River, 145-147
Dead Sea, 174-175
Delamain, General, 66
DeNogales, Rafael, 100, 104
Dera, 174-175, 195, 198
Derbent, 192
DeRoebeck, Admiral, 78, attacks on the Dardanelles, 79-80
Dilman, 185, 192
Diyala River, 165, 176
Diyarbakir, 62-63, 99, 128-130
Dobruja, 143-146
Doğubeyazit, 105, 184-185
Dortyol, 98
Drama, 148-149
Dunsterforce, 191-192, 203
Dunsterville, Major General L. C., 191-192

El Arish, 71, 161
Elişkirt valley, 97, 105, 107-108, 131, 182; battle of, 107-108, *see also*, Ottoman Army Plans, Bull's Eye Directive
Emir Ali, 175
Enver Paşa, 2, 4-5, 25, 28-34, 36-37, 46, 52-55, 58-65, 68, 80-81, 85, 88-89, 93-96, 100-103, 107-108, 114, 119-123, 127-129, 131, 135, 138, 143, 146, 148, 150, 152-153, 159-161, 163, 166-168, 171, 176, 179-189, 192-193, 194; biography, 217-218; secret orders, 48
Enzeli, 191-192
Erivan, 97,193

Erzincan, 98, 104, 119-120, 131, 133, 135, 183
Erzurum, 5, 6, 39, 41, 54-55, 62-64, 79, 98-99, 101, 104-105, 107, 199-123, 127-128, 130, 133, 138, 182, 183; fall of, 124-128; fortress of, 123-124; forts: Cobandede and Dalangoz, 125
Esat Paşa, 76, 81-85, 87, 90-91, 187; biography 218
Euphrates River, 42, 66, 100, 110-115, 164-167, 203

Fahri Ferik Nuri Paşa, 189
Fahri Paşa, 155
Faik Pasa, 89
Falkenhayn, Field Marshal Erich von, 123, 138, 142-143, 147, 159, 166-169, 171-173, 193-195, 200
Feldman, Major, 55
Ferit, Major, 53
Fethi Bey, 4, 30
Fevzi Paşa, 171, 173, 174; biography 218-219
France, influence of, 98, 99, 147-148, 182
Frankenberg, Colonel von, 69

Galicia, 137-142, 169
Gallipoli, 10, 76-95, 101, 103, 108, 119, 121, 123, 127; battle of, 75-95; casualties, 94-95; Canakkale Fortified Area Command, 76, 77, 78, 81, 89, 94; Italian intervention, 93
Gas attacks, Galicia, 141; Second Gaza, 163
Gaza, 45, 161-164, 167-169, 171-173; battle of Third Gaza,172-173; battles of First and Second Gaza, 161-164
Geehl, Lieutenant Colonel, 115
Georgia, 183, 185, 187, 189
German Army, 153, 155, 167, 169, 186
  Army Group F, 168
  Army South, 139
  Danube Army, 143
  Ninth Army, 143, 147
  1st Reserve Division (Bavarian), 139
  36th Infantry Division, 140
  55th Infantry Division, 139
  146th Infantry Regiment, 232
  185th Infantry Regiment, 140
  228th Infantry Regiment
Asia Corps, 169, 196, 232; composition of, 169
German General Staff, 6, 138, 148
German military assistance, 231-234; treaties, 231-234
German Military Mission, 11-12; 1914 staffing, 11
Giers, Ambassador, 31, 46
Giresun, 182
Goeben, SMS, 27, 33, 35, 64
Goltz, Marshal von der, 8-9, 46, 81, 91, 114-115, 150-151
Graf von Bothmer, General, 139-140
Greece, 32, 33, 39, 146-149
Greeks, Ottoman, 52, 82, 96, 100, 182, 184
Guse, Major, 53-54, 59, 104, 120, 127

Hafif Hakki Bey, 35, 39, 40, 46, 54-55, 59, 61-62, 68, 104; campaign plans of 39; death of, 104
Haifa, 199
Halil Paşa, 62-63, 150-151, 164-167, 171, 176, 187, 191-192; biography, 219
Halit, Major, 79
Hamadan, 152, 153, 176, 191
Hamdi, Lieutenant Colonel, 144
Hamidiye (cruiser), 64
Harput, 62
Harsova, 146
Haspi, Major, 79
Hassan Izzet Paşa, 53
Hedjaz railway, 155, 195
Herwig, Holger H., *The First World War, Germany and Austria-Hungary, 1914-1918*, 137
Hinis, 126
Humus, 201
Hüsamettin, Major, 182
Hüseyin Hüsnü, 2, 144
Hyderpaşa, 169, 171

Indian Army, 67, 71, 110-115, 149-151, 164, 195-196; effect on Allenby's army, 196
  6th (Poona) Infantry Division, 67, 113, 149-151
Ismail Hakki Bey, 203

Jaffa, 174
Jandarma, 6, 30, 37, 96, 100, 103-104, 111; 1914 strength, 5
Jerusalem, 160, 173-174, 198; capture of, 174
Jordan River, 174, 193, 195-196, 198-199; battle of First Jordan, 195; battle of Second Jordan, 195

Kaiser Wilhelm, 168
Kantara, 155
Karakilis, 184
Karasu River, 131
Karind, 152
Kars, 54, 97, 131, 184-185, 189; seizure of, 185
Katia, 155; battle of, 155
Katma, 130
Kayseri, 98
Kazim Bey, 30, 63, 81, 165
Kermansah, 152
Konya, 99
Köprüköy, 46, 96, 121-123, battle of, 121-122
Kornes, 124; incident at, 124
Kotur, 65, 184
Kress von Kressenstein, Colonel, 69, 71, 153, 155, 161, 169, 171-174, 186
Kurds, 99, 104, 133
Kut Al Amara, 110-112, 128, 152; battle of First Kut, 110-112; battle of Second Kut, 164-166; siege of Kut, 149-151; surrender of, 151

Lange, Major, 53
Lawrence, T. E., 198
Lazistan, 125, 128-129; V Corps offensive in the Pontic Alps, 129-131
Libyan War, 2
Liman von Sanders, General Otto, 5, 11-12, 23, 25, 28-30, 34, 46, 62, 80-85, 87-91, 93-94, 138-139, 193, 193-196, 198-201
Limpus, Admiral Arthur, 30
Lossow, Otto von, 186, 193
Ludendorf Offensive, 195, 199

Macedonia, 147-149, 169
Mackensen, Field Marshal August von, 143-147
Mahit Fahri, Lieutenant Colonel, 146

Mahmut Kamil Paşa, 104, 121-122, 124, 127; relief of 127
Mahmut Şevket Paşa, 2, 3, 29, 96
Malazgirt, 104-105, 107-108, 125, 131, 136, 183; battle of, 105-106
Marshall, General, 203
Maude, General Stanley, 160, 164-166
Maummer Bey, 100
Mecidiye (cruiser), 54, 64
Medina, 155, 174-175
Meggido, 198-199, battle of, 198-199
Mehmed Fazil Paşa, 68
Mehmet Ali Paşa, 91
Mehmet Vehip Paşa, 89-91, 93, 127-129, 131, 135, 180, 182-184, 186-187; biography, 221-222
Mersin, 176
Mesopotamia, 39, 42, 62-68, 99, 101, 103, 110-115, 121, 123, 128, 138, 142, 149-152, 159, 164-168, 171, 176, 180, 194, 203
Milne, General, 203-204, effect on Ottomans, 203-204
Ministry of the Interior, Ottoman, 5, 98, 101-104; Intelligence Division of, 98
Ministry of War, Ottoman, 4, 5, 35, 100, 104
Morgenthau, Ambassador Henry, 33
Mosul, 64, 66, 112, 152, 164, 166, 169, 187, 203
Mudros, Armistace at, 203-204
Muhammed Amin, 66
Muhlmann, Carl, *Deutschland und Die Turkei*, 26
Musa Dağ, 103
Muslims, 70, 182; massacres of, 103, 182, 183; refugees, 101
Mustafa Hilmi Paşa, 91, 143, 147
Mustafa Kemal Paşa, 2, 4, 28, 30, 78, 83, 85, 90-91, 128-129, 133, 135, 167-168, 171-173, 196, 199, 201; biography, 220-221
Muş, 97, 105, 106, 133

Nablus, 174, 198, 199
Nazareth, 199
Neu Hammer (Silesia), 169
Nikolai, Lieutenant Colonel, 12, 84-85
Nurettin Paşa, 111-114, 149, 150

Oltu, 58, 61, 64, 105

Oppen, Colonel von, 196
Osmaniye Gap, 63, 130, 176, 201
Ottoman Army: Gonullu systemi, 9; Ihtiyat 8; maneuvers (1910), 6; mobilization, 7-11, 22, 32-34, 40; Nizamiye, 8; organization, 225; Redif, 8; structure, 5; reconstitution (1914) 33-40, retirement of officers (1913), 72
  Anatolian Army Group, 135
  Caucasus Army Group, 167, 180
  Eastern Army Group, 187
  Şevki Paşa Group, 183-185, 187
  Yildirim Army Group, 159-160, 166-174, 180, 193-203, 207; activation of, 193-195; treaties supporting, 232; See also German Army Group F
  First Army, 9-10, 12, 20, 41, 52, 80-81, 85, 91, 104, 121, 139, 193, 194
  Second Army, 9, 12, 20, 41, 52, 68, 80, 85, 89-91, 93, 104, 121, 127-129, 131-133, 135, 161, 172, 180, 194, 201
  Third Army, 10, 12, 39-41, 44, 46, 52-55, 58-65, 97-99, 102, 104, 105-109, 120-138, 149, 160-161, 172, 180, 182, 184-185, 187, 189; Right Wing Group of, 107; First, Second, Third Regions of, 129; regions divided into zones, 136
  Fourth Army, 41, 47, 69, 71, 98-99, 153, 160-161, 163, 167-168, 171, 175, 194, 196
  Fifth Army, 81-95, 119, 143, 171; activated, 81; ammunition expenditures, 88; Anafarta Group, 91; Ari Burnu Group, 91, Asia Group 91, Seddelbahir Group 91, Southern Group, 90, Willmer Group, 91
  Sixth Army, 66, 110-115, 149-151, 164-167, 171, 187, 194, 203; activation of, 110
  Seventh Army, 167, 168, 171-174, 196, 199, 201
  Eighth Army, 171-174, 196, 198-199
  Ninth Army, 187, 189, 191-193
  Army of Islam, 189, 191-192
  I Corps, 10, 12, 39, 40, 63, 91, 98
  II Corps, 10, 40, 63, 80, 98, 131, 196

II Corps, 10, 39-40, 44, 76-78, 81-82, 85, 98, 130-131, 133, 169, 172, 196, 200-201; strength (1914), 77
IV Corps, 40, 46, 62, 80, 98, 130-131, 133, 180, 182-185, 187
V Corps, 39, 46, 62, 87, 90, 98, 127-130, 135
VI Corps: 12, 32, 42, 44, 46, 68, 91, 94, 142-147, 183-184, 187, 189
VII Corps, 40
VIII Corps, 39, 69-71, 153, 174-175, 196
IX Corps, 40, 42, 53-55, 57-59, 61, 64, 105-109, 121-122, 124, 127, 129, 131, 135
X Corps, 12, 40, 42, 53-59, 61, 64, 105-109, 121-122, 124, 127, 129, 131, 135
XI Corps, 42, 53-59, 61, 64, 105-109, 121-122, 124, 127, 129, 131, 135
XII Corps, 3, 39, 42, 46, 66-68, 153, 174, 176, 201
XIII Corps, 39, 42, 46, 66-67, 110, 114, 149-153, 164, 176
XIV Corps, 90, 94, 144
XV Corps, 81, 82, 139-142, 169, 201
XVI Corps, 90-91, 128-131, 133, 135
XVII Corps, 91, 144
XVIII, 110, 149-153, 164-165, 203
XX Corps, 148-149, 163, 172, 174, 193, 196, 201
XXII Corps, 163, 172, 174, 196, 198-199
1st Caucasian Corps, 135-136, 180, 182-184, 187
2nd Caucasian Corps, 135-136, 180, 182-184, 187
1st Infantry Division, 90, 130-131, 172, 174, 193, 196, 201
2nd Infantry Division, 87, 90, 150, 152-153, 176
3rd Infantry Division, 12, 54, 63, 81, 84-85, 87-88, 155, 161, 163, 172
4th Infantry Division, 87, 90, 152, 176
5th Infantry Division, 12, 81, 82, 84-85, 88, 128, 130-131, 180, 183, 185, 187, 189, 191
6th Infantry Division, 90, 152-153,

176
7th Infantry Division, 10, 76-78, 81-82, 84-85, 90-91, 130-131, 163, 173, 196, 198-199
8th Infantry Division, 10, 68-69, 71, 76-77, 90, 130-131, 153
9th Infantry Division, 10, 76-77, 81-83, 85, 87, 90, 130, 136
10th Infantry Division, 12, 68-71, 90, 127, 136, 153
11th Infantry Division, 81, 84-85, 87-89, 131, 193, 201
12th Infantry Division, 87, 90-91, 130-131, 180, 183, 187, 192
13th Infantry Division, 87, 89-90, 127, 130-135
14th Infantry Division, 90, 130, 131, 165, 203
15th Infantry Division, 87, 90-91, 143-147, 182, 189, 191-192
16th Infantry Division, 87, 90, 161, 163, 172, 196
17th Infantry Division, 59, 107, 136
18th Infantry Division, 53, 122, 136
19th Infantry Division, 77-78, 81-83, 85, 139-142, 169, 172, 196, 198-199
20th Infantry Division, 139-142, 169, 196, 198
22nd Infantry Division, 69
23rd Infantry Division, 69-70, 176, 201
24th Infantry Division, 91, 94, 169, 172, 193, 195-196, 200
25th Infantry Division, 69-71, 91, 94, 144-147, 153
26th Infantry Division, 91, 94, 146-147, 193, 196, 200
27th Infantry Division, 69-70, 172, 174
28th Infantry Division, 59, 99, 107, 135
29th Infantry Division, 58-59, 107, 136
30th Infantry Division, 135
31st Infantry Division, 136
32nd Infantry Division, 59, 136
33rd Infantry Division, 54, 122, 135
34th Infantry Division, 54, 122, 127, 136
35th Infantry Division, 68, 111-114, 149-150, 152, 164
36th Infantry Division, 104, 106-107, 121, 125, 135
37th Infantry Division, 66, 105, 182-183
38th Infantry Division, 9, 66-68, 111-114, 125, 164
41st Infantry Division, 72, 94, 176, 201
42nd Infantry Division, 172
43rd Infantry Division, 72, 176, 201
44th Infantry Division, 72, 176, 201
45th Infantry Division, 111-114, 149-150, 165
46th Infantry Division, 148-149, 164, 203
47th Infantry Division, 130-131
48th Infantry Division, 130-131, 175, 195-196, 201
49th Infantry Division, 130
50th Infantry Division, 148-149, 169, 171
51st Infantry Division, 111-114, 149-150, 164-165
52nd Infantry Division, 111-114, 149-150, 152, 164-165
53rd Infantry Division, 130-131, 163, 172-174, 193, 196, 200
54th Infantry Division, 163, 172, 174
58th Infantry Division, 176
59th Infantry Division, 169, 171
5th Caucasian Infantry Division, 135-136, 182, 187, 189, 192
9th Caucasian Infantry Division, 135-136, 187
10th Caucasian Infantry Division, 136, 183, 187, 191
11th Caucasian Infantry Division, 136, 182, 187
36th Caucasian Infantry Division, 136, 187
37th Caucasian Infantry Division, 136, 183, 187
Van Jandarma (Infantry) Division, 39, 42, 53, 65, 99, 105-108, 184; composition, 53
1st Expeditionary Force, 63-65, 99, 105-107, 112, 121
5th Expeditionary Force, 62-65, 105-107, 112, 121
Hejaz Expeditionary Force, 176

1st Provisional Force, 175
2nd Provisional Force, 175
Desert Force, 153
Left Wing Group, 196
Mosul Group, 152-153
River Group, 165
Şeria Group, 196
Şerştal Group, 196
2nd Regular Cavalry Division, 55-56, 58, 61, 64, 105-107, 121, 125, 129
3rd Regular Cavalry Division, 130-131, 161, 163, 172-174, 195-196, 201
2nd Caucasian Cavalry Division, 172, 174, 180, 196
1st Reserve Cavalry Division, 9, 37, 39, 42, 53, 64
2nd Reserve Cavalry Division, 9, 37, 39, 42, 53, 64
3rd Reserve Cavalry Division, 9, 37, 39, 42, 53, 105
4th Reserve Cavalry Division, 9, 37, 39, 42, 53
3rd Infantry Regiment, 165
8th Infantry Regiment, 12, 55, 64
26th Infantry Regiment, 66, 83
31st Infantry Regiment, 155
32nd Infantry regiment, 155
37th Infantry Regiment, 62
39th Infantry Regiment, 155
40th Infantry Regiment, 62
43rd Infantry Regiment, 62
44th Infantry Regiment, 64
56th Infantry Regiment, 145
57th Infantry Regiment, 83
59th Infantry Regiment, 145
61st Infantry Regiment, 140
64th Infantry Regiment, 165
75th Infantry Regiment, 145
110th Infantry Regiment, 199
123rd Infantry Regiment, 182
177th Infantry Regiment, 148
178th Infantry Regiment, 163
Baghdad Infantry Regiment, 106-107
4th Reserve Cavalry Regiment, 96
Light Reserve Cavalry Regiments (Hamidiye), 5
3rd Artillery Regiment, 12
8th Artillery Regiment, 78-79
9th Artillery Regiment, 76
Aviation Squadrons, 227-230

Irak Area Command, 66, 68, 98, 101, 112
Bis divisions, 9
Ştanke Bey Detachment, 55-57
Ledabor Detachment, 140-141
Ottoman Army Plans: Concentration Plan, 42-46; Bull's Eye Directive, 107; Mobilization Plan, 37-41, 64; Primary Campaign Plan, 37-40; Primary Mission Continues Plan, 64; restructuring the army 1919, 207-208; Sarikamiş, 54-57; war plans, 37-47
Ottoman Empire: communications, 19; economic conditions, 13-17; resources, 13-17; war aims, 25-27
Ottoman General Staff, 4-7, 29, 32, 35, 40-41, 45-46, 54, 63, 76, 80, 88-89, 93-94, 97-101, 104, 110, 119-123, 128, 130, 138, 142, 144, 146, 148-149, 159-160, 164-165, 167, 180, 182-183, 193, 199-200, 207, 208; Aviation Inspectorate, 227-230; Operations Division, 98; organization of, 223; Railroad Directorate, 144
Ottoman military performance, 211-215; casualties, 235-241; myths, 214-215

Palestine, 10, 69, 123, 153, 155, 159-160, 167-168, 171-175, 180, 193-203
Pallavinci, Ambassador, 31
Pan-Turanism, 53, 65, 97, 185-187, 189
Persia, 9, 65, 114, 119, 152-153, 166-168, 176, 184-185, 187, 189, 192-193; first invasion, 65; second invasion, 152-153; withdrawal, 192-193
Petrovsk, 192
Poti, 186
Pozanti, 129
Prisoners of War, returned from Russia, 189

Qurna, 67, 110-111

Railroads, 103, 123, 128-130, 138, 144, 148, 155, 169; Baghdad Railroad, 102; operational rate, 17; transport of 8th and 9th Infantry Divisions, 129-

130; transport of 24th Infantry Division, 169
Ramadiye, 166, 171
Rauf Bey, 28
Refet, Colonel, 89
Rifat, Major, 79
Rize, 128
Rodoslavov, Ambassador, 31
Romania, 40, 78, 119-120, 142-147, 193; Romanian Army, 142-147
Royal Navy, 46, 63, 39, 71, 79, 87, 114, 148, 163, 173-175
HMS Agamemnon, 203
Russian Army, 58, 97-99, 101, 103, 105-109, 121-147, 152-153, 166, 176, 180, 189, 191
Sarikamiş Group, 57
19th Turkistan Army, 65
3rd Turkistan Infantry Division, 139
47th Infantry Division, 139
113th Infantry Division, 139
Russian Navy, 88, 120, 182, 192

Sait Halim, 3, 26-231, 34, 36, 168; proposals, 27
Salonika, 147-149
Salonika Group, 1
Sami, Colonel, 83
Samsun, 130
Sannaiyat, 165
Saray, 65, 184, 189
Sarikamiş, 39, 54, 57-58, 60, 65, 98, 108, 184; campaign 52-65; losses, 59-60; operations plan, 55; Turnagel Wood, 59
Sarrail, General, 148
Schulenberg legend, 72
Seeckt, Major General Hans von, 182, 186, 193
Selman Pak, 112
Serbia, 32, 122, 139, 147-148
Shaiba, battle of, 110
Sherif Faisal, 153, 175
Sherif Hussein, 153, 155, 175
Sinai, 9, 45, 68-72, 119, 153, 155; first invasion 68-72; second invasion, 153
Sinop, 120
Sivas, 98, 130
Sodernstern, Colonel von, 82, 85
Souchon, Admiral Wilhelm, 27, 29-30, 33-36

Stange, Captain, 12, 55, 60, 64-65, 106. *See also* Ottoman Army, Ştanke Bey Detachment
Suez Canal, 33, 39, 40, 66, 69-72, 153, 155, 168; first attack on 68-72
Suvla Bay, 90-91; landings, 90; Kuçuk and Buyuk Anafarta, 90
Süleyman Askeri Bey, 66, 68, 110
Süleymaniye, 100, 152-153
Symrna, 130, 144
Syria, 9, 32, 68-69, 99, 123, 168, 171-172, 175-176, 200-203; campaign in, 200-203

Şefik, Lieutenant Colonel, 139
Şükrü Ali, Colonel, 144
Şükrü Naili, Colonel, 148

Tabriz, 62, 65, 105, 108, 187, 189, 192-193
Talat, 1, 3, 29-31, 34, 36, 95, 203
Tannenberg, battle of, 54
Tarsus, 201
Taurus Mountains, 130
Taylor, A. J. P., *The Struggle for Mastery in Europe*, 20, 28, 36
Tehran, 63, 65, 176
Tekirdag (Rodosto), 76, 78
Thrace, 10, 31, 33, 37, 42, 62, 80, 119, 128, 138, 203
Tigris River, 42, 66, 110-115, 150, 164-167, 176, 203
Tiflis, 182, 185-186
Tortum, 99, 105
Townshend, General Charles, 111-115, 149-151, 203
Trabzon, 104, 119, 127-131, 138, 183, 185-186
Trans-Caucasian Federation, 180, 183, 185
Treaties of:
Brest-Litovsk, 180, 186
Bucharest, 3, 23
Bulgaria-Ottoman Empire, Secret Treaty of Alliance, 31, 37-38
Germany-Ottoman Empire, Secret Treaty of Alliance, 25-26, 28, 32
London, 3, 23
Tronnier, Colonel, 12
Trumpener, Ulrich, *Germany and the Ottoman Empire*, 20, 28, 30, 31

Urfa, 100
Usedom, Admiral von, 77
Uzunkopru, 91, 144, 146

Van/Lake Van, 55, 62, 64-65, 96, 98-101, 103-104, 106, 108, 121, 127, 182, 184; battle for, 105. See also, Armenian Rebellion
Vardar valley, 9, 148
Varna, 144

Wangenheim, Ambassador Hans von, 25, 27-28, 30, 34, 36
Weber, Colonel, 77, 82, 84, 89
Weber, Frank, *Eagles on the Crescent*, 20, 28, 31
Wehrle, Colonel, 78
Westenek, Dutch Attache, 59
Willmer, Major, 90
Wilson, President Woodrow, 203

Yahya Çavus, 83-84
Yakup Şevki Paşa, 139-141, 183, 185, 192; biography 221
Yasin Hilmi, Colonel, 139
Yildirim Army Group. See Ottoman Army, Yildirim Army Group
Young Turks, 1-2, 30, 95; Second Young Turk Congress, 1. See also Committee of Union and Progress
Yudenich, General, 106-107, 121
Yusuf Izzet, 59

Zadernstorn, Colonel, 11
Zistrovi, 146
Ziya Gök Alp, 97
Ziya Paşa, 53, 55, 129
Zlotalipa River, 139-141

About the Author

EDWARD J. ERICKSON teaches social studies at Norwich High School in Norwich, New York. After serving as an infantry noncommissioned officer in airborne assignments, he was commissioned in the field artillery and served with divisional and corps artillery units in the United States, Germany, Italy, Turkey, and in Operation Desert Storm.